TRAFFICKING AND PROSTITUTION RECONSIDERED

New Perspectives on Migration, Sex Work, and Human Rights

TRAFFICKING AND PROSTITUTION RECONSIDERED

New Perspectives on Migration, Sex Work, and Human Rights

SECOND EDITION

edited by
Kamala Kempadoo
with
Jyoti Sanghera and Bandana Pattanaik

Paradigm Publishers
Boulder • London

Copyright © 2012 Paradigm Publishers

Published in the United States by Paradigm Publishers, 2845 Wilderness Place, Boulder, CO 80301 USA.

Paradigm Publishers is the trade name of Birkenkamp & Company, LLC, Dean Birkenkamp, President and Publisher.

Library of Congress Cataloging-in-Publication Data

Trafficking and prostitution reconsidered: new perspectives on migration, sex work, and human rights / edited by Kamala Kempadoo, Jyoti Sanghera, Bandana Pattanaik. — 2nd ed.
      p. cm.
   Includes bibliographical references and index.
   ISBN 978-1-59451-988-8 (hardcover: alk. paper)
   ISBN 978-1-59451-989-5 (pbk. : alk. paper)   1. Human smuggling—Asia.   2. Human trafficking—Asia.   3. Prostitution—Asia.   4. Forced labor—Asia.   5. Transnational crime.   6. Asia—Emigration and immigration.   I. Kempadoo, Kamala.   II. Sanghera, Jyoti.   III. Pattanaik, Bandana, 1960–
   HQ281.T618 2012
   306.74095—dc23
                                                                                      2011035982

Printed and bound in the United States of America on acid free paper that meets the standards of the American National Standard for Permanence of Paper for Printed Library Materials.

Designed and Typeset by Straight Creek Bookmakers.

16 15 14 13 12   1 2 3 4 5

Contents

Introduction

Abolitionism, Criminal Justice, and Transnational Feminism

Twenty-first-century Perspectives on Human Trafficking

Kamala Kempadoo

A belief about human trafficking as a contemporary global problem made its way into public consciousness at the start of the twenty-first century, pressed mainly by governments and feminists. It has since become sedimented in everyday life and is regularly broadcast in the media, yet the problem it points to is not new and has been a concern of Western nations since the mid-nineteenth century. At the turn of the twenty-first century, human trafficking was identified by the United Nations as a transnational crime, and was cast by political leaders, alongside terrorism and drug trafficking, as one of the three "evils" to haunt the globe. Beliefs about human trafficking have also created a veritable anti-trafficking industry as well as a set of durable narratives.[1] These narratives have informed law enforcement efforts to control immigration and transnational organized crime, state policies and interventions to closely survey and regulate sex industries, and an array of social work and other activities aimed at undocumented migrants, sex workers, and bonded laborers. Indeed, by 2003, over 900 entities worldwide, including nongovernmental human rights, women's rights, anti-violence, sex-worker rights, and health-care organizations,

government organizations, international agencies, and university depart-
ments, drew from the narratives and were involved in combating human
trafficking (Change 2003). This anti-trafficking activity has since deepened
and expanded, with the academic world adding considerable weight and
legitimacy to the various narratives. In 2010 alone, around 140 academic
books and journal articles were published that explicitly dealt with the in-
tersection of human trafficking and prostitution and many more appeared
dealing with subjects such as "modern-day slavery," organized crime, child
prostitution, forced labor, and international labor migration. The number
of publications over the span of the first decade of the twenty-first century
is much vaster. Forensic nurses, HIV and other health specialists, social
workers, pastors, sociologists, psychologists, criminologists, anthropolo-
gists, political scientists, and economists, as well as scholars in women's,
gender and sexuality studies, development studies, labor studies, migration studies, black slavery studies, and Latin American and Asian studies
have all added their voices to what Emma Goldman coined a century ago
as a "righteous cry" against human suffering (1911).

In reflection upon this explosion of interest during the first decade of
the twenty-first century and upon what it has managed to accomplish since
the first edition of this book in 2005, some common themes continue and
new ones emerge. First, there remain different and competing narratives
about human trafficking, which now constitute quite distinct conceptual
frameworks or paradigms, with little consensus or agreement among
scholars, policy makers, and activists about the problem. Few new narratives have been added, but contestation over the existing ones appears
to have become fiercer, due in part to academic interventions. Second,
while descriptions and analyses of the perceived problem have become
considerably more sophisticated, with expanded areas of social life being
implicated, there is a surprising lack of any theoretical breakthroughs since
the start of the century. Rather, earlier perspectives are rehearsed, applied
to specific national contexts and within new academic disciplines, and used
to reveal different shades of the problem. This has led to a deepening of
the various narratives but not to any significant shifts in paradigm.[2] Third,
while a conflation between human trafficking and prostitution underlies
some narratives, "sex trafficking" has emerged as a term that many employ to speak to the nexus between two, and to point to that area that is
considered one of "the most severe forms of trafficking." Sex trafficking
is now the metaphor par excellence for analysis of the degraded state of
humanity in the twenty-first century and has become a central vehicle for
academic critique of a variety of contemporary social relations of power
at local and global levels. Nevertheless, the term is attached to a particular
feminist narrative about violence to women and carries a specific meaning.
Finally, much of what is debated in the name of a struggle against human
rights violations still carries troubling consequences for many people

around the world. In particular, the migrant woman in prostitution is taken up—explicitly or not—to express a growing unease with an array of social injustices, but her silence, especially that of women from the global South, is overwhelming. In the outpouring of outrage, condemnation, and claims to human rights, she is spoken for and represented, but rarely does she find voice. The migrant woman sex worker becomes the ground for competing claims and theories, silenced by not only the master narratives but also the Western gaze (Doezema 2001; Downe 2007; Mohanty 2003).

We tend to forget that the global South, specifically South and Southeast Asia, is the area of the world where the contemporary international interest in human trafficking originated, and that it is persons from the global South who are disproportionately represented in transnational migration flows in the twenty-first century.[3] This book takes these starting points seriously. Views, experiences, and perspectives of women of the global South, especially Asia, frame this collection and are foregrounded throughout. It attempts to disrupt the dominant trend where white westerners—many feminists included—occupy most of the space in the debate and set the academic and political terms around which the debate takes place. The collection also presents ways in which human trafficking is conceptualized, defined, and made operational by people who have worked in the field for many years. It documents human trafficking as *the movement, trade, and exploitation of labor under conditions of coercion and force*, analyzed from the lives, agency, and rights of women and men who are involved in a variety of activities in a transnationalized world. It offers critical examinations of abolitionist and international governmental definitions of trafficking, while proposing alternatives for study, research, and intervention. The writings—by persons who advocate for the rights of migrants and sex workers, especially in and of the global South—shed light on everyday circumstances, popular discourses, national policies, and grassroots struggles for change. The essays and analyses link theory and praxis in ways that are often overlooked by researchers and academicians who have recently joined the anti-trafficking industry and who attempt to intervene in debates from their ivory towers or political platforms.

The contributions here draw from grounded research, activism, and debates that have taken place since the 1990s, focusing on people's livelihood strategies and struggles for change under new forms of globalization, in which gender, race, ethnicity, sexuality, and citizenship are central organizing principles. The collection was initially inspired by workshops on feminist participatory action research in 2000 and 2001 held by the Global Alliance Against Traffic in Women (GAATW) in Thailand, at which research projects and perspectives on trafficking in a number of different countries were presented and discussed. All three editors of this collection were part of the workshops as resource persons and had some attachment to the GAATW organization at the time.[4] The understanding that had developed from extensive participatory research and work with nongovernmental organizations (NGOs) presented by the majority of the participants in the workshops was that "trafficking," or aspects of the phenomenon, were evident in various migration processes and sites of work and not just in sex industries. This shared conceptualization of the problem was striking, as it offered an alternative perspective to the radical feminist, predominantly Western, view that dominated international debates at the time. From the realization that the researchers were articulating a complex redefinition of human trafficking based on grounded observations and local realities, we set out to make this perspective more visible through publication. Simultaneously, through the GAATW network we solicited other writings from people working in the anti-trafficking field. This book is a culmination of that effort, and although GAATW was a central fomenter in the process, the following chapters do not represent that organization's perspective but draw from a far broader movement.

The centrality of women to this collection can be taken in different ways. On one hand, it can be argued that this focus maintains the gendered divide around which earlier definitions of trafficking settled and thus reinforces the general, dominant image of trafficking as pertinent only to the lives of women and girls. On the other hand, reformulations of the concept of trafficking—to encompass a gendered quality of labor migration, exploitation, and oppression—combine with the knowledge that women are disproportionately represented among the poor, the undocumented, the debt-bonded, and the international migrant work force, and this leads to a foregrounding of women's lives and experiences. Gendered inequality remains a central feature that guides research and investigations, with situations of poor women and girls becoming a main concern for those in this book. Thus, although the issue of the trafficking of men and boys is gaining some significance in international debates and a broader notion of the trafficking in *persons* is popular, gendered relations of power and gendered difference remain central to examinations of migration and sex work.

Due to the varying ideas about human trafficking represented here, this collection does not claim to offer a singular solution to the problem. Some authors imply that the notion of human trafficking should be completely jettisoned, viewing the issue as one that is primarily about national anxieties, conservative sexual positionings, undocumented migration and forced labor, and global inequalities. Others critique the concept for its ability to highjack attention away from structural forces that produce exploitation, violence, and the coercion of (migrant) workers, or for its ability to obscure other aspects of women's lives and identities, and therefore seek to redefine and refocus it. Still others wish to make it more precise and applicable to empowerment work among migrants and sex workers. However, even with these different emphases, all authors in this book share a critical stance toward the narratives on human trafficking that locate migrants and sex workers as victims, advocate a politics of rescue, or call for greater criminalization of human life. They all advance an approach to trafficking that supports the humanity, agency, rights, and perspectives of labor migrants and sex workers and seek to open up borders and spaces rather than tighten or foreclose them.

THE MAIN NARRATIVES

The genealogy of a discourse on human trafficking has been traced and retraced in a number of works such that it must by now be quite familiar to most academics and activists in the field and so will not be repeated here. Instead the history is linked to the production of a set of narratives that have become quite stable, are attached to different subject positions and different assumptions about or conceptualizations of the problem, and constitute quite distinct frameworks or paradigms. Three main frameworks—identified here as the abolitionist, the criminal justice, and the transnational feminist—are reviewed, in order to better locate this collection and to make visible the global politics of knowledge that is involved in twenty-first-century debates and activities. While three frameworks are identified and discussed below, it is important to keep in mind that they are not discreet and sometimes overlap or blend eclectically in various activities, analyses, or strategic alliances. Moreover, although it can be argued that a concern about human rights forms the common ground for all anti-trafficking work, notions about what constitutes human rights appear in the three frameworks in different ways. There may also be other narratives that fall outside this tripartite analytic, especially those that are specific to one particular locale or language, and not all three frameworks will be present or recognizable in every place. Nevertheless, a review of the literature in the field suggests that the three paradigms are primary ways in which trafficking is approached, defined, and combated globally in the twenty-first century, in countries as diverse as Thailand, Australia, Cambodia, Brazil, and the US, in regions such as the EU, and in international contexts.[5]

ANTI-MIGRATION, ANTI-PROSTITUTION BEGINNINGS

The idea about human trafficking has strong anti-migration, anti-prostitution foundations, and its emergence is generally located in concerns in Western Europe and North America about late-nineteenth/early-twentieth-century cross-border migrations by women. These migrations constituted part of the large-scale international relocations and displacements of people that followed the abolition of slavery in the nineteenth century, and which accompanied the internationalization of waged labor embedded in the period of globalization between 1850 and 1914 (Stalker 2000; Tilly 2004). Predominantly poor and working-class men and women crossed borders, clandestinely or not, to find new futures, enduring systems of bonded labor and indentured servitude that positioned and maintained them as cheap, disposable labor forces. Women sought to independently move or were moved through organized channels—commonly as sexual and domestic partners, but also as workers in their own right—servicing and reproducing the migrant work force, sometimes obtaining new freedoms through non-marital sexual relations and work that could include prostitution (Guy 1991; Walkowitz 1980; White 1990). Nevertheless, narratives about the mobility and trade of women's labor and bodies under nineteenth-century contract labor, indenture, and debt-bondage systems ignored the impacts of colonialism and demands of patriarchal, racialized capital, and linked the emergence of migrant women in prostitution to notions of "loose" sexual relations, degraded feminine sexuality and the immorality of migrant men. In the nineteenth-century narratives, women were often portrayed as coerced, deceived, lured, trapped, kidnapped, and forced into prostitution, explained by the "natural" sexual depravity and uncivilized character of (im)migrant communities. Consequently, as occurred for Chinese women in West Coast cities in the United States under the Page Act of 1875, in Canada during the latter part of the nineteenth century, and for Indian women under British colonial indentureship systems in the Caribbean after the abolition of slavery, the women's lives and movements were subjected to laws and policies that restricted or even banned their migration.[6]

The nineteenth-century narratives on gendered international migration patterns set the stage for what a number of scholars have identified as a racialized social panic about the "White Slave Trade."[7] The ever-growing number of women traveling abroad for work and new life opportunities caused great anxiety and suspicion among middle classes and elites, and even though a major concern was the arrival in the global North of men and women from Asia and other places in the global South, it produced ideologies about the entrapment and enslavement of, particularly, white, Western European and North American women in prostitution.[8] The panic instilled in the European-American imagination a notion of the barbaric, uncivilized, non-Western Other who brutalized and violated white women, while serving to restrict all women's mobility and sexual freedoms (Doezema 2000; Findlay 1999). Narratives about the white slave traffic came to dominate international attention around the subject of women's international migration and mobility and led to a series of international debates and conventions in the early twentieth century, starting with the 1904 "International Agreement for the Suppression of the White Slave Traffic." The international agreement, which was initially formulated to halt "the procuring of women or girls for immoral purposes abroad," gave rise to a plethora of nationally defined law enforcement and policing efforts to eradicate prostitution. It was a campaign to abolish the morally defined "social evil" of prostitution through control of women's movements, and in effect exercised control over women's sexuality. Moreover, as Emma Goldman—a staunch advocate of women's sexual autonomy—astutely noted, the anti-white slavery crusade that became synonymous with an anti-prostitution campaign was supported, if not led, by Western European and North American middle-class feminist reformists who sought to "save" their "fallen" sisters.[9] The anti-prostitution feminist approach imparted an imperialist bourgeois logic to early anti-trafficking campaigns, containing a very particular script about women's sexuality.

SEX TRAFFICKING AND CONTEMPORARY ABOLITIONISM

Between the two world wars in the twentieth century, the moral panic over women's mobility and involvement in the sex trade appears to have subsided. In the post–World War II era, with the new surge of capitalist globalization and Western economies in recovery, male labor migration was often demanded for new and expanding industries in the global North, with women being pushed (back) into family-building arrangements and domesticity, their mobility and sexuality severely restricted to the home and nation. The containment of women's sexuality to specific spheres was reinforced through the passing of the 1949 United Nations Convention for the Suppression of the Traffic in Persons and of the Exploitation of the Prostitution of Others, which replaced the earlier international agreements on white slavery and which continued to take the abolition of prostitution as its main objective. Interest in the subject of trafficking was revitalized in the 1970s, highlighted in the first instance by feminists concerned with the social impacts of the reconstruction and development of the Southeast Asian region in the aftermath of the Vietnam War and the continued stationing and servicing of US military troops in the region. Sex tourism, mail-order bride arrangements, militarized prostitution, and coercions and violence in the movement of women from poorer to more affluent areas at home and abroad for work in leisure, relaxation, and sex industries were paramount in the early campaigns (ISIS-wicce 1990/91). "Sexual slavery" was claimed, from a radical feminist perspective, especially from within the US women's movement, to be central to this understanding of trafficking, and it was taken to epitomize the very worst of patriarchal oppression and the greatest injury to women.[10] The patriarchal institution of prostitution—but also marriage and the family—was defined in this feminist approach as inherently violent and abusive for women, and those who participated in such institutions were believed to be deceived victims of male power and privilege. The conceptualization of "woman-as-victim" that was deployed by the US women's movement during the 1970s to demand recognition of the injustices of patriarchy, and which borrowed from political struggles and definitions in the 1960s that stressed black victimization at the hands of a white racist society, formed an integral part of the narrative (Barry 1984). Women's freedom rested then on the complete abolition of those institutions that enslaved and victimized women, prostitution included.

While the idea of sexual slavery could immediately arouse horror and indignation through the invocation of the experience of black slavery, and allied comfortably with liberal concerns and anxieties about human rights abuses under late-twentieth-century conditions, by 2000 it was exchanged for the term "sex trafficking." Established through the US Trafficking in Persons Act to designate a "severe form of trafficking in persons," the notion of sex trafficking was popularized through the advocacy and writings of feminist scholars and activists such as Janice Raymond and the US-based Coalition Against Trafficking in Women (CATW) (Hynes and Raymond 2002). The exchange of terms did not, however, change the paradigm, but enabled anti-prostitution analyses and sentiments to fully reinsert themselves into a discourse that, as Lin Chew points out in chapter four, was increasingly becoming defined as a labor migration issue. Since its appearance, the notion of sex trafficking has come to dominate this particular narrative on human trafficking, specifying the exploitation of (migrant) labor in the sex trade as intrinsically harmful to all women. Anti-trafficking campaigns designed within this perspective advocate the abolition of prostitution, a greater criminalization of various aspects of trafficking, and the "rescue" of young women and girls from international and national cross-border sex work.[11] Migrant women and sex workers, as agents who may consciously and willingly cross borders in undocumented status in search of a livelihood or a better way of life, and/or who exchange sex as part of this process, are classified in this framework as "sex slaves" or "trafficked victims."

Sex trafficking narratives in the twenty-first century differ little from the earlier white slavery and sexual slavery beliefs, despite the quite differing global conditions of their emergence. Similar to yesteryear, the narrative takes to heart the abolition of prostitution, and makes an appeal for an end of violence to women or, in contemporary terms, "gender-based violence," from an approach in which certain acts or situations are considered always and inevitably oppressive to women, such as female genital surgery, veiling, or rape. Universality, as Wendy Hesford and Wendy Kozol point out in their discussion of twenty-first-century women's human rights discourses, "provides the framework for understanding acts of violence and oppression against women within national and global contexts," where it is considered that "some acts are so heinous that anywhere and anytime we can recognize them as such" (2005, 16–17). The sex trafficking approach does not operate independently, but has developed in conversation with, or has drawn its power from, other movements and narratives. Building from the white slavery and sexual slavery narratives, it too depends upon the history of black people in the Americas to speak about conditions of forced labor, and similarly reproduces the uneasy, often exploitative, historical relationship between white feminist and black emancipation movements. In the following chapters Josephine Ho and Melissa Ditmore point out other reliances and alliances in, respectively, Taiwan and the US. Both authors describe the meeting ground around the issue of "sex trafficking" between liberal and radical feminists on the one hand and neoconservative governments and Christian fundamentalists on the other, which in both countries has led to demands to curb women's struggles for sexual self-determination and autonomy. The marriage of twenty-first-century US feminist ideas about sex trafficking to neoliberal abolitionist formulations about "modern-day slavery" adds to this picture. The modern-day antislavery approach dwells on the abolition of institutions and conditions of force and violence that enslave humans, prostitution being identified as one of the main institutions that violates women and girls and restricts freedom.[12] A defense of a notion of universal human rights stands front and center in the work of the "modern-day slavery" abolitionists. Defining the alliance as "contemporary abolitionism," Elizabeth Bernstein describes it as "the growing cadre of evangelical Christian and secular feminist humanitarian projects that have emerged to reclassify all or certain forms of sexual labor as 'slavery,' to press for laws that punish the individuals who are deemed responsible for this captivity, and to vigorously pursue sex workers' rescue" (2007, 129). The movement appeals to a particular morality about how sexuality should be expressed, about who has a right to citizenship, and about who may have access to the benefits and wealth accrued from capitalist exploitation of the globe. Sex trafficking abolitionism claims a moral high ground and mobilizes a universalizing concept of human rights, and the narrative finds easy resonance in neoliberal feminisms worldwide, as well as in humanitarian projects that are implemented in a variety of contexts.[13]

The panic that these twenty-first-century abolitionist movements have whipped up about "sex trafficking" and "modern-day slavery" supports the intensification of the policing of local communities, internal and national borders, as it is presumed that only through close surveillance and regulation can "traffickers" be rooted out and punished and "victims" rescued and saved. This commitment to political agendas of criminalization and punishment by the new abolitionists coincides neatly with other state and international efforts to regulate the cross-border flows of people around claims of securitizing the nation, and supports both war and peacekeeping efforts designed to eradicate "terrorism" and instill Western humanitarian values and discourses of democracy worldwide.[14] In many countries extensive anti-trafficking units patrol the borders and streets and conduct raids on sex industries, searching for undocumented migrants, all in the name of protecting humanity from the "evil" of "sex trafficking." Moreover, in countries such as the US, the intense focus on sex industries for delivering victims is strengthened by the definition of all inter-state movement for sex work as trafficking, and leads to a fixation on the lives and activities of national sex workers.[15] Denise Brennan, in her research on forced labor, concludes that the reorientation to the domestic sphere that has taken place through US law and policy has led to a growing lack of attention for hyperexploitation and forced labor in sectors of the economy and labor markets that are not attached to sex industries, an intensification of interest in underage prostitution, as well as an inflated estimate of the number of trafficked persons (2008). Anti-trafficking in this approach appears completely synonymous with legal efforts to curb immigration and prostitution, once again limiting the mobility of migrant women workers. In the UK and other parts of Europe, the attention paid to "child sex trafficking," which covers any minor in prostitution, accompanies the anti-immigration thrust of anti-trafficking policies and activities, giving rise to a racialized panic around the "sexual grooming" of white girls by immigrant men.[16] On both sides of the Atlantic, the original "white slave" narrative is reinstalled in full glory and, as with its earlier incarnation, even while the "sex slaves" are of various ethnic and national descents, it is the image of the ruin of the (white) national body that is invoked. This contemporary white slave narrative in the global North maps almost seamlessly onto the intensely nationalistic, anti-prostitution, child protection governance models that have been erected to regulate, police, and discipline feminine sexuality in other parts of the globe.[17]

THE CRIMINAL JUSTICE APPROACH

At the turn of this century a shift in the global governance regimes around human trafficking emerged through the introduction of the 2000 UN Protocol to Prevent, Suppress and Punish Trafficking in Persons, Especially Women and Children, which replaced the 1949 Convention, and which was attached to the UN Convention on Transnational Organized Crime. Thus, whereas the early-twentieth-century approach primarily focused on prostitution, by 2000 trafficking was subsumed under the heading of international criminal activity. The trafficking of persons was also located as akin to the trafficking of drugs and weapons and defined as being of almost equal magnitude, taking place in a range of industries, only one of which is the sex industry. Anti-trafficking in this framework was made synonymous with a war on international crime and the prosecution of those who moved or employed persons, weapons, or drugs in defiance or by circumvention of legal boundaries and borders. The understanding that human trafficking was a criminal activity—whether as organized gang activity or as the "illegal" movement and employment of people—placed greater emphasis on immigration and border controls and on detecting underground activities than on prostitution. It is fundamentally a criminal justice approach that lends authority to international law and national efforts for the criminal prosecution of traffickers (Smith 2010). In this framework, protection of the nation-state against incursions that might unsettle or disrupt its security is paramount (Schaeffer-Grabiel 2010). The UN framework nevertheless also continues to criminalize the "exploitation of the prostitution of others" when that involves cross-border and forced activities, yet does not criminalize all prostitution, to allow for differences in national legislation on the issue.

The legal approach of the UN Protocol to human trafficking is lodged in a criminal justice framework framed within international law that assumes human rights to be transhistorical or "natural," yet which translates not into the promotion of universal rights, but, as various legal scholars point out, into the universalization of the liberal Western legal tradition.[18] This rights discourse draws from a paradigm that was originally constructed around distinctions between "civilized" and "non-civilized" nations, emboldening a civilizing mission that is considered to be still present in the neoliberal international legal regime into which is encoded the main governing concepts and categories, such as modernity, progress, development, emancipation, and rights.[19] Moreover, as has been repeatedly pointed out, this "international" human rights discourse derives from a system of state sovereignty through which claims to rights are made on national citizenship criteria, excluding "non-citizens" such as refugees and undocumented migrants who are positioned as having no rights and who "are no longer even recognized or treated as humans."[20] The legal tradition produces a "reluctance" of governments to embrace a human rights approach to human trafficking and supports a prioritization of the prosecution of criminals "over the protection of the human rights of those it defines as 'trafficked victims'" (Gallagher 2010; Smith 2010)—a tension that is also identified as "the gap between the founding principles and real practices of liberal democratic states" (O'Connell Davidson 2010, 258).

The international legal/criminal justice framework is echoed in a variety of national and regional policies, laws, and initiatives that have been adopted by governments around the world and signal growing attention by the international political community and national governments to issues of unregulated migration flows and underground profitable, cross-border activities through law enforcement.[21] As well, a variety of international agencies such as the International Migration Organization (IOM) have taken up the criminal justice approach, mostly focusing on the management of "irregular" international migration flows.[22] Strengthening this approach are analyses by criminologists and legal scholars, who in recent years have vigorously taken up the issue of human trafficking as a law and order problem, and who often call for more legislation, increased policing and surveillance, a greater focus on clients, traffickers or criminal networks, or more assistance for "trafficked victims."[23] Some have framed the discussion in terms of the securitization of the nation-state or of human rights (Friesendorf 2009). Others critically relate the development of a criminal justice approach to the reorganization of citizenship, particularly in the European Union (Andrijasevic 2010).

Some national laws such as the US Trafficking Victims Protection Act (TVPA) have folded the sex trafficking and criminal justice paradigms into one, and some governments have attempted to impress this conflation onto others. As Melissa Ditmore details in her chapter here about the construction of the UN Protocol, US abolitionists fought hard to insert their anti-prostitution framework into the international arena. Although only partially successful at the UN level, they are considered to have been more successful at the national level due to the conservative political climate, backed up by a powerful media.[24] The criminalization of prostitution is one outcome in the US legal context that is enforced through its annual international anti-trafficking reporting system as well through its international aid and development policies. In the EU and South Asia, a trend toward the equation of trafficking with prostitution in government laws and policies is also discernible.

"THIRD WORLD" FEMINIST AND SEX WORKERS' RIGHTS ALLIANCES

In the 1990s a feminist shift away from a sexual slavery perspective became more audible and visible, grounded in grassroots activities and action research projects with "trafficked women," particularly in and from the global South. Initially articulated through collaborations between certain "Third World" feminists and sex workers' rights activists, it offered nuanced and different analyses, and indicated that although many women were indeed coerced and violated in the global sex trade, their situations were in many ways similar to those of other migrant women who sought to make a livelihood for themselves and their families in a world shaped by unequal relations of power around various axes.[25] Taking into account such new approaches and understandings of the subject, the UN Special Rapporteur on Violence against Women, Radhika Coomaraswamy, commissioned a worldwide research project on trafficking in 1996 to reestablish the parameters of the problem.[26] The report marked an important shift in international definitions of trafficking, as Lin Chew describes in her essay here, culminating in advice by the Special Rapporteur to the United Nations to delink processes of recruitment and transportation under coercion from the sex trade: that is, to conceptually separate the traffic of women from prostitution. Moreover, prostitution was defined as a legitimate form of work, inspired heavily by the global sex workers' rights movement and claims by migrant women in sex industries as well as by analyses of women's labor in "Third World" non-Western, postcolonial contexts (Kempadoo and Doezema 1998; Truong 1990; Wijers and Lap-Chew 1997). "Trafficking of women" was complexly seen to be shaped by hegemonic and local patriarchies, globalized capitalism, and the widening gaps in income and wealth, as well as by reconfigurations of empire under late-twentieth-century globalization that reinscribed international hierarchies around notions of racial, religious, and national difference. From a perspective that combined analyses of sexual labor and gendered migration, the global sex trade was defined as one, but not the only, site in which human trafficking could be located. Sectors that required unskilled or semi-skilled non-sexual labor, such as domestic service and manufacturing, as well as the racialization and feminization of the global work force and migration processes produced through the globalization of capitalism, became relevant to the analysis.[27] The redefinition rested upon an understanding of the imbrication of force and violence in conditions and processes in which poor, predominantly brown and black, women were involved in the search for social and economic security in the new world order.[28] Taking migrant women and sex workers as agents in their own right, with complex identities and subjectivities, was a critical dimension of the equation. This definition of human trafficking continues to inform many analyses and research by, on, and about women migrants and sex workers, especially in and of the global South, and continues to underpin the GAATW work.[29]

Even while it is overshadowed by the criminal justice and sex trafficking abolitionist paradigms, and in some places is almost invisible, this third perspective that threads through this collection of essays is distinct. Due in part to the sustained claim of prostitution as "work" or sexual labor, made by national and international prostitutes' rights groups, and combining with feminist analyses of international migration, a central focus of the approach is on racialized gendered labor migrations and working conditions in multiple sectors and sites.[30] Injustices and violence to women are taken to be widespread, created or exacerbated by UN, governmental, and western humanitarian anti-trafficking initiatives (Hua and Ray 2010). The critique of international and local state discourses on trafficking, which follows from such analysis, shares a common interest in a new agenda for humanity that reverberates in perspectives articulated by political and social movements that emerge from "the grassroots," "the subaltern," or "the multitude."[31] A common concern among such scholars and activists is that contemporary abolitionist, as well as criminal justice, frameworks, support neoliberal economic and political interests of major multilateral agencies and national governments, rather than those of the world's working and poor people. Current global economic policies calling for free trade and unqualified access by large transnational corporations to an unlimited supply of natural resources and raw materials, it is argued, guarantee, and defend, the rights of socially powerful elites—the propertied, managerial, cosmopolitan, and professional classes—while they limit the access, movement, and rights of the dispossessed and the economically weak and powerless. In this arrangement, a continual regulation of the supply of cheap, flexible wage-labor is paramount, with immigration laws and policies playing a critical role in controlling flows of labor.

Although dimensions of the third framework are echoed and expanded in various ways, the fuller articulations of the perspective emerge from an explicit grounding in the lives and subjectivities, struggles, and collective action of migrant and sex-working women. Experiences of migrant women and sex workers thus form the substance for the critique of the dominant paradigms and narratives on human trafficking, while also providing new categories, concepts, or different ways of approaching the problem. This framework contains then a methodology for constructing alternate discourses on sexuality, prostitution, and trafficking, and more generally on human rights and women's liberation. The methodology is located within a longer-standing principle of research that relies upon participatory action, "listening to," collaboration, or "partnership with" the marginalized, whose lives are the subject of social research and theorizing. In a discussion of the significance of participatory methodologies for exploring counter-discourses, researchers in the UK note that "sex worker's rights, unionization, advocacy and research that evidences the complexity of women's lived experience not only challenges dominant discourses but also creates space for discussions to take place around inclusion, citizenship and policy change" (O'Neill et al. 2008, 88–89). A feminist participatory action research (FPAR) approach is also central to the GAATW work, as exemplified in the chapters here by Jan Boontinand and Rebecca Napier-Moore. For some scholars and activists, being attentive to "non-Western" and migrant sex workers' definitions of their own situation enables us to see past or through existing (Western) categories and to rethink some of the core concepts within the trafficking–prostitution debate. Laura Agustin for example concludes, "The most interesting new conceptualization comes from the Durbar Mahila Samanwaya Committee [a sex workers' organization] of Kolkata, West Bengal, India" (2008, 83). In other instances, sex workers' own experiences and definitions of their lives and activities are used to interrogate the concept of work, exposing the limitations in the common Western language of freedom (Day 2010). Rutvica Andrijasevic and others note that a claim to "the right to hold rights" that was a centerpiece for sex workers in the EU was mobilized around their collective experience and understanding of exclusion and marginalization from instituted human rights for European citizens, offering a possibility for the expansion of the notion of citizenship and human rights (Andrijasevic et al. 2010). Similarly, in an ethnography among sex workers in Sonagachi India, women's conceptions and views are mobilized to illuminate the existence of complex rule networks, which include formal law "in constant interaction with several other legal orders including social norms, customs, community based dispute resolution mechanisms, social practices, and market structures" as well as conditions of "illegality" (Kotiswaran 2008, 584). Limitations of the dominant legal frameworks and discourses are thus brought into view through this close engagement with (migrant) sex workers, predominantly of non-Western origin, and it is through careful attention to their understandings, struggles, and perspectives that foundations are laid for redefinitions and alternative views.

The third perspective also stands in conversation with a discourse on human rights, albeit in ways that differ from the other two paradigms. It contests the conventional, liberal discourse of the universality of human rights, even while deploying a claim to rights. Many feminists have long raised the point that the Western liberal discourse of human rights has often worked in contradictory ways for the non-Western women it is supposed to liberate. For example, American, Canadian, or European campaigns under the banner of human rights to "save Afghan women" or rescue African women from female genital mutilation have been exposed not only for the disrespect they hold for the women involved, but for the power they hold to co-authorize new imperialist foreign policy and interventions.[32]

In examinations of the ways in which the mobilization of a universalizing discourse on human rights carries many dangers for women, including "trafficked" women in the sex trade, some argue for contextually appropriate concepts and strategies of cultural advocacy that then enable another form of human rights activism (Hesford and Kozol 2005; Collins et al. 2011). Jyoti Sanghera, in articulating the GAATW position, notes that "a sharper analytical perspective needs to be employed which goes beyond the template prescribed by the UN standards and even the human rights discourse," arguing that at the very core of the definition of rights in this framework must be "the voice and agency of trafficked and migrant women," where it is acknowledged that the women "are the architects of their own future and know best what kind of a structure they would like to live in" (2007, viii). Recognizing that the subaltern subject, including the transnational migrant and sex worker, "provides a normative challenge to the subject of liberal rights discourse," feminist legal scholar Ratna Kapur argues for a re-envisioning of the subject of women's human rights discourse from an acceptance of the value of rights without the celebration of colonial and postcolonial processes that have justified or continue to justify imperialist interventions (2005, 27, 135). Furthering these arguments, in a reflection upon new directions in feminism and human rights, Dana Collins et al. argue that "transnational feminist inquiry both brings to light, and works alongside, the longstanding tension between the universal and the particular in human rights debates by 're-engaging the local' and by attending to the cultural and representational politics of human rights deployments" (2011, 308). This third framework thus locates the claim to "rights" within the specific discursive context in which collective struggles for recognition, citizenship, and justice take place, and which is seen not to flow automatically or linearly from a Western, individualistic human rights discourse but instead to derive from collective subjectivities, experiences, norms, and perspectives of the marginalized and oppressed.

However, within this third perspective we are also cautioned against "the treachery of authenticity" and of falling into the trap of constructing an essentialist unitary notion of the Other—the Third World woman, the migrant, or sex worker—who is valorized and represented as pure and unentangled, and who, in such a representation, is ultimately silenced.[33] It recognizes that migrant women and sex workers are complicated subjects whose experiences and stories "challenge easy distinctions between innocent and knowing, between mere exploitation and severe abuse" (Chapkis 2003, 935; Parrenas Shimizu 2010). Migrant women and sex workers may then, for example, be victim and agent simultaneously, or at different stages in the process of migration, and are not simply represented as free individuals outside of wider contexts of structural oppression or coercion. Likewise, the perspective warns against dichotomizing the local and the global through essentialist configurations of the local "as the space of oppositional consciousness" and the global "as an oppressive network of dominant power structures."[34] Recognition of the complex and sometimes contradictory subjectivities, positionalities, and claims of migrants and sex workers is critical to this framework.

Accompanying the anti-essentialist stance is a self-reflexive practice that is commonly raised by researchers engaged in empirical fieldwork, but which is also relevant to other scholarly, activist, or policy work. From research on migrant sex workers in Barbados, Pamela Downe affirms the idea that we have to be conscious of the frame we employ and proposes that "we would do well to wrestle with it and to turn our analytical gaze to why we are attending to a particular story as we do" (2007, 570). Thus, she continues, "Despite the powerful grip of the compelling master narrative, it is clear that if we want to better understand how those involved in crossborder sex trades construct meaning in their lives and how they see themselves as healthy or unhealthy, safe, or vulnerable, we must try to make our engagement with this narrative as explicit as possible. In doing so, we can rewrite the dominant script so that the silences it creates are broken" (2007, 567). Such critical reflection on the researchers' own frame of reference, positionality, and engagement with the subject has been a strong tradition within subaltern, feminist, and postcolonial studies, and even while a difficult project to complete, has led some scholars to conclude that we must continue to be vigilant about our research practice through scrupulously "acknowledging complicity," "unlearning dominant systems of knowledge and representation," "learning to learn from below," "establishing an ethical relationship with our research subjects," and "working without guarantees."[35] From an examination of Canadian women in development work in Africa, Barbara Heron contends that this type of work, or "the performance of goodness" in international arenas, "is deeply about the making of the white bourgeois subjectivities at home and abroad," impressing upon us that it is critical that northerners, especially white women drawn by a "helping imperative," recognize and unpack their investments in such work (2007).[36]

Reflexivity—on the relations of power we inhabit, the narratives we produce, or the silences we create or break—is a continuous theme in this third perspective. As Doezema notes in the conclusion of her book about global trafficking discourses, reflexivity may lead to "bringing to the forefront alternative ways of thinking about 'sex work' that have lingered at the margins of the movement and may enable the incorporation of settings and experiences that are difficult to fit within a 'sex worker rights' framework" (2010, 176). Attention to marginalized experiences, struggles, and lives may then illuminate the boundaries of certain categories and concepts, as well as the boundaries of law, sovereignty, citizenship, and human rights, engendering possibilities not just for shifting the debate but for an epistemological shift toward other ways of thinking about prostitution and trafficking. This third perspective might then, as Kapur writes, "provide that alternative and possibly transformative cosmology we are seeking to move towards" (2005, 136).

LIMITATIONS OF ABOLITIONIST AND CRIMINAL JUSTICE PARADIGMS

The sex trafficking abolitionist and criminal justice paradigms are the two that dominate the global debate, and they are the most widely taken up or critiqued by scholars and activists. A number of themes run through the critiques of these paradigms. For example, the criminalization of greater areas of social life that both demand is seen to fail to significantly reduce undocumented migration or the causes for cross-border movement. Instead, it changes some avenues for migration and for securing work in another place or country, and pushes many activities further underground. It creates, for example, what Phil Marshall and Susu Thatun describe in chapter three as a "push down–pop up" effect, where interventions serve to suppress trafficking in one geographical location or community and cause it to resurface elsewhere. A displacement rather than an eradication of the problem takes place, and practices morph and mutate in unpredictable and untraceable ways. Some communities or groups may, then, be "saved" by anti-trafficking efforts, yet at the same time, new communities or younger generations are found to supply the demand for cheap services and labor. New and more sophisticated techniques for screening and apprehending border-crossers at official checkpoints furthermore compel "coyotes" or "carries" to find new avenues for their charges, and alternative entry points and modes of cross-border smuggling are tried. Sanghera observes in chapter one that new sites or venues are also found, as well as more repressive forms of confinement. In gallant rescue attempts—usually broadcast on television and the Internet, but also increasingly forming the substance of entire books—large sums of money may be handed over to secure the release of individual "slaves," generating new sources of income and new business arrangements for small-time recruiters, people-smugglers, and employers (Kristof 2004). In addition, policies developed within a framework that stresses the tightening of immigration controls tend to empower anti-immigrant sentiments and xenophobic acts. Apart from the various examples in the following essays, right-wing, armed vigilante groups complement US state and federal forces' efforts to deter and detain undocumented border-crossers (Cooper 2003).

Another striking effect that has been documented and commented upon widely is that while trafficked persons/migrants are designated "victims" under various policies and laws, they are more commonly treated as illegal immigrants and criminals, and as threats to national security. Access to documented status and residency in the destination country—that is easily afforded to categories of highly skilled workers, technocrats, business-elites, and those with enough financial clout—is not extended to the working class, and growing numbers of poor immigrants add to the already large number of persons who are processed through criminal justice systems, with increasing numbers being detained or incarcerated for non-violent crimes (Bhattacharjee 2002; Lindsley 2002; Dewey 2008). From the vantage point of migrants who are classified as trafficked, visas created for them may appear as a "stay of deportation," as they simply allow the individual to remain in the destination country for as long as required for criminal proceedings against the persons who brought them into the country for work (Pearson 2002; Gallagher and Pearson 2010). Assistance out of forced labor situations then is conditional upon cooperation with law enforcement officials (Dotteridge 2007).

As is also well documented, including by several authors in this book, along with the primary ways in which trafficked women, men, girls, and boys are dealt with in destination countries through arrest and detention measures, once "rescued" they are most commonly deported under the charge of being undocumented or "illegal." Once home they then face the shame and humiliation that accompanies deportee status. In addition, there is a fear that the family or home community is made aware of a woman's involvement in criminalized, stigmatized activities, such as prostitution. John Frederick also shows here in chapter seven that in Nepal, young "rescued" women who have been returned home from brothels in India are commonly institutionalized in safe houses or special homes indefinitely, as they no longer fit the model of the "good Nepali woman" and are left with inadequate psychological and social care to enable them to settle back into their home community or to reconstruct a life for themselves.

NGO involvement and efficacy in anti-trafficking work is also increasingly problematized. For example, Lin Chew in chapter four raises the question of whether the explosion of interest for trafficking among NGOs and other groups in the twenty-first century has to do with a real increase in the problem or with other interests, particularly international funding. Evaluations of anti-trafficking campaigns go a long way in addressing this question. In an extensive review of institutional responses to sex trafficking in Armenia, Bosnia, and India, Susan Dewey concludes that the construct of the trafficked woman is "hollow," "an empty figure to be filled up with the assumptions of relatively privileged staff members at most international organizations, governments and nongovernmental organizations," with NGOs becoming "little more than hollow fronts for donor funding" (2008, 164). Similarly in the US, abolitionist NGOs and faith-based organizations have been found to be "amply rewarded" by the government (Foerster 2009, 165). Moreover, the dependency on external funding for anti-trafficking activities by NGOs makes their efforts often unsustainable, ad hoc, and quite ineffective (Samarasinghe and Burton 2007). Economic rewards and interests appear then to profoundly shape much anti-trafficking NGO and institutionalized activity, often superseding the humanitarian dimensions of the work.

In response to the disregard for migrant women's lives, their rights to mobility, and rights to livelihood that underpins or results from dominant anti-trafficking campaigns, several authors here argue that state policies and interventions need to create systems that allow for "safe migration" in order that violation and injustices in processes of migration be eliminated, and the right to freedom of movement be guaranteed for all. As the majority of the authors in this collection point out, efforts to repress migration, to keep people at home, or to "push them back," often do greater harm than good, and run counter to the interests of the migrant person. Migrant women and men who are deported for infringing upon national immigration laws (even though they may be "rescued") are generally forced through state anti-trafficking interventions to return to the same conditions that initially prompted their move. Global structural inequalities in the distribution of wealth and in access to education, employment, healthcare, and social security; militarized conflicts and occupations; dispossessions from the land and environmental disasters; and gender-based or religious violence and ethnic conflicts, all of which underlie the movement of women into particular labor market sectors, are not eradicated in the sex trafficking abolitionist or criminal justice approaches to trafficking. Conditions at home remain for the most part unchanged. Returned or deported migrants may then make new attempts to leave, and are once again made vulnerable to smuggling, deception, or coercion in the migration process, debt-bondage, and/or violence from employers, law enforcement officials, and clients. Thus, even though the rescue and assistance of "trafficked victims" is advocated in the dominant narratives, it has come to the attention of many involved with migrants and marginalized communities, and especially migrant sex workers, that human rights violations have not abated under anti-trafficking policies and legislation.[37] The wider economic and political global conditions thus remain pressing issues, which, according to authors here, are crucial issues for the international community to take up.

In addition to the violence that the anti-trafficking fervor promotes, the two dominant approaches primarily identify foreign gangs and "source" countries as the main culprits, criminals, and beneficiaries in the trafficking business. Given that the majority of "destination" countries are claimed to be postindustrial countries in Western and Northern Europe and North America, as well as the industrialized or militarized centers in Asia, such as Japan, Taiwan, and South Korea, this creates international divides around nationality, ethnicity, and race. And while it has been established that most of the undocumented migration occurs not for underground sex industries run by criminal elements, but for sweatshops, farming, service, and domestic work that are attached to formal sectors of the economy, state and public attention is quickly drawn to groups of middle-persons who are held up as the "real" menaces—recruiting agents and those who assist others to move without legal documents or money—who are commonly identified as greedy, immoral men from or of the global South and postsocialist states (O'Neill 1999; Surtees 2005). Media and research reports on trafficking worldwide often reproduce this focus. The main profiteers in the dominant narratives are racialized, ethnic Others, with the victims poor brown or black women from Asia, Africa, and Latin America, or young women from Eastern Europe and Russia.

The dominant anti-trafficking paradigms also ignore to a large extent the enmeshment of legal sectors in organized crime. As pointed out in studies of twenty-first-century transnational organized crime, one of the more obdurate characteristics of organized crime is that established (legalized) and underground (criminalized) sectors stand in a symbiotic relationship (Beare 2003). Without assistance from "legitimate" businessmen, lawyers, police and other law enforcement officials, politicians, and

CEOs of large corporations, organized crime is largely unsuccessful. Yet, an elision of this relationship has occurred, and instead anti-trafficking campaigns are promoted through a politics that rests upon the prosecution and punishment of those considered to be lawless and ruthless. The crediting of trafficking to the foreign "Other," who is configured as a threat to Western societies and civilization, serves thus as a scare tactic to corral racist, nationalist sentiments and to obfuscate the interaction between the state, corporate capital, and underground sectors. To some researchers and policy makers this problem in the dominant paradigms can be corrected through attention for "the demand side"—clients of sex workers, such as advocated in the "Nordic model"—as well as for police and state military complicities, and through investigations into investment and gains made by established "legal" social and political institutions.[38]

Many of the claims made about sex or human trafficking are based on sensationalist reports, hyperbole, and conceptual confusions. Even those who wish to incite moral indignation through use of the trope of slavery indicate that debt-bondage, indentureship, and hyperexploitative contractual arrangements are the most common forms of contemporary forced labor practices.[39] Slaves are said to make up the smallest proportion of those who are smuggled or cross borders in undocumented status, and/or engaged in forced labor and debt-bondage.[40] A distinction between different labor regimes is important to recognize, for whereas slavery is premised on property relations—the permanent and legal ownership of one human being by another and the power invested in the owner to command that property at will—debt-bondage, indentureship, and forced labor are lodged in contractual, wage relations and principles of free labor power and its market exchange value. Examinations of contract labor and debt-bondage conditions of the nineteenth and early twentieth centuries, including the indentureship of people from India, China, and Indonesia, as well as Britain and Portugal, on plantations in the Americas could, for example, tell us a great deal about capitalist development since the abolition of slavery, its need for cheap, disposable labor, and the systems it erects to ensure a steady supply of labor. Such examinations could produce historically informed and less moralistic analyses of forced labor and processes of migration that have taken place since the mid-nineteenth century (Sandy 2010).

Despite efforts to prove human trafficking, it is generally acknowledged that claims about the problem are largely unsubstantiated. Nevertheless, the lack of evidence does not deter anti-trafficking campaigns. The US State Department effort stands as an exemplar on this score. The campaign revolves around an annual evaluation and ranking of national interventions to combat trafficking into three tiers, according to standards set by the US State Department. Countries that do not comply with the US standards are placed in the lowest tier and are subject to sanctions.

However, since its inception, the system has been plagued by a lack of evidence, unsystematic data collection, and a lack of analysis.[41] This glaring tendency has led to conclusions that some nations are punished "only on the basis of insufficient evidence."[42] That Tier 3 is mostly composed of countries that the US considers to be unruly, undemocratic, and/or terrorist states, such as Cuba, Venezuela, North Korea, Burma, and Iran, most clearly illustrates the political intention of the ranking. Regarding this political character of the US ranking system, former UN anti-trafficking officer Anne Gallagher concludes from an extensive review of a decade of US reporting on trafficking:

> The Reports are political creatures, produced through a political process and serving specific political ends ... it is naïve to expect that country narratives will always be able to maintain an objective distance from the two sharp ends of US foreign relations policy.... Political and ideological opponents of the USA may never be moved from Tier 3, no matter how much they try to conform to the TVPA minimum standards. (2010, 12)

As several of the authors here argue, analyses of immiseration, structural violence, and social injustice in the world today must be lodged in real, material conditions. Hyperbole, unsubstantiated claims, and sensationalism, while perhaps useful for rustling up indignation and moral condemnation about inhumane treatment and exploitation and for advancing particular national political agendas, can, and often do, lead to greater abuse and violations, even in the hands of well-meaning anti-trafficking policy makers and activists. And as Anderson, Sharma, and Wright also point out, the hyperbole masks the ways in which increasing exclusionary practices and contradictions that are central to the working of the neo-liberal state not only affect migrants, but citizens as well. Thus, restrictive immigration policies, including anti-trafficking immigration controls, shore up "ideological, even fantastical, re-presentations of the 'nation,'" and not only serve to accord fewer migrants status that comes with rights but to rob citizens of civil liberties (Anderson, Sharma, and Wright 2009, 7).

ON MATTERS OF AGENCY

Evident in the criminal justice paradigm, and particularly emphasized in the sex trafficking abolitionist narrative, is the idea that those who are subject to trafficking are "victims." This designation has implications for the advancement of women's rights and freedoms, and connects to wider debates about the conceptualization of gender oppression. The notion of "victim" immediately captures the principle that women's subjugation and oppression is not of their own making, but rather a consequence of masculine power and male dominance. However, the objectifying dimensions of the definition and its ability to dismiss any conception of agency have also been recognized by feminist researchers and theorists.[43] Thus in much contemporary transnational and other feminist theorizing the gender category "woman" is neither exclusively object nor subject, but seen to be constructed under variable conditions or systems of domination such as patriarchy, colonialism, racism, and imperialism, and to always include some notions of resistance, agency, subjectivity, and self-determination. "Woman" in the twenty-first century is a category in most feminist work that is constituted simultaneously as "victim" and "agent." However, the almost exclusive reliance on the notion of "victim" in dominant anti-trafficking paradigms ignores this trend, privileging external forces in the conceptualization of the trafficked person, and denying women any agency or subjectivity in the process (Schwenken 2003).

Such a conceptualization sustains an image of women as pure, unblemished, and innocent prior to the trafficking act, as clean passive slates that are consequently imprinted and given character by and through the actions of "evil" men. Ditmore argues in this volume that the gendered distinction between, on the one hand, women as victims, and on the other, men as actors, is also acutely visible in the UN Protocols on trafficking and smuggling. Whereas the former primarily speaks about women and children, the latter refers most commonly to men. Women and children by definition are trafficked—kidnapped, transported against their will over borders, and held in inhumane conditions—due to their presumed innocence, purity, and inability to take action on their own behalf, while it is men who are thought to actively seek to be smuggled, and hence are viewed as implicated subjects.[44]

The ability of the concept "victim" to rob the (feminized) individual of any notion of agency and subjectivity, and to ideologically locate the migrant woman or sex worker as helpless and pitiful, has strong implications for how change is imagined or taken up in policies and interventions. Victims, who by this definition are passive and child-like, are deemed incapable of undertaking any action, thus requiring "rescue" or "saving" from their circumstances by others who stand outside of the trafficking process and who, it is believed, "know best" (Skrobanek et al. 1997, 18). The construction of, and changes to, the trafficking myth in Nepal, discussed in chapter seven, illustrates how even the work of local well-intentioned nongovernmental organizations can fall into this trap, lending to the process of the objectification and further victimization, or even a retraumatization of women. Moreover, as has been repeatedly documented and observed, many so-called trafficked persons tend to define themselves not as "victims of trafficking" but as "migrant workers who have had some bad luck as a result of a bad decision" (Pearson 2002; GAATW 2007; Gallagher and Pearson 2010). The term "trafficked victim" does not always generate recognition or self-identification, and may be counterproductive in everyday human rights and social justice work. Chapter 13 draws from participatory action research among "trafficked women" around the world underscores this limitation.

Migrant women's and sex workers' "victimhood" is thus used to mobilize anti-trafficking sympathy and to make humanitarian appeals, as well as to secure funds, increase policing and law enforcement, and to monitor borders, while their own subjectivity, decisions, and "choices" are denied legitimacy.[45] A critique of the victim approach of much of the contemporary anti-trafficking narratives is an important aspect of this book. Many of the authors argue here that it is not prostitution per se that is harmful to women, but rather that under the ruse of anti-trafficking interventions, migrants' and prostitutes' rights to work, migrate, receive health-care, social benefits, and respect are violated. Moreover, even while diverse identifications are employed throughout this book, such as "trafficked persons," "affected women," "sex workers," "undocumented migrants," or "transnational migrant subjects," it is a commitment to ending the exploitations, injuries, and injustices with these populations in mind that underwrites these essays.

CHANGES IN THE SECOND EDITION

This second edition, like the first, focuses on the ongoing re-articulation of the trafficking discourse that began through mainly feminist definitions since the mid-1990s. It continues to shift attention away from state drives for greater immigration control, global policing, and the criminalization of prostitution, and to foreground the needs, agency, struggles, and rights of migrant and sex working communities. The first three sections have undergone little revision or change, as the original texts represent developments, ideas, and data that continue to be pertinent to contemporary situations and debates. The original arguments and analyses are immensely helpful in demonstrating that very little that is theoretically innovative or substantively groundbreaking has been brought to the debate over the past decade, even while the field has expanded and a wealth of studies on trafficking now exists. Ratna Kapur's chapter, "Cross-border Movements and the Law: Renegotiating the Boundaries of Difference," has, however, been updated to address some of the more recent global initiatives, including recent UN and US laws and conventions. Her chapter provides, once again, a comprehensive critique of the dominant trafficking discourse through an examination of the workings of the global legal order and its implications for the transnational migrant subject.

A fourth section has been added to this new edition, which contains two new chapters. In chapter 13, the alliance that gave shape to the original edition reflects upon what has been accomplished over the past decade and a half of anti-trafficking activity and sketches out future directions. Arguing that anti-trafficking work has become overspecialized and trapped within policy and NGO silos, Rebecca Napier-Moore, who writes on behalf of the GAATW, points out that much of the work is now inadequate for attending to the needs of "trafficked women." She goes on to highlight aspects of recent GAATW feminist participatory action research that stitch back together those elements that have become virtually severed in the dominant, compartmentalized interventions, namely, migration, labor, and women's rights. The chapter also describes how, through an alternative, holistic approach, women's own understandings about identity, experiences, migration, and future prospects become visible and can lead to sustainable and meaningful grassroots change. The concluding chapter is a compilation of reflections, observations, notes, and ideas about the field of anti-trafficking by several of the contributing authors and editors of this book. It gives some insight into what has (not) been accomplished over the past decade, and ideas about what could be done in the field. A fundamental shift away from the dominant paradigms is, it would seem, still an imperative. Nevertheless, as with the first edition, we hope that in examining trafficking with respect for migrant and sex worker rights, agency, and humanity, this book continues to provide alternative ways of thinking about the subject and to offer insights that can inspire future theory, policy, and action.

NOTES

1. Jo Doezema (2010) refers to these and similar narratives as "myths" within a wider discourse of human trafficking.

2. In a review of the two dominant US discourses on trafficking Jennifer Musto notes, "while the ability to name and categorize human rights abuses like trafficking have grown more sophisticated, such naming practices have, to date, proven limited in translating modes of suffering . . . into theoretical and political strategies that prevent their emergence" (2009, 286).

3. Recent data on legal international migration compiled by the UN state that "most legal migrants in the more developed regions [defined as Europe, North America, Australia, New Zealand, and Japan], originate from the less developed regions [defined as Africa, Asia (excluding Japan), Latin America and the Caribbean, Melanesia, Micronesia, and Polynesia]." United Nations, Department of Economic and Social Affairs, Population Division (2009). *International Migration, 2009 Wallchart* (United Nations publication, Sales No. E.09.XIII.8). Rhacel Parrenas also reminds us that "migrant women workers from the Philippines . . . represent one of the largest labour migrant groups in the world today" (2006, 146).

4. At the time of the compilation of the first edition of this book Bandana Pattanaik was research project coordinator, Jyoti Sanghera was a member of the GAATW board, and this author was a member of the GAATW working group on research methodology.

5. See for example, Seagrave (2009) on Thailand and Australia, Sandy (2007; 2010)

on Cambodia, Amar (2009) on Brazil, Chuang (2010) on the US, and Andrijasevic and Anderson (2009) on the EU.

6. Anna-Louise Crago argues that a precursor to the twentieth-century discourse on human trafficking is lodged in the ideologies and laws that were constructed in the United States around Asian immigration. She notes that in West Coast American cities, it was widely believed that "Oriental" women were involved in prostitution due to the immoral nature of the immigrant populations. Consequently, efforts were made to curb the migration of the women and to prevent such "immorality" from further corrupting the nation. The first US act to explicitly address the issue was passed in 1870 and prohibited the importation of "Mongolian," Chinese, and Japanese women. In 1875, the US Congress passed the Page Law which forbade the entry of prostitutes, felons, and Asian contract laborers into the United States and specifically prohibited immigration from "China, Japan or any Oriental country" for so-called lewd and immoral purposes. Crago observes, "Chinese (and more broadly, 'Oriental') immorality and depravity, as 'proven' by the presence of prostitution, were marshaled in support for the 'Yellow Peril' panic and the 1882 Chinese Exclusion Act in the United States, as well as similar laws in Canada, which cut off legal immigration to all but a tiny elite minority" (Unpublished paper, presented at the conference *Mapping Insurgencies: Sex, Race and Globalization,* Committee on Lesbian /Gay /Bisexual Transgender Studies, University of Arizona–Tucson, April 25–26, 2003). See also Bisnauth (2000), Reddock (1985), and Shepherd (2002) for accounts on the regulation of Indian women's labor under indentureship regimes in the Caribbean.

7. See for example, Grittner (1990), Guy (1991), Walkowitz (1980), Doezema (2000; 2010), Kempadoo (2004), Weitzer (2007), and Dewey (2008).

8. Emma Goldman was quick to point out that the trade in women was not merely about white women, but involved "yellow and black women" as well ("The Traffic in Women," 1911).

9. For Emma Goldman's views on prostitution, the trafficking of women, the women's movement, and reformist morality, see her essays "The Traffic in Women," "The Tragedy of Women's Emancipation," "Victims of Morality," and "Woman Suffrage," originally published in 1910 and 1913, reprinted in Shulman (1996). Judith Walkowitz was one of the first feminists in the late twentieth century to revisit the subject.

10. "Radical feminist" is used here following Alison Jaggar and others who classified the main feminist frameworks of the "second wave" according to their underlying assumptions about gender relations. Thus radical feminism refers to the framework that locates women's oppression as caused by patriarchy, which is taken as a universal and primary form of domination.

11. Recent examples of this perspective are found in Hughes et al. (2007) and Hoffer (2010). Regarding this approach Halley et al. argue that there has been a "profound turn in American feminism to criminal/social control visions of law, traceable in feminist legal theory over the 1990s and persisting today" (2006, 342).

12. See for example Bales (1999), Skinner (2008), and Kara (2009) as examples of the "modern-day slavery" approach, and O'Connell Davidson (2010) for a recent critique.

13. Chuang (2010) also traces this development using the notion of "neo-abolitionism" to refer to this coalition. Weitzer and Ditmore (2008) refer to it as a modern-day "moral crusade." See also Sayeed (2006).

14. Through careful ethnographic research and analysis, Bernstein (2010) locates the modern-day abolitionists at the meeting point of "militarized humanism" and "carceral feminism."

15. This redefinition was made in the reauthorizations of the US TVPA in 2005 and 2008, in which all commercial sex acts were defined as trafficking. See for example, Weitzer and Ditmore (2008).

16. In the flurry of attention around the publication of a report on child sex trafficking in the UK, and the claim that Asian men were sexually grooming young white English women, the authors of the report attempted to counter this racialized panic by pointing out that the majority of the women harmed were young women of color ("Warning of Racial Stereotyping over 'Sexual Grooming' Gangs." *Guardian Weekly,* Jan. 14, 2011, p. 16). Likewise, despite the arrest of predominantly Asian men on suspicion of grooming young girls, the concern is said to be about "white, black and Asian children" ("Groom Gloom" *Guardian Weekly,* Jan. 21, 2011, p. 15).

17. See also chapter 5 by Josephine Ho on shifts in the Taiwanese discourse.

18. Kapoor (2008, 34). See also Kapur for a critique of the Western liberal legal framework especially as it relates to women of the global South, and who argues that the law is taken "as an objective external neutral truth that propels us into the future, providing stability to the societies in which it operates and steering us carefully along the path of maturity, development, and civilization" (2005, 21).

19. Anghie (1999, 71). See also Hua and Ray (2010) for an incisive critique of the ways in which the UN Protocol enables neoliberal, including "neo-universal feminist," understandings of subjectivity, freedom, and humanity, and which locate certain transnational female bodies as always and already in need of rescue. In contrast, Veronica Hayes' 2010 analysis of anti-trafficking debates around the Olympics and other world sports events is a typical example of scholarly work where a commitment to combating "sex trafficking" is tied to an uncritical adoption of the Western discourse on human rights.

20. Kapoor (2008, 4–35), drawing from Hannah Arendt.

21. See for example *Alliance News* 18, July 2002 for the full coverage of earlier plans and conventions such as the South Asian Association for Regional Cooperation (SAARC) Convention on Preventing and Combating Trafficking in Women and Children for Prostitution, and the Asian Regional Initiative Against Trafficking (ARIAT) Regional Action Plan Against Trafficking in Persons, Especially Women and Children.

22. See for example ASI (2003), EU (2002), ILO (2001), IOM (2003), Laczko (2005), and Mahmoud and Trebesch (2010).

23. Scholars such as Leman and Janssens argue that "to combat human trafficking it is crucial to combat criminal networks in their entirety" (2008, 448). See also Surtees (2008), Goodey (2008), Gallagher and Holmes (2008), Farrell and Fahy (2009), Lebov (2010), Simeunovic-Patic and Copic (2010), and Perrin (2010).

24. In writing about the "moral crusade" of the abolitionist feminists, Weitzer and Ditmore note that under the George W. Bush administration "antiprostitution gained tremendous influence over policymaking" to the extent that "abolitionist forces helped to transform the campaign against sex trafficking into an official government campaign against prostitution" (2008, 327). Schaeffer-Grabiel (2010) provides an analysis of the role of the media in this process.

25. Lin Chew's chapter in this volume documents some of the early history of this feminist movement. See also Brussa (1991), Skrobanek et al. (1997), and Wijers and Lap-Chew (1997).

26. The commissioned report was published as Wijers and Lap-Chew (1997).

27. Research on migrant women's lives, such as Sassen (1998), Chang (2000), Louie (2001), Parrenas (2001), and Ehrenreich and Hoschchild (2002) provided important insights into conditions for "Third World" women in the global labor marketplace.

28. In an earlier essay, I referred to this "alternative" perspective on trafficking as a "transnational feminist" approach (Kempadoo 2005). Transnational feminism I take to mean the body of analyses, methods, and activities that emerged from the convergence of distinct areas—cultural and postcolonial studies, Third World feminism, and women's activism in the late 1990s. It is defined as a theory and practice within women's studies

and the women's movement that acts as an umbrella framework for a range of analyses and activities that self-consciously and critically address contemporary global material inequalities and relations of power, new flows and linkages in the global economy, and the ways in which gender is mediated by race, class, nationality, sexuality, and religion. It is located in a diverse set of social realities and struggles for and by women in very diverse conditions, from postmodernity to postcoloniality, yet takes the relations of domination and subordination that appear within and across these contexts as central for both analyzing and changing these conditions. (See also Kempadoo, *Recuperations and Re-visionings: Theories and Practices in Transnational Feminism*. National Women's Studies Association 22nd Annual Conference, Minneapolis, USA, June 13–17, 2001, for an earlier delineation of the framework.)

29. Although this third paradigm has been called for and developed since the late 1990s (Kempadoo and Doezema [1998]; Wijers, cited in Doezema [2000]), some scholars, particularly those who have more recently joined the debate and who seem to be unaware of this history, also come to the conclusion that dominant discourses are quite inadequate and that another perspective is needed. For example, Seagrave argues for "an alternative framework" that "begins with the shifting political, economic, labour and migration patterns that have emerged under conditions of globalisation, including the patterns of women's movement across national and international borders and the feminisation of the low skilled, low-wage workforce in both the Global North and the Global South" (2009, 255). See also Limoncelli (2009), who proposes a feminist political economy approach, and Musto (2009).

30. This direction has been expanded through research into connections between sex work and other forms of women's migrant labor, especially domestic work. See for example O'Connell Davidson (2006), Brennan (2010), Truong (2008), Kim and Fu (2008), Jacobsen and Stenvoll (2010), Andrijasevic and Anderson (2009), Sandy (2007), Papanicolaou (2008), and Boris et al. (2010), who have repeated a call for, or deepened, a labor analysis of sex work. It could be argued that research on sexual labor or prostitution that locates the activities within contexts of labor migration constitutes another paradigm or a distinctly different narrative. However, given that analysis of sex work as labor is integral to this third paradigm from the start, through both the study by Thanh-Dam Truong and the analysis by Carole Leigh in the 1980s, a focus on labor is included as one dimension of the transnational feminist paradigm. Moreover, labor migration has been critical to this third perspective from the outset, and continues to be one of many factors that complicates our understanding of women in the global sex trade (see for example Kempadoo and Doezema [1998], and Agustin [2006; 2007]). This is not however to foreclose the possibility that a more stable set of narratives will appear around either labor or migration, or both, and in the future will constitute distinct paradigms on the subject.

31. As identified by scholars such as Appadurai (2000), Panitch and Leys (2003), Wright (2003), and Sharma (2006).

32. Godec, for example, critiques militarized humanitarian peacekeeping interventions for the devastating effects they have on women—in Kosovo, but also Kuwait, Afghanistan, and Iraq—noting that the "'saving women' rhetoric is disjunctive from the reality of women's lives" (2010, 256). Regarding feminist support for such military interventions, she concludes, "The convergence of interventionist doctrine with the feminist concern about systematic sexual violence, underscored by 'saving women' and 'heroic' narratives, has proved to be a relationship of inequality" (2010, 258). Similarly, in an analysis of media reports on US military camptowns in South Korea, Cheng concludes, "the spectacle of victimization in the report narrowly contains Third World women in roles of one-dimensional victims who are powerless and scared, awaiting the rescue of the White knight who will arrive in the form of the journalist-hero. The representational obliteration of these women's agency eliminates the possibility of including their own assessment of what they need and their

analysis for solving the problems of their human rights violations. Instead, the women's power is transferred to the middle-class American journalist who can travel across national borders in a flash and has direct access to U.S. government officials, who know best" (2008, 15). Heron (2007) points out that this relationship is repeated through development discourses and interventions, where the "helping imperative" is mobilized by white North American women.

33. Gayatri Spivak, in her pivotal 1988 essay "Can the Subaltern Speak?" argued that due to the dominance of particular discourses, shaped by patriarchy and imperialism, not only is the voice and the figure of the subaltern/Third World/Indian woman unable to be heard and seen, but that any notion of an "authentic" voice disappears. Similarly, Sylvia Wynter (1990) contends that for Caliban's/Caribbean/Black women, the ground from which she self-represents is itself constituted through dominant discourses.

34. Grewel and Kaplan, cited in Hesford and Kozol (2005, 19).

35. Kapoor (2008), echoing Spivak's ideas about research and work with "the subaltern."

36. Similarly Agustin calls for greater self-reflection on the part of "helpers," noting that "social agents and their projects remain at the centre of attention while failing materially to improve the situation of people who sell sex" (2007, 186).

37. While this was the conclusion drawn in the first edition of the book in 2005, it has since been supported in many other research reports and writings on trafficking. See for example, GAATW (2007), Agustin (2007), Maynard (2010), and Dewey (2008).

38. See for example, Keren-Paz and Levenkron (2009). Godec (2010) also points to the need to investigate UN peacekeeping interventions as part of the problem of trafficking.

39. This is acknowledged by well-established abolitionists, such as Hynes and Raymond (2002), but also by others who have recently joined the crusade against modern-day slavery, such as Pennington et al. (2009).

40. See for example Bales (1999), Viuhko (2010), Haynes (2009), and Cole (2009).

41. Gallagher (2001), Marshall (2001), Human Rights Watch (2003), GAATW (2007), Gallagher (2010).

42. Shah (2002), Kempadoo (2007; 2009). In 2009 the US rankings were immediately contested by the Caribbean governments of St. Vincent and Guyana governments on the basis of a lack of evidence. The TIP (Trafficking in Persons) designation was considered unfair and unfounded, with no recognition for what was being done locally to address the problem. Even countries that were placed in Tier 2 objected to the US State Department's ranking, such as the Bahamas where the Ministry of Foreign Affairs issued a statement claiming "there is no positive evidence" of the trafficking of women from Jamaica for sex work, and that incidences of forced labor could not by themselves be taken as evidence to prove that persons were being trafficked. The resentment reflects the position often taken by Caribbean governments that the US should not try to control or influence affairs in postcolonial, independent nations.

43. See for example, the work of Michel Foucault, Pierre Bourdieu, Sherry Ortner, Judith Butler, and Aihwa Ong.

44. Dotteridge (2007) notes that because men are rarely identified as trafficked victims they lose access to the resources or assistance that are put in place by anti-trafficking interventions, even when it is clear that they have been subjected to forced labor. Dennis's 2008 analysis of 166 published social science articles reveals an acute invisibility of men in the global sex trade—trafficked or not—and concludes that in the event that they are mentioned, they are accorded more agency than women.

45. Nevertheless, a large body of work that deepens examinations of migrant women's subjectivity and agency in relationship to migration and "trafficking" for the sex trade has arisen since the first edition of this book, including Agustin (2007), Sandy (2007), Downe (2007), Lévy and Lieber (2008), Oso Casas (2010), Jacobsen and Skilbrei (2010), Penttinen (2010), Brennan (2010), Chimienti (2010), Zheng (2010), and Andrijasevic (2010).

xxxvi   *Kamala Kempadoo*

REFERENCES

Agustin, Laura Maria. "The Disappearing of a Migration Category: Migrants Who Sell Sex." *Journal of Ethnic and Migration Studies* 32 (2006): 29–47.
———. *Sex at the Margins: Migration, Labour Markets and the Rescue Industry.* London and New York: Zed Books, 2007.
———. "Sex and the Limits of Enlightenment: The Irrationality of Legal Regimes to Control Prostitution." *Sexuality Research & Social Policy* 5 (2008): 73–86.
Amar, Paul. "Operation Princess in Rio de Janeiro: Policing 'Sex Trafficking,' Strengthening Worker Citizenship, and the Urban Geopolitics of Security in Brazil." *Security Dialogue* 40 (2009): 513–541.
Anderson, Bridget, Nandita Sharma, and Cynthia Wright. "Editorial: Why No Borders?" *Refuge: Canada's Periodical on Refugees* 26 (2009): 5–18.
Andrijasevic, Rutvica. *Migration, Agency and Citizenship in Sex Trafficking.* Basingstoke: Palgrave Macmillan, 2010.
Andrijasevic, Rutvica, and Bridget Anderson. "Anti-Trafficking Campaigns: Decent? Honest? Truthful?" *Feminist Review* 92 (2009): 151–155.
Andrijasevic, Rutvica, Claudia Aradau, Jef Huysmans, and Vicki Squire. "Unexpected Citizens: Sex Work, Mobility, Europe." ENACT, Open University, 2010.
Anghie, Anthony. "Finding the Peripheries: Sovereignty and Colonialism in Nineteenth-Century International Law." *Harvard International Law Journal* 40 (1999).
Appadurai, Arjun. "Grassroots Globalization and the Research Imagination." In *Globalization,* edited by Arjun Appadurai. Durham, NC: Duke University Press, 2000: 1–21.
ASI. "The Migration-Trafficking Nexus: Combating Trafficking Through the Protection of Migrant's Human Rights." London: Anti-Slavery International, 2003.
Bales, Kevin. *Disposable People: New Slavery in the Global Economy.* Berkeley/Los Angeles: University of California Press, 1999.
Barry, Kathleen. *Female Sexual Slavery.* New York: New York University Press, 1984.
Beare, Margaret E. "Introduction." In Margaret E. Beare, editor, *Critical Reflections on Transnational Organized Crime, Money Laundering, and Corruption.* Toronto: University of Toronto Press, 2003: xi–xxix.
Bernstein, Elizabeth. "The Sexual Politics of the 'New Abolitionism'." *Differences: A Journal of Feminist Cultural Studies* 18 (2007): 128–151.
———. "Militarized Humanitarianism Meets Carceral Feminism: The Politics of Sex, Rights, and Freedom in Contemporary Antitrafficking Campaigns." *Signs* 36 (1), 2010: 45–71.
Bhattacharjee, Anannya. "Private Fists and Public Force: Race, Gender and Surveillance." In J. Silliman and A. Bhattacharjee, editors, *Policing the National Body: Race, Gender and Criminalization.* Cambridge, MA: South End Press, 2002.
Bisnauth, Dale. *The Settlement of Indians in Guyana 1890–1930.* London: Peepal Tree Press, 2000.
Boris, Eileen, Stephanie Gilmore, and Rhacel Parrenas. "Sexual Labors: Interdisciplinary Perspectives Toward Sex as Work." *Sexualities* 13 (2010): 131–137.
Brennan, Denise. "Competing Claims of Victimhood? Foreign and Domestic Victims of Trafficking in the United States." *Sexuality Research & Social Policy* 5 (2008): 45–61.
———. "Key Issues in the Resettlement of Formerly Trafficked Persons in the United States." *University of Pennsylvania Law Review* 158 (2010): 1581–1608.
———. "Thoughts on Finding and Assisting Individuals in Forced Labor in the USA." *Sexualities* 13 (2010): 139–152.
Brussa, Licia. "Survey on Prostitution, Migration and Traffick in Women: History and Current Situation." European Committee for Equality between Women and Men. Council of Europe, Strasbourg, 1991.
Chang, Grace. *Disposable Domestics: Immigrant Women Workers in the Global Economy.* Boston: South End Press, 2000.

Change. "Combating Trafficking in Persons: A Directory of Organisations." Anti-trafficking Programme, London, 2003.

Chapkis, Wendy. "Trafficking, Migration and the Law: Protecting Innocents, Punishing Immigrants." *Gender and Society* 17 (2003): 923–937.

Cheng, Sealing. "Muckraking and Stories Untold: Ethnography Meets Journalism on Trafficked Women and the U.S. Military." *Sexuality Research & Social Policy* 5 (2008): 6–18.

Chimienti, Milena. "Selling Sex in Order to Migrate: The End of the Migratory Dream?" *Journal of Ethnic and Migration Studies* 36 (2010): 27–45.

Chuang, Janie A. "Rescuing Trafficking from Ideological Capture: Prostitution Reform and Anti-trafficking Law and Policy." *University of Pennsylvania Law Review* 158 (2010): 1655.

Cole, Helen. "Human Trafficking: Implications for the Role of the Advanced Practice Forensic Nurse." *Journal of American Psychiatric Nurses Association* 14 (2009): 462–470.

Collins, Dana, Sylvanna Falcón, Sharmila Lodhia, and Molly Talcott. "New Directions in Feminism and Human Rights: Introduction." *International Feminist Journal of Politics* 12 (2011): 298–318.

Cooper, Marc. "On the Border of Hypocrisy: The Unintended Consequences of Getting Tough in Illegal Immigration." *LA Weekly*, December 5–11, 2003.

Day, S. "The Re-emergence of 'Trafficking': Sex Work between Slavery and Freedom." *Journal of the Royal Anthropological Institute* 16(4), 2010: 816–834.

Dennis, Jeffrey P. "Women are Victims, Men Make Choices: The Invisibility of Men and Boys in the Global Sex Trade." *Gender Issues* (2008): 11–25.

Dewey, Susan. *Hollow Bodies: Institutional Responses to Sex Trafficking in Armenia, Bosnia, and India*. Sterling, VA: Kumarian Press, 2008.

Doezema, Jo. "Loose Women or Lost Women? The Re-emergence of the Myth of White Slavery in Contemporary Discourse of Trafficking in Women." *Gender Issues* 18 (2000): 23–50.

———. "Ouch!: Western Feminists' 'Wounded Attachment' to the 'Third World Prostitute'." *Feminist Review* 67 (2001): 16–38.

———. *Sex Slaves and Discourse Masters: The Construction of Trafficking*. London and New York: Zed Books/Palgrave Macmillan, 2010.

Dotteridge, Mike. "Introduction." In *Collateral Damage: The Impact of Anti-Trafficking Measures on Human Rights around the World*, edited by GAATW. Bangkok: Global Alliance Against Traffic in Women, 2007: 1–28.

Downe, Pamela J. "Strategic Stories and Reflexive Interruptions: Narratives of a 'Safe Home' Amidst Cross-Border Sex Work." *Qualitative Inquiry* 13 (2007): 554–572.

Ehrenreich, Barbara, and Arlie Russell Hoschchild. *Global Woman: Nannies, Maids, and Sex Workers in the New Economy*. New York: Metropolitan Books, 2002.

EU. "Campaign Against Trafficking in Women." Council of Europe Parliamentary Assembly, 2002.

Farrell, Amy, and Stephanie Fahy. "The Problem Of Human Trafficking in the U.S.: Public Frames and Policy Responses." *Journal of Criminal Justice* 37 (6), 2009: 617–626.

Findlay, Eileen J. Suarez. *Imposing Decency: The Politics of Sexuality in Puerto Rico, 1870–1920*. Durham, NC: Duke University Press, 1999.

Foerster, Amy. "'Contested Bodies': Sex Trafficking NGOs and Transnational Politics." *International Feminist Journal of Politics* 11 (2009): 151–173.

Friesendorf, Cornelius, editor. *Strategies against Human Trafficking: The Role of the Security Sector*. Vienna: National Defence Academy and Austrian Ministry of Defence and Sports in cooperation with Geneva Centre for the Democratic Control of Armed Forces, 2009.

GAATW. *Collateral Damage: The Impact of Anti-Trafficking Measures on Human Rights Around the World*. Bangkok: Global Alliance Against Traffic in Women, 2007.

Gallagher, Anne. "Human Rights and the New UN Protocols on Trafficking and Migrant Smuggling: A Preliminary Analysis." *Human Rights Quarterly* 23 (2001): 975–1004.

————. "Improving the Effectiveness of the International Law of Human Trafficking: A Vision for the Future of the US Trafficking in Persons Reports." In *Human Rights Review*. Springer Science+Business Media B.V., 2010.

Gallagher, Anne, and Paul Holmes. "Developing an Effective Criminal Justice Response to Human Trafficking: Lessons From the Front Line." *International Criminal Justice Review* 18 (2008): 318–343.

Gallagher, Anne, and Elaine Pearson. "The High Cost of Freedom: A Legal and Policy Analysis of Shelter Detention for Victims of Trafficking." *Human Rights Quarterly* 32 (2010): 73–114.

Godec, S. T. "Between Rhetoric and Reality: Exploring the Impact of Military Humanitarian Intervention upon Sexual Violence: Post-conflict Sex Trafficking in Kosovo." *International Review of the Red Cross* 92 (2010): 235–258.

Goldman, Emma. "The Traffic in Women." In *Anarchism and Other Essays*. New York and London: Mother Earth Publishing Association, 1911.

Goodey, Jo. "Human Trafficking." *Criminology & Criminal Justice* 8 (2008): 421–442.

Grittner, Frederick K. *White Slavery: Myth, Ideology and American Law.* New York: Garland Press, 1990.

Guy, Donna J. *Sex and Danger in Buenos Aires: Prostitution, Family, and Nation in Argentina.* Lincoln: University of Nebraska Press, 1991.

Halley, Janet, Prabha Kotiswaran, Hila Shamir, and Chantal Thomas. "From the International to the Local in Feminist Legal Responses to Rape, Prostitution/Sex Work, and Sex Trafficking: Four Studies in Contemporary Governance Feminism." *Harvard Women's Law Journal* 29 (2006): 335.

Hayes, Victoria. "Human Trafficking For Sexual Exploitation at World Sporting Events." *Chicago-Kent Law Review* 85 (2010): 1105–1146.

Haynes, Dina F. "Exploitation Nation: The Thin and Grey Legal Lines Between Trafficked Persons and Abused Migrant Laborers." *Notre Dame Journal of Law, Ethics & Public Policy* 23 (2009): 1–69.

Heron, Barbara. *Desire for Development: Whiteness, Gender and the Helping Imperative.* Waterloo: Wilfred Laurier University Press, 2007.

Hesford, Wendy S., and Wendy Kozol. *Just Advocacy? Women's Human Rights, Transnational Feminisms, and the Politics of Representation.* New Brunswick, New Jersey and London: Rutgers University Press, 2005.

Hoffer, K. M. "A Response to Sex Trafficking Chicago Style: Follow the Sisters, Speak Out." *University of Pennsylvania Law Review* 158 (2010): 1831.

Hua, Julietta, and Kasturi Ray. "The 'Practice of Humanity'." *Feminist Media Studies* 10 (2010): 253–267.

Hughes, Donna, Catherine Y. Chon, and Derek P. Ellerman. "Modern-Day Comfort Women: The U.S. Military, Transnational Crime, and the Trafficking of Women." *Violence Against Women* 13 (2007): 901–922.

Human Rights Watch. *U.S. State Department Trafficking Report Undercut by Lack of Analysis.* Human Rights Watch, 2003. Available: http://www.hrw.org/press/2003/06/traffickingreport.htm.

Hynes, H. Patricia, and Janice Raymond. "Put in Harm's Way: The Neglected Health Consequences of Sex Trafficking in the United States." In J. Silliman and A. Bhattacharjee, editors, *Policing the National Body: Race, Gender and Criminalization.* Cambridge, MA: South End Press, 2002: 197–230.

ILO. "Trafficking of Children: The Problem and Response Worldwide." International Labour Organization, Geneva, 2001.

IOM. "World Migration 2003: Managing Migration—Challenges and Responses for People on the Move." International Organization on Migration, Geneva, 2003.

ISIS-wicce. 1990/91. "Asian Campaigns." *Women's World*, 1990/91, 9–11.

Jacobsen, Christine, and May-Len Skilbrei. "'Reproachable Victims'? Representations and Self-representations of Russian Women Involved in Transnational Prostitution." *Ethnos* 75 (2010): 190–212.

Jacobsen, Christine, and Dag Stenvoll. "Muslim Women and Foreign Prostitutes: Victim Discourse, Subjectivity, and Governance." *Social Politics* 17 (2010): 270–294.

Kapoor, Ilan. *The Postcolonial Politics of Development.* London and New York: Routledge, 2008.

Kapur, Ratna. *Erotic Justice: Law and the New Politics of Postcolonialism.* London: Glass House Press, 2005.

Kara, Siddharth. *Sex Trafficking: Inside the Business of Modern Slavery.* New York: Columbia University Press, 2009.

Kempadoo, Kamala. *Sexing the Caribbean: Gender, Race and Sexual Labor.* New York: Routledge, 2004.

———. "Victims and Agents: The New Crusade Against Trafficking." In Julia Sudbury, editor, *Global Lockdown.* New York: Routledge, 2005.

———. "The War on Human Trafficking in the Caribbean." *Race and Class* 49 (2007): 79–84.

———. "Prostitution, Sex Work and Transactional Sex in the English, Dutch and French-Speaking Caribbean: A Literature Review of Definitions, Laws and Research. Final Report." PANCAP/CARICOM, 2009.

Kempadoo, Kamala, and Jo Doezema. *Global Sex Workers: Rights, Resistance, and Redefinition.* New York: Routledge, 1998.

Keren-Paz, Tsachi, and Nomi Levenkron. "Clients' Strict Liability towards Victims of Sex-trafficking." *Legal Studies* 29 (2009): 438–463.

Kim, Joon K., and May Fu. "International Women in South Korea's Sex Industry: A New Commodity Frontier." *Asian Survey* 48 (2008): 492–513.

Kotiswaran, Prabha. "Born unto Brothels: Toward a Legal Ethnography of Sex Work in an Indian Red-Light Area." *Law and Social Inquiry* 33 (2008): 579–629.

Kristof, Nicholas D. "Stopping the Traffickers." *New York Times,* January 31, 2004.

Laczko, Frank. "Introduction: Data and Research on Human Trafficking." *International Migration* 43 (2005): 5–16.

Lebov, Korin. "Human Trafficking in Scotland." *European Journal of Criminology* 7 (2010): 77–93.

Leman, Johan, and Stef Janssens. "The Albanian and Post-Soviet Business of Trafficking Women for Prostitution: Structural Developments and Financial Modus Operandi." *European Journal of Criminology* 5 (2008): 433–451.

Lévy, Florence, and Marylène Lieber. "Northern Chinese Women in Paris: The Illegal Immigration–Prostitution Nexus." *Social Science Information* 47 (2008): 629–642.

Limoncelli, Stephanie A. "The Trouble with Trafficking: Conceptualizing Women's Sexual Labor and Economic Human Rights." *Women's Studies International Forum* 32 (2009): 261–269.

Lindsley, Syd. "The Gendered Assault on Immigrants." In J. Silliman and A. Bhattacharjee, editors, *Policing the National Body: Race, Gender, and Criminalization.* Cambridge, MA: South End Press, 2002: 175–196.

Louie, Miriam Ching Yoon. *Sweatshop Warriors: Immigrant Women Workers Take on the Global Factory.* Cambridge, MA: South End Press, 2001.

Mahmoud, Toman Omar, and Christoph Trebesch. "The Economics of Human Trafficking and Labour Migration: Micro-Evidence From Eastern Europe." *Journal of Comparative Economics* 38 (2010): 173–188.

Marshall, Phil. "The Trojan Horse and Other Worries." *Stop by Stop: Newsletter of the UN Inter-Agency Project on Trafficking in Women and Children in the Mekong Sub-region,* Third Quarter (2001): 3.

Maynard, Robyn. "Sex Work, Migration and Anti-Trafficking." *Briarpatch* 39 (2010): 28.

Mohanty, Chandra Talpade. *Feminisms Without Borders: Decolonizing Theory, Practicing Solidarity.* Durham, NC: Duke University Press, 2003.

Musto, Jennifer Lynne. "What's in a Name? Conflations and Contradictions in Contemporary U.S. Discourses of Human Trafficking." *Women's Studies International Forum* 32 (2009): 281–287.

O'Connell Davidson, Julia. "Will the Real Sex Slave Please Stand Up?" *Feminist Review* 83 (2006): 4–22.

———. "New Slavery, Old Binaries: Human Trafficking and the Borders of 'Freedom'." *Global Networks* 10 (2010): 244–261.

O'Neill, Amy Richard. "International Trafficking in Women to the United States: A Contemporary Manifestation of Slavery and Organized Crime." Center for the Study of Intelligence, DCI Exceptional Intelligence Analyst Program, U.S. Government, 1999.

O'Neill, Maggie, Rosie Campbell, Phil Hubbard, Jane Pitcher, and Jane Scoular. "Living with the Other: Street Sex Work, Contingent Communities and Degrees of Tolerance." *Crime, Media, Culture* 4 (2008): 73.

Oso Casas, Laura. "Money, Sex, Love and the Family: Economic and Affective Strategies of Latin American Sex Workers in Spain." *Journal of Ethnic and Migration Studies* 36 (2010): 47–65.

Pajnik, Mojca. "Media Framing of Trafficking." *International Feminist Journal of Politics* 12 (2010): 45–64.

Panitch, Leo, and Colin Leys. *The New Imperial Challenge: Socialist Register 2004.* London and New York: Merlin Press and Monthly Review Press, 2003.

Papanicolaou, Georgios. "The Sex Industry, Human Trafficking and the Global Prohibition Regime: A Cautionary Tale from Greece." *Trends in Organized Crime* 11 (2008): 379–409.

Parrenas, Rhacel Salazar. *Servants of Globalization: Women, Migration, and Domestic Work.* Stanford: Stanford University Press, 2001.

———. "Trafficked? Filipino Hostesses in Tokyo's Nightlife Industry." *Yale Journal of Law and Feminism* 18 (2006): 145–180.

Parrenas Shimizu, Celine. "Screening Sexual Slavery? Southeast Asian Gonzo Porn and US Anti-Trafficking Law." *Sexualities* 13 (2010): 161–170.

Pearson, Elaine. "Human Traffic, Human Rights: Redefining Victim Protection." Anti-Slavery International, London, 2002.

Pennington, Julia R., A. Dwayne Ball, and Julia N. Soulakova. "The Cross-National Market in Human Beings." *Journal of Macromarketing* 29 (2009): 119–134.

Penttinen, Elina. "Imagined and Embodied Spaces in the Global Sex Industry." *Gender, Work and Organization* 17 (2010): 28–44.

Perrin, Benjamin. "Just Passing Through? International Legal Obligations and Policies of Transit Countries in Combating Trafficking in Persons." *European Journal of Criminology* 7 (2010): 11–27.

Reddock, Rhoda. "Freedom Denied: Indian Women and Indentureship in Trinidad and Tobago, 1845–1917." *Economic and Political Weekly* 20 (43), 1985: 79–87.

Samarasinghe, Vidyamali, and Barbara Burton. "Strategising Prevention: A Critical Review of Local Initiatives to Prevent Female Sex Trafficking." *Development in Practice* 17 (2007): 51–64.

Sandy, Larissa. "Just Choices: Representations of Choice and Coercion in Sex Work in Cambodia." *The Australian Journal of Anthropology* 18 (2007): 194–206.

———. "'Behind Closed Doors': Debt-Bonded Sex Workers in Sihanoukville, Cambodia." *The Asia Pacific Journal of Anthropology* 10 (2010): 216–230.

Sanghera, Jyoti. "Preface: Lessons From the Poetry of Departures." In *Collateral Damage: The Impact of Anti-Trafficking Measures on Human Rights around the World,* edited by GAATW. Bangkok: Global Alliance Against Traffick in Women, 2007: vii–x.

Sassen, Saskia. "Notes on the Incorporation of Third World Women into Wage Labor

Through Immigration and Offshore Production." In S. Sassen, editor, *Globalization and Its Discontents: Essays on the New Mobility of People and Money*. New York: The New Press, 1998.

Sayeed, Almas. "Making Political Hay of Sex and Slavery: Kansas Conservatism, Feminism and the Global Regulation of Sexual Moralities." *Feminist Review* 83 (2006): 119–131.

Schaeffer-Grabiel, Felicity. "Sex Trafficking as the 'New Slave Trade'?" *Sexualities* 13 (2010): 153–160.

Schwenken, Helen. "RESPECT for All: The Political Self-organization of Female Migrant Domestic Workers in the European Union." *Refuge: Canada's Periodical on Refugees* 21 (2003): 45–52.

Seagrave, Marie. "Order at the Border: The Repatriation of Victims of Trafficking." *Women's Studies International Forum* 32 (2009): 251–260.

Sharma, Nandita. *Home Economics: Nationalism and the Making of "Migrant Workers" in Canada*. Toronto: University of Toronto Press, 2006.

Shah, Dimple R. "Trafficking in Human Beings: The U.S. Department of State Issues 2002 Trafficking in Persons Report." *Migration Enforcement* 18, no. 8 (2002).

Shepherd, Verene A. *Maharani's Misery: Narratives of a Passage from India to the Caribbean*. Kingston: University of the West Indies, 2002.

Shulman, Alix Kates, ed. *Emma Goldman Speaks: An Emma Goldman Reader*. New Jersey: Humanities Press, 1996.

Simeunovic-Patic, Biljana, and Sanja Copic. "Protection and Assistance to Victims of Human Trafficking in Serbia: Recent Developments." *European Journal of Criminology* 7 (2010): 45–60.

Skinner, E. Benjamin. *A Crime So Monstrous: Face-to-Face with Modern-day Slavery*. New York: Free Press, 2008.

Skrobanek, Siriporn, Nattaya Boonpakdi, and Chutima Janthakeero. *The Traffic in Women: Human Realities of the International Sex Trade*. London: Zed Press, 1997.

Smith, Heather M. "Sex Trafficking: Trends, Challenges, and the Limitations of International Law." *Human Rights Review* (2010): 1–16.

Stalker, Peter. *Workers Without Frontiers: The Impact of Globalization on International Migration*. Boulder, CO: Lynne Rienner, 2000.

Surtees, Rebecca. "Human Trafficking in SE Europe." *Intersec* 15 (2005): 336–338.

———. "Traffickers and Trafficking in Southern and Eastern Europe." *European Journal of Criminology* 5 (2008): 39–68.

Tilly, Charles. *Social Movements 1768–2004*. Boulder and London: Paradigm, 2004.

Truong, Thanh-Dam. *Sex, Money and Morality: The Political Economy of Prostitution and Tourism in South East Asia*. London: Zed Books, 1990.

———. "Human Trafficking and New Patterns of Migration." *Gender, Technology and Development* 12 (2008): 5–8.

Viuhko, Minna. "Human Trafficking for Sexual Exploitation and Organized Procuring in Finland." *European Journal of Criminology* 7 (2010): 61–75.

Walkowitz, Judith R. *Prostitution and Victorian Society: Women, Class and the State*. Cambridge: Cambridge University Press, 1980.

Weitzer, Ron. "The Social Construction of Sex Trafficking: Ideology and Institutionalization of a Moral Crusade." *Politics and Society* 35 (2007): 447–475.

Weitzer, Ron, and Melissa Ditmore. "Sex Trafficking: Facts and Fictions." In Ron Weitzer, editor, *Sex for Sale*. New York: Routledge, 2008: 325–351.

White, Luise. *The Comforts of Home: Prostitution in Colonial Nairobi*. Chicago: University of Chicago Press, 1990.

Wijers, Marjan, and Lin Lap-Chew. *Trafficking in Women, Forced Labor and Slavery-like Practices in Marriage, Domestic Labor and Prostitution*. Utrecht: STV, 1997.

Wright, Cynthia. "Moments of Emergence: Organizing by and with Undocumented and

Non-citizen People in Canada after 9/11." *Refuge: Canada's Periodical on Refugees* 21 (2003): 5–16.

Wynter, Sylvia. "Beyond Miranda's Meanings: Un/Silencing the 'Demonic Ground' of Caliban's 'Woman.'" In Carole Boyce Davies and Elaine Savory Fido, editors, *Out of the Kumbla: Caribbean Women and Literature.* New Jersey: Africa World, 1990: 355–372.

Zheng, Tiantian, editor. *Sex Trafficking, Human Rights and Social Justice.* London and New York: Routledge, 2010.

PART I

SHIFTING PARADIGMS
Globalization, Labor Migration, and Human Rights

1

Unpacking the Trafficking Discourse

Jyoti Sanghera

Trafficking is a subject open to fierce debate, yet it also lends itself to critical reflection and honest conversation. In the following I offer an overview and analysis of the dominant discourse on trafficking by reflecting on the assumptions, interventions, and approaches followed by its practitioners. This essay is written in the spirit of an invitation for a collective reflection on the mainstream anti-trafficking paradigm with its package of interventions developed over the past decade or more, particularly in Asia. It is also a plea to think beyond and outside of the box, for this box has incarcerated and inhibited creative thinking and practice for far too many years. I draw confidence for my candor—which might seem to some audacious arrogance, but in all honesty is nothing more than a brutal reflection on our collective anti-trafficking practice—from the unwavering commitment of groups and allies to foreground the rights of those women whose struggle for a life of dignity they purport to support. In their commitment, these mindful practitioners have not shied away from abdicating their own strategies of engagement when these were found to be detrimental or lacking. It is no secret that the anti-trafficking arena is a beleaguered one. It has been made murkier by the melding together of complicated categories, constructs, and players. Issues of migration, trafficking, and sex work are peppered with constructs of sexuality, gender, and vulnerability; threaded through with categories of victim and agent, consent and coercion; and stirred together in a cauldron by cooks, who are far too many in number, much too disparate in their culinary skills, and have at their disposal a budget which is far too lavish for a mere broth. These "too many cooks" have not only managed to spoil the broth, but some of them have also ended up bonking each other with their spatulas. I locate myself squarely within the company of these cooks and after several years of engagement and serious reflection, humbly offer some suggestions for improving the recipe.

Central to this reflection process is calling a spade a spade, and not a snake. In the context of anti-trafficking work, this merely means eschewing the moral panics and jettisoning the practice of categorizing social reality under mutually exclusive dichotomies. That trafficking in persons is a critical issue is not the contestable point in this discussion. What is under question is the manner in which the trafficking discourse has been constructed and the assumptions and myths that have underscored this construction. The trafficking debate has rendered itself too quickly to a simplistic association with the prostitution debate, the reasons for which will be discussed later. However, the outcome of this conflation has resulted in the ideological burdens of the prostitution and sex wars transmigrating into the anti-trafficking arena. It has also resulted in a dead-end scenario with a pro- and anti-prostitution position. Critical thinking and reflection, and hence hope, emerge from a growing and disparate range of players located in the middle, who consciously seek to complicate their analyses in commensuration with the layered reality of trafficking. At present, their plea for questioning, challenging, and complicating may simply be dismissed as a pro-prostitution position. However, it is from this forum of reflective practitioners that the praxis of embodying rights for women in the arenas of sexuality and labor will emerge.

Mythologies of Trafficking: Stating the Problem

My thoughts are based upon the premise that there is a problem with the manner in which the "problem of trafficking," especially within the Asia-Pacific region, has been addressed by a majority of players over the past decade or so. This problem is connected to the construction of the discourse of trafficking or the manner in which the trafficking story is being told within the Asian region (Frederick 1998). The dominant anti-trafficking discourse, and consequently understanding, is not evidence-based but grounded in the construction of a particular mythology of trafficking. As a result, the interventions and programs flowing from this understanding have rarely led to the desired or expected results, i.e., the reduction of trafficking. Hence, despite the spate of heightened activity within the last decade on the part of a plethora of actors to curb the trafficking of women, and the investment of huge amounts of funds on the part of a host of donors, the common refrain among the same community of donors and grantees is that trafficking is "rapidly increasing," and acquiring "monstrous dimensions."[1] This begs the logical question: If all the energies and monies deployed to curb trafficking are not resulting in its reduction but, on the contrary, leading to an increase of it, then where are we going wrong?

The dominant discourse of trafficking is based upon a set of assumptions. These, in a large measure, merely flow from unexamined hypotheses, shoddy research, anecdotal information, or strong moralistic positions. The issue is not whether they are true or false, but simply one of pushing conclusions that are not supported by rigorous empirical research and a sound evidence base. This faulty methodology of disseminating a flow of information and data whose origins are questionable contributes to the construction of both the dominant paradigm or discourse of trafficking, as well as the mythologies of trafficking.

Some of the dominant assumptions that inform the mainstream trafficking discourse are:

1. Trafficking of children and women is an ever-growing phenomenon;
2. Increasing numbers of victims of trafficking are younger girls;
3. Most trafficking happens for the purpose of prostitution;
4. Poverty is the sole or principal cause of trafficking;
5. Trafficking within the Asian subcontinent and the region is controlled and perpetrated by organized crime gangs;
6. All entry of women into the sex industry is forced and the notion of "consent" in prostitution is based upon false consciousness or falsehood;
7. Based on the assumption that most women in prostitution are coerced and trafficked, it is then assumed that they would be only too happy to be rescued and reintegrated with their families, or rehabilitated;
8. Rehabilitation into families and communities is viewed as an unproblematic strategy for it is assumed to provide adequate protection and safety to the victims of trafficking;
9. Brothel-based prostitution is the sole or major form through which sex trade in the region is conducted;
10. Police-facilitated raids and rescue operations in brothels will reduce the number of victims of trafficking in the prostitution industry;
11. Absence of stringent border surveillance and border control is the principal reason for facilitation of transborder trafficking;
12. Anti-migration strategies based upon awareness-raising campaigns which alert communities to the dangers of trafficking by

instilling fear of strangers, and fear of big metropoles and cities, will curb migration and hence trafficking;

13. Strategies which club women and children together will be equally beneficial to both in extending protection against trafficking and redress after being trafficked;

14. All persons under 18 years of age constitute a homogenous category—children, devoid equally of sexual identity and sexual activity, bereft equally of the ability to exercise agency, and hence in need of identical protective measures;

15. Law enforcement is a neutral and unproblematic category and all it needs is sensitization and training on issues of trafficking in order to intervene effectively to curb the problem of trafficking.

These fifteen assumptions are the major founding blocks of the dominant discourse on trafficking. In challenging the dominant discourse of trafficking, my intention is not to deny the existence of trafficking as a problem in Asia—far from it. There is no denying the fact that with growing insecurity of food and livelihoods and shrinking avenues for regular migration, several harms, including that of trafficking, may be on the rise. Rather, my intention is to unravel the puzzle of why the trafficking story is shrouded in mystery; to unpack the elements of the trafficking discourse; to comprehend why a spade is not called a spade; and to examine some persistent maladies of the paradigm in order to generate deeper analysis, understanding, and, consequently, action.

A critical tool that enables a spade to be called a spade is the lens through which it is viewed. This, in effect, holds true of any social phenomenon. Here the trafficking discourse is analyzed through the lens of a rights-based approach, which incorporates within its core both a gender and development perspective as well.

THE CONTEXT OF TRAFFICKING

Trafficking in women and girls is acknowledged by the international community as a global problem today. Reportedly, millions of children and women are said to be trafficked across borders and within countries, and the profits accruing from this trade are alleged to be phenomenal, exceeding, according to some estimates, the clandestine gains made from the underground trade in arms and narcotics.[2] There is general consensus that trafficking in women and children has become a significant facet of transnational organized crime, and the growth of such activities has been referred to as the "dark side of globalization."[3]

We learn, through an endless cycle of stories, how trafficked women are separated from their families, and sexually exploited by means of coercion, violence, or abuse of authority. Their ability to seek help is severely constrained, especially if they are minors (UNICEF-EASRO 2001; Estes and Weiner 2001). In addition, trafficked women and minors are often further disadvantaged if they are undocumented migrants or immigrants; refugees or displaced; or if they belong to a marginalized ethnic, cultural, or religious social group. Poverty and lack of sustainable livelihood are common conditions of those who become victims of trafficking. These trafficked persons are often uneducated, unskilled, and debt-ridden.

Women are trafficked for a variety of reasons, including for the purposes of prostitution, domestic work, marriage, industrial and agricultural work, and trade in human organs. All victims of trafficking are not necessarily subjected to commercial sexual exploitation. Some of the purposes for which trafficking occurs, such as prostitution, pornography, sex tourism, and the marriage market, are by their very nature marked by commercial sexual exploitation. However, other sites into which trafficking feeds might result in other types of exploitation, forced labor, and abuse. It has been reported that even when women and minors are not ostensibly trafficked for the purpose of commercial sexual exploitation, their trafficked status renders them highly vulnerable to sexual exploitation and sexual abuse (UNICEF Innocenti Research Centre 2003).

The growth of trafficking in persons has been attributed to many causes, including poverty, lack of sustainable livelihoods, structural inequities in society, gender discrimination, war and armed conflict, and other forms of natural or constructed disasters. However, it is critical to understand that these factors are not in themselves the causes of trafficking; they merely exacerbate the vulnerability of marginalized and disadvantaged groups and render them increasingly more susceptible to a variety of harms. Factors such as lack of livelihood options, conflict, and structural inequities create conditions for the displacement and mobility of populations and, hence, contribute to the "freeing up" of marginal and vulnerable groups, thereby creating a potential supply of migrants and livelihood-seekers. The sites of work that draw this supply of migrant livelihood-seekers are contingent upon demand from particular sectors of the economy for certain types of labor that would enable maximization of profit. Trafficking for commercial sexual purposes is tied to the expansion and diversification of the sex entertainment industry as well as to the expansion of marketable, intimate services and arrangements, including marriage.

The drive for maximizing profit under a competitive economic regime fields a demand for workers who are the most vulnerable and therefore the most exploitable and controllable. Children, followed by women, fit this description perfectly. It must be remembered that trafficking of persons is, most importantly, a demand-driven phenomenon. And yet the majority of anti-trafficking interventions in the arenas of rescue, repatriation, rehabilitation, and even prevention are targeted only toward the supply of trafficking or the victims. This is a serious gap in the sphere of interventions.

THE NEXUS OF VULNERABILITY AND ILLEGALITY

A close examination shows that the recent impetus for transborder trafficking, as well as smuggling or other clandestine forms of labor recruitment, is connected to striking imbalances between the increasing supply of unskilled, indigent jobseekers on the one hand and the availability of legal and sustainable work in places where the jobseekers have legal rights to residence or citizenship on the other. A recent International Labour Organisation (ILO) study supports this view and maintains that "labor trafficking should not, in theory, take place if the jobseeker has freedom of geographical movement and freedom of access to employment" (ILO 2001, 53). Lack of legal rights to mobility and to legally accepted forms of livelihood compel marginal and vulnerable groups to lead underground lives, enhancing manifold their vulnerability to harms such as trafficking, bondage, slavery-like working and living conditions, and HIV/AIDS. This is the "quintessential knot" in the nexus of vulnerability where prevailing vulnerabilities of age, gender, and socio-economic status forge a complex relationship with newer vulnerabilities, such as widespread and unprecedented insecurity of food and livelihood.

This nexus of vulnerability is increasingly cemented by the "illegality factor," where practically everything about the victim of trafficking is covered by a shroud of illegality. It may seem that the discussions on legality of work and freedom of movement are irrelevant for minors because, in principle, they should not be migrating as jobseekers. However, the reality is that minors, perhaps more than anyone else, are marked most by the illegality factor because they too are an integral part of the vast pool of mobile jobseekers. Their inherent vulnerability as minors is often exacerbated several-fold by the formal and informal sanctions against child labor. As far as women are concerned, we do have enough statistics to show that, especially in Asia, a majority of the migrants today are women, moving not as part of a family unit but in their independent capacity (Asis 2003; Sanghera 2003).

The illegality factor taints almost every aspect of the trafficked person's life. Hence, the work done by this trafficked person is often considered "illegal" in the informal sector—her age may be below the legally stipulated age of employment; her status within the country of residence may be undocumented; the conditions of work under which she labors may be illegal or not up to legal standards; the hovels, slums, or brothels in which she resides may be unlicensed or exist on squatted land; and several of her partners in business or life may be defined as "illegal," such as agents, pimps, madams, other sex workers, children, and siblings. (While both females and males are victims of trafficking, the term "her" is used here to foreground a gender approach, as well as to underscore the specific vulnerability of girls and women.) In being compelled to lead "illegal" lives, victims of trafficking are simultaneously converted into criminals. Their illegalization keeps them from accessing most of the freedoms and rights that are extended to all as human beings. These trafficked persons invariably live hidden and invisible lives. Much of their energy is spent upon averting either state agents such as law enforcement officers from apprehending them, or non-state agents such as their employers and exploiters from squeezing them further.

Any strategy to address the issue of trafficking of persons from a rights-based perspective must address their illegalization and criminalization. A preventive strategy in this regard entails exploring options for legal employment as well as ensuring that existing forms of illegal work are made consistent with legally stipulated standards of labor. With special regard to minors this discussion enters a controversial arena since child labor is a contentious issue. However, in principle it has been seen that in order to remove the illegal status of a victim and empower her, it is vital to simultaneously address all those locations of her existence that imbue her with this illegality and ultimately render her a criminal in the eyes of the law. In addition to employment, it is also crucial to address the issue of mobility and the right to freedom of movement. This is tied in integrally with questions of migration and the rights of migrants. In the context of transborder movement of people and border controls exercised by nations, questions regarding the illegality of migrants are complex ones. Nonetheless, concerns related to rights of a person regardless of citizenship and nationality remain to be taken up in a systematic fashion within the dominant anti-trafficking discourse. At the same time, the debate on the rights of young people to migrate has been kept largely at bay.

UNPACKING THE MYTHOLOGIES OF TRAFFICKING

Naming and Defining the Problem

Until the finalization of the UN Trafficking Protocol Supplementing the UN Convention Against Transnational Organized Crime at the end of the year

2000, there was no comprehensive international definition of trafficking whose basic elements were acceptable to State parties and key stakeholders. Therefore, until recently the term "trafficking" was employed to describe varied and disparate phenomena, processes, and outcomes.

Historically and most commonly, trafficking has been conceptually conflated with prostitution and illegal migration, and more recently with the commercial sexual exploitation of children (CSEC). In fact, the reason for equating child trafficking and CSEC can be logically traced to the practice of equating trafficking in women and children with prostitution over the past several decades. It is not a coincidence that a majority of the anti-trafficking laws in most countries are also prostitution laws, which seek to variously criminalize or regulate the sex trade.

A commonly agreed upon definition of trafficking is now contained in the UN Protocol to Prevent, Suppress and Punish Trafficking in Persons, Especially Women and Children, supplementing the UN Convention Against Transnational Organized Crime, which was adopted in 2000. The UN Convention came into force in September 2003, and the Trafficking Protocol in December 2003.

In the recent past, the need to expand the definition of trafficking to include purposes other than prostitution, such as forced labor, forced marriage, and slavery-like practices,[4] has also been recognized. This is reflected in the new UN protocol on trafficking. An acknowledgment of the key understanding that trafficking is a problem of human-rights violation, and not of law and order or public morality related to prostitution, is of recent origin, and gaining currency in some quarters. However, despite this growing realization, in actual practice crime prevention and concerns with public morality continue to be foregrounded as the core of the anti-trafficking discourse.

TRAFFICKING, MIGRATION, AND PROSTITUTION

The dominant trafficking paradigm rests upon an absence of the critical distinction between trafficking and migration on the one hand and trafficking and prostitution on the other. What are the implications of conflating and collapsing the categories of migration and prostitution with trafficking? And what are the implications when these concepts are often value-loaded, with an inherent bias that marginalized people who migrate are vagrants, and women who migrate into the sex industry are sexual delinquents?

Curbing Migration to Prevent Trafficking

Equating trafficking with migration has led to simplistic and unrealistic solutions within the mainstream anti-trafficking paradigm. As a result,

in order to prevent trafficking there is a ɪ
those who are considered vulnerable to tɪ
migration is not a stated programmatic foɪ
to dissuade women and girls from moving
harm. Hence, conflating trafficking with n
manner results in reinforcing the gender bi
constant male or state protection, and theɪ
exercise their right to movement.

Curbing migration has not and will n
on the part of some practitioners to implɪ
and surveillance on the Indo-Nepal bordeɪ
passports or other measures, merely serveɕ ... . ɯɛ aɕuviɪy ɪurtner
underground, and make it still more invisible (Sanghera and Kapur 2001).
This outcome has been repeatedly underscored in all those instances where
states have proceeded to enforce increasingly stringent immigration control
as a response to heightened trafficking in persons and narcotics. Borders
cannot be impermeable, and stricter immigration measures have merely
resulted in pushing the trafficked persons further into situations of violence
and abuse, and rendering them more inaccessible.

Banning Prostitution to Prevent Trafficking

There has been a continued persistence among anti-trafficking players
within the dominant discourse to conflate trafficking with prostitution.
By collapsing the process with the purpose, the abuse and violence inherent in trafficking is mistaken for the actual site of work and form of
labor. Furthermore, trafficking for all other purposes is largely ignored,
and targeting trafficking for prostitution becomes the principal agenda of
anti-trafficking interventions, policies, and laws.

To provide protection and redress to women and girls who are trafficked, a clear distinction needs to be made between the abuse and human-
rights violations committed during the entire process of recruitment, transport, and confinement via coercion to exploitative labor conditions on the one
hand, and the form of employment or purpose of trafficking on the other. In
the case of trafficking for the purpose of domestic work, forced marriage, or
work in carpet factories, the objective of anti-trafficking interventions must
be to target the abuse, forced labor, and violation of rights that is endured by
those affected by trafficking and not to eradicate marriage as an institution,
or domestic work and the carpet industry as sectors of employment. Similarly, attempting to eradicate the sex industry in a bid to prevent the harm
of trafficking may be an unrealistic agenda. Not all victims of trafficking are
prostitutes, nor are all prostitutes victims of trafficking.[5]

Figures on the scale of trafficking are often derived from small-scale
surveys based upon disparate methodologies, or sources such as police

rmation, or media reports which cannot be statistically or empirically sound. These calculations are based on many umptions. Most data on the number of trafficked persons are peculation and projection. To date, there is no sound methodol- calculate the numbers of those who have been trafficked.

The United Nations estimates that, in the last 30 years, trafficking in omen and children for sexual exploitation in Asia alone has victimized more than 30 million people.[6] There are few statistics which distinguish the number trafficked according to the age of the victim. In South Asia it has been noticed that several of the statistics on trafficked victims have remained unchanged over the years. To elucidate this point the case of Nepal serves as a good example. The figure of 5,000–7,000 Nepali girls trafficked into India each year, with 150,000–200,000 in Indian brothels, has remained unaltered over the past 15 years.[7]

When trafficking is equated with migration on the one hand and prostitution on the other, then it logically follows that the number of victims of trafficking is equal to the number of those who have migrated or those who are engaged in prostitution. This logic operates particularly in the case of adolescent girls and women migrants, and not in the case of men. This practice has resulted in an extremely flawed methodology for conducting baseline surveys on trafficking in "risk-prone" and "affected districts." Household surveys have been conducted in South Asia by well-meaning community-based organizations (CBOs) and researchers, for example, on the number of women and girls who are absent from their villages. These persons may have migrated voluntarily or under deception—however, there are no methodological variables to ascertain this information. Absence of women or girls is routinely considered tantamount to "missing persons," and therefore, trafficked (Sanghera and Kapur 2001). In this context a pressing query begs a response: Why are female migrants considered to be trafficked by anti-trafficking stakeholders while male migrants are considered to be simply that—male migrants?

For all of the above reasons statistical data are highly questionable and contestable, and consequently the weakest link as far as the issue of trafficking in persons is concerned. And yet, statistics of trafficked women and children constitute one of the legs upon which the dominant trafficking paradigm stands. Victims of trafficking are presented as the fastest growing population under globalization, and the "trafficking problem" is portrayed as a formidable and heinous serpent, constantly tightening its coils around vulnerable women and girls of poor and marginalized communities, especially of the Third World. A statement by a Third World activist aptly sums up this fear: "Because everything becomes marketable, and everything becomes a commodity in the new world of globalization, men can travel thousand of miles just to buy girls from poorer countries" (Shifman 2003). In this dominant frame, men prey upon women, the rich countries gouge out resources, including women, of the poorer ones, poor women are not human beings but merely commodities, and on and on... This is the trope and the principal refrain of the saga of unmitigated victimization of the dominant discourse on trafficking.

Equating Children with Women

The UN Protocol on Trafficking and the US Trafficking Victims Protection Act 2000, as well as a majority of the major documents and laws addressing the issue of trafficking, fail to make a distinction between the trafficking of women and children. In commenting upon the SAARC (South Asian Association for Regional Cooperation) Draft Convention on Trafficking, which clubs children and women together, the previous UN Special Rapporteur on Violence Against Women stated, "The legal regime surrounding women should be based on a framework of rights and the concept of coercion when it comes to trafficking. The legal regime with children must be completely different" (Coomaraswamy 2000).[8] The issue of consent for children with regard to certain arenas of work, including prostitution, is deemed irrelevant. This is in accordance with the Convention on the Rights of the Child (CRC), whereas treating women like children or in accordance with similar norms infantilizes women and denies them both their right to autonomy and to make decisions. "Some women may have been trafficked while they were under age. In such a case a woman should be entitled to a legal remedy for any harm she may have endured as a child, whether it is in the form of child sexual abuse, slave labor, or coerced work while still a minor. Providing such remedies is different from setting up a legal regime that treats all women like children" (Sanghera and Kapur 2001, 24).

Why are women and children clubbed together in anti-trafficking legislation and the dominant trafficking paradigm when in all other instances, including labor laws, great care is being taken to separate child labor from adult labor? The Convention on the Rights of the Child is a clear statement on the ideological, strategic, and operational need to make distinctions between children and adults. This distinction is based on the principle that the development of children as human beings is a process and is not complete so long as they are minors. Children are deemed "innocent" and in need of special protection and assistance in making decisions. It is believed that minors cannot be expected to act in their own best interest as their ability to exercise full agency is not yet entirely developed.

The category of children with regard to "consent" will be complicated in a subsequent section of this paper; however there should be no dispute over the fact that women, as adults, have a full right to all their freedoms, including the freedom to exercise their agency and to seek a livelihood. Why then are they clubbed together with children in anti-trafficking laws? The fact that a woman may have been trafficked as a minor in the past does not justify her continued treatment as a child past the age of majority.

POST-FACTO NATURE OF THE CRIME OF TRAFFICKING

One of the key problems in understanding and dealing with the problem of trafficking is that it is deemed a crime only after it has happened. Herein lies its operational and conceptual complexity. There are three interlinked core elements involved in the operation of trafficking based upon its definition: (i) Movement of a person; (ii) under deception or coercion; (iii) into a situation of forced labor, servitude, or slavery-like practices (GAATW 2001).

The first of these elements, namely movement, involves both recruitment and transportation of the person. In present times, many trafficked women migrate voluntarily or willingly in their desire to better their life situation. Therefore, agents or traffickers do not encounter much difficulty in recruiting or transporting their victims within or across borders. In fact, it may be said that most victims actively collude in their own trafficking through cooperation with traffickers during the process of transportation. The traffickers pose as well-wishers offering to deliver the innocent persons into lucrative situations of work or marriage. Hence, the first phase of trafficking is achieved oftentimes with little coercion or force; various forms of deception and false promises are employed in this phase.

Coercion, sometimes of an extreme nature, is evident at the point of destination in the trafficking process. At the destination end, the process of trafficking entails consignment to, and continued confinement in, the situation of forced labor, servitude, or slavery-like practices. At the point of destination the person who, during the process of recruitment and transport, is a willing collaborator and migrant, becomes a victim of trafficking. This chain process is characterized by the involvement of one or more agents/traffickers—recruiter, transporter, broker, employer—who derive profit through this activity.

Given the nature of the process of trafficking—namely, recruitment, transportation, and confinement—it is difficult to determine the crime during its earlier phases. At its commencement, trafficking is indistinguishable from agent-facilitated voluntary migration or smuggling. It can only be established as a crime once it has happened and the person has been trapped and confined to exploitative conditions. At the destination point the trafficking process enters its most clandestine and invisible phase; it simultaneously puts on its criminal face. Just as trafficking becomes a crime in its final stage, the jobseeker and willing migrant becomes a victim at the destination point. And as the crime of trafficking goes underground into invisibility, the victim of trafficking becomes increasingly inaccessible. It is critical to grasp that the process of trafficking, while transforming itself into a crime, simultaneously transforms the seeker of a better life into a victim. In fact, if her situation is suffused with illegalities,[9] as argued earlier, then she is transformed paradoxically into both a victim and a criminal. And thus, in a desire to expand and enjoy her rights as a human being, the victim of trafficking might experience a brutal and systematic violation of her rights.

The complexity of the process of trafficking, where the crime can be ascertained only post-facto, complicates any endeavor to formulate an effective, rights-based response to address it at the point of origin and transportation, and indeed, poses a great challenge to all anti-trafficking advocates. To establish "intent" of trafficking and apprehend the trafficker or recover the potential victim during the phase of recruitment and transportation is fraught with immense challenges and pitfalls. In fact, it is extremely difficult to design apprehension or recovery interventions during this first phase of the process. Although there may be "suspicion," there is a lack of a systematic or verifiable methodology to ascertain that the woman crossing the border is a potential victim and that her companion is a trafficker. Intense interrogation of the suspected "victim" has often proven to be extremely intimidating, and detention of her chaperone without adequate grounds of proof of the crime, unconstitutional. Therefore, a rights-based intervention especially during the phase of recruitment and transportation needs very careful consideration. And yet the dominant discourse on trafficking does not adequately acknowledge nor address these complications.

ORGANIZED CRIME GANGS OR THE GUY NEXT DOOR?

Who are the traffickers? The new UN Convention that deals with trafficking through one of its protocols is entitled the UN Convention Against Transnational Organized Crime. It is obvious that encoded within the title of the new convention is an understanding that trafficking of children and women is perpetrated by members of organized crime, and it is a transnational problem. There is certainly evidence to prove that in some instances in certain parts of the world, organized crime gangs are involved. However, in view of the overall paucity of evidence on the issue of trafficking globally, it is near impossible to make a claim that trafficking is entirely or even largely a problem of organized crime. Neither is there enough evidence or data to establish the extent or nature of involvement of members of organized crime in various countries.[10] A number of tentative studies and case profiles from both Asia in general and South Asia in particular reveal that contrary to the commonly held impression of the existence of highly organized national and transborder networks of crime gangs, the perpetrators of trafficking in the form of recruiters and agents are primarily small-time operators functioning mostly in an individual capacity, and are based upon personal and sometimes familial sets of relationships.

Evidently, the definition of a trafficker is too broad and open-ended to be legally operationalized with ease. To establish the "intent" to traffic, until the crime is committed, is difficult. However, once the crime of trafficking is committed the trafficker(s), if apprehended, could be charged for a variety of crimes, including debt-bondage, fraud, assault and battery, rape, torture, abduction, sale of human beings, unlawful detention, murder, deprivation of labor rights, child abuse, and exploitation through enforcement of child labor. All countries have laws against these crimes, thus all countries do have some laws that can be used to prosecute traffickers. And while some traffickers commit all of these crimes, very few are prosecuted or punished for committing them. It has been observed that, more commonly, traffickers are tried for migration-related offenses that are less serious and carry milder sentences. It has also been observed that in the case of trafficking into the sex industry, traffickers are prosecuted for laws relating to prostitution, such as procurement, rather than for the serious harm often inflicted upon trafficked persons, including physical, sexual, and psychological violence; physical incarceration; and debt-bondage and other forms of forced labor and slavery-like conditions.

Rescue, Repatriation, and Rehabilitation

A review of the dominant anti-trafficking paradigm and work reveals that the largest number of players are clustered around rescue and rehabilitation activities, primarily in the arena of prostitution. Rescue operations conducted in conjunction with police authorities in various brothel areas are the anti-trafficking activity most highlighted by the media, as well as by anti-trafficking practitioners. It needs to be stated at the outset that the recovery of trafficked persons from situations of abuse, forced labor, and slavery-like practices is indeed a very legitimate and necessary anti-trafficking intervention. However, such an activity needs to be carefully designed, taking into account all aspects of holistic recovery based integrally upon a rights-based approach. A close analysis of interventions in this sector reveals that there is a marked absence of any clear anti-trafficking rescue and rehabilitation strategy. In addition, there is little rescue happening from other sites into which people are trafficked; an exception may be the greatly publicized case of boys who have been apprehended while being trafficked to the Middle East as "camel jockeys." A few cases of young girls rescued from forced marriages have also come to light. Notwithstanding these exceptions, there is no doubt that the most favored site for rescue operations continues to be brothels in major red-light areas.

Implicit behind these rescue operations are the assumptions that (i) all trafficked girls are to be found in the sex industry, and (ii) all prostitution, especially in South Asia, is confined to brothels in red-light areas of cities. Both these assumptions are not based upon a realistic understanding of either trafficking or prostitution. New research reveals that many women and young people are trafficked to sites other than the sex industry. At the same time sex trade in the region takes many diverse forms, including street-based prostitution, sex trade sites along major highways, casual sex service-provision in rental buildings, guest-house and hotel-based sex trade, tourist industry-based sex trade, call-girl operations, and independently run arrangements. The proportion of sex trade conducted through brothels in the region is unknown, but it is known that a myriad of other forms and arrangements exists within the sex industry.[11]

An assessment of rescue initiatives in Asia clearly shows that rescues are commonly conducted in brothels of big cities. There are few services planned or implemented for women who may be trapped in other forms of prostitution. Almost all rescue operations are conducted through police-facilitated raids in which "seemingly minor-looking girls" are picked up and consigned either to government remand homes or to shelters run by NGOs. The reason for this exclusive focus on brothels for rescue work is not difficult to comprehend—it is relatively easy to engage in such rescue operations, as the brothel is a distinct physical location which houses residents of a certain profession. In addition, the police, who are indispensable partners of NGOs in rescue operations, know the ins-and-outs of these locations, not the least on account of the fact that many of their members are allegedly the beneficiaries of the regular payoffs and commissions received from brothel owners. Therefore, all-in-all, the relative ease of rescue work in brothels, coupled with the high-publicity potential of this activity and the assistance of the police, has made this kind of rescue work a favored anti-trafficking activity. Demonstrable impact in terms of the numbers of women scooped out of brothels provides immediate proof of the anti-trafficking work, unlike prevention or reintegration activities which are extremely long-term, arduous, and consume vast amounts of money and time.

And yet, despite the focus on rescue of victims of trafficking from brothels, we need to ask ourselves whether there is any tangible reduction in the incidence of trafficking into prostitution? On the contrary, such highly publicized and single-focus activity might actually result in a change of venue on the part of traffickers for their activities.[12] In addition, perpetrators of trafficking may end up devising more repressive forms of confinement which render the victims even more inaccessible. However, in view of this discussion, it must not be concluded that comprehensive, rights-based recovery initiatives operations are unnecessary and therefore should not be conducted. This analysis merely alerts anti-trafficking advocates to diversify their interventions to other sites as well, while at the same time devising more innovative strategies for recovery.

Reintegration has been the most difficult stage within the anti-trafficking process, especially in the case of women and girls returning from the sex industry. The incidence of reintegration at the family and community levels has been low and painstakingly slow. Recognizing the nexus between sexual abuse of girls and their commercial sexual exploitation, reintegration within the family or community may not even be desirable when sexual abuse is perpetrated within intimate family settings. However, alternative forms of recovery and reintegration, which are both innovative and rights-based and can be emulated as models, have been slow in emerging. In addition, the development of non-institutional support in terms of foster homes and alternative community care has not gone very far.

Therefore, in the area of rescue and reintegration in particular, there is an urgent need to think outside the box and to think beyond prescribed and existing templates of anti-trafficking interventions. Innovative, rights-based strategies must be developed for alternative recovery and reintegration programs.

Groping in the "Gray Zone"—The Problem of "Consent"

This section of the paper attempts to enter a rather gray zone by complicating the categories of "child" and "consent." By virtue of its very nature this discussion will consciously stray into a minefield of controversy for the purpose of pushing the boundaries of analysis and thinking. However, from this discussion the reader is cautioned against drawing simplistic conclusions and assuming that this paper (i) advocates support of child prostitution, or (ii) assumes that consent is without limits and boundaries.

According to the Convention on the Rights of the Child (CRC), a child is "every human being below the age of 18, unless under the law applicable to the child, majority is attained earlier." No distinction is made in the convention between a four-year-old and a seventeen-year-old. Both are defined as children and therefore, "need special safeguards and care, including appropriate legal protection" (CRC). Common sense, experience, and social research tell us that, in reality, the concept of "childhood" varies according to social, cultural, historical, religious, and relational norms, as well as according to one's personal circumstances. Marriage confers adult status on a person. In many countries a girl is married off at a younger age than a boy, and often below the age of eighteen. Hence, in her particular social context, she acquires the status and responsibilities of an adult before she reaches eighteen years of age. If she becomes a mother as well, then her adulthood is further confirmed. However, pregnancy and adulthood are tied to marital status, and if this very girl were to become pregnant before being married she would not automatically be assigned adulthood. The legal age for sexual consent in many countries is below the age at which the CRC deems a child to be an adult. Therefore many countries allow sexual activity and recognize sexual agency in young people below the age of eighteen years. Ironically, the legal age of sexual consent in many countries is also below the legal age of independent access to contraceptives, abortion, and sexual health services. Thus, young people may be accepted as sexually active but denied safe-sex measures.

In contrast to trafficking in adults wherein the question of consent is contested, there is a broad agreement that the issue of "consent" is irrelevant in the case of children under eighteen years of age when considering commercial sexual exploitation and hazardous forms of labor. It is held that children cannot give consent in these sectors of work. One commentator points out the possibility that any minor who has reached the legal age limit for having a (part-time) job or having sexual intercourse—which usually is set below the age of eighteen, for instance at the age of sixteen or fourteen—could also agree to his/her exploitation in labor or sex (Vermeulen 2001). However, the author also mentions that even in the Netherlands, where the exploitation of prostitution in brothels has been decriminalized since October 2000, protection through criminal law against sexual exploitation has been fully maintained for all persons below the age of eighteen, irrespective of their actual consent or legal ability to consent to sexual intercourse at a lower age.

Trafficking of children, unlike that of adult women, does not need to involve means of coercion, deception, or any form of illicit influence, in order to meet the conditions of criminality. The UN Trafficking Protocol provides that the recruitment, transportation, transfer, harboring, or receipt of a child for the purpose of exploitation shall be considered "trafficking in persons" even if this does not involve any of the means set forth in the article, and that "child" shall mean any person under eighteen years of age.

It needs to be pointed out that what is deemed illegal under law may be socially and culturally acceptable in many instances. Hence, girls from traditional occupational groups, such as the Bedias, Devadasis, or Nats in India, who are engaged in sex entertainment and prostitution, may be socially acceptable but criminalized by law. Similarly Thai girls engaged in sexual activity to support their families may be socially honorable but punishable under the law. On the other hand, girls having sex before marriage may be legally acceptable depending on the legal age of consent but socially impermissible. Social stigma and vulnerability are integrally linked to social status and privilege. It has been seen that in the mainstream reformist discourse the children who are the most disadvantaged, including poor and street children, are considered the most vulnerable. And yet, they are subjected to the maximum degree of institutional surveillance, the minimum of institutional protection, and severe legal-punitive action against sexual and economic activities undertaken mostly for self-preservation and familial responsibilities. These "most-vulnerables," including street children, are also the most stigmatized.

It must be borne in mind that millions of street children and youth may have no unit such as a family, nor any responsible person or institution to depend on. As such they are minors but non-dependents. Laws against legitimate employment of these young non-dependents leave them no alternative but to resort to occupations that are illegalized and criminalized and to work sites that are unprotected and underpaid.

An analysis of the legal and other initiatives reveals that under the dominant reformist-protectionist approach, protection of the "young-vulnerables" has not created an expansion of opportunities and choices for them. On the contrary, vulnerable young people have been criminalized for exercising autonomy in the economic and sexual spheres, stripped of all powers to exercise agency and independent choices, reduced to deeper vulnerability due to lack of viable alternatives, rescued and confined in dead-end remand homes, rehabilitated into abusive situations, which they fled from in the first place, and above all, stigmatized.

To sum up this brief description of the complexities involved around the issue of consent and coercion in relation to the age of majority, some crucial questions emerge. I wish to reiterate that the argument forwarded here must not be assumed to advocate support for youth prostitution or labor. The objective is merely to complicate the discussion on "consent" and autonomy with regard to young people. These questions become all the more pressing when one perceives the actual ground reality of many underage persons engaged in labor for survival, when often this labor may be exploitative. According to the UN Convention Against Transnational Organized Crime and the protocols supporting it, all youths under the age of eighteen years would be deemed trafficked if they ended up in sexual arrangements which were exploitative—even if it was marriage—or in exploitative work situations. Similarly, all such young people who were undocumented migrants could be considered trafficked, especially if they were also engaged in labor. And parents who consented to the migration of their children on the children's behalf would be criminalized as traffickers, especially if the children ended up in exploitative situations. The fact that a number of terms such as youth, young persons, adolescents, minors, underage persons, children, etc., are in currency, and sometimes used interchangeably, underscores the complexity of this issue as well. The principal motive in generating this far-from-easy discussion with regards to minors and consent stems from the concern related to how best to promote the rights and agency of young people while ensuring that they stay out of harm's way.

Concluding Comments

The inherent complexity of the issue of trafficking, combined with lack of data on the one hand, and a heightened commitment to urgently rectify the problem on the other, has resulted in overenthusiastic responses in many instances. Such responses are predicated on the assumption that "tightening the screws" will alleviate the crime. However, contrary to their goal, several of these responses have not achieved the aim of promoting the human rights of those trafficked. The ambit of antitrafficking initiatives is further weakened by the relative lack of rigorous indicators for evaluating the impact of interventions at various levels. A paucity of reliable data and the gap in devising a rigorous research methodology for procuring good data on trafficking continues to pose a major challenge.

A "tightening the screws" strategy, which has tended to underpin overenthusiastic and dominant responses to trafficking, is noticeable in the arenas of policy and legislation, rescue and repatriation, and interception of "seemingly potential victims" at border points during the process of transportation and migration. A number of increasingly stringent laws with draconian measures and harsh punishments have been implemented. At the same time, aggressive and intrusive rescue operations with little regard to the personhood, wishes, or rights of the trafficked person have been conducted. Judicial procedures which are not rights-based have been employed during trials, with little attention to witness protection in many cases. Evidence reveals that in some instances prevention initiatives at source have been tantamount to restricting womens' and girls' right to freedom of movement, reinforcing thereby the patriarchal practice of keeping them trapped within the four walls of the home as a measure of protection. Surveillance and watchdog committees at the community level have gone overboard in their enthusiasm to police young girls and women, and in their intent to protect, have been responsible for violating the rights of the girls deemed to be vulnerable. Rehabilitation has sometimes meant nothing more than a change in venue of the victim's incarceration from a brothel to a shelter.

The purpose of this analysis of anti-trafficking strategies and interventions, and the identification of gaps, is not to construct a dismal picture. Nor do I seek to demolish the work and commitment of well-intentioned practitioners. My attempt here is to merely put out a strong cautionary note that in forging ahead on the beaten track of anti-trafficking work, it is vital to stop and engage in a systematic stock-taking of both the theory and the practice.

NOTES

1. The common refrain in most anti-trafficking fora is the ever-increasing and mounting terror of trafficking. The document prepared by the Government of India for the Yokohama Congress states that trafficking "has never before reached the proportions as in the world today, not under slavery, not in feudal times" (in *Protecting Children from Trafficking and Sexual Abuse: Initiatives in India,* Department of Women and Child Development, Ministry of Human Resource Development, Govt. of India, December 2001).

2. The profits accruing from the international trade of trafficking in persons are estimated to range between US $5–7 billion annually (see Jonas Widgren, *Multinational Cooperation to Combat Trafficking in Migrants and the Role of International Organisations,* IOM Seminar on International Responses to Trafficking in Migrants and Safeguarding Migrant Rights, Geneva, October 26–28, 1994).

3. Communiqué of the Ministerial Conference of the G-8 Countries on Combating Transnational Organized Crime, Moscow, October 19–20, 1999.

4. See the Beijing Platform for Action, 1995, Strategic Objective D3 130 (b), which states, "trafficking in women and girls for prostitution and other forms of commercialized sex, forced marriages and forced labor."

5. The misplaced conflation of trafficking with prostitution has a historical basis. For decades, the problem has been defined by governments and advocates alike as "sex trafficking in women and children" or the "immoral traffic in women." This belies a concern which stems from a protectionist agenda and in some instances, is based entirely on a welfare and charity approach where the "fallen need to be uplifted."

6. http://www.unicef.org/programme/cprotection/trafficking.html.

7. The article which first published these statistics was written by Dr. I.S. Gilada of the Indian Health Association in Mumbai, and was presented at a workshop in 1986. Subsequently, a version of this piece was published in the *Times of India,* 2 January 1989. These figures have since then been recycled by innumerable reports and articles on trafficking in Nepal.

8. Radhika Coomaraswamy, "Addendum, Mission to Bangladesh, Nepal and India on the issue of trafficking of women and girls" (28 October–15 November 2000), *Integration of Human Rights of Women and the Gender Perspective: Violence Against Women, Report of the Special Rapporteur on Violence Against Women, Its Causes and Consequences,* in accordance with the Commission on Human Rights resolution 2000/45: GE. 01-10865 (E)

9. See discussion under the section of this article on "The Nexus of Vulnerability and Illegality."

10. A study carried out by the IOM (International Migration Organization) in Cambodia on the recruitment of girls and women for the purpose of prostitution leads to quite the opposite conclusion. Evidence from South Africa, many parts of Asia, and Latin America supports the finding as well that local-level operators and individuals are mostly involved

in the trafficking of children. See the report by the organization Molo Songololo: *The Trafficking of Children for the Purposes of Sexual Exploitation*, South Africa, 2000. In Europe and to some extent in Southeast Asia, organized international criminal groups are reportedly more prevalent. Chinese, Japanese, and Vietnamese criminal networks, as well as Russian and Albanian gangs and the Italian mafia, are among the major traffickers of underage persons and women.

11. Ongoing research by CARE India reveals that in Mumbai, the core of the sex trade has moved out of brothels into beer bars and parlors in the recent past. It is estimated that currently, only about 10–20 percent of the sex trade in Mumbai is conducted out of brothels (conversations with the CARE India Assistant Country Director). Such patterns are emerging as well in other Indian cities, as well as in Nepal. In the state of Kerala in Southern India, there is no brothel-based sex trade; most of it is street-based or conducted through beer bars (based on information provided by the Foundation for Integrated Research in Mental Health, Kerala).

12. Experience with ongoing raids for rescue of women and girls on the GB road brothels in 2002 in Delhi, India, clearly revealed that many brothel keepers shifted their businesses out of the brothel area into apartments and houses in general residential areas of Delhi.

REFERENCES

Asis, Marija M.B. "When Men and Women Migrate: Comparing Gendered Migrations in Asia," presented at the *Consultative Meeting on Migration and Mobility and How This Movement Affects Women*, organized by the United Nations Division for the Advancement of Women, held at the World Maritime University, Malmo, Sweden, 2–4 December 2003.

Coomaraswamy, Radhika. "Addendum, Mission to Bangladesh, Nepal and India on the issue of trafficking of women and girls" (28 October–15 November 2000), *Integration of Human Rights of Women and the Gender Perspective: Violence Against Women*. Report of the Special Rapporteur on Violence Against Women, Its Causes and Consequences, in accordance with the Commission on Human Rights resolution 2000/45: GE. 01–10865 (E).

Estes, Richard, and Neil Allan Weiner. *The Commercial Sexual Exploitation of Children in the US, Canada and Mexico*, University of Pennsylvania, September 2001.

Frederick, John. "Deconstructing Gita." *Himal*. Kathmandu, October 1998.

GAATW (Global Alliance Against Traffick in Women). *Human Rights and Trafficking in Persons: A Handbook*. Bangkok, 2001.

Government of India, Department of Women and Child Development, Ministry of Human Resource Development. *Protecting Children from Trafficking and Sexual Abuse: Initiatives in India*. New Delhi, 2001.

International Labour Organisation. *Stopping Forced Labour*. Global Report under the follow-up to the ILO Declaration on Fundamental Principles and Rights at Work, International Labour Conference, 89th Session 2001. Available at http://www.ilo.org.

Sanghera, Jyoti, and Ratna Kapur. *Trafficking in Nepal: Policy Analysis—An Assessment of Laws and Policies for the Prevention and Control of Trafficking in Nepal*. Sponsored by the Population Council, New Delhi, and the Asia Foundation, Nepal, 2001.

Sanghera, Jyoti. "The New Borderlanders: Enabling Mobile Women and Girls for Safe Migration and Citizenship Rights." Presented at the Consultative Meeting on Migration and Mobility and How This Movement Affects Women, organized by the United Nations Division for the Advancement of Women, held at the World Maritime University, Malmo, Sweden, 2–4 December 2003.

Shifman, Pamela. "Trafficking and Women's Human Rights in a Globalised World." *Gender and Development: Women Reinventing Globalisation*. An Oxfam Journal, vol. 11, No. 1 (May 2003): 125–132.

Songololo, Molo. *The Trafficking of Children for the Purposes of Sexual Exploitation.* South Africa, 2000.

UNICEF Innocenti Research Centre. *Trafficking in Human Beings, Especially Women and Children, in Africa.* Florence, 2003.

UNICEF-EASRO. *Analysis of the Situation of Sexual Exploitation of Children in the Eastern and Southern Africa Region,* Partnership Project on Sexual Exploitation of Children's Rights. Bangkok, October 2001.

UNICEF-ROSA. *South Asia Consultation for the Second World Congress Against Commercial Sexual Exploitation of Children, Summary Report,* Nepal, October 2001.

United Nations. *Beijing Platform for Action.* New York, 1995.

Vermeulen, Gert. *International Trafficking in Women and Children,* International Association of Penal Law, First International Congress of the Young Penalists Section, Siracuse, June 2001.

Widgren, Jonas. "Multinational Cooperation to Combat Trafficking in Migrants and the Role of International Organizations." IOM Seminar on International Responses to Trafficking in Migrants and Safeguarding Migrant Rights, Geneva, October 26–28, 1994.

2

Cross-border Movements and the Law

Renegotiating the Boundaries of Difference

Ratna Kapur

The current moment of globalization is witnessing an extraordinary movement of people, legitimate and illegitimate, across national and international borders. These movements are exposing the porosity of borders, the transnational reality of migrant existence, and the contingent foundations of international law. And this global movement of people has created a panic across borders—a panic which is manifesting itself in the strengthening of border controls, tightening of immigration laws, and casting of the "Other" as a threat to the security of the nation-state. In this essay, I discuss how the issue of cross-border movements is being displaced onto a First World/Third World divide, which has the effect of keeping the "Rest" away from the "West," and is premised on liberal exclusions and understandings of difference. I also examine how laws encounter with these constitutive "Others," quite specifically the transnational migrant subject, which disrupts and disturbs the universalist premise of international law.

Over the past decade, there has been an extraordinary proliferation of law regulating cross-border movements, in the area of trafficking as well as people smuggling. The issue of trafficking and clandestine cross-border movements is regarded as a major contemporary human-rights challenge by the United Nations Secretary General as well as the High Commissioner for Human Rights (Report of the Secretary General to the Commission on Human Rights 2002). This concern has been reflected in part in the Protocol

25

to Prevent, Suppress and Punish Trafficking in Persons, Especially Women and Children (hereinafter, the Trafficking Protocol), supplementing the UN Convention Against Transnational Organized Crime, which came into force on December 25, 2003. A Protocol Against the Smuggling of Migrants by Land, Air and Sea, which came into force on January 28, 2004, was also adopted under the Convention Against Transnational Organized Crime. Another reflection of this concern is in the appointment by the UN Commission on Human Rights of a Special Rapporteur for trafficking in persons, in 2004. In 2007, organizations as diverse as the International Labour Organisation, the Office of the United Nations High Commissioner for Human Rights, the United Nations Children's Fund, the United Nations Office on Drugs and Crime, the International Organization for Migration, and the Organization for Security and Cooperation in Europe came together to set up the UN Global Initiative to Fight Human Trafficking (UNGIFT). The Council of Ministers for the European Union, the Parliamentary Assembly of the Council of Europe, and the Parliamentary Assembly of the Organization for Security and Co-operation in Europe have all issued directives, recommendations, and resolutions on the subject of trafficking (Council of Europe 2000). In 2008 the Council of Europe's Convention on Action against Trafficking in Human Beings entered into force. An International Convention on the Protection of the Rights of All Migrant Workers and Members of Their Families is the first convention to deal specifically with the issue of the rights of documented and undocumented migrant workers, and came into force on July 1, 2003. These initiatives all deal with the extraordinary movement of people, legitimate and illegitimate, across national and international borders, and have been brought into being with the support and advocacy of non-governmental organizations, women's groups, and other social-justice groups.

At one level there is an outward sense of progress, of something being done, of a social-justice project being pursued in the name of the human rights of these have-nots. Yet, this sense of progress is emerging as a somewhat disingenuous and illusory project. Indeed, the legal project pursued in the context of cross-border movements is perhaps the most explicit example we have to date of how our good intentions, passions, and progressive swords of human rights advocacy may have turned into boomerangs; of how international law's promise of progress, emancipation, and universalism has been exposed by these new global subjects as myopic, exclusive, and informed by a series of new global panics (Brown and Halley 2002, 4). These panics include a panic about the survival of the nation, manifesting itself partly in legal responses that focus on strengthening border controls, tightening immigration, and casting the "Other" as a threat primarily to the security of the (First World) nation-state. There is also a moral panic that partly underlies responses to trafficking and also feeds the anti-sex work agenda of feminists, evangelicals, the religious right, and orthodox voices.

And finally there is a cultural panic that treats the "Other" as some form of cultural contaminant who is disrupting a nation's social and cultural cohesion and destroying the authentic fabrics which constitute cultures. In this essay, I address how these panics are informing the legal responses to cross-border movements and today's new global subjects—the transnational migrant. Most of these legal initiatives have been taken ostensibly in the interest of the migrant, out of concern for the abuse, exploitation, or victimization they may experience. Yet an interrogation of the assumptions on which these laws are based exposes how they are invariably designed to shore up the borders of the nation-state, to maintain social and cultural cohesion, and at times, to return to some nostalgic dream of a long-lost golden era of cultural cohesion, family values, and a conservative sexual morality. This paper addresses three areas of concern in the context of the legal regulation of cross-border movements. First, I set out the context in which cross-border movements are taking place. Secondly, I examine how international law's current engagement with difference in the context of cross-border movements reflects the insecurity and instability that is being produced by the disruptive emergence of this new global subject, which is challenging the very identity of the sovereign state and the sovereign citizen. Thirdly, I discuss how recent legal responses to cross-border movements have been partly informed by the "War on Terror," which has converged with the xenophobic discourse of the conservative right and turned it into a hostile, antagonistic fear of the "Other" who is threatening the security of the nation. And finally, I propose some constructive ways in which we can engage with law and legal boundaries, to promote a more liberating and constructive response to the transnational migrant subject.

The Context

According to the United Nations, nearly 214 million migrants are crossing borders in our world today—from rural towns to urban centers, from the periphery into the metropolis, from the global South into the global North (United Nations 2009). These crossings are profoundly challenging some of the most basic notions of women's reproductive labor, family, community, nation, culture, and citizenship. Transborder and in-country movements and migrations are occurring for a plethora of reasons: the reconfiguration of the global economy, the ability to travel, displacement and dispossession of marginalized populations, the awareness through consciousness-raising that there are better options elsewhere, armed conflict, and of course the basic human aspiration to explore the world (Hollifield 1998; Weiner 1995). The global patterns of economics and trade have also increased the demand for low-wage labor, as well as the demand of poor countries for remittances from immigrants in the global North that assist in social welfare that the state is neither able nor willing to provide (Rittich 2000). The World Bank estimates that migrant remittances to developing countries reached $316 billion in 2009 and that these remittances constituted a significant proportion of the GDP of many developing countries (World Bank's Migration and Development Brief 2010). Poorer countries thus have little interest in controlling outward movement, legal or illegal (IOM 2003; Buch, Kucklenz, and Le Manchec 2002).

Although migration is a fact of a globalized economy, this movement has yet to be adequately addressed within the discourse of market management or international migration or labor law. It is addressed primarily in and through the international legal order by initiatives dealing with trafficking, human smuggling, law and order, border controls, security, and sexual morality. The impact of these different initiatives on cross-border movements is mediated by gender, class, religion, and sexual and marital status. The failure of international law to adequately address the reality of the migration phenomenon has given rise to a growing market for clandestine migration services under a migrant-mobility regime (Sanghera 2002, 6). The clandestine regime is produced in part by the failure of States to recognize the need for marginalized groups to migrate and to facilitate such movement through the provision of safe, legal passage. At the same time there is an increasing demand for cheap, exploitable labor that is being produced by market processes (Ghosh 1998, 53). The emerging legal regime with its focus on border controls, security, and law and order is in part producing a clandestine migrant-mobility regime, which provides a host of "services" to those who cross borders, including the facilitation of smuggling, illegal migration, and underground travel, and the provision of false passports, visa permits, and identity papers (Beare 1997, 22). The regulatory edifice of the law with its punitive consequences is being confounded by the emergence of this clandestine migrant-mobility regime.

INTERNATIONAL LAW AND THE POLITICS OF DIFFERENCE

The international legal responses to cross-border movements are based on three assumptions about these new global subjects. First, they are either weak, submissive, and incapable of looking after themselves—that is, they are victims; secondly, they can be assimilated and brought into the mainstream; and thirdly, they are capable of the most terrifying violence, and must be incarcerated, detained, or even eliminated.

Trafficking

Anti-trafficking initiatives have been adopted or enacted at the international and domestic levels at an extraordinary rate over the past few years, and the impetus behind these initiatives stems from a variety of concerns and locations. In some contexts, the trafficking agenda has come to be increasingly influenced by a conservative sexual morality. For example, the evangelical right in the United States specifically called on George W. Bush to foreground the issue of trafficking in his speech to the United Nations General Assembly on September 12, 2003 (Bumiller 2003). In other contexts, a protectionist approach toward women informs the trafficking agenda, which results in casting women as victims and justifies at times protective detention (Kapur 2002). Such initiatives are being enacted ostensibly and primarily for the protection of women who are perceived as vulnerable to the designs of traffickers and criminal networks which force women across borders primarily for the purpose of engaging in sex work and for sexual exploitation. However, it is extremely difficult to determine the real dimensions of the trafficking phenomenon due to the lack of both qualitative and quantitative research in this area. Most of the information currently available is anecdotal and based on small-scale surveys and studies (Wijers and Lap-Chew 1997). There is also a tendency to accept unverified statistics and data that are available without further interrogation.[1] An example of this is the data collection efforts by the U.S. to measure global trafficking in its annual Trafficking in Persons Report. As its own internal audit has found, the data collection methods are highly "questionable" and their accuracy is in doubt because of "methodological weaknesses, gaps in data, and numerical discrepancies" (United States Government Accountability Office [GAO] 2006, 2).

These questionable statistics have been combined with other confusions between trafficking, migration, and sex work. In contemporary discourse, human trafficking has come to be variously and yet integrally interwoven with migration—mainly illegal—clandestine border crossing, and smuggling of humans. On a parallel plane, trafficking in women and girls is resoundingly conflated with their sale and forced consignment to brothels in the sex industry. For example, the South Asian Association for Regional Cooperation Convention on Preventing and Combating Trafficking in Women and Children for Prostitution, 2002, which was ratified by all member states in 2006, defines trafficking as the "moving, selling or buying of women and children for prostitution within and outside a country for monetary or other considerations with or without the consent of the person subjected to trafficking" (Article I [3]). The conflation of trafficking in persons with various manifestations of migration and mobility on the one hand, and with prostitution and sex work on the other, lies at the very core of the confusion that underpins the contemporary discourse on trafficking of women and girls globally, regionally, and nationally.

Equating trafficking with migration leads to simplistic and unrealistic solutions—in order to prevent trafficking there is a conscious or inadvertent move to stop those who are deemed vulnerable from migrating. Even when curbing migration is not a stated programmatic focus, an inadvertent impetus is to dissuade women and girls from moving in order to protect them from harm. For example, after concerns were raised regarding the trafficking of Burmese women to Thailand to feed into its sex industry, the Burmese government put in place rules to prevent women aged 16–25 from traveling without a legal guardian (Belak 2003). Such conflation of trafficking with migration results in reinforcing the gender bias that women and girls need constant male or state protection from harm, and therefore must not be allowed to exercise their right to movement or right to earn a living in the manner they choose.[2]

Secondly, curbing migration will not stop trafficking, but merely drive the activity further underground, and make it more invisible.[3] This lesson has been learned from states that have proceeded to enforce increasingly stringent immigration controls as a response to heightened trafficking in persons and narcotics. Borders cannot be impermeable, and stricter immigration measures have resulted in pushing the victims further into situations of violence and abuse. The response to this by the international community has been to create legal frameworks to criminalize the smuggling of migrants through the Protocol (to the UN Convention Against Transnational Organized Crime) Against Smuggling of Migrants. This serves to further exacerbate the vulnerability of the migrant.

Thirdly, when no clear conceptual or operational distinctions are drawn between migration and trafficking, and in fact, when migration is considered equal to trafficking, then it logically follows that the number of victims of trafficking is equal to the number of those who have migrated voluntarily (Kaye 2003). This logic operates particularly in the case of adolescent girls and women migrants, and not in the case of men. This practice has resulted in an extremely flawed methodology for conducting baseline surveys on trafficking in "risk-prone" and "affected districts" in different South Asian countries (Asia Foundation 2001, 28). If women are not present in a locality or district they are invariably deemed to have been trafficked away. Hence, even women's consensual migration comes to be viewed primarily through the lens of trafficking (see also Sanghera in chapter one).

The trafficking initiatives are also characterized by racial and gendered dimensions. The discourse often reproduces a First World and Third World divide, with the assumption that the problem exists over "there" in the Third World, or postcolonial world, and proposes strategies that reinforce the image of a truncated, seriously battered, culturally constrained, and oppressed subject that needs to be rescued and rehabilitated by a civilizing West (Mohanty 1991). Both governmental and non-governmental initiatives reinforce the images presented in the media that promote stereotyped construction of the trafficked victim as foreign, innocent, and ignorant (Doezema 2001). Simultaneously these images vilify Third World governments and single out alien criminal gangs. This image, and the dichotomous understanding on which it is constructed, fails to comprehend the complex reality and nature of trafficking. Trafficking needs to be understood within the broader context of globalization and the increase in female migration from the Third World, and as a part of the repressive consequences of anti-trafficking strategies that are constructed along binaries and stereotypes of the Third World.

And finally, there has been a continued persistence among anti-trafficking players to conflate trafficking with sex work/prostitution (Hughes and Roche 1999).[4] For example, upon signing the Trafficking Victims Protection Reauthorization Act 2005 (TVPRA) George W. Bush stated that "we're attacking this problem aggressively. Over the past four years, the Department of Homeland Security has taken new measures to protect children from sexual predators, as well as pornography and prostitution rings." Another example of the conflation of trafficking with prostitution was the 2006 proposed amendment to the Immoral Traffic (Prevention) Act. Section 5A of the Act sought to limit the definition of "trafficking in persons" to trafficking for prostitution (see Hundred Eighty-Second Report on the Immoral Traffic (Prevention) Amendment Bill, 2006, ¶11).

By collapsing the process with the purpose, the abuse and violence inherent in trafficking are mistaken for the actual site of work and form of labor. Furthermore, trafficking for all other purposes is largely ignored, and targeting trafficking for prostitution becomes the principal agenda of anti-trafficking interventions, policies, and laws. This dimension of the issue has recently been challenged by the Trafficking Protocol, which emphasizes that there are several sites of exploitation, and that trafficking is not confined merely to prostitution or sex work.

The conflation of trafficking with prostitution also serves to reinforce dominant sexual morality regarding prostitution through measures to control trafficking. This is especially true of the U.S., which does not recognize prostitution as a valid form of employment for the purposes of its trafficking policies. It also specifically considers curbing prostitution as an essential measure of trafficking control. As a result, in ranking countries in its annual Trafficking in Persons reports, it uses state efforts to curb prostitution as one of the proxies for a state's commitment to anti-trafficking measures (US Trafficking in Persons Report 2010, 8).

The focus of anti-trafficking initiatives at the domestic, regional, and international level is rarely on providing women-who-move with human rights—the tools that are critical to fighting abuse, violence, and harm they may experience in the course of movement. The inability of states to control their borders and fears about security have led to an unprecedented cooperation between nation-states to share information and develop strategies to improve border controls and strengthen law enforcement (Advisory Council of Jurists 2002, 8).[5] The issues of trafficking and clandestine movement are regarded especially by powerful countries of destination as a problem of migration, law and order, and transnational organized crime, rather than an issue of human rights. The fact that the Trafficking Protocol was negotiated within the framework of the UN Convention Against Transnational Organized Crime and outside the human-rights system highlights the criminal justice and security approach and states' interests in maintaining border integrity. The failure to foreground the human-rights aspects of trafficking has resulted in further pushing the activity underground, and centering the security of the State at the cost of the security of the migrant subject. This might be changing, however, at the international level at least, with the appointment of a Special Rapporteur on Trafficking in Persons by the UN Commission on Human Rights (see Report by Special Raporteur 2010, 18).

Assimilation

A second legal response is to attempt the assimilation of those who cross borders. The strategy of assimilation is a familiar device by which to deal with those who are different. During the period of the colonial encounter, assimilation was advanced through the educational curriculum, where the native subject learned to mime, and walk and talk like an "Englishman" (Vishwanathan 1989). Strategies of assimilation remain present even in the current moment. States throughout Europe are enacting new citizenship and nationality laws to enable these subjects to be part of the universal project of rights and acquire legitimacy through the process of assimilation. One example is the recently enacted British Nationality, Immigration and Asylum Act 2002, which targets the transnational migrant subject through new cultural, emotional, and citizenship criteria. The primary objective of the act is to build social cohesion and a sense of British identity in "an increasingly diverse world" (UK Home Office 2002, 11). It thus requires that people who want to become UK citizens take a compulsory English-language test and an exam on the ways of British life, British society, and British institutions (UK Home Office 2002, 32–33). These measures are justified by the Home Secretary in the following terms: "Our future social cohesion, economic prosperity and integrity depends on how well we rise to the global challenge of mass migration, communication and flight from persecution" (UK Home Office 2002, 3; Hodge 2002; Cantle 2003).

Another objective of the act is to meet the economic challenge partly by ensuring that people who want to work in the United Kingdom can do so without entering into the country through illegal routes. These two challenges are to be confronted under a policy of "managing migration" (UK Home Office 2002, 19). Managing migration is designed to set up a system of entry into the country that is orderly and organized. It is also directed toward assisting in the integration of migrants into the British economy and society in ways where they will be welcomed by the existing population. These migrants are to be managed in the crossing of borders, as well as in terms of their identity construction once they have crossed the borders.

Another recent example of assimilation is the proposal to ban head-scarves in France—which, though taken in the name of secularism, is but another shift by which to pressurize the minority immigrant community to conform to the practices of the majority (Sciolino 2004). These assimila-tionist moves are also prevalent in India, where Muslims and Christians, who are constructed as outsiders or foreigners because their holy lands lie outside of India, are being pressured by the Hindu Right to surrender their identities; surrender their places of worship, educational spaces, and even customary practices; and merge with the majority; read "Hindu majority" (Kapur and Cossman 2001).

These measures provide the "Other" with an opportunity to be embraced by the universal project, through his/her willingness to as-similate. It provides the possibility for the "Other" to metamorphose into someone who is familiar and recognizable. And access to rights and benefits is contingent on the ability of the transnational migrant to reinvent himself/herself, to become recognizable, comprehensible, and hence, non-threatening.

Demonizing the "Other"

Finally, there is the legal response that promotes incarceration, deten-tion, even annihilation or elimination. In these contexts, the migrant is cast as a transgressor, incomprehensible, and existing completely outside of the framework of liberal democracy, and is defined as a threat to the nation-state and as backward, uncivilized, and dangerous. We find these responses present in the explicit policy of incarceration of asylum-seekers in Australia, illustrating how the migrant subject is being transformed into a manipulative, dangerous, and contaminating force against which state and individual sovereignty must be protected (McMaster 2000; McMaster 2002). In the United Kingdom, the Home Secretary recently proposed that the children of rejected asylum-seekers be taken from their care as a way to pressurize them to leave (Hinsliff 2003). The proposal does not reveal the double objective of the UK government in quietly allowing the immigra-tion of the economically valued while ensuring the politically oppressed are treated as criminals and despised.

However, this approach is not confined to the West—it has become an increasingly effective tool in the hands of countries in the South, including Malaysia, Thailand, and even India, where the right wing is intent on eliminating or removing those who do not conform to the new cultural-authenticity, nationalist agendas. One example is the proposal by the Bhartiya Janata Party, the political wing of the Hindu Right that led the coalition government from 1999–2004, to deport undocumented Bangladeshi migrants from India—they number anywhere from 13 to 20 million people. The argument time and again is that these migrants pose a potential threat to the security of the nation-states (Samaddar 1999). There is at the same time a clear distinction drawn by the Hindu Right, between Hindu and Muslim migrants (Kaur 2003). Hindu migrants are referred to as refugees; that is, those who are in need of State support and regarded as victims of intolerance in a Muslim country, namely Bangladesh. In contrast the Muslims are referred to as infiltrators; that is, they are regarded as aliens suspected of crossing the border with the objective of threatening the security of the Indian (read "Hindu") nation, even though in fact most of them are economic refugees (Kapur 2010).[6]

THE GLOBAL "WAR ON TERROR"

The situation of those who cross borders has been aggravated by the recent global "War on Terror." The issues of trafficking and migration are now being taken up within the overarching concern with security of the nation and the global War on Terror. The perceived link between trafficking, immigration, and national security was underscored in the context of the U.S. when its Immigration and Naturalization Services, which implements U.S. policy on immigration (and therefore makes key determinations regarding trafficked persons) was transferred to the Department of Homeland Security (Huckerby 2007, 246). The War on Terror has acquired a supernatural life and existence outside of the international legal order, while simultaneously being pursued in and through the processes and institutions of the international regime. The UN Security Council and the General Assembly have been deployed to foreground the security and sovereignty of some nation-states through the abrogation of the security and sovereignty of other nation-states. The legal mechanisms endorsed in pursuit of this endeavor have resulted in the enactment of laws at the domestic and international level that have further cauterized cross-border movements, and justified going after anything and anyone one does not like.

Numerous countries have passed regressive anti-terrorism laws that expand governmental powers of detention and surveillance in ways that threaten basic rights (Amnesty International 2004). There has been a continuing spate of arbitrary arrests and detentions of suspects without due process (Human Rights Watch 2002). For example, in the United States, suspects have been charged or brought before a court in only a handful of cases. Hundreds remain in detention without charge at Guantanamo Bay, in military custody inside the United States, or at other U.S. bases or undisclosed locations around the world. Almost every "alien" entering the

U.S. is suspect, though in varying degrees, subject to fingerprinting and photographing at ports of entry. In many European Union countries, new laws and policies have undermined fundamental human-rights protections, including the right to seek asylum and prohibitions against arbitrary detention and torture (ECRI [Denmark] 2001; ECRI [Austria] 2001). In India, the Prevention of Terrorism Act has been used against political opponents, and quite specifically religious minorities. In Indonesia, new legislation and presidential decrees threaten fundamental rights, invoking broad definitions of terrorism that could be used to target political opponents. What is most troubling is how anti-terrorism has now come to structure militarized reaction, not war anchored in national sovereignty.

These legal responses need to be read with the fact that, globally, we are witnessing a heightened anxiety about the "Other," who is perceived as a threat or someone who is dangerous to the security of the nation. The boundary line of difference is being redrawn along very stark divides—between friend and enemy, those who are good and those who are evil. Although these concerns are most explicitly voiced by the extreme right or religious right, less noticed is the more uniformly pervasive emergence of similar forms of conservatism within mainstream discourses. The "alien migrant," here and there, has become one of the primary casualties of the failure to define either the purpose or limits of the War on Terror. This failure forces migrants to continue to move through illicit channels, and remain vulnerable, stigmatized, and illegitimate.

The new War on Terror has created space for a more strident and alarming response to the global movements of people, reducing it at times to nothing more than an evil threat. And once again this new war is not being pursued only in the United States—it is rather alarming how enthusiastically it is being embraced by states in many different parts of the world. The breadth and scope of this war remain undefined and ambiguous. It would include a situation where, if terrorism was defined as a transnational crime, then by merely committing the crime of seeking illegal movement and illegal entry these people could be defined as terrorists. Because the smugglers offer travel services to undocumented migrants, they would easily fall within the category of transnational organized crime, criminals, and potential terrorists. These simple equations again lead to a disjuncture between reality of the illegal migrant and the issue of terrorism.

The War on Terror has resulted in legal reforms that alienate those who have been cast as the "new enemy" and justifies resorting to punitive measures on the grounds that these people are evil or dangerous and not entitled to due process or rights. The conflation of the migrant with the terrorist is not new, but it has received greater attention since September 11, 2001; it has afforded more space for the representation of the "Other" as a fanatic and dangerous and opposed to freedom (Porras 1994); and it has pushed us further away from addressing the complexity of cross-border movements and the equally complex legal and political responses required to address the issues raised by such movements.

The space for the migrant is being eroded through the discourse of trafficking and through the discourse of terrorism and threats to the security of the nation. Yet criminalizing or victimizing those who cross borders forces these people to continue to move through illicit channels, and to remain vulnerable, stigmatized, and illegitimate. It seems unlikely that the security of what is left of the nation-state can be achieved at the cost of the security of the alien migrant. Indeed it will only serve to encourage the construction of a paradox, where the security of the alien migrant is perhaps less threatened by people-smugglers and clandestine migrant-mobility regimes than by the current international system of protection offered to people who move as migrants, refugees, or asylum-seekers.

TOWARD RENEGOTIATING BOUNDARIES

The legal interventions in the lives of the transnational migrant have been articulated primarily from the perspective of the host country. The voices of the migrant subject are omitted from these conversations and yet these are the voices that can assist in untangling the conflations and confusions that are taking place between trafficking, migration, and terrorism in the international and domestic legal arenas.

At a practical level we need to take up the issue of cross-border migration within the framework of migration and globalization. This means doing much more to publicize and lobby for the Migrant Workers Convention (MWC). The MWC is, however, full of ambiguities and incapable of addressing the full range of human-rights concerns implicated in cross-border movements. Although the convention affirmatively grants recognition to the rights of the migrants (a welcome change to the earlier attempts to address the issue of migration), it fails to consider migration from the point of view of the migrant.[7] It is critical to develop guidelines in relation to the MWC that would foreground the rights aspects of the convention, and build a framework for interpretation of the convention's provisions.

Secondly, the human rights of migrants must also be located in the vortex of human-rights norms and read against the spectacular array of rights that already exist in the form of the ILO conventions, the Convention on the Elimination of All Forms of Discrimination Against Women, the International Convention on the Elimination of All Forms of Racial Discrimination, and the two covenants on civil, political, economic, and cultural and social rights.

Female migration also needs to be more adequately addressed in law. Women's cross-border movements continue to be addressed primarily within the framework of trafficking, victimization, and a conservative sexual morality. The agency of women needs to be foregrounded and their complex subjectivity consciously addressed in the legal and policy approaches being pursued at the national and international levels. Women's choices to cross borders need to be viewed within the context of empowerment and their search for better economic market opportunities. Their movement must be linked with migration, and the harms they experience in the course of movement specifically addressed.

Women's consent needs to be located in the matrix of the global economy, market demand, and cross-border migrations. Currently, their cross-border movements are largely located and addressed within normative understandings about women's sexuality, the security of the nation, and criminal law. A woman's choice is reconfigured through international legal processes, and she is either rendered a victim, to be repatriated to her home country; or a criminal, a trespasser, to be prosecuted along with traffickers and terrorists for having exposed the porosity of national borders. Legal barrier methods fail to attend to the complex factors that induce migration, and instead target the individual as being exclusively responsible for the problem of transnational migration. The receiving country is not implicated in this migration phenomenon, and is justified in resorting to methods of containment and confinement. These punitive measures constitute migrant women as outlaws, and compel them to live illegal lives. The international legal order has failed to facilitate women's freedom of mobility and safe migration, especially, though not exclusively, from the South to the North. A woman's consensual movement is rendered illegal, through the foregrounding of the security of the nation-state, the conservative sexual morality that informs anti-trafficking laws, and the xenophobic responses to global movements that increasingly inform immigration laws.

Regardless of why women move, their assertion of the right to mobility, self-determination, and development must not be confused with the violence, force, coercion, abuse, or fraud that may take place in the course of migration or transport. The crime rests in the elements of abuse and violations that are committed against women along the continuum of women's migration, and not in the movement or mobility per se.

At a normative level, there are certain shifts that also need to be made. What is most evident from even this rather brief evaluation of the legal regulation of cross-border movements is how the interests of those who cross borders and states are opposed to one another. The migrant is regarded as either a terrorist, or as a victim, rather than a complex subject who is affected by global processes and seeking safe passage across borders. These subjects are exposing the need for us to think about law and rights in ways that are not confined to the boxes of sovereignty, the nation-state, and the autonomous subject of liberal rights discourse.

The liberal state and the liberal subject are based on the idea of fixed borders, with clearly identifiable interests and identities. Yet globalization, which produces the challenge of migration and non-state actors to the legitimacy of the borders of the sovereign state and the autonomous subject, indicates otherwise. The complexity of new global formations and the dynamic character of transnational migrants challenge any notion that the state and individual are hermetically sealed and capable of exercising control through self-contained power (Brown 2001). The inability to distinguish those who constitute national subjects from those who are alien or foreign is blurred because of the proliferation of races, cultures, and ethnicities within national borders. It is difficult to locate a distinct national entity with distinct borders and a distinct, clearly delineated national subject. Social cohesion, unity, and sovereignty are all becoming blunt in the face of a more complex and integrated world and global economy, and the challenge posed by the transnational migrant subject.

The role of law, at the international and domestic level, should be to address how broader transnational processes affect flows or movements of people and are an integral feature of globalization. This in turn requires radical rethinking and a renegotiation of legal and normative boundaries. As long as these issues are not viewed through the complex lens of globalization, market demand, and the (in)security of the nation-state, the rights and legitimacy of these people will remain unaddressed or compromised, and contribute to the growing instability of both the host country and this itinerant population. Cross-border movements have been caught within the framework of a "war" fought along the simple binaries of good versus evil, civilization versus barbarism. A response to border crossings cannot be adequately addressed through such binaries. Indeed this myopic response will do little to discourage the illegal crossing of borders or the determination of those who want to move.

Current legal strategies have produced responses that have not advanced the rights of the transnational migrant subject, nor produced a liberatory politics or progressive end. Engagements with international and human-rights law require a monitoring of the way in which rights are introduced, pursued, and implemented. Good intentions—to protect migrants, and specifically women, from harm—are not sufficient for pursuing a rights strategy, and can indeed reinforce dominant assumptions about the "Other" and protectionist and patronizing assumptions about women, especially those who move from the global South. The international and human-rights legal terrain and their respective institutions are contested, non-democratic, and informed by economic, military, and political considerations. We cannot abandon these spaces of engagement; we simply have to learn how to engage with them differently.

Cross-border movements must be addressed against the broader canvas of transnationalism. Transnational movements require a transnational response and analysis—they cannot be caught within older frameworks. If it is possible to invent a response in the course of twenty-four hours that allows a state to invoke its right to self-defense against a terrorist, non-state actor, then it is surely also possible to pursue a vision by which law centers the transnational migrant, rather than the State. The transnational migrant is living the global reality, forcing us to revisit current legal responses to cross-border movements, and to acknowledge the fact that people will move illegally if legal means are not made available to them.

NOTES

1. For example, the Coalition Against Trafficking in Women, Asia Pacific, sets out the numbers of women trafficked in a number of countries, without citing any research or sources of their statistics: See Coalition Against Trafficking in Women—Asia Pacific at http://www.catw-ap.org/. Similarly, the 1995 Human Rights Report on Trafficking between Nepal and India states that "At least hundreds of thousands, and probably more than a million women and children are employed in Indian brothels" (Human Rights Watch, *Rape for Profit: Trafficking of Nepali Girls and Women to India's Brothels,* 1995: 1). This same group's report on trafficking between Burma and Thailand states that "there are an estimated 800,000 to two million prostitutes currently working in Thailand" (Women's Rights Project, Human Rights Watch, *A Modern Form of Slavery: Trafficking of Burmese Women and Girls into Brothels in Thailand,* 1993: 1).

2. Policies that appear to be initiated for the *benefit* of women often contribute to further victimization and infantilization of female migrants. For example, in the early 1990s, Bangladesh, India, and Indonesia imposed minimum age limits for women workers going abroad for employment. In 1998, Bangladesh banned women from going abroad as domestic workers. In 2002, the government of Bangladesh announced that it was considering removing the ban; however, to date the ban appears to have remained in effect. In 2003, the Indonesian government similarly announced the imposition of a temporary ban on female migrant workers. See Irene Fernandez, *Ban on Female Workers by Indonesia Is Not the Solution,* March 3, 2003 (online) accessed May 27, 2004. Available at http://www.december18.net/web/papers/view.php?paperID=672&menuID=41&lang=EN. In the same vein, although not entirely prohibiting migration by women, the Nepal Foreign Employment Act, 2042 (1985) prohibits issuance to women of employment licenses to work overseas without the consent of the woman's guardian. Similarly, the government of Burma, reacting to publication of a report by Human Rights Watch about the trafficking of Burmese women and girls into Thailand's sex industry, imposed rules prohibiting all women in this area between the ages of 16 and 25 from traveling without a legal guardian (Brenda Belak, "Migration & Trafficking of Women & Girls," in *Gathering Strength: Women from Burma and Their Rights* [Images Asia, Thailand], June 2003 [online] accessed May 27, 2004. Available at http://www.ibiblio.org/obl/docs/GS12.migration-and-trafficking.pdf).

3. Report of the Special Rapporteur on Violence Against Women, Its Causes and Consequences, Radhika Coomaraswamy, on trafficking in women, women's migration, and violence against women, E/CN.4/2000/68, 29 February 2000; see also Population Council, *Trafficking and Human Rights in Nepal: Community Perceptions and Program Responses,* joint research summary of Horizons and Asia Foundation, Washington, D.C., and Delhi, 2001,

accessed May 27, 2004. Available at http://www.popcouncil.org/horizons/ressum/traffickingsum1_key.html.

4. For example, in Nepal, the Ministry of Women, Children and Social Welfare's draft of the Traffic in Human Beings (Offences and Penalties) Bill, 1999, came under criticism for failing to distinguish trafficking from a number of sexual offenses, including prostitution, pornography, and sexual abuse. Similarly, in Thailand, the Measures of Prevention and Suppression of the Trafficking in Women and Children Act, 1997, prohibits the selling, buying, luring, sending, receiving, detaining, and procuring of women and children to perform sexual acts with or without the consent of the woman or child. The South Asian Association for Regional Cooperation (SAARC) Convention on Preventing and Combating Trafficking in Women and Children for Prostitution was adopted by SAARC in January 2002. The issue of trafficking is specifically linked to prostitution, and trafficking for purposes other than prostitution remains unaddressed in the convention. Furthermore, in several of these initiatives, the consent of the woman is deemed irrelevant, thus conflating consensual and non-consensual movement, treating all movement of women as involving trafficking.

5. Report of the Special Rapporteur on Violence Against Women, Its Causes and Consequences, UN Doc E/CN.4/2000/68 at para 54.

6. This argument was in fact accepted by the Indian Supreme Court in *Sonowal v. Union of India*, and was a basis on which India's Illegal Migrants (Determination by Tribunals) Act, 1983 was struck down (*Sonowal* 2005).

7. See the United Nations Press Release, "Convention on Protection of Rights of Migrant Workers to Enter into Force Next July," March 19, 2003, which states that "[t]he Convention reflects an up-to-date understanding of migratory trends *as seen from the point of view of both States of origin and host States* of migrant workers and their families" (emphasis added).

REFERENCES

Advisory Council of Jurists. *Consideration of the Issue of Trafficking: Background Paper.* New Delhi: Asia Pacific Forum of National Human Rights Institutions, 2002.

Amnesty International. *Amnesty International Report, 2004.* London: Amnesty International, 2004.

Asia Foundation. *Prevention of Trafficking and the Care and Support of Trafficked Persons in the Context of an Emerging HIV/AIDS Epidemic in Nepal.* Kathmandu and New Delhi: Horizons, 2001.

Beare, Margaret. "Illegal Migration: Person Tragedies, Social Problems or National Security Threats?" *Transnational Organized Crime* 3(4) (1997): pp.11–41.

Belak, B. "Migration and Trafficking of Women and Girls." In *Gathering Strength: Women from Burma and Their Rights.* Thailand: Images Asia Online, 2003. Available at http://www.ibiblio.org/obl/docs/GS12.migration-and-trafficking.pdf.

Brown, Wendy. *Politics Out of History.* Princeton and Oxford: Princeton University Press, 2001.

Brown, Wendy, and Halley, Janet. "Introduction." In Brown, Wendy, and Halley, Janet (eds), *Left Legalism/Left Critique.* Durham and London: Duke University Press, 2002: pp 1–37.

Buch, Claudia M., Kucklenz, Anja, and Le Manchec, Marie-Helene. "Worker Remittances and Capital Flows." Kiel Institute for World Economics, Working Paper No. 1130, 2002.

Bumiller, Elizabeth. "Evangelicals Sway White House on Human Rights Issues Abroad." *New York Times,* 26 October 2003.

Cantle, Ted. *Community Cohesion: A Report of the Independent Review Team.* London: Community Cohesion Unit, Home Office, 2003.

Council of Europe. Trafficking in Human Beings: Compilation of the Main Legal Instruments and Analytical Reports Dealing with Trafficking Human Beings at International, Regional, and National Levels, Volume 1, International and Regional Texts, 2000: 91–193.

Doezema, Jo. "Ouch! Western Feminists' 'Wounded Attachment' to the 'Third World Prostitute.'" *Feminist Review* No. 67, 2001: 16–38.

ECRI. *European Commission Against Racism and Intolerance, Second Report on Denmark.* Adopted June 16, 2000 CRI (2001).

Ghosh, Bimal. *Huddled Masses and Uncertain Shores: Insights Into Irregular Migration.* The Hague: Kluwer Law International, 1998.

Hinsliff, Gaby. "Asylum Children May be Forced into Care." *The Guardian,* 23 November 2003.

Hodge, Warren. "Britain's Nonwhites Feel Un-British, Report Says." *New York Times,* 4 April 2002.

Hollifield, James. "Migration, Trade and the Nation-State: The Myth of Globalization." *UCLA Journal of International Law and Foreign Affairs,* Volume 3, No. 2 (1998): 595–696.

Huckerby, Jayne. "United States of America." In *Collateral Damage: The Human Rights Impact of Anti-Trafficking Policies around the World.* Bangkok: Global Alliance Against Traffic in Women, 2007: pp. 230–256.

Hughes, Donna, and Roche, Claire (eds). *Making the Harms Visible: Global Sexual Exploitation of Women and Girls: Speaking Out and Providing Services.* Coalition Against Trafficking in Women, 1999.

Human Rights Watch. *World Report, 2002.* New York: Human Rights Watch, 2002.

———. *Rape for Profit: Trafficking of Nepali Girls and Women into India's Brothels,* 1995.

———. *A Modern Form of Slavery: Trafficking of Burmese Women and Girls into Brothels in Thailand,* 1993.

IMF. *International Monetary Fund, Balance of Payments Statistics Yearbook, 2002.* Washington: IMF, 2002.

IOM. "Facts and Figures on International Migration." *Migration Policy Issues,* Volume 2, No. 1 (2003).

———. *World Migration Report, 2000.*

Kapur, Ratna. *Makeshift Migrants: Gender, Belonging and Postcolonial Anxieties.* New Delhi: Routledge, 2010.

———. "The Tragedy of Victimization Rhetoric: Resurrecting the 'Native' Subject in International/Postcolonial Feminist Legal Politics." *Harvard Law Review,* Volume 15, No. 1 (2002): 1–37.

Kapur, Ratna, and Cossman, Brenda. *Secularism's Last Sigh? Hindutva and the (Mis)Rule of Law.* New Delhi: Oxford University Press, 2001.

Kaur, Naunidhi. "Right-Wing Politics at Play." *Frontline Magazine,* Volume 20, No. 4 (2003): 102–103.

Kaye, Mike. *The Migration-Trafficking Nexus: Combating Trafficking Through the Protection of Migrants' Human Rights.* London: Anti-Slavery International, 2003.

McMaster, Don. "Refugees: where to now?: White Australia to Tampa: the politics of fear." *The Academy of the Social Sciences in Australia Dialogue,* Volume 21, No. 1 (2002):3–9.

———. "Asylum-seekers and the insecurity of a nation." *Australian Journal of International Affairs,* Volume 56, No. 2 (2000): 279–290.

Mohanty, Chandra Talpade. "Under Western Eyes: Feminist Scholarship and Colonial Discourses." In Mohanty, Chandra Talpade, Russo, Ann, and Torres, Lourdes (eds), *Third World Women and the Politics of Feminism.* Indianapolis: Indiana University Press, 1991: pp. 51–80.

Parliamentary Standing Committee on Human Resource Development. *Hundred Eighty-Second Report on the Immoral Traffic (Prevention) Amendment Bill, 2006.*

Porras, Ileana. "On Terrorism: Reflections on Violence and the Outlaw." In Danielson, Dan and Engles, Karen (eds.), *After Identity: A Reader in Law and Culture.* New York: Routledge, 1994: pp. 294–313.

Report of the Secretary General to the Commission on Human Rights. "Traffic in Women and Girls." UN Doc. E/CN.4/2002/80.

Report submitted by the Special Rapporteur on trafficking in persons, especially women and children, Joy Ngozi Ezeilo, A/HRC/14/32 (4 May 2010).

Rittich, Kerry. "Transformed Pursuits: The Quest for Equality in Globalized Markets." *Harvard Human Rights Journal*, Volume 13 (2000): 231–261.

Samaddar, Ranabir. *The Marginal Nation: Transborder Migration from Bangladesh to West Bengal.* New Delhi: Sage, 1999.

Sanghera Jyoti. "Enabling and Empowering Mobile Women and Girls: Strategy Paper on the Safe Migration and Citizenship Rights of Women and Adolescent Girls." ASEM meeting on Gender, Migration and Trafficking, sponsored by Swedish Department for International Cooperation and UNIFEM, Bangkok, October 2002.

Sciolino, Elaine. "French Assembly Votes to Ban Religious Symbols in Schools." *New York Times*, 3 February 2004.

Tempest, Mathew. "Blunkett Defends Asylum Proposals." *The Guardian*, 17 December 2003.

UK Home Office. *Secure Borders, Safe Haven.* Home Office White Paper. London: HMG, 2002.

United Nations, Department of Economic and Social Affairs, Population Division. *Trends in International Migrant Stock: The 2008 Revision* (United Nations database, POP/DB/MIG/Stock/Rev.2008), 2009.

US Government Accountability Office. *Report to the Chairman, Committee on the Judiciary and the Chairman, Committee on International Relations, House of Representatives: Human Trafficking: Better Data, Strategy, and Reporting Needed to Enhance U.S. Antitrafficking Efforts Abroad, 2006.*

Viswanathan, Gauri. *Masks of Conquest: Literary Studies and British Rule in India.* London: Faber & Faber, 1989.

Weiner, Myron. *The Global Migration Crisis: Challenges to States and to Human Rights.* Reading, MA: Addison Wesley Publishing Company, 1995.

Wijers, Marjan, and Lap-Chew, Lin. *Trafficking in Women: Forced Labor and Slavery-Like Practices in Marriage, Domestic Labor and Prostitution.* Utrecht: STV, 1997.

World Bank. "World Bank's Migration and Development Brief 12: Outlook for Remittance Flows 2010–11." April 23, 2010. Available online at http://go.worldbank.org/SSW3DDNLQ0.

3

Miles Away

The Trouble with Prevention in the Greater Mekong Sub-region

Phil Marshall and Susu Thatun

Despite significant and growing efforts against human trafficking on a local, national, and global scale, most practitioners believe that the scope and magnitude of the problem continues to increase. The Greater Mekong Sub-region (GMS), covering Cambodia, Lao PDR, Myanmar, Thailand, Vietnam, and Yunnan Province in China, is no exception. Several regional initiatives and numerous local and national programs have yet to show strong signs of impacting on the problem.

This paper examines the response to trafficking in the region and suggests that this response to date has been undermined by three inter-related shortcomings in how the issue is conceptualized and understood. These are: lack of acknowledgment and understanding of a "push-down, pop-up phenomenon" that is taking place around trafficking; faulty construction of the concept of prevention (including misunderstanding of what is being prevented); and inaccurate assessment of the root causes of trafficking. Taken together, these shortcomings serve to focus attention on migration—particularly cross-border movements—rather than on the fundamental abuses of women, men, and children that trafficking involves. While the analysis is based on the authors' own experience and knowledge of the GMS, it is submitted that the problems underlying the response to human trafficking in this part of the world are present, to a greater or lesser degree, in all other regions.

PUSH-DOWN POP-UP

There is now growing acknowledgment of the displacement, or *push-down pop-up* (PDPU)[1] effect surrounding trafficking. This term is used to describe a phenomenon whereby the problem is reduced or pushed down in one place, only to emerge somewhere else. Trafficking is a dynamic phenomenon and traffickers can quickly adjust to changing environments, in particular, but not only, by shifting the geographic focus of their activities. Evidence of PDPU raises questions about the efficacy of a range of current programs and its acknowledgment is fundamental to developing more effective interventions.

The push-down pop-up effect manifests itself in several different ways. One relates to the vulnerability of communities as a whole. Research from South Asia (Horizons Project 2001) has indicated that some community-level trafficking interventions which appear successful on the surface may simply be moving the problem from one community to another—that pushing the issue down in one community may lead to it "popping up" somewhere else. These findings are consistent with analysis in the GMS, particularly as it relates to the sex trade in Thailand. With notable but insufficient measures to reduce demand for children, there are reports that successful programs to prevent Thai children from Northern Thailand entering the sex trade are displacing the problem to ethnic minority children, and to the neighboring countries of Lao PDR and Myanmar.

A second version of this PDPU effect relates to individual vulnerability, and concerns rescue and return efforts. Rescuing a person from a situation of exploitation has high "feel-good" value and lends itself to positive media coverage (and, by extension, fundraising efforts). Given problems with raids of establishments into which people are trafficked, including the rescue of those who do not wish to be rescued (see below), many agencies understandably prefer to focus on rescuing individuals without necessarily taking action against the establishment. However, unless strong, deterrent action is taken against those involved in the exploitation of the trafficked person, it is extremely likely that she or he will simply be replaced. Where the rescue has been undertaken by buying a person out of their trafficking situation, this actually helps to perpetuate the business, providing what amounts to working capital to the traffickers to recruit more people. In at least one country in the GMS, Thailand, this last approach has reportedly generated a new type of business, with brothel owners offering to sell trafficked persons to potential "saviors."

A corollary to the PDPU effect is found at the community level, with regard to repatriation. Considerable resources have been put into this area to date and the services offered to those trafficked in places such as Thailand are certainly a vast improvement on the summary deportations of trafficked persons as undocumented migrants that continue to take place in many countries. However, the ultimate value of repatriation efforts may be limited unless they are accompanied by measures that make a significant impact on the economics of the trafficking business. The success criterion for repatriation efforts is generally that the person returned is not retrafficked. This is often confused with a person not leaving their community again, rather than a person regaining control over her life. Leaving that aside, however, the fact that a person is not retrafficked is often more an indication that the traffickers have simply taken somebody else in their place. For example, there has been a systemic and compassionate repatriation of more than 500 Cambodian children taken to Thailand in organized begging rings. Despite more than two-thirds of these returned children remaining in their communities over a one-year period (IOM and MOSALVY 2003), this program has failed to have a noticeable impact on the overall number of Cambodian child beggars in Thailand.

A third example of the PDPU phenomenon is the targeting of small-scale people-movers as part of anti-trafficking campaigns, often reflecting a tendency to conflate traffickers and smugglers. (This is covered in more detail below.) These people are mostly women and generally poor. A significant number have been trafficked themselves, while others are unaware of exploitative intentions behind the larger process of which they are a part (ARCPPT 2003, [3]).

It is worth noting that in Myanmar, the local term for those involved in the movement of people across borders is the "carry." While some of these carries are directly complicit in an end outcome of trafficking, most are not (UNIAP 2003 [1]). In fact, these people are seen as providing an important community service in helping members of the community cross the border to Thailand. There, they are able to help potential migrants to fill the demand for an estimated one-and-a-half-million genuine jobs (Martin 2002), for which there is currently no way to migrate legally.

Regardless of their level of complicity, however, it is clear that these people—the primary focus of the limited law enforcement efforts to date—are generally small links in the trafficking chain. Just as the supply pool of potential victims is very large, so too is the pool from which potential people-movers can "pop up," including communities denied opportunities for legal employment, such as ethnic minority groups.[2] In the GMS context, making such people the primary focus of law enforcement efforts has therefore had little impact on the trafficking problem. Further, it has also served to take the spotlight off those who have perpetuated the most exploitative aspects of the trafficking process, and those who have obtained the greatest financial benefit.

These PDPU effects have significant implications for the response to trafficking, particularly in terms of the broad area that is generally known as prevention. This paper will now briefly examine three main approaches to prevention and the rationale behind these, and suggest an alternative way of looking at preventing trafficking.

THE PROBLEM WITH PREVENTION

Many trafficking programs focus on "prevention," often at the community level in places that are known or thought to be vulnerable to trafficking. The rationale behind many of these programs appears to be that if people don't move, they can't be trafficked. These programs generally look to address issues of vulnerability, which are most commonly held to be poverty, lack of education, and/or a lack of awareness about trafficking and the risks of migration. In the following section, we discuss three common responses based on this analysis—poverty alleviation, awareness raising, and tougher border controls.

The Poverty Alleviation Response

Where the problem is taken to be one of poverty, trafficking prevention strategies generally cover poverty alleviation and alternative livelihood activities, such as skills training, microcredit, and employment creation. It is certainly true that many people do leave their communities because they cannot meet their basic needs, be it in terms of food and water supply, or in terms of human security. However, it does not necessarily follow that such basic issues of survival should, first and foremost, be characterized as a trafficking problem. From a wider perspective, programs to address these issues are worthy in and of themselves, and they certainly have a role to play in anti-trafficking responses. Yet with regard to the prevention of trafficking, where it occurs—as in the GMS—within a framework of substantial out-migration, there are a number of concerns.

First, research from all over the world indicates that it is generally neither the poorest of the poor, nor the least educated, who migrate. Those who struggle to cover subsistence needs do not have ready access to money or collateral to help pay for travel to another country, and usually stay close to home (see, for example: Harris 2002; Stalker 2000). They are less likely then to be cross-border migrants. Within the GMS, this is borne out by recent research including a study in the Kayin State, Myanmar, which found that of over 300 migrants interviewed, more than two-thirds came from middle-income and better-off families, while just 2 percent of the migrants came from families categorized as very poor (UNIAP 2003, [2]). Information gathered from the interview indicated that those in the poorer categories, more or less in the state of "absolute poverty," had little means to facilitate the process of migration. Similarly, out-migration from poorer ethnic minority groups in Lao PDR is very small compared to that of the lowland Lao population, and there is further evidence that those who migrate among lowland Lao are not the poorest (ARCPPT 2003, [2]).

The situation is similar with regard to education levels. The Myanmar survey also notes that the level of formal education for migrant workers is concentrated, not at the bottom levels, but at primary and secondary levels. Household interviews and focus-group discussions indicate that people with no education often lack the confidence to take the risks identified with migration. Again these findings are consistent with evidence from Lao PDR (Chamberlain et al. 2001) and from other parts of the world (Harris 2002).

One inference from this information is that an increase in people's level of income and education might actually increase the incidence of migration, and again there is some evidence to back this up. Research by the International Labor Organization-International Program on the Elimination of Child Labor (ILO-IPEC) in Lao PDR, for example, suggests higher than average migration levels among villages that have been the focus of international development activities. Higher incomes bring raised expectations and through television, romanticized images of foreign places. Some young people leave home because friends come back with money, and others simply out of boredom due to an absence of meaningful opportunities at home. Similarly, many of the skills learned by those in employment-creation programs in rural areas can actually bring more effective reward in the cities and hence add to the impetus to migrate. Some microloan schemes also contribute to migration, either by providing the means, or by creating pressure to repay the debt. If the rationale of programs is to reduce trafficking by reducing migration, it seems possible that some of the poverty alleviation interventions might therefore actually be having the opposite effect.

There is also another flaw in the assessment that poverty, at least in absolute terms, and lack of education lie at the heart of the trafficking problem; that they are, as is often quoted, its root causes. Neither factor, taken alone or together, is able to explain why, as is widely held to be the case, trafficking would have been rapidly increasing over the past decade or so. In the same period, levels of absolute poverty have been falling, and education levels have been rising (UNDP 2002). Even the addition of a myriad of issues around gender equality and relations, while helping to explain some of the factors which contribute to trafficking, fails to provide significant justification for the apparent substantial increase in the trafficking problem.

Further, the attribution of trafficking to poverty fails to explain why some places, such as Thailand, are both points of destination and points of origin for trafficking. Rather, it seems clear that the problem of relative poverty (inequality) is more relevant to trafficking. Addressing the issue of inequality is likely to take generations and, in fact, may prove to be an impossibility within the current global political and economic structures. Growing inequality has been a key feature of globalization. This is not surprising. The process of globalization is distinguished by increased focus on "competitive" markets. Such competitive markets tend to be characterized by considerable inequality in incomes and wealth, favoring strong and established businesses on the one hand, and encouraging location of businesses in areas with the lowest labor standards on the other (Marshall 2001). It is this inequality, this disparity that is the main driving force behind migration. Most people would prefer not to travel too far from home. If there were no expectation that better opportunities were available elsewhere, there would be little cause to migrate.

The Awareness-raising Response

A second approach to prevention is raising awareness about the risks of trafficking. The rationale behind awareness-raising programs is essentially that people are trafficked because they are unaware of the dangers. If people are educated about the risks, then, this reasoning goes, they will be much less likely to leave home. The most obvious thing to be said about this activity is that, to be useful, it needs to take place in tandem with alternative-livelihood options. It is no good discouraging people from moving if they simply do not have a realistic alternative.

Most awareness-raising campaigns are couched in terms that migration is highly risky. The biggest problem with this message is that evidence does not generally support it. Notwithstanding the many horror stories and the hardships faced by many migrants—those who have been deceived, coerced, or forced into a trafficked situation, those who have died in the attempt to migrate for a better life—the majority of people who migrate, even from poorer communities, appear to improve their lives by doing so. In addition, any messages will be set against not only an individual's perception of their existing situation but against other information they have collected. It would seem of little use to tell a young person from Lao PDR that if they go to Thailand they are likely to be trapped on a fishing boat or locked in a brothel, if their friends have come back with money in their pockets and tales of adventure, true or otherwise.

Like poverty-alleviation and alternative-livelihood activities, awareness raising is important, and if properly done, can greatly reduce vulnerability, particularly where the recruiters in the communities concerned are highly complicit in the end outcome of trafficking. However, as with any intervention, programs based on raising awareness must realistically aim to provide honest information and genuine choices. This will require such programs to allow for the possibility that people may still choose to migrate and to equip them with skills that will be useful if they do so. In recognition of this, many organizations in the GMS are now incorporating awareness raising into a broader life-skills package. This often includes providing young people with a realistic assessment of the risks of migration, while equipping them with skills in areas such as HIV/AIDS prevention to reduce their vulnerability if they decide to move. It is important to note that many communities do in fact develop their own coping mechanisms over time, independently of outside intervention, to reduce the risks of migration, identifying safe routes, good employers, mechanisms to remit money, and ways of dealing with difficult situations.

Importantly also, while at least one UN organization, the UN Office on Drugs and Crime, has attempted to develop a global awareness-raising campaign, it should be obvious that awareness-raising messages need to be highly contextualized and based on an understanding of local situations. In fact, somewhat ironically, given that it is the communities' awareness that practitioners are trying to raise, it is our own understanding of local situations, and in particular, the decision-making processes behind decisions to migrate, that is often lacking. One of the reasons for this is the tendency of many governments, Western and otherwise, to deport the evidence by sending trafficked persons home as undocumented migrants. Failure to identify trafficked persons as such not only ignores their basic rights but also detracts significantly from the information we could be collecting to assist in better targeting our responses.

When more information is available we may well find that, far from lacking an understanding of the situation, people and communities often have more knowledge than is realized. For example, one survey in Northern Thailand examined how women from certain communities ended up in debt bondage in the Japanese sex trade (Sobieszczyk 2002). Contrary to the initial expectations, most of these women were not ignorant, either of the work they would be doing, or of the risks involved in such debt-bondage arrangements. For many, however, debt bondage at the point of destination was actually seen as a risk-minimization strategy, as the cost of a failed attempt to reach Japan was borne by the employer. Should a woman borrow the necessary US$5,000 or so locally and be turned back, she would return to the community with a huge debt and no way of paying this off, other than attempting to migrate again. Further, those concerned would have preferred to migrate for other work if this had been viable. *The major risk factor here is not a lack of knowledge but the lack of legitimate and safe opportunities for labor migration.*

As with alternative-livelihood options, appropriate and accurate awareness-raising activities are an important component of a holistic response to trafficking. It is clear though that raising awareness of the dangers of migration and trafficking will not stop people moving, particularly when reports of these dangers are not consistent with their own experiences. Activities such as poverty reduction and awareness raising therefore fall much more accurately under the heading "vulnerability reduction" than under "prevention."

At the same time, it stands to reason that, in addition to providing alternatives to migration, and advising people of the risks, migration needs to be made safer. And yet, much of what is being done in the name of anti-trafficking programs is actually making migration considerably less safe.

Prevention Through Tougher Border Controls

The rationale behind increased border controls is an adjunct to the idea that if people cannot move, they cannot be trafficked. It supposes that if fewer people can be smuggled across borders, fewer people will be trafficked. Just as the assignation of poverty as the root cause of trafficking allows many development agencies to continue with existing programs under an anti-trafficking banner and funding source, the border-control theory has the compelling advantage of allowing destination countries, particularly some of the donor countries, to pursue anti-smuggling policies under the guise of trafficking prevention—using trafficking as a kind of "Trojan horse" for tougher controls on migration. This can be clearly seen, for example, in the Asian Ministerial Regional Conferences on People Smuggling, Trafficking in Persons and Related Transnational Crime, and even in the UN Trafficking Protocol itself. The first of the above conferences, in 2002, was attended by forty-three ministers from thirty-seven countries of the Asia-Pacific region. Two high-level meetings to date have seen an almost complete conflation of trafficking and smuggling, symbolized by the coining of the term "victims of smuggling." The follow-up work to the conference continues to highlight the supposed importance of tougher border controls to reducing trafficking. The main difficulty with this approach is that it is demonstrably incorrect.

Empirical evidence indicates that moves to restrict the movement of people assist trafficking, rather than hinder it. This evidence comes from all parts of the world. Tougher controls on the US-Mexico border, for example, have diverted the flow of migrants away from established migration routes to the most dangerous and least populated areas, such as the Arizona desert, or to more organized forms of smuggling. This has not only led to a rise in organized crime, but has resulted in a large increase in the number of deaths associated with crossing the border, reaching an average of almost one a day in 1999 (Harris 2002). The situation is similar in Europe; the death of 58 Chinese would-be immigrants en route from Belgium to the United Kingdom in 2000 is the most well-known, though not numerically the worst example of the tragedies that occur as people seek to find a better life. In the GMS, the situation and vulnerability of migrants likewise worsen whenever border controls are tightened. A recent "closure" of Thailand's border with Myanmar, for example, did not stop people crossing the border, but it became more dangerous and potential migrants were forced into using more organized criminal groups. One of the consequences was that the cost for crossing the border increased from some 50,000 Kyats (US$50) to over 100,000 (US$100), doubling the level of potential debt faced by the migrant and therefore the time needed to pay it off (UNIAP 2003, [2]).

Tougher migration policies also impact on families. In Thailand, as elsewhere, during times of greater tolerance for migrant workers, families have been able to migrate together, reducing vulnerability on a whole range of fronts. However, crackdowns on migrants often lead to a host of vulnerable situations, such as separation of families, with parents being deported to their home countries while children remain in the country of destination, or children being unable to access education and taking highly exploitative jobs in the shadow labor market. Ironically, evidence from the GMS and elsewhere indicates that *tougher border controls, rather than encouraging migrants to remain in the country of origin, tend to encourage migrants to remain in the country of destination.* Once the border crossing has been undertaken, it is often too risky and/or too expensive to make a visit home.

A further example is on the Chinese side of the China-Vietnam border, where conflation of smuggling and trafficking has led to indiscriminant deportations of Vietnamese women as undocumented migrants, regardless of their personal circumstances, in the name of anti-trafficking interventions. In many cases, these circumstances involve consensual marriage to a local man and a family. As well as separation from the husband, deportation (whether from forced or consensual marriage) inevitably involves separation from the children, who are not recognized as Vietnamese citizens under Vietnamese law.

Other, more specific forms of movement restriction have been attempted as a response to trafficking. One such policy, attempted in several countries in Asia, is to restrict the movement of young women. Again this serves primarily to push already vulnerable young women into more dangerous forms of movement. It is also a further discrimination against women, who are often already heavily discriminated against in migration policy. Most legal migration channels are strongly biased toward work that is traditionally done by men, while two very common areas of migration for women, domestic and entertainment work, have very little protection under labor laws. Another approach is to restrict movement from the village by imposing sanctions such as fines. However, as Ginzburg (2002) notes, the relatively heavy fine in some communities in Lao PDR sends mixed messages. On the one hand, it says, "what you are doing is wrong," while on the other, "it is easy to make money across the border."

Added to evidence that tighter border controls exacerbate trafficking, there is also evidence that the converse holds true, that liberalized border controls can have an opposite effect. In the European Union, new visa-free entry enjoyed by women from EU-candidate countries (Hungary, Poland, Czech Republic, Slovenia) has reduced the level of exploitation of those in the sex trade to similar levels to local women (Davies 2003). Women from outside this region (notably Albania, Romania, and Moldova) are still subject to much worse degrees of exploitation. As noted above, it is also risky and expensive for the latter group to go home and those with freedom of movement are actually spending less time in the destination countries than those without it (Davies 2003).

Although the existence of legal migration channels in itself does not preclude trafficking, the need for many migrants, and asylum-seekers, to resort to irregular forms of movement greatly increases their vulnerability. Current migration policies have created an underclass of people with little or no access to basic rights, and therefore limited access to protection. With regard to trafficking, it is the *vulnerability of migrants that is important, not the vulnerability of people to migrate*. While governments may have other justifications for border-control activities, anti-trafficking funds should clearly not be directed into this area.

PREVENTION, VULNERABILITY REDUCTION, AND THE ASSIGNMENT OF RESPONSIBILITY

While it should be clear that tougher migration policies contribute to the existence of trafficking rather than its prevention, and thus have no place in anti-trafficking programs, there clearly remains a role for poverty-alleviation and awareness-raising activities. However, neither basic analysis nor available evidence suggests that these are more than a partial solution. Even when these programs work in themselves, increasing incomes and opportunities in villages, and through this reducing the vulnerability of individual communities, this does not mean that we are reducing trafficking in absolute terms. Recruiters are not passive agents—they will target the most vulnerable communities, and the most vulnerable within communities—children from broken homes are known to be at greater risk, for example, but so are children from larger families

(Aye 2002). Again there is a push-down pop-up effect. The supply pool is huge, with more than half the world's population earning under US$2 a day, less than the earnings of an average European cow under the current system of massive agricultural subsidies. We may have reduced vulnerability in a particular community but it does not necessarily follow that we have prevented trafficking.

On the surface, the distinction between the terms *prevention* and *vulnerability reduction* may seem like a question of semantics. However, there is more to it than that. The current use of the term *prevention* generally assigns responsibility for dealing with gross violations of persons to places hundreds or thousands of miles from where these violations are taking place.

It thus tends to imply that the five-year-old Khmer child being forced to eat the flowers he cannot sell on the streets of Bangkok is primarily the responsibility of Cambodia; that Thailand is to blame for the young Thai woman suffocating on her own vomit in an Australian detention center after years of forced prostitution; that Vietnam is responsible for the young Vietnamese girls and boys forced into the sex trade in Cambodia, for use by both local and foreign child sex offenders.

The assigning of responsibility for trafficking in this way is reflected in, as an example, the US State Department's annual "Trafficking in Persons (TIP) Report." This report divides countries into three tiers according to their efforts to comply with minimum standards for the elimination of trafficking. Tier One is the highest, denoting full compliance, while Tier Three is the lowest, and those countries in Tier Three face sanctions. In the 2002 TIP report, there were eighteen countries in Tier One, seventeen of which are destination countries, with Colombia the only sending country assigned to this tier. Several of these Tier One countries have few or no services for trafficked persons.

Such an implicit apportioning of responsibilities perhaps helps to explain the overemphasis on the movement aspects of the trafficking process, taking the focus off the gross exploitations of people that are often taking place with impunity. The implication that trafficking can be "prevented" at its source also tends to take the focus off what governments really need to do to disrupt the economics of the trafficking business—much of which must take place at the point of destination. While countries develop elaborate anti-trafficking plans, attention is diverted from core issues, such as increasing protection and access to justice for vulnerable groups and appropriate targeting of law enforcement to remove the impunity of those who benefit most, coupled with and complemented by measures to reduce community tolerance for the abuses which currently persist.

Such a construction also takes the focus off the highly restrictive migration policies operated by most destination countries. While there is much evidence that bringing migration policies more closely into line with labor market realties would be the single greatest step a country could take against trafficking, this is generally lacking from most anti-trafficking strategies. Extraordinarily, despite the potential serious implications of the US TIP report, in terms of possible sanctions for countries that do not match up to certain minimum standards, a realistic migration regime is not even one of the criteria.

It is worth noting that, within the broad field of international development, this apportioning of responsibility is not confined to trafficking. Pupavac (forthcoming) has noted a similar tendency in the area of human rights more broadly, noting that:

> in effect, it is the weaker, poorer societies of the South, which are held morally culpable for the harsher conditions prevailing there, and whose populations become objects of corrective interventions by the international community of the more powerful prosperous Northern states... While the international human rights regime's imperative to secure the good is undermining universal equal rights, it is not securing global justice. The prospects of securing justice globally are effectively deferred, since the international human rights model fails to address the inequalities between the North and actually reinforces them.

Recently we have also seen poverty reduction strategies becoming popular as part of the donor countries' approach to development assistance. Again, however, such strategies tend to focus on conditions within lower-income countries. Ignored are key global issues such as the removal of agricultural subsidies and other trade barriers, and more realistic and fairer migration policies, each of which would have much greater impact. The next section discusses the migration issue in more detail because of its direct impact on trafficking.

MIGRATION AND DEVELOPMENT

Harris (2002) notes that "seeking to end migration has nowhere been successful, but it is least successful for open economies with a strong demand for unskilled workers and few on offer." The International Labor Organization goes further, asserting that:

> tighter border controls have not halted migratory flows nor have they had projected results in reducing the number of workers crossing borders. Instead they have put more pressure on those who migrate. With few options available for legal migration in the face of strong pull-push pressures, irregular migration channels become the only alternative, and one which presents lucrative "business" opportunities for helping

people arrange travel, obtain documents, cross borders and find jobs in destination countries. (Taran and Geronimi 2002)

In other words, as with any market with sufficient supply and demand (other examples include drugs, alcohol, and commercial sex), the record of direct control through law enforcement is not convincing. Rather, current controls provide ready-made conditions for criminal activity and serve to greatly increase the vulnerabilities inherent in the migration process.

Like all forms of organized crime, trafficking is a business arising out of a response to market forces. If we really wish to prevent this crime, we need to look at how to undermine this market. This would mean developing an international migration system which facilitates the movement of labor to places of legitimate demand, crowding out many of the opportunities for smuggling and trafficking and providing protection for the rights of migrants. And yet, while most developed countries extol the virtues of unfettered movement of capital, technology, and information across the globe, very different rhetoric and policies are used when it comes to the freedom of labor movement. The irony about this is that more liberalized migration policies benefit not only sending countries, but also receiving ones. In the GMS, for example, the ongoing prosperity of Thailand in particular remains heavily dependent on continued cheap labor from neighboring countries. As noted above, one arguably conservative estimate in 2002 suggested that at least 1.5 million foreign workers were required. Demographic factors will also continue to lead to spatial differences in demand and supply. Developed countries, with ageing populations, will require more and more migrant labor, while differing sex ratios between neighboring countries (there are significantly more women than men in Cambodia and Vietnam, the opposite is true in China) will continue to encourage an increase in cross-border marriages. The increasing number of women desiring to maintain careers outside of the home will continue to increase the demand for foreign domestic labor.

A more liberalized migration regime would also benefit the sending countries in the forms of remittances and more frequent circulation of labor, with the accompanying opportunities for skill-sharing. Rubens Ricupero, Secretary-General of the United Nations Conference on Trade and Development (UNCTAD), has called migration "the missing link between globalization and development" (see IOM 2001), while in 1992 the United Nations Development Programme (UNDP) estimated that the potential benefits for a more liberalized migration regime could be in the order of $250 billion a year, an amount which dwarfs current aid flows (UNDP 1992).

Migration from areas of lesser to greater opportunity has in fact long been recognized as an important part of development, even a specific phase of the development process. In fact, the World Bank's first report on China in the early 1980s highly criticized the Government of China's tight controls on the internal movements of its people as locking them into poverty (Harris 2002). Such migration patterns will continue to play an important part in economic development and poverty reduction, but in an increasingly globalized world, will naturally extend beyond national borders.

While a more appropriate and equitable migration system is a long-term goal, there is growing acknowledgment that more could be done in the shorter term about providing legal, well-monitored alternatives to irregular migration. This is something that governments within the GMS are starting to work on, with support from agencies such as the International Organization for Migration (IOM), ILO-IPEC, and the UN Inter-Agency Project on Human Trafficking (UNIAP). Recent labor migration agreements between the Government of Thailand and the Governments of Cambodia, Lao PDR, and Myanmar, respectively, present an important step along the way, laying the groundwork for increased recognition of the rights of migrants.

Prevention at the Point of Destination

A more realistic and equitable migration regime is a central component of an effective response to trafficking. Apart from the benefits to both sending and receiving countries, this will greatly facilitate the protection of the rights of migrants, allowing for migrants to organize supportive networks and obtain access to legal recourse and justice without automatic repatriation/deportation. There is also evidence that a spin-off of a more liberal regime would be a reduction in the pressure on the refugee system as many refugees are highly skilled and would have the opportunity to help themselves by finding their own employment, bypassing the cumbersome asylum-seeking procedures (see Hayter 2000). At the same time, as amply demonstrated by the experiences of women and men from South Asia in the Middle East, regularized and legal migration channels in themselves do not necessarily provide a guarantee against cross-border trafficking. Nor is migration policy a significant factor in internal trafficking, which is prevalent in many countries in the GMS.

Thus, while the undocumented nature of much migration lies at the heart of much migrant vulnerability, it is not the sole cause of that vulnerability. Further, it does not account for why people take advantage of that vulnerability to place and maintain others in situations of gross exploitation. Reducing this exploitation means moving the focus of prevention efforts to places where the exploitation is occurring—the destination communities. There are few efforts in this direction at the present time. Much more could be done in terms of improved law enforcement and increased access to rights for those trafficked, two concepts which are often seen as conflicting but are inherently complementary and are discussed below under the heading of criminal justice. More also needs to be done in working with destination communities.

Criminal Justice Responses

As noted previously, trafficking is a business, with the activities of traffickers motivated primarily by profit. Law enforcement therefore has a key role to play in changing the economics of this business by increasing the risks, in particular removing the impunity currently enjoyed by those at the end of the trafficking chain, and reducing the benefits. Yet in most countries in the GMS, the law enforcement response to date has been limited, and has focused on the irregular migration aspects of the trafficking process. This is understandable. While "supply-side" interventions such as poverty reduction and awareness raising tend to be relatively straightforward in their planning and execution, measures aimed at making trafficking a less profitable and more risky undertaking for all beneficiaries tend to represent the "hard edge" of the response. Human trafficking must compete for attention with a range of other priorities, noticeably drug trafficking, which generally has a higher profile and higher rewards for those on the front line of law enforcement. Human trafficking is also by nature a particularly difficult crime to investigate.

In addition, there is the potential (and, in some cases, actual) involvement of law enforcement officials in this crime. Such involvement can be indirect (e.g., through corrupt practices such as overlooking trafficking cases in exchange for payment) or direct (e.g., ownership of, or involvement in, businesses into which people are trafficked). Growing inequalities, discussed elsewhere in this paper, help to fuel growing corruption, whether it be a poorly paid low-level policeman who is simply trying to improve the life of his family, or a high-level official who sees the "opportunity cost" of being honest go up exponentially as criminal groups are in a position to offer him larger and larger amounts of money.

These constraints are not an excuse for inaction. Much more could be done, particularly in countries of destination, where the worst abuses generally take place, and where law enforcement tends to be stronger. However, as efforts to target the movement of people have been shown to facilitate crime and exploitation rather than to reduce it, a change in emphasis is needed. Law enforcement efforts need to move away from targeting movers to targeting exploiters. Obviously there is an overlap between the two. Some brokers or people-movers are highly complicit in the exploitation of those they are moving and need to be brought to justice.

There is also a general need for people-movers to take more responsibility for the end outcome of the migration process. Distinctions need to be made between those who are complicit in trafficking, those who are ignorant or uncaring as to the end fate of those they are helping to move, and those who are effectively providing a service by providing access to genuine, safe employment opportunities.

Much more impact would, however, be achieved by focusing on those who own and manage the establishments in which people are abused, exploited, and kept in slave-like conditions. This needs to be done in a way that undermines the profitability of the business. In this regard, more emphasis might be placed on the area of asset confiscation. While obviously in cases of violence, and with regard to less "business-like" areas, such as domestic work, a prison term might also be appropriate, asset confiscation has three advantages. First, unlike detention, it requires a one-off action—in most countries it is more difficult for an influential person to recover an asset than to find their way out of prison. Second, the confiscation of assets is likely to provide more of a disincentive to other owners. Given that his purpose is to make money, the possibility of losing the entire business is likely to seem more immediate than the possibility of going to jail. Both of these directly undermine the "perfect business" of trafficking. Third, the assets used in confiscation can be used for anti-trafficking programs, including compensation of trafficked persons.

Hand-in-hand with better targeted and more effective criminal sanctions goes human rights. Criminals cannot adequately be brought to justice unless those affected have appropriate ways in which to bring their abuses to notice and have them acted upon. Also, effective law enforcement responses are currently heavily witness-dependent in all but a very small number of countries around the world. Sensitive, appropriate handling of witnesses is crucial to maximizing the usefulness of victim testimony and thereby ensuring successful prosecutions. Yet few countries provide mechanisms for trafficked persons to help themselves in any way. Even where this is possible, the end outcome of such an action will inevitably be that the person concerned, whether or not they are acknowledged as trafficked, ends up having to return to their country of origin.

Further, in many countries, victims of trafficking, particularly foreign victims, do not have the right to leave shelters. In Thailand, for example, most victims come to notice after being arrested as an undocumented migrant and placed in an international detention center. Once there, they may be screened and identified as a trafficked person. If so, they will be removed and placed in a special welfare shelter. They must remain in the shelter until their families have been traced and an assessment carried out as to the likelihood of a successful integration back into their communities. Where they are involved in legal proceedings the process may take longer. While the return process is generally referred to as repatriation, it is worth noting that, like in almost all other countries, it is only voluntary if the person actually wants to go. Trafficked persons are repatriated whether they wish to be or not. This is not repatriation, but deportation. Many trafficked persons, like other expatriates, do not wish to return home, often for the same reasons they left in the first place. They simply wish to escape their immediate situation. The combined possibility of detention in shelters and then automatic return home acts as a major disincentive to come forward.

The other main form of identification of trafficked persons is rescue from an entertainment establishment or brothel. Well-targeted raids, followed up by strong deterrent action against the owners and managers of the establishments, are an important intervention. In the current policy context, however, there is a problem that raids rescue people whether they want to be rescued or not. Few establishments consist solely of trafficked women and girls. Raids in Thailand have rescued migrant women working in a non-forced situation.[3] A line is drawn at age eighteen—based on international conventions to which those affected, never having had a vote, are hardly party—and those under it are automatically identified as trafficked and go through the welfare channels. Those over eighteen are generally charged, sometimes placed in prison (where they may be abused), and deported. While a strict upholding of the law, this is not exactly a humanitarian intervention.

Few methods currently exist which recognize the agency of trafficked persons or witnesses of this crime by providing avenues to bring these events to notice and seek redress. More mechanisms are required, such as hotlines with access to interpreters and linked to nationwide service networks to support trafficked persons. At the same time, it must be recognized that it is often difficult to separate the rights of trafficked persons from the rights of all migrants. A young foreign woman locked in a brothel is an undocumented migrant and often involved in an illegal trade, until such time as somebody in a position of authority decides that she has been trafficked, something that may or may not occur. At the time she most needs to access her rights as a trafficked person, she has often not yet been classified as such. There needs to be wider recognition, in principle and in practice, that the illegal nature of a person's entry into a country does not take away their basic human rights, regardless of whether or not they have been trafficked.

Community Attitudes

Perhaps more fundamentally, as our understanding of the issue evolves, it is becoming clearer that, while it is disparity that fuels much of the movement involved, it is the pervasiveness of racism, linked with gender and class distinctions, which is providing the underlying conditions for the gross exploitation of human beings which is trafficking. As Gallagher notes, "trafficking affects the least powerful groups within national societies including women, children, migrants, and stateless persons. Social practices and community attitudes towards these groups reinforce and extend their vulnerability to being trafficked and also serve to shape responses to this crime" (Gallagher 2002). Often the issue is marked with hypocrisy. Politicians and officials complain about the influx of foreigners while a foreign maid irons their shirts at home. Foreign development expatriates, most of whom share with undocumented migrants the desire to migrate in search of a better job and a more interesting life, express surprise that these migrants do not want to return home. Societal norms accept that good men have many sexual partners but good women do not, facilitating the development of the sex trade, and then stigmatizing and discriminating against those who work in this trade, denying them basic rights such as security, health coverage, and time off. Western governments bluster about the treatment of children in developing countries while doing little about, and sometimes even protecting, their nationals involved in the sexual exploitation of these children. At other times, discriminatory attitudes appear to be based more on ignorance, such as when the public erroneously complains that migrants are taking local jobs or when they fail to understand the role that migrants are playing in their own prosperity. Traditional beliefs, such as those concerning a child's responsibility to his/her parents, also play a role, as of course do those around gender, attitudes which are well documented elsewhere (see ARCPPT 2003, [1]).

Much more attention needs to be paid to the attitudes that enable people to distance themselves from others in a way that allows them to behave in such an exploitative manner, and to the systems that reinforce this. Yet, while many resources are put into community campaigns to raise awareness of the risks of migration, there are few examples of campaigns tackling prejudice and discrimination at places of destination. Reducing discrimination based on sex, ethnicity, age, and class, and the interrelationship between these, is obviously a long-term issue but one that should be near the forefront of any response.

As an example of what can be done working with destination communities, one small local NGO in Cambodia is working with local authorities and restaurant owners to reduce trafficking by monitoring conditions in each of the entertainment venues in the province. To complement these efforts, the NGO has engaged the wider community, developing a network of motorbike-taxi drivers, boat paddlers, and "reliable neighbors" to report incidents relating to trafficking and sexual exploitation. This has brought some small but notable successes and suggests possibilities for larger such interventions. The Cambodian Ministry of Women's and Veterans' Affairs is also working on campaigns to address community attitudes regarding the treatment of children and the abuse of women in the sex trade. These are obviously long-term measures but would ultimately address the heart of much of the exploitation that surrounds trafficking.

CONCLUSION

It is generally acknowledged that the many anti-trafficking activities in the Greater Mekong Sub-region have failed to make a noticeable impact on the problem to date. While it is still relatively early in the response, activities would be greatly assisted by more clarity over both the underlying causes of the issue and the efficacy of various responses. In particular, the current construction of prevention is not only empirically inaccurate, but enables destination countries to gloss over the lack of an authentic response to human-rights violations happening within their borders, while blaming countries of origin for the rational desire of their citizens to improve their lives.

The recategorization of many of the current prevention activities under the rubric of vulnerability reduction would make a significant difference to the way this issue is perceived. This needs to be accompanied by a general acknowledgment that increased border controls, per se, do not belong in either of these categories; that migration is an important and legitimate poverty/disparity reduction strategy, and that more realistic and fairer migration policies are central to a more effective local, national, and global response to trafficking.

In terms of specific action, priorities in the GMS, as elsewhere, are for the institutional and political changes needed to reduce the opportunities for trafficking to flourish. These include bringing immigration policies into line with labor market realities, creating channels for safe migration, and improving the terms and conditions of employment, particularly in the most vulnerable sectors of domestic labor, factory work, and entertainment.

In addition, law enforcement efforts must be refocused toward undermining the profitability of the business by targeting those at the point of exploitation, recognizing the central role that trafficked persons play in assisting with this process. Avenues must be created for those trafficked to access justice. And ultimately there must continue to be a challenging of attitudes about race, class, and gender that provide the enabling environment for this crime throughout the world.

NOTES

1. The term "push-down pop-up" actually comes from drug trafficking, although it is more commonly known as the "balloon effect." Its lack of acknowledgment by decision-makers in this area has helped lead to policies which have had disastrous effects on the lives of some of the most vulnerable communities in the world, including in some instances an increase in trafficking (Feingold 1996). It is essential that the same mistakes are not made in the response to human trafficking.

2. See Lertharoenchok (2001) on the impact of Thailand's citizenship policies on these groups.

3. Several documented examples of this exist in Thailand. See, for example, Empower 2003.

REFERENCES

Anh, N. (ed.) *Migration in Vietnam: Theoretical Approaches and Evidence from a Survey.* Hanoi: Transport Communications Publishing House, 2001.

Archavanitkul, K. *Trafficking in Children for Labour Exploitation Including Child Prostitution in the Mekong Sub-region.* Bangkok: ILO-IPEC, 1998.

Asia Regional Cooperation to Prevent People Trafficking Project. *Gender and Development Strategy.* Bangkok: ARCPPT, 2003 (1).

———. *Gender, Trafficking and Criminal Justice Process in Myanmar.* Bangkok: ARCPPT, 2003 (2).

———. *Gender, Trafficking and Criminal Justice Process in Myanmar.* Bangkok: ARCPPT, 2003 (3).

Aye, N. "Can We Outsmart Traffickers?" *Step by Step,* Issue 8. Bangkok: UNIAP, 2002.

Caouette, T. *Needs Assessment on Cross-Border Trafficking in Women and Children in the Mekong Sub-region.* Paper for UN Working Group on Trafficking. Bangkok, 1998.

Chamberlain, J., et al. *Trafficking of Women and Children in the Lao PDR: Initial Observations.* Bangkok: UNIAP, 2001.

Davies, J. "The Role of Migration Policy in Creating and Sustaining Trafficking Harm." Presentation to UNIAP Working Group, Bangkok, January 2003.

Empower. *A Report On The Human Rights Violations Women Are Subjected to when "Rescued" by Anti-Trafficking Groups Who Employ Methods Using Deception, Force and Coercion.* Chiang Mai: Empower, 2003.

Feingold, D. "The Hell of Good Intentions: Some Preliminary Thoughts on Opium and the Political Ecology of Trade in Girls and Women." Draft paper. Hong Kong: Centre of Asian Studies, 1996.

Gallagher, Anne. "Consideration of the Issue of Trafficking." Background paper for the Advisory Council of Jurists, Asia Pacific Forum of National Human Rights Institutions, 2002.

Ginzburg, O. *Lao PDR—Building Projects on Assumptions.* Bangkok: UNIAP, 2002.

Harris, N. *Thinking the Unthinkable: The Immigration Myth Exposed.* London: IB Taurus, 2002.

Hayter, T. *Open Borders: The Case Against Immigration Controls.* London: Pluto Press, 2000.

Horizons Project, Population Council. *Prevention of Trafficking and the Care and Support of Trafficked Persons.* Kathmandu: The Asia Foundation, 2001.

International Organization for Migration. *The Link Between Migration and Development in the Least Developed Countries.* Geneva: IOM, 2001.

International Organization for Migration, and MOSALVY. *Database Report on Children Trafficked from Cambodia to Thailand, 1 September 2000–31 March 2003.* Bangkok: IOM, 2003.

Lertharoenchok, Y. "Searching for Identity." *Step by Step,* Issue 5. Bangkok: UNIAP, 2001.

Marshall, P. *Globalisation, Migration and Trafficking: Some Thoughts From the South-East Asian Region.* UNIAP Occasional Paper No.1, Bangkok, 2001.

Martin, P. *Thailand: Improving the Management of Foreign Workers.* Bangkok: International Labor Organization and International Organization for Migration, 2002.

Pupavac, V. "Gender, Human Rights and Therapeutizing Development." *Development and Change,* forthcoming.

Sobieszczyk, T. "Risky Business: Debt Bondage Migration from Northern Thailand." *Step by Step,* Issue 6. Bangkok: UNIAP, 2002.

Stalker, Peter. *Workers Without Frontiers: The Impact of Globalization on International Migration.* Boulder, CO: Lynne Rienner, 2000.

Taran, P., and Geronimi, E. *Globalization, Labour and Migration: Protection Is Paramount.* Geneva: ILO, 2002.

United Nations Development Programme. *The Human Development Report 1992.* New York: UNDP, 1992.

———. *The Human Development Report 2002.* New York: UNDP, 2002.

UN Inter-Agency Project on Human Trafficking in the Greater Mekong Sub-Region. *Annual Report 2002.* Bangkok: UNIAP, 2002.

UN Inter-Agency Project on Human Trafficking in the Greater Mekong Sub-Region and Food Security Project, Myanmar (UNDP-FAO). "Pilot Study on Out-migration of Women and Children in the Dry Zone." Myanmar: UNIAP, 2003 (1).

UN Inter-Agency Project on Human Trafficking in the Greater Mekong Sub-Region. *Partnership Against Trafficking.* Bangkok: UNIAP, 2003 (2).

4

Reflections by an Anti-trafficking Activist

Lin Chew

A Global Start: Some Thirty Years Ago

In 1982 I joined a Dutch women's group that was attached to a local development education center, concerned with "Women and the Third World." This was a way, I thought, to combine my own personal situation as a woman and migrant in the Netherlands with concern for the situation of women in my home region, Southeast Asia. The issue, which at that time offered an avenue for concrete action, was "prostitution tourism." Women's organizations, development NGOs, and various action groups, especially in the regions—for example, Southeast Asia—where mass tourism was becoming the alternative paradigm for development, were awakening to the fact that not only the natural resources but also the human resources, namely the young women, of their countries were being traded for foreign exchange.

In the Netherlands there had been sporadic actions and publicity against tour organizations offering sex tours as package deals, sometimes with a "bride" included in the price. Travel brochures and advertisements which offered "exotic" women from Thailand and the Philippines as subservient and eager to please "rich white males" enraged us—by now a growing group of Dutch and Asian women. This was imperialism, sexism, and racism rolled into one; the issue symbolized for us the total exploitation of womankind—sexual, economic, and cultural. When news of an organized sex tour to Thailand leaked out, we organized a demonstration at the airport when the tour was to leave. Coincidentally, the then-Coordinator of the Foundation for Women (a non-governmental organization based in Bangkok), Siriporn Skrobanek, was studying in the Netherlands. Thus, immediate contact could be established and a demonstration was ready to meet the tour when it arrived at Bangkok Airport. This action launched the campaign against prostitution tourism and trafficking in women in the Netherlands and in Thailand simultaneously. In the Netherlands the action was a political success. The issue was quickly picked up, not only by a wide range of women's, developmental, and solidarity groups, but also by state policy-makers.

In 1982, preparatory to the formulation of state policy guidelines to address the issue of sexual violence, the then-Ministry for Social Affairs in the Netherlands organized a study conference to gather the opinions of women's organizations across the board. Violence in prostitution was one of the areas under scrutiny. As representative of my group, I participated in the conference workshop on prostitution, and succeeded in pushing through a demand for an official investigation into the phenomenon of what was perceived to be the reverse side of prostitution tourism: the trafficking of women into the Netherlands for prostitution.

In 1983, the "Global Workshop to Organize Against Traffic in Women" was held in Rotterdam.[1] This was a significant point—the beginning of the international anti-trafficking activities. It was also significant for me, being quite new in this field, and as I greedily and actively participated, I was unaware of the tensions that were already underlying the whole organization of the workshop, namely, the tension between pro-prostitutes' rights advocates and some of the organizers of the workshop.[2] At that workshop, the various manifestations of violations of women's human rights were identified and discussed, including the "trafficking" in women for work as domestics, as au pairs, as brides, and for prostitution; the focus, however, was on women from developing countries being trafficked into prostitution. I came away convinced that I was not against the women who worked as prostitutes, but that the patriarchal institution of prostitution should be dismantled. The connection with "trafficking" was still tenuous and unclarified, but I took that in good faith—we would research, investigate, and expose how it all worked, starting in the Netherlands.

But soon I was to learn, through direct and regular contact with women in prostitution, that it was not possible to maintain a distinction between the "workers" and their "profession," and at the same time to maintain an unconditional attitude of personal acceptance and respect. It also became clear to me, through many long hours of reflection and discussions with colleagues as well as women in prostitution, that the only way to break the stigma and marginalization of prostitutes was to accept the

work that they do as exactly that—a form of work, with its own specificities of risks and benefits, but no more or no less special than other forms
of work. Furthermore, with deeper understanding of the workings of the
"patriarchal system" within social and personal relationships came the
understanding that prostitution is not the only "patriarchal institution" that
should be dismantled if at all possible. The specific fundamental character
of the relationship between prostitute and customer—the rendering of
sexual service in return for cash payment—also underlies any relationship
where the exchange of sexual favor for any form of benefit (status, security,
friendship, etc.) takes place. And if one is honest, one has to admit that this
exchange takes place, unspoken and camouflaged or open and blatant, in
all forms of relationships, and more systematically than we would like
to acknowledge. The "institution of patriarchy," therefore, is insidiously
integrated into more social and personal relationships than just prostitution. However, only women in prostitution are being subjected to such
extreme stigmatization and marginalization as the arch-collaborators with
"patriarchy." The personal struggle for me was to overcome the mainstream
moral hypocrisy into which I had been socialized, and to understand
prostitution as one of the institutions within our contemporary patriarchal,
socioeconomic system, next to, for example, marriage.

ANTI-TRAFFICKING ACTIVISM IN EUROPE

In 1985, the report of the "Investigation into the nature, global scale and
channels through which women are trafficked into the Netherlands,"
commissioned by the Ministry for Social Affairs, as mentioned earlier, was
published. The researchers could not come up with very concrete statistics
to indicate the scale on which trafficking into the Netherlands was taking
place, because there were no records in police files, and the issue had not
been systematically addressed until then. Nevertheless they were quite
convinced of the reprehensible nature of trafficking in women. The report
concluded thus:

> trafficking in women is definitely not a marginal phenomenon; . . . it
> transpires in a clearly criminal sphere, whereby deception, coercion and
> violence are used to transport women to the Netherlands, and to bring
> them into prostitution and keep them in prostitution. The victim is in
> a situation of exploitation, in *violation of all basic human rights and of the
> right to sexual liberty, physical and emotional integrity* . . .[3]

This report signified important political recognition of the seriousness of
the issue and opened the way to obtaining government support for the first
initiative to address this issue in a systematic way. The Foundation Against

Trafficking in Women (STV) was officially formalized and funded by the then-Directorate for Coordination of Emancipation within the Ministry for Welfare and Work Opportunities in 1987. At that time trafficking in women and minors was simply defined as unlawful in the Dutch Penal Code (Art. 250 ter), punishable by a prison sentence of not more than 5 years (in 1993 this was raised to 6 years). But although this legislation had been in existence for nearly a century, trafficking was not precisely defined and there were no guidelines as to what the punishable elements were; thus, there were very few cases listed under "trafficking in women" in police and court files. In terms of strategy, litigation was one area where concrete action could be taken; legal proceedings against traffickers would serve three purposes: first, the victim could obtain some sense of redress if the trafficker was convicted; second, precedents of cases would help in clarifying the issues involved in trafficking and lead to more effective detection and prosecution of trafficking; third, the publicity around prosecutions would keep the issue in the public awareness and on the political agenda. For this, women who felt they had been victimized had to press charges. Most women we talked to were afraid of reprisals from the traffickers, and absolutely afraid that news of their predicament would reach their families back home. At the same time foreign women found working in prostitution by the Aliens Police were simply being sent back to their countries without any investigations being made into how they had gotten into the business in the first place. Needless to say, they did not even get time to recover, much less to consider pressing charges.

The first campaigns undertaken by STV—in 1987 and 1988—were thus aimed at refining the instruments for addressing trafficking in women at the level of legislation and litigation. The first advocacy action was to obtain a ruling under the Aliens Laws to prevent migrant women who may have become victims of trafficking from being deported before investigations have been done. As a result, in August 1988, a special ruling was inserted in the Dutch Aliens Law. It was then called "paragraph 1322" but in January 1994, with the passing of a new Aliens Law, this was changed to "paragraph 1317." This paragraph stated that if there was at the least suspicion of trafficking, a woman should be allowed time to consider pressing charges. When she had done so, she should be allowed to stay in the Netherlands until the whole juridical procedure had been completed. In 1993 this provision was extended to witnesses who were willing to testify for the prosecution in cases of trafficking.

The second necessary action was to sharpen the juridical definition of "trafficking," in order to facilitate prosecution of traffickers. In 1989 the Attorney-General's office formulated a new definition which stated that a person is guilty of *traffic in persons*: "who induces another into prostitution by violence or an act of violence or by threatening violence or an act of violence, or by using his ascendancy ensuing from an actual relationship or by misrepresentation, or who undertakes any action which he or she knows or could reasonably suspect, may bring the other into prostitution."[4] This definition introduced the element of the "dependency" of the victim-survivor as a reasonable basis to presume that trafficking has taken place.

The success of these campaigns was due to the fact that two women—from Indonesia and the Philippines—who had been trafficked into prostitution in the Netherlands bravely filed charges and persisted, in the face of slanderous character attacks and intimidation from the traffickers and their cronies. Their cases were exemplary: one illustrated the difficulties that victims of trafficking faced if they were to be sent home immediately, the other showed the reluctance of the juridical authorities to prosecute trafficking and the difficulties of successful litigation based on the then-inadequate definition of trafficking. They were prepared to speak before parliamentary committees, and to face the media, albeit anonymously. The publicity and political value of these cases was crucial for the first successes achieved in the field of government policies.

The 1993 extension of the "1322" (now "1317") provision to include witnesses was obtained after a successful lobby campaign to prevent a South American prostitute who had reported a case of trafficking from being evicted. She had gone to the police when she could not stand seeing her Polish colleague being physically assaulted and coerced, when she obviously was not happy working. In return she was held in the lock-up as an illegal alien!

INTERNATIONAL ADVOCACY: WOMEN'S RIGHTS ARE HUMAN RIGHTS

In Europe, the collapse of the Iron Curtain at the end of the 1980s released a stream of women—young and old, college graduates and rural emigrants—traveling westward, looking for that lucky strike, and often falling prey to the parallel stream of job and marriage agencies and brokers who offered their services to the uninitiated migrants, to circumvent the obstacles and complicities of immigration laws and travel hazards.

Meanwhile, the Foundation For Women (FFW) in Bangkok, under the leadership of Siriporn Skrobanek, was also developing its anti-trafficking activities, which included research, legal advocacy in Thailand, and support of women who were pursuing prosecution cases, in collaboration with organizations in the countries where trafficking prosecutions were being initiated. By then the campaign in Thailand had expanded, and simultaneously, a network of organizations who were in some way addressing "trafficking" was growing in other countries in Asia. FFW was becoming the center of anti-trafficking activity, and it logically became the "host" of the Global Alliance Against Traffic in Women (GAATW) when it was formed in 1994.

The international advocacy campaign started with preparations for and participation in the World Conference on Human Rights in Vienna, June 1993. I participated in the Global Tribunal on Women's Human Rights and read out a testimony on trafficking, describing the (anonymous) case of one of the clients of STV. The event was part of the international women's campaign for the recognition of women's rights as human rights. The strategy was to present concrete cases—many at firsthand—of different forms of violence against women and combine them with analyses based on the relevant human rights standards in order to get recognition that violence against women is a violation of human rights. It was tremendously successful! Trafficking was specifically mentioned. In the concluding statement, the Vienna Declaration and Program of Action states:

> Gender-based violence and all forms of sexual harassment and exploitation, including those resulting from cultural prejudice and *international trafficking* are incompatible with the dignity and worth of the human person, and must be eliminated. This can be achieved by legal measures and through national action and international co-operation in such fields as economic and social development, education, safe maternity and health care and social support.[5]

The inclusion of gender violence (including trafficking in women) on the human rights agenda was a political victory. It was a recognition that the subordinate position of women is construed and maintained by patriarchal interests, ideologies, and institutions, and therefore could be broken down. Strategically, nation-states could now be held accountable for their efforts, or lack of efforts, to suppress gender violence.

At the end of 1993, STV and the GAATW started to participate in the preparatory events leading up to the Fourth World Conference on Women as strategic lobbying moments. Participation in these activities helped to expand the international network, identifying partners working from the same principles of respect for human rights in order to form a strong lobby for pro-rights measures to prevent and combat trafficking.

GAATW WAS OFFICIALLY LAUNCHED

The Global Alliance Against Traffic in Women was officially launched in October 1994, in Chiangmai, Thailand. This happened during an International Workshop at Chiangmai University, attended by 75 women activists, social workers, researchers, policy-makers, jurists, and civil servants, coming from 22 countries and representing some 40 organizations. Significantly, the workshop concluded that national governments in both sending and receiving countries played a significant role in exacerbating the situation by (a) promoting "migrant labor export" without any regulations or supervision to protect the rights and welfare of the workers; (b) neglecting to secure the rights and protection particularly of women migrants in their respective states, thus rendering them dependent on "third parties" and middle-men; and (c) denying women migrants opportunities to work in the formal, regulated sectors by upholding repressive immigration and migrant labor laws.

GAATW now moved more and more toward a broader concept of trafficking than only for prostitution and started to advocate a *pro-rights framework* to analyze and strategize against trafficking in women. Sharing in this vision, member organizations of the Alliance in different countries are engaged in victim support work, running crisis centers, and providing education and information work in prevention projects, as well as advocacy for women migrant workers' and sex workers' rights, and for reform of legislation and policies to better defend the rights of women. The International Secretariat in Bangkok evolved into a facilitating and training center—initiating and coordinating research, refining research methodologies, and organizing human rights training sessions. The research findings as well as the experiences gathered through direct assistance given to victims of trafficking were valuable as a reliable foundation for input into international advocacy campaigns.

An important strategic tool developed by GAATW is the Human Rights Standards for the Treatment of Trafficked Persons (HRS). This formulation of the rights of trafficked persons and the responsibilities of states to guarantee and protect these rights has proven extremely useful in lobbying and, as well as training support workers, human rights advocates, lawyers, etc., in illustrating the human rights content of GAATW strategies.

HUMAN RIGHTS ARE ALSO WOMEN'S RIGHTS: TRAFFICKING IN WOMEN ON THE WOMEN'S AGENDA

Two positive developments just before the Beijing Women's Conference were the adoption of the Convention on the Elimination of Violence Against Women by the United Nations General Assembly in December 1993, and the appointment of a Special Rapporteur on Violence Against Women in April 1994, in whose mandate "forced prostitution and trafficking" was included as one of the issues she should investigate. The supreme "lobby moment" of the last decade was the UN World Conference on Women in Beijing. The successful lobby of STV and GAATW in Beijing is reflected in the relevant texts of the Platform for Action (Section I. par. 230(n) and Strategic Objective D.3, par. 130(a–d). The positive elements in these paragraphs are that states are called upon to use human rights instruments, which give a better guarantee that measures based on these principles will be more respectful of the rights of the women concerned. There is recognition that there are other manifestations of trafficking in women than that in the sex industry (thus, there are more forms of exploitation than "sexual") and that "forced marriages" and "forced labor" are root factors which must be addressed in order to eliminate trafficking. Unfortunately, the Beijing+5 assessment did not show positive improvement in the status of women in the world, not to mention in the combat of trafficking in women.

Immediately after the Beijing Conference, STV and GAATW started to implement the International Report Project. Strategically, this report was initiated as a response to a request from the Special Rapporteur (SR), Ms. Radhika Coomaraswamy, for information about the global situation concerning trafficking. This gave the conclusions and recommendations a special "status," as well as made sure that the SR could not ignore the recommendations made in the report. The report was significant in that it provided the factual and moral basis for reexamination of old concepts and standards in order to evolve new ones which are more relevant to modern realities. Most importantly, the report offered a working definition of "trafficking" which distinguished the process of recruitment and transportation under coercion from the conditions encountered at the actual site of work. This process of recruitment and transportation could, in principle, be for many purposes besides work in the sex industry. This definition presumed acceptance of the sex industry as legitimate work, while at the same time de-linking the concept of trafficking from prostitution. On the other hand, the concept of "trafficking" became more entrenched in the migration paradigm. This was a breakthrough for advocates who were trying to get away from traditional anti-prostitution concepts and to develop more rights-based strategies which would address the exploitative conditions of work of migrant women.

In her report to the Commission on Human Rights (March 1997), the Special Rapporteur acknowledged the main conclusions of the report, reiterating that "prostitution is an income-generating activity." She noted the main issues that needed to be resolved among and by NGOs. Important was the lack of consensus within the international community regarding the definition of "trafficking." Coomaraswamy noted two basic controversies that arose from the historical definition of trafficking as "the trade in women for the purpose of prostitution." One revolved around the scope of the definition and whether it included or excluded contemporary forms of trafficking for domestic work, marriage, and sweatshop labor.

The second controversy arose from the existence of two main positions regarding prostitution—one, the abolitionist position which is based on the moral rejection of prostitution and defines prostitution per se as abuse and prostitutes as victims to be rescued and rehabilitated, was diametrically opposed to the position of those who view prostitution as work and wish to see it regulated as such. At the same time, the failure of the 1949 Convention on the Suppression of Trafficking in Persons and the Exploitation of the Prostitution of Others—because of its ill-defined and broad terminology, weak enforcement mechanisms, and its abolitionist perspective—gave rise to the need to reformulate international standards which would be relevant to the modern reality, and which included a new definition of "trafficking" as well as principles to guide national and international action. These controversies have persisted, and were a great obstacle in the ongoing negotiations in Vienna in 1999–2000 over the formulation of a protocol on trafficking to supplement the UN Convention Against Transnational Organized Crime.[6]

The Special Rapporteur also gave examples of State strategies that not only were ineffective in stopping exploitation of migrant women, but could actually harm women and increase their vulnerability to exploitation. For example, the Philippines and Bangladesh had both placed bans on women leaving to work as domestic workers in the Middle East, following reports of the bad treatment they received from employers, but this did not stop recruitment agencies from seeking and finding other channels, albeit illegal ones. This increased dependency of women on these agencies, and thus also the danger of exploitation and abuse by them.

In her second report on trafficking in women, presented to the Commission on Human Rights in April 2000, Coomaraswamy again cautioned states to abandon their "paternalistic" actions, and instead to develop strategies that truly respect and strengthen the human rights of trafficked persons. She offered a new rights-based definition of trafficking, which derived from the Human Rights Standards[7] definition and unequivocally criticized the 1949 Convention for its inability to protect the rights of women. She explicitly recommended that States and the international community utilize the Human Rights Standards. Also at this session, the newly appointed Special Rapporteur on the Rights of Migrants presented her first report, in which she promised to work closely with the Special Rapporteur on Violence Against Women on trafficking issues.

THE BEGINNING OF A NEW MILLENNIUM: THE NEW TRAFFICKING PROTOCOL

In December 2000, the long-awaited new international instrument on trafficking in persons was promulgated, in the form of the Protocol to

Prevent, Suppress and Punish Trafficking in Persons, Especially Women and Children (henceforth called the Trafficking Protocol), as a supplement to the United Nations Convention Against Transnational Organized Crime. The most important aspect of the protocol is its definition of "trafficking in persons," which emphasizes the use of *"threat of or use of force or other forms of coercion, abduction, fraud, deception, the abuse of power or (the abuse of) a position of vulnerability, the giving or receiving of payments or benefits to achieve the consent of a person having control over another person, for the purpose of exploitation."*[8]

The Trafficking Protocol is a big step forward in that it offers a comprehensive description of what constitutes the crime of trafficking, so that prosecution of the crime is facilitated, and states which have signed the protocol can use it as a basis to enact national legislation to combat trafficking. An important aspect of this definition is that it names "forced labor" as one of the characteristics of the situation of "exploitation" from which domestic workers should be protected: "Exploitation shall include, at a minimum, the exploitation of the prostitution of others or other forms of sexual exploitation, forced labor or services, slavery or practices similar to slavery, servitude or the removal of organs."

According to the *Annotated Guide*, a national legislation enacted on the principles of the protocol must have as the core of its definition the criminalization of the intent to recruit, transport, receive, or harbor someone in a situation of forced labor, slavery, or slavery-like practices.[9] It is not necessary to include all the "means" listed in the protocol definition, since it is clear that no one can consent to forced labor or slavery, making the listing of the coercive means with regard to these situations superfluous. At the same time, although the protocol focuses on the "transnational" nature of trafficking, a national legislation can also include internal cases of trafficking.

TRAFFICKING AND MIGRATION

The relation of trafficking to migration is that trafficking is a crime that occurs in the context of the movement of people—both within and across national borders. Exploitation and migration are, of course, not essentially linked, but we are here trying to address the forms of exploitation which take place when people are on the move, and in general, it is those who are not from the privileged class, gender, or race who face the most obstacles when they attempt to exercise independently their freedom of movement. It is the dependence of aspirant migrants on others to facilitate their movement which renders them vulnerable to any eventual criminal intentions of those who offer work opportunities in foreign countries and organize all the travel requirements.

The activities of recruitment, transportation, transfer, harboring, or receipt of persons do not constitute trafficking in themselves when they are carried out in a proper manner; that is, when the worker is fully informed about the nature and conditions of work for which she/he is contracted and under concrete and negotiated contractual agreements as to payments and other obligations of both parties. These activities are punishable when they are carried out "with the intent of" placing or keeping a person in an exploitative situation, characterized by "forced labor or services, slavery and slavery-like practices."

TRAFFICKING, CRIME PREVENTION, AND HUMAN RIGHTS

Trafficking as it is now defined in the UN Trafficking Protocol is a crime, which has a concrete and unambiguous description, under which forced labor in the domestic work sector can be prosecuted. With the proper and efficiently implemented national investigatory instruments—both legislation and mechanisms—in place, it should be possible for a court of law to determine the nature and extent of the criminal violations committed against the complainant. In such cases, the trafficking laws in place should also ensure that the protective and supportive mechanisms recommended in the Trafficking Protocol are available and accessible to the trafficked person.

The fact that trafficking is formally integrated into the sphere of the combatting of transnational organized crime does not mean that it has nothing more to do with human rights. Serious crimes which violate the physical or psychological integrity of persons, or their life-security, are ultimately violations of human rights, and every society must take every step within the legal system that is operable to combat these violations and protect everyone whose rights are thus violated. It is a recognized principle of international human rights law, reflected in Article 2.3 of the International Covenant on Civil and Political Rights and Articles 2 and 3 of the Convention on the Elimination of All Forms of Discrimination Against Women (CEDAW), that States have a duty to protect the rights of individuals to exercise their human rights, investigate alleged violations of human rights, punish violators, and provide effective remedies to victims of human rights violations. Conversely, for their sense of justice done, victims of violations should be encouraged to demand redress and reparation or compensation, for which it is necessary that the relevant legal mechanism, including the relevant legislation, exists and is accessible.[10]

The issue then becomes one of the professionalism and efficiency of the local criminal justice system and its willingness to act upon the complaints of migrant workers in any labor sector. Upon this hang their rights to redress and compensation, and to protection from further exploitation and abuse. Human rights advocacy demands that action should be taken to reform and improve the workings of the whole judicial system since the rights to due process, to redress and restitution, are basic to the enjoyment of all human rights. Outside the realm of crime prevention, trafficking remains a priority subject of concern of the office of the UN High Commissioner for Human Rights, where a special task force on trafficking is functional. This office has recently submitted "Recommended Principles and Guidelines on Human Rights and Human Trafficking" to the Economic and Social Council (E/2002/100).

AND, WHAT NEXT. . . ?

I would like to see anti-trafficking work develop toward more active pro-rights action and advocacy. Real "prevention" of violations of rights of migrant workers through real freedom of movement across internal as well as external borders; transparent, non-discriminatory, and non-exploitative practices regarding recruitment, transport, and acquiring jobs; and the prevention of forced labor in the sectors where migrant women work, starting with the recognition of migrants' employment as work. This work, at the moment largely in the informal economy, should be regulated under the state labor laws, taking into consideration the specificities of each sector, for example, domestic work in private homes or work in the sex industry.

One positive development is the recognition by the International Labour Organisation of the inherent link between trafficking and forced labor. In 1998, the ILO promulgated the Declaration on Fundamental Principles and Rights at Work, exhorting all members to renew their commitment to respect, promote, and realize the four fundamental principles and rights of workers; that is, freedom of association and the effective recognition of the right to collective bargaining; the elimination of all forms of forced or compulsory labor; the effective abolition of child labor; and the elimination of discrimination in respect to employment and occupation.

The first Global Report in the Follow-up to the ILO Declaration *Stopping Forced Labour*, issued in June 2001, focuses on the domestic work sector, explicitly linking domestic work, forced labor, and trafficking: there is a link between modern trafficking and modern forms of bondage through indebtedness, which makes trafficking a form of forced labor.

> Forced labour as such has not really caught the world's attention. It takes different forms—and their common features might seem abstract at first

glance. Yet forced or compulsory labor makes headlines almost daily in stories of trafficking in persons, imprisonment in sweatshops and the slavery-like conditions on some plantations and even in private homes.[11]

The report specifically describes the forced labor situation of domestic workers:

> Domestic work per se is of course not forced labour. But it can degener-ate into forced labour when debt bondage or trafficking is involved—or when the worker is physically restrained from leaving the employer's home or has his or her identity papers withheld...When the domestic workers are international migrants, the problems are compounded further ... primarily in developing countries, most often girls and some-times boys spend long hours toiling in private homes instead of attend-ing school...most common in urban areas, with children having been lured from poor rural areas. Even adult domestic workers are subject to the same fraudulent and coercive recruiting practices as those faced by rural workers, and themselves come from the countryside . . . Once on the job, domestic workers tend to work in isolation, creating ample opportunity for disregarding labour legislation, if it applies to them in the first place. Indeed, domestic workers suffer prejudice on account of their frequent exclusion from the coverage of labour legislation (in developed and developing countries alike) and the obstacles they face in exercising freedom of association. This combination makes it all the more difficult for them to extract themselves from situations involving forced or compulsory labour.[12]

I would like now to see the work that was started by the International Report Project proceed to the next stage: the integration of anti-trafficking policies and legislation into labor policies and legislation, as instruments to address conditions of forced labor and slavery-like practices. This means that the basic strategy should be to address the specificities of the sectors in which most women work; for example, the nature and physical state of the workplace, working hours, leave days, and payment of wages (scales and methods of payment), and to regulate them in such a way as to preclude conditions of forced labor. Such a strategy requires the establishment and monitoring of the channels for recourse when these conditions are violated (e.g., by clear national legislation based on the Protocol definition of traf-ficking for forced labor), either by specific agents and employers or as a result of discrimination against migrant workers on grounds of ethnicity or work sector. Ultimately, as in all labor issues, the workers must be enabled to organize both formally into trade unions and informally in their own communities, to demand and defend their rights.

WHAT HAS CHANGED?

In general, there has definitely been an explosion of anti-trafficking activity, from all sectors and at all levels. When I started, 30 years ago, we had to introduce the subject of trafficking and explain every time what it meant, as best we could. Nowadays, at every meeting that has to do with women, violence, migration, development, or human rights, at least one or two groups mention that they are working on trafficking, whatever they may mean by the term. It is still unclear to me whether this is because there has been a real increase in the phenomenon of trafficking itself, or that the consciousness of the activists and development agencies to the issue has increased, or that they have discovered that trafficking is a popular issue, especially with development funders.

I think that there has been an evolution in the public response to trafficking—from moralistic outrage at the physical (sexual) violation of women's bodies to a more "ethical" concern for the poor conditions of work, especially of migrant women. As more knowledge is gathered about the impact of gendered migration flows on women's lives and work, there is also the realization that in the worsening global economic and political climate for the advancement of any rights, let alone women's rights, one has to accept all the forms and strategies for survival as such, and to improve the basic conditions of work as much as possible.

There is, in general, more acceptance of prostitution as "sex work," as well as understanding that trafficking encompasses more than prostitution, although there is still some lack of clarity about the precise definition of trafficking, and how to go about getting legal and social redress for victims. Sex-worker rights and migrants' organizations now distinguish between the different anti-trafficking cohorts, and realize that there is no antagonistic contradiction between being "pro-rights" and "anti-violence," and that the two must inherently coexist as two sides of the same coin. For example, this is evident in the fact that migrant workers' organizations and networks are collaborating more and more with GAATW, even inviting them to make presentations on the situation of migrant sex workers. This is a recognition of the validity of GAATW's basic thrust—the promotion and defense of the rights of migrant workers in all labor sectors as the most potent strategy in anti-trafficking activism. There is, thus, a growing collaboration between migrants' rights groups and GAATW on the basis of struggle to achieve basic human rights and eliminate violence.

As I write this, I am reminded that this is exactly how we started in the Netherlands. In the 1980s alliances were being forged between feminists and prostitutes. In 1985, the same year that the report on trafficking was published, the Dutch prostitutes' organization, "Red Thread" (Rode Draad), and the feminist solidarity movement for prostitutes, "Pink Thread" (Roze Draad), were launched, *and* the first meeting of the International Committee for Prostitutes' Rights was held in Amsterdam.

Right from the beginning, the initiators of the prostitutes' rights movement and the anti-trafficking campaigners felt the tension between the two approaches. There was tacit acknowledgment of the legitimacy of each other's point of departure, and an intuitive conviction that the one did not exclude the other. But, to keep the analogy of the "thread," the two strategies remained stretched away from each other at two ends of the same "thread"… of the movements, lives, and work of women.

At the Second International Prostitutes' Congress held in Brussels in October 1986, I represented the Foundation against Trafficking in Women, together with Nena, a woman from the Philippines, who had started the tortuous process of bringing her traffickers to justice. We wanted to emphasize that recognition of the right of a person to choose her work, including prostitution, must imply the collateral right of another to refuse that work; thus forced prostitution (which was how we initially defined trafficking) should also be a concern of prostitutes' rights organizations. We held strongly that "the right to say YES" implied "the right to say NO" and both rights must be equally defended and advanced.

The statement that Nena read out then, in 1986, placed the issue of trafficking within the context of migration:

> We migrant women have left our countries and our families for various reasons: some, because we married foreign men, some to look for work to keep ourselves and our families. Leaving our countries in itself has been difficult, and in general we feel strange and lonely in a foreign country and isolated because we do not speak the language.
>
> Our situation is complicated by the fact that as migrant women we are dependent on either our spouses or other friends or agencies to help us organize the necessary immigration papers. In almost every western country Third World women are denied independent working and resident permits. We are subject to control in very discriminating manners at borders. This is especially severe for workers in the sex-industry.
>
> Because of this, many of us have been cheated and deceived by (internationally) organized traffickers who either promise us jobs or marriage and then coerce us into work which we do not choose to do, or do not pay us justly for our work…
>
> We are here today to bring to the attention of this conference that many migrant women are being coerced, under conditions of servitude and violence, to work in different branches of the sex-industry. Migrant women working voluntarily in prostitution are often under great control and suffer violence and are not free to determine how and where and when to work. Most of the money we earn is taken away from us…

This is still my basic conviction today. After more than thirty years of anti-trafficking activism, my commitment remains to the struggle to establish the basic human rights universally for every human being. The change I have undergone, through all the personal and working experiences and insights gained throughout the years is, I hope, the maturity and wisdom to understand and acknowledge the various ways that people, in any specific context, must negotiate and compromise because the conditions are not present for the exercise of absolute rights. The work that must continue unabated is the identification and removal of the obstacles to the exercise of rights and freedoms within the community. This is a work that must be done in principle, by the people concerned themselves, for the concrete exercise of rights is in the very struggle to achieve or defend those rights.

NOTES

1. "International Feminism: Networking against Female Sexual Slavery." Report of the Global Workshop to Organize Against Traffic in Women, Rotterdam, the Netherlands April 6–15, 1983. Edited by Kathleen Barry, Charlotte Bunch, and Shirley Castley.

2. Many of the participants of this Rotterdam workshop would later form the Coalition Against Trafficking in Women, an aggressively abolitionist group, which rejects any notion of women's agency in prostitution and advocates for the abolition of prostitution.

3. Ministry of Social Affairs. "Investigation into the nature, global scale and channels through which women are trafficked into the Netherlands." The Hague: Ministry of Social Affairs and Employment, 1985.

4. Since then, new legislation has been passed, decriminalizing prostitution for Dutch women and women from EC countries, and a parallel legislation on trafficking for prostitution, which absolutely forbids the employment of women from non-EU countries in prostitution. This in spite of persistent lobbying and arguments from STV and other supporters.

5. Vienna Declaration and Program of Action, as adopted by the World Conference on Human Rights on 25 June 1993. United Nations General Assembly. A/CONF.157/23, 12 July 1993, Paragraph 1/18. Emphasis added.

6. GAATW was fully engaged in this lobby effort, together with the Human Rights Caucus, an international group formed specially to influence this process. The Human Rights Standards (see note 7) was used as the basic lobby document to make clear to the delegates the importance of, again, a clear definition, and of integrating such standards into the Protocol mechanisms in order to guarantee respect for and defense of the rights of victims and witnesses.

7. See GAATW (Global Alliance Against Traffic in Women). *Human Rights Standards for the Treatment of Trafficked Persons.* Bangkok: GAATW, 1999.

8. Protocol to Prevent, Suppress and Punish Trafficking in Persons, Especially Women and Children, supplementing the United Nations Convention Against Transnational Organized Crime. United Nations Assembly A/55/383, Article 3 (a).

9. Jordan, Ann. *The Annotated Guide to the Complete UN Trafficking Protocol.* Washington, DC: International Human Rights Law Group, 2001.

10. Haverman, Roelof, and Marjan Wijers. *Review of the Law on Trafficking in Persons in Ukraine.* Geneva: International Organization for Migration (IOM), 2001.

11. *Stopping Forced Labour.* Global Report under the Follow-up to the ILO Declaration on Fundamental Principles and Rights at Work. International Labour Conference, 89th Session. Report 1 (B) Geneva: International Labor Office, para. 305.

12. Ibid., para. 83, 84, 85.

PART II

COMPLICATING THE "PROBLEM" OF SEX WORK

5

From Anti-trafficking to Social Discipline

Or, the Changing Role of "Women's" NGOs in Taiwan

Josephine Ho

Gail Hershatter has noted that prostitution usually does not dominate public discourse or attention, except at certain critical moments when it suddenly becomes the center of social concern as "a metaphor, a medium of articulation" through which various emerging social forces and social anxieties play out their displaced existence (Hershatter 1997, 4). As such, prostitution, as a recognizable "social problem," signifies very different practices and populations and involves quite different ramifications in changing social contexts. One such extended process of signification has taken place since the 1990s in Taiwan, when the anti-trafficking discourse, previously understood as an effort to eradicate forced prostitution of aboriginal girls, found itself losing relevance in the fast-liberalizing youth culture of post–martial law, consumption-oriented Taiwan. Christian groups then revamped the cause, articulating broad parental anxieties and building up an intricate web of social discipline that also embodies "a vision of global governance."[1] As the sex work rights movement's persistent struggle finally culminated in actual progress toward decriminalization in 2009, the anti-trafficking discourse is now revived to mobilize ethnic and economic anxieties surrounding global

83

migration into a line of resistance against possible favorable changes in the status of sexual transactions. The present paper documents this long process in order to demonstrate the changing scope of the anti-prostitution cause that continuously metamorphoses itself into new forms of social control.

I

The mid-1980s were the last years of the notoriously repressive Taiwanese martial law, as well as the height of Taiwan's struggling democratization process. And it was within this delicately volatile political milieu[2] that "anti-trafficking," as a moral and humanitarian imperative became "incidentally" hooked to a human rights imperative[3] and came to provide a legitimate cause through which various social forces could rally for social demonstration. The central figure in the initial formation of the anti-trafficking cause was the politically militant Presbyterian Church of Taiwan.[4] Presbyterian relief workers serving the aboriginal tribes had noted the string of girls, 13 to 16 years of age, who were sold into city brothels as collateral damage to a bankrupt aboriginal economy in the midst of a booming Taiwanese economic miracle.[5] As the advocacy of children's rights became the central focus of international organizations in the mid-1980s,[6] the Presbyterian Church in Taiwan saw an opportunity to link up the local with the international. For the first time in church history, aboriginal girl prostitutes were featured prominently in a report on tourism and prostitution at the Asian Church Women's Convention held by the Presbyterian Church in Taiwan in November of 1985.[7]

Determined to stop the spread of this terrible sin among the disadvantaged ethnic groups, the Presbyterian Church set up the "Rainbow Project" the following year to advocate the rescue of aboriginal girls. Presbyterian relief workers would conduct regular missionary visits to families in the aboriginal area and take note of missing daughters so as to provide information to the police and urge the latter to put out searches for the girls. They were often frustrated because many policemen were rumored to have taken bribes from the traffickers and were not too enthusiastic about looking for the girls, not to mention bringing known traffickers to justice. More troubling was the worry that selling underage daughters to the brothels no longer seemed to be taken very seriously by aboriginal families, and many of the girls even willingly returned to the trade after being rescued.[8] For the Christian workers of the Rainbow Project, this was a sign of the total collapse of moral values in the villages. To save "the future mothers" of the aboriginal peoples, the Rainbow Project began appealing to nascent Taiwanese NGOs to join in and pressure the government into eradicating what was then termed "the child prostitution problem."[9]

The invitation by the Presbyterian Rainbow Project met with warm support among NGOs in the loose political opposition alliance.[10] Labor issue–oriented progressives saw a cut-and-dried case of exploitation and oppression of aboriginal girls being forced to work in the brothels. Human rights groups, which had been treading cautiously under the martial law to defend the rights of political dissidents, saw the issue of child prostitution as a fully justified and potent case to accelerate the discourse of universal human rights. Nascent "women's" groups saw the helpless minority girls living in a state of enslavement as a clear-cut case of gender oppression that could work to mobilize more women into political activism.[11] Religious groups of other denominations or other faiths were also supportive of the cause to rescue poor, helpless girls and rid society of this terrible disgrace. As protests and rallies were still deemed unlawful political gatherings under martial law, the groups gathered around the anti-trafficking cause to stage a small-scale march, titled "Face Up to Trafficking: Concern for the Child Prostitutes." The march would highlight not only the plight of underage prostitutes, but also the evil doings of heartless traffickers, as well as the indifference of the police. The target of the march was the Gweilin Precinct of Taipei Metropolitan Police, which oversaw a specific red-light district notorious for harboring aborigine girl prostitutes.

The march, organized and headed by the Presbyterian Rainbow Project, took place under martial law on January 11, 1987. Over 100 marchers gathered in front of the police station, demanding that the police make a genuine effort to rescue child prostitutes and put a stop to the operation of traffickers. Slogans that condemned traffickers were chanted over and over again. Afterward, the marchers went into the red-light district and called out in the aboriginal dialect to the girls in the brothels to leave the business and go home. Although the brothel doors remained shut during the march and it was not certain whether any of the girls heard the call, the march was significant because this was the first time a social cause, rather than a political cause, mobilized the Taiwanese people into the streets. And as police integrity and performance were profiled and questioned by this act, which did not make the government look too good at that delicate moment of political volatility (four months before the lifting of martial law), authorities responded by announcing a special project effective March 1987 (known as the "Correcting the Customs Project"). The government promised that not only would more police force be devoted to obscenity sweeps directed at the sex trade, but those police stations that failed to wipe out child prostitution in their own districts would face austere punishment. The later execution of the policy proved to be far from satisfactory, but at least the issue of underage prostitution was formally admitted into public view.

At this initial stage of collaboration of the social movement groups, the general framework of reference for this united front was "rescue," with a two-pronged goal to urge the nonchalant police to rescue the girls from their immediate predicament and to crack down upon the trafficking crime rings. The police were seen as at least partially responsible for leaving the girls trapped in the vicious circle of trafficking and prostitution. In the meantime, the united front hoped to raise funds that would help the girls leave the sex industry permanently, learn a useful trade or continue with their education, return to their homes in the aboriginal tribes, and eventually become productive members of society.[12]

It is significant that at this initial stage, the anti-trafficking cause limited its targets to the evil traffickers and the inept police, and maintained a rather pragmatic attitude toward the tenacious existence of the sex industry as a whole. The banner that led the march boldly read: "the human rights of prostitutes."[13] In their First Joint Statement of Cause, the anti-trafficking alliance, instead of calling for the total eradication of the sex industry, offered "supervision" and "unionization of sex workers" as part of the short-term plan to deal with prostitution, so that other prostitutes could at least enjoy some basic protection and autonomy before the eventual abolition of prostitution (Fang 2003, 4). The Joint Statement of Cause thus cited its rationale for rescue efforts from the United Nations' 1948 *Universal Declaration of Human Rights,* Article 4: "No one shall be held in slavery; slavery and the slave-trade in all their forms shall be prohibited." In other words, anti-trafficking at this stage in Taiwan was more *anti-slavery* than anti-prostitution, with a strong human rights concern for the enslavement of a specific segment of prostitutes, the underage minority girls.

Such a pragmatic and humane effort would gradually harden as Taiwan's sociopolitical arena continued to change its scope. In order to meet Taiwan's pressing need for economic liberalization in the new globalizing world market, which at the same time necessitated the liberalization of the political sphere, martial law was finally lifted in May of 1987. Post–martial-law atmosphere afforded a lot of opportunities for hitherto forbidden social mobilization, including labor activism that organized to resist Taiwan's capitalistic exploitation, human rights activism that advocated the right to political dissidence, feminist activism that promoted the idea of gender equality, independence activism that worked toward reconsideration of Taiwan's nation-state status, etc. As social forces bubbled for outlets, the persistent ineptitude and insincerity of the police (as well as local legislators) to stop the traffic of aboriginal girls was taken to be a symbol of the utterly inefficient and indifferent authoritarian state. The anti-trafficking cause thus aimed at revamping the whole legal system needed to be amended to ensure that traffickers and brothel owners would be dissuaded from such acts of victimization once and for all. Tougher sentences would be instituted against trafficking, and reforms to the criminal code were to be included as one of the goals of the anti-trafficking rescue effort. In addition to stopping up the supply channel through these practical measures, the anti-traffickers believed that the demand side should also come under the auspices of law. Actions directed at legal reform and at eliminating the clients thus became the main focus of the second anti-trafficking march one year later in 1988.

As public demonstrations gained increasing legitimacy under the rubric of democratization after the lifting of martial law, the anti-trafficking cause also found more grounds to work from than simple religious humanitarianism. When the second rescue march was held on January 9, 1988, in the same red-light district in Taipei, the central organizers had become the Awakening Foundation, the feminist intellectual NGO that was developing discourses to turn the problem of child prostitution into an issue of profound *gender* oppression. Collaborating with the Awakening Foundation on the organization work was the recently established Taipei Women's Rescue Foundation, an NGO devoted specifically to the cause of rescuing unfortunate women and girls who had fallen victim to domestic violence or human trafficking.[14] Now discursively well-armed and politically righteous, the core organizers first lobbied the Ministry of Justice as well as the Judicial Yuan on the morning of the day of the march, demanding stiffer penalties for "the bad guys"—the traffickers and the brothel owners, as well as the johns. In the afternoon, a total of more than 300 people representing various NGOs (including academic groups, "women's" groups, aboriginal groups, and Christian groups) joined a march titled "The Second March to Rescue Child Prostitutes."

This time, as the marchers entered the red-light district, they chanted slogans directed not only at the traffickers but also prominently at the clients who frequented the brothels. As the marchers increasingly chastised the johns alongside the traffickers, what had begun as a humanitarian or human rights gesture a year ago was refiguring itself into a moral crusade against immoral men who brutalized young girls through the sex industry. Reflecting (and venting) the crowds' increasing impatience with the indifference of an authoritarian government, the general mood of the march was not so much "rescue" of the innocent but *"punishment" of the guilty (sinful).* Unfortunately, that impatience also translated into a different position on sex work as a whole. The First Statement of Cause in the previous year had accommodated a distinction between the short-term goal of rescuing the aboriginal girls and the long-term goal of the eventual abolition of prostitution. But the Second Statement of Cause in the following year dropped the conciliatory discourse that had called for more supervision of the brothels and unionization of existing prostitutes, leaving the whole discourse leaning toward the goal of total abolition of sex work (Fang 2003, 5).

II

The gradual foregrounding of the abolition stance had its historical context too. After the lifting of martial law in 1987, as competing loyalties or affiliations emerged and began organizing crowds for various urgent social issues, the continued operation of the anti-trafficking cause fell into the hands of mainly conservative and religious NGOs searching for more effective ways to curb the child prostitution problem as well as to reinstate moral values in the changing times of the early 1990s.[15] They believed that a whole new special law would be needed to coordinate the various clauses of various codes and various agencies of the government into a concerted effort to not only punish those who were responsible for the trafficking of aboriginal girls into prostitution, but also to establish a sort of preemptive/protective network to keep *all* girls from ever coming into contact with the perils of sex work.

The grand project of putting a new legislation into place called for a different kind of ballgame for NGOs, one that would involve heavy lobbying and advocacy strategies. One aggressive religious/children's welfare group, Garden of Hope (GOH), took the lead in 1992 to organize a task force of lawyers and social workers that would help draft the special law.[16] The new cause was also helped along by pressure from international organizations that were actively setting up a minimum framework of rules to tackle regional problems deemed to have global significance. The International Campaign to End Child Prostitution in Asian Tourism (established in Thailand in 1990, renamed in 1997 as End Child Prostitution, Child Pornography & Trafficking of Children for Sexual Purposes and broadened to include the rest of the world, but still abbreviated as ECPAT) joined UNICEF in disclosing horrendous figures for children involved in sex tourism or prostitution in Asian countries.[17] Proud of its own economic miracle but embarrassed to find itself listed among economically and politically "backward" countries such as India, Sri Lanka, Thailand, and the Philippines for harboring child prostitution, the aspiring Taiwan government scrambled to improve its image and international reputation, thus creating a new window of opportunity for the legislative efforts launched by anti-child-prostitution groups.

As rescue efforts turned into legislative efforts, their scope of applicability also underwent significant transformations. The key justification of "rescue" efforts had depended upon the rescued girls testifying that they had been "forced" into prostitution. Yet, out of a complex of varied considerations, many rescued girls chose not to incriminate their own parents or the brothel owners.[18] Without the element of coercion, the trafficking charges brought against traffickers or brothel owners often ended in acquittals and the girls were returned to their guardians or their parents, before moving back into the sex trade again. The erosion of the "forced prostitution" premise left many frustrated anti-traffickers determined to change the terms of indictment so as to get rid of this seeming "loophole." Another factor that urged anti-traffickers to consider overstepping the question of consent was the realization, supported by quite a few contemporary studies, that an increasing number of the so-called underage prostitutes were no longer aboriginal girls sold into prostitution. Instead, many newly found underage prostitutes were simply ordinary girls who, helped along by the liberalizing attitudes toward sex in a sexually charged social context, chose to enter the trade for the lucrative profits it offered.[19] Faced with this emerging moral crisis amid the deep and rapid structural changes in the socioeconomic-political fabric of Taiwanese society in the early 1990s, worried anti-traffickers resolved that the work of *aggressive and comprehensive "prevention"* would make more sense than the work of reactive and isolated "rescue." This significant change in approach and outlook would reveal itself later as a nationalist middle-class child-protection agendum that took giant strides to institute its own punitive-preventive measures of social control.

Several important transformations were thus effected in the process of legislation in the early 1990s. To begin with, the rescued girls' testimonies of their own consent to do sex work would no longer be taken into the equation. Instead, the *act* of sexual contact and the *age* of the girl involved would be sufficient criteria for an indictment, thus effectively erasing the subjectivity of the girls, and most significantly broadening the meaning of "trafficking." One woman lawyer from the Taipei Women's Rescue Foundation who worked closely with the drafting of the new law stated the basic spirit of the law bluntly: "Those under 16 are weak and shallow in their thoughts, and lack adequate power of judgment in relation to sexual acts." Consequently, she believed that those who commit sexual contact or perform obscene acts with such minors should receive severe penalty "whether or not monetary exchange takes place" (Shen 2002, 26).[20] Two significant expansions had been effected here: first, penalty would be applicable to any obscene contact, not just sexual intercourse; second, penalty would be applicable even when no monetary transaction took place. In other words, the target of the new law was no longer just trafficking or prostitution that involved minors, but *any kind of sexual contact with (or even between) juveniles.*

Moreover, penalties for the perpetrators of child-prostitution crimes were not only heavier according to the new law but also applicable to parties other than the traffickers and brothel owners. It would include: anybody who gave shelter to the girls (for any reason at all), the landlord who (whether knowingly or unwittingly) rented the property that was later used as a brothel, even the person who unknowingly lent money to a girl who then used it to take a taxi to a love motel to conduct a sexual transaction, etc. To safeguard the girls from reentering the sex trade after being returned to their parents, the new law would also allocate great sums of funding for halfway schools and other protection facilities that would keep the girls for a certain period of rehabilitation, monitor their progress, and eventually determine whether they were ready to be returned to normal life. Moreover, in order to prevent other "high-risk" girls from entering the trade, whether voluntarily or forced, the law decreed that a monitoring network be established whereby schools and police stations would be required to report and track down girls who dropped out of school without a good reason. The girls would then be consigned to relief workers and social workers to be "counseled" back onto the right track of life.

In other words, the anti-trafficking and anti-slavery line, even the whole framework of "rescue," was being displaced by an *anti-prostitution* line that aimed to eliminate all that seemingly helped connect young girls to sex work, all that materially sustained the continued existence of such girls outside the supervision and jurisdiction of paternalistic families— while at the same time empowering the anti-prostitution NGOs in very substantial ways. Significantly, as anti-trafficking moved along this process of legislation, the class/ethnic outlook in the original rescue efforts was quietly eclipsed by a *gender/age outlook* that further affirmed the *woman-child protection-prevention dyad* which reached deep into all sectors of social life.[21] An ever-broadening circle of control had conveniently displaced an originally humanitarian rescue effort.

Riding on an issue that had the potential to become a moral as well as nationalistic imperative, the anti-child-prostitution cause "consciously" adopted "strategic marketing" to lobby leaders of the Taiwanese society, including policy makers, legislators, opinion leaders, religious leaders, artists, and celebrity performers (Chi and Zheng 2002, 43–45). Staff members were successful in recruiting people of influence to the politically righteous anti-child-prostitution cause, or at least getting them to sign the Anti-Child-Prostitution Covenant drafted by Nan-Chou Su, the editor of the Christian journal *Wilderness.* Besides approaching influential figures, the cause also campaigned in front of popular department stores and collected signatures from shoppers in order to apply pressure to the notoriously opportunistic legislators. A total of 70,000 signatures were turned over to the Legislative Yuan, which not only highlighted the importance of the issue but also greatly enhanced Garden of Hope's public image and influence, from a Christian social service organization to a socially active NGO. More than US$300,000 in donations was collected through collaboration with the famous convenience store chain 7-Eleven. A total of more than 55 task force discussions, public hearings, press conferences, reviewing sessions, and petitions were used to publicize the issue and lobby relevant legislators between May 1993 and July 1995 when the special law finally passed—which was record speed for any legislation in Taiwan's history. And all this time, an effective media campaign, including radio programs, slogans, and rescue hotline numbers displayed in non-profit ads on TV, kept the issue and relevant activities alive in public view.

The eventual transformation of the anti-child-prostitution cause since 1987 was clearly dramatized in one grand event. Before the proposed new legislation moved into the political process in 1993, a third massive march through the brothel district was organized by the anti-child-prostitution cause to christen the effort. But in contrast to the first two marches, which were distinctively NGO in nature, namely, small in size, consisting of marginalized NGO groups, and viewed by the government with suspicion; the third march—the so-called Anti-Child-Prostitution Jog[22]—took place on November 14, 1993, and was attended by all the key government officials, legislators representing various political parties, educators, celebrities, and other social leaders, amounting to more than ten thousand people. Leading the jog were the Minister of Justice, Minister of the Interior, Minister of Finance, Director of Government Information Office, and other officials of the government, as a gesture of state support for such a noble cause. Instead of being the targets of criticism for corruption and indifference toward the child-prostitution issue, politicians and law enforcement officers were now running alongside anti-child-prostitution movement organizers and crowds, declaring war on the traffickers, brothel owners, and clients, and pledging to rid Taiwan of this unmentionable national shame.[23]

While the public show of resolve was still riding on the strong sentiment against the trafficking of underage girls, the legislation was expanding far beyond the issue with successive expansions added on by opportunistic politicians, who were urged on by concerned anti-child-prostitution NGOs as they responded to the evolving social realities of Taiwan.[24] In the end, the version that was passed no longer contained much reference to human trafficking, but something much broader. In addition to broadening the category of punishable acts from sexual intercourse to all forms of "obscene acts," ranging from heavy petting, oral sex, and masturbation to posing for pornographic films, another new category of punishable crimes was also added to the law to truncate teenagers' increasing accessibility to information that was believed to lead to sex work. Advertising for sex-related work, advertising for pornographic materials, even provision or display of pornographic materials would be considered "solicitation," liable for sentencing of up to five years of imprisonment and $1 million in fines. The information control also brought with it a whole set of knowledge/power formations that not only demonized perpetrators, but also pedagogized children and juveniles. The law would provide detailed classification of relevant crimes, and perpetrators would be categorized, labeled, and assigned differential degrees of punishment, thus creating a whole new conceptual framework for the so-called child prostitution ring. The newly drafted law also imposed a clear demarcation on the age of the child or juvenile in question—differential punishments would be applied to the clients in direct proportion to the age and gender of the juvenile involved, with 14 (for girls) and 16 (for boys) as the benchmark ages. In short, a new parental and pastoral power concerning the sexuality of the young was gradually moving into place.

This parental and pastoral power was not only manifested in the punishment applied to traffickers and johns, but more concretely embodied in the administrative power that would now be invested in the anti-prostitution NGOs. For, instead of turning a blind eye to the petition of NGOs, various state agencies—including the Ministry of Justice, Bureau of Health, Ministry of Communication and Transportation, Ministry of Education, Ministry of Defense (!), and Ministry of Economic Affairs—would be bound by the law to actively seek, inform, investigate, place in protective custody, and provide medical care and consultation for those girls suspected of doing sex work. Moreover, the performance of government agencies on such matters would be subjected to regular evaluations by a monitoring alliance formed by none other than the anti-child-prostitution NGOs and their sympathetic lawyers and scholars. Now legally endowed as "watchdog agencies," these NGOs had the right to directly or indirectly report cases, interview suspected child prostitutes, bring lawsuits against perpetrators, set up placement institutions or halfway schools, and hold regular meetings with government agencies. The easy access to state information and power, plus preferential access to state-provided funding and resources, added onto their original image as non-profitable religious charity/social service organizations, would greatly improve the anti-prostitution NGOs' sustained power to institute and monitor/supervise the implementation of the laws, not to mention increase staff and budgets through both government funding and public donations.[25]

At the historical moment when the Law to Suppress Sexual Transaction Involving Children and Juveniles was passed in 1995, what had begun as an anti-trafficking effort initiated for aboriginal peoples eight years before had now been formally and legally transformed into a national establishment that held immense power and resources to regulate sexual associations as well as sexual expressions of those under the age of 16. The formation and operation of such a "power of the civil society" would prove to be instrumental in urging the Taipei city government to ban legalized prostitution in 1997, which, to the government's surprise, sparked off Taiwan's first prostitutes' rights movement, made up of 128 middle-aged, minimally literate, licensed prostitutes. Once again, marginal sex workers came into public view, but this time not as young helpless victims to be rescued by anti-trafficking "women's" groups, but as mature sexual subjects resisting regulation by the now-powerful anti-prostitution "women's" NGOs.[26] The ironic turn of events reflected not only the emergence of a new subjectivity of sex workers in the Taiwanese context (from victims of trafficking to prostitutes demanding their right to work), but also the rising social status of mainstream "women's" NGOs in the increasing bourgeoisization of Taiwanese society.[27]

III

As one key woman lawyer in the anti-prostitution camp put it: "The law will have to be continuously revised to keep up with the emerging forms of sex work for juveniles."[28] True enough—since 1995, the Law to Suppress Sexual Transaction Involving Children and Juveniles has gone through several major amendments. Each amendment was heralded as necessary in order to curb newly emerging social ills, and each further widened the web of social discipline.

Most noteworthy of all were amendments introduced in 1999. In response to media reports of Taiwanese men taking advantage of sexual tourism in other countries (whether it involves minors or not), amendments to Articles 9, 22, and 34 added penalties for such acts even if the country where the sexual transaction took place does not consider such acts as criminal. To make enforcement feasible, the amendment mandates tour guides or tourist agencies to become whistle-blowers or watchdogs, thus extending the long arm of Taiwanese law far beyond its borders. Amendments to Article 33, furthermore, made media agencies liable for the ads they carry in their publications or broadcasts, thus effectively forcing the media agencies to take on censorship functions that greatly impinge on the freedom of speech and expression. The media's compliance would be further ensured by the anti-prostitution NGOs' watchdog mechanism that would monitor, evaluate, and report on media performance regularly.

The most devastating amendment to the law had to do with Article 29, which has now become the most broadly and effectively enforced article. The original article had aimed to prevent those establishments in the sex industry (ranging from night clubs, escort services, porn production companies, underground pubs, and sexual karaokes, to telephone clubs) from putting up commercials to lure teens into the sex trade.[29] So the original article read:

> Those who use advertisement, publication, radio, television, or other media to publish or broadcast *commercials* in order to induce, broker, imply or by other means *cause people to be involved* in sexual transactions

shall be punished with imprisonment of no more than five years and alternatively coupled with a fine of no more than one million NT dollars. [italics added]

But the 1999 amended version greatly extended its scope of applicability:

Those who use advertisement, publication, radio, television, *electronic signal and internet,* or other media to publish or broadcast *messages* that induce, broker, imply or by other means *cause people to be involved* in sexual transactions shall be punished with imprisonment of no more than five years and alternatively coupled with a fine of no more than one million NT dollars. [italics added]

When the applicability of the law was extended to include "electronic signal and the internet" and far beyond the category of "ads and commercials," the highly individualized and variegated communications in the cyberworld were conveniently subsumed under the auspice of the law. Now, any "messages" on the Internet, even those posted by individual Net citizens in the clearly marked adult chat-rooms or discussion boards, that could be read as "hinting/implying" sexual invitations which "might" then evolve into sexual transactions were to be indicted.[30] In fact, just between 1999 and 2003, a total of more than 2,000 cases of alleged efforts to conduct *enjo-kosai* (a Japanese term meaning compensated companionship or casual sex work) have been indicted and convicted.[31] Many of the perpetrators were merely young people who were seeking sexual relationships on the Internet and had done nothing other than using the fashionable and highly seductive term *enjo-kosai* to distinguish themselves in the vast ocean of "Netters."[32] Still, the enforcement of Article 29 was so pervasive that even online discussions of *enjo-kosai* as an academic subject could be subjected to the same scrutiny if the discussion did not toe the orthodox line of condemnation of casual sex. In short, whereas it used to be the *act* of sex for money that constituted punishable behavior, now, even *speech* about sex for money is liable to be indicted.[33]

The Internet has become a focal point of contestation not only because it has provided limitless possible connections for sexual contacts and sexual transactions, but also because of its easy circulation of so-called pornographic materials.[34] Adults are all the more alarmed because of their own unfamiliarity with and ineptness on the Internet. Protection-minded "women's" NGOs thus took up the crusade to "make the Internet safe" for children and juveniles.[35] ECPAT Taiwan, the NGO that still retains the anti-child-prostitution concept in its Chinese name but is now concentrating on anti-pornography campaigns, acquired state funding to start an online pornography-monitoring campaign called Web 547 in 1999. The campaign recruited volunteers, put them through a 3-day training program on how to use the computer and how to "recognize" pornographic or other illegal material on the Web, and then assigned them to monitor communications and postings on the Internet. Statistics and figures of the "amazing inundation by pornographic material" were then made known not only to the government but also to the media to alarm the public of the pervasiveness of pornography and to urge more control and screening of the Internet.[36] But the target of such "purity campaigns" spans far beyond sexual transaction or pornographic materials. In its May 2002 campaign of "guarding angels on the internet," ECPAT encourages children to adopt the principle of three "No's" while surfing the Internet: "to say no to selling, buying, distributing, posting, or forwarding pornography"; "to say no to prostitution"; and most interestingly, "to say no to one-night-stands." The incongruence of the third term is symptomatic of ECPAT's expanding goal: To end child prostitution now means to curb sexual explorations by the young. In that sense, measures taken by such NGOs are aiming much less at forced child prostitution than at containing the immense sexual impulses and curiosity demonstrated by today's youths.[37]

Since 1995, the once-anti-trafficking NGOs have evolved into mainly children's welfare or child-protection agencies, with more than two dozen subsidiary care centers or halfway houses. Child protection has proven to be a much more potent and profitable concept than anti-trafficking. Garden of Hope, ECPAT Taiwan, Taipei Women's Rescue Foundation, and Catholic Good Shepherd Sisters have been aligned since the anti-trafficking days, presenting themselves not only as the moral high ground but as the "heart" of Taiwan society. Now recognized as key "women's groups," they can reform the world in the name of a "fiercely protective motherhood." In addition to gains in the judicial arena where new laws are being added to consolidate the control over sexual contacts through the Internet, these NGOs are also increasing their presence in the education arena. New proposed amendments in 2003 included clauses that require all schools to initiate preemptive reports on "high-risk" students who "look like" they "might" get involved in casual sexual transactions; decisions may then be made to put them away in halfway houses for their "protection." On a grander scale, government committees that oversee gender-related laws and gender/sex education programs continuously include these NGOs as regular members or advisors,[38] thus giving such groups even more access to not only the design of education policies but also the regulation of the education Internet, which effectively controls the activities of numerous Net users. Still, the child-protection groups continue to expand the scope of their cause: New revisions to the Child Welfare Act entered the review process in 2010 that would further elevate the child-protection issue into a "children's rights-and-welfare issue," thus not only greatly increasing the size of the national budget that would go into related provisions most conveniently located under the auspices of the Christian groups but also putting the whole of media and adult life under scrutiny and control according to standards deemed conducive to "the growth and well-being of children."

In retrospect, the late-1980s "discovery" of "aborigine child prostitution" and attendant local and international (religious) fervor of anti-trafficking efforts in Taiwan have over the years become the terrain whereupon a nationalist middle-class consolidation of social and moral values is taking place via the policing of sex as well as the eradication of all forms of sex work in the name of child protection.

Aside from the justified deployment of disciplinary powers that these child-protection NGOs helped put into place in Taiwan, a major part of the welcome enjoyed by these NGOs in government matters must also be attributed to the opportunity of international participation that they have helped provide the Taiwan government. The child-protection NGOs' affiliations with international anti-child-prostitution organizations often carry further links to other international non-governmental and intergovernmental organizations (such as Interpol, World Tourism Organization, and various United Nations agencies, especially UNICEF and ILO-IPEC),[39] a connection network that the aspiring Taiwan government is eager to tap into in order to promote affirmation of its envisioned independent nation-state status. The NGOs themselves benefit from such a network too, for connections are set up for exchange of skills, information, and advocacy purposes between organizations in the developed countries and those in the developing countries, which quickly and dramatically enhance the effectiveness of local efforts as well as their power of influence. International events hosted or promoted or assisted by the international organizations give strength and credibility to local groups.[40] Furthermore, the organizations share their work plans with one another, mutually strengthening each other's projects. Linkages with all these organizations bring external pressures to bear on national governments to implement measures suggested by international organizations, thus effectively consolidating the "global governance" that the UN is aspiring for.

The Convention on the Rights of the Child, deemed as "a *universally agreed* set of *non-negotiable* standards and obligations," is the most recent example of such consolidating efforts that work to identify national laws and practices that need to be brought into conformity with UN standards. The Taiwanese Legislative Yuan has passed joint amendments to the Children's Welfare Act and Juveniles' Welfare Act, effective June 1, 2003, in order to "bring the Acts in line with United Nations' definition of children."[41] The amendments not only broadened the Acts' applicability to those under the age of 18, thus greatly increasing the number of youngsters that come under the auspices of the law in the name of children's welfare,[42] but also more rigidly regulated the whole of social and virtual space *in the name of children*. The Internet and other media have to be rated and, if found to be broadcasting materials unsuitable for children, would be subjected to heavy fines and temporary suspension of licenses. Furthermore, parents and guardians are now held responsible for the activities of their children: If children under 18 are found to have come into contact with unsuitable materials, visited sex-related recreational businesses, or lingered at gambling, pornography, or violence-related video arcades, then the parents or guardians will be charged and fined.[43] Protection of children can even extend to before they were born: pregnant mothers are now prohibited by law from smoking, drinking, using drugs, chewing betel nuts, or conducting other activities deemed harmful for the fetus. It is speculated that as "gender mainstreaming" gains international momentum, more new rules and regulations concerning men's and women's daily lives are going to be prescribed in Taiwan to further consolidate the encroaching project of global governance.

IV

It is a historical irony that, while the original anti-trafficking fervor dissipated and transformed into a large-scale project of social discipline, the actual "trafficking" of humans in Taiwan at the present moment is being conducted on a much larger scale than ever imagined. Thousands of migrant laborers from, for example, Thailand, Vietnam, Indonesia, Philippines, and most recently Mongolia, are being legally brought in to satisfy the needs of both government construction projects and industries in the private sector, as well as the need for domestic help by middle-class families.[44] Thousands of migrant marriages have also taken place as a result of dramatically changed global and local economic conditions since the early or mid-1990s (with foreign brides coming mostly from Vietnam and Indonesia, negotiated through professional matchmaking agencies at a cost, in addition to a huge number of Mainland China brides).[45] Viewed in this context, when conservative "women's" groups, in an effort to demand more stringent laws in the name of anti-trafficking, continue to invoke the history and memory of trafficking in terms of a traditional familial custom in times of economic poverty (the "selling" of daughters, daughters-in-law, etc.), it serves only to effectively displace/deny today's massive legalized trafficking on the state level, as well as the discriminatory laws in relation to Mainland brides.[46] On the other hand, the term "human trafficking" is always invoked in another specific context: the continuous flow of migrant women from Mainland China, or more recently from Russia, in search of better economic possibilities through sex work in this wave of rapid globalization. To describe such women in terms of trafficking—evoking lingering images of helpless women in the hands of heartless traffickers, brothel owners, and pimps—serves not only to distort/erase the subjectivity/agency of such migrating sex workers but also to demonize the political regimes from whence they come.[47] In other words, the cause of "anti-trafficking" can still serve multiple political functions—as a means to stabilize and consolidate state- and family-oriented projects (in state-sponsored construction work or the flow of brides from Third World regions), as well as a continued effort to defeat women's transgressive search for economic betterment outside the confines of marriage relationships.

In the past, astronomical figures that document the rapid growth and spread of the sex industry in monetary terms have been constantly cited by anti-prostitution groups to justify the legislation of more laws and ordinances that impinge on the life of every citizen in the name of child protection. Yet, what we have witnessed in Taiwan in the past 10 years is the incredible growth and power of an *"anti-sex industry"* that thrives upon the imagined evil existence of trafficking and the sex industry, as well as the convoluted aspirations for national-global governance. Such a web of normalizing knowledge/power conglomerate that continues to reduce the widely varied faces and practices of Asian sex work to nothing but the trafficking of women and children is bound to constitute more obstacles for the emerging subjectivity and agency of sex workers as well as the prostitutes' rights movements in Asia. And it is this national/global governance that has to be resisted.[48]

NOTES

1. Tani E. Barlow has also discussed this concept in relation to the universalization of the gender analytic by Chinese women's NGOs working in unison with the United Nations in the post–Cold War era. See Tani Barlow, "Asia, Gender and Scholarship Under Processes of Re-Regionalization," *Journal of Gender Studies,* No. 5 (2002), 8.

2. Researchers have also detected that concern over prostitution flares up usually at moments of intense social or political tension. Cf. Lucy Bland, *Banishing the Beast: Sexuality and the Early Feminists* (New York: The New Press, 1995), 95–123; Gail Hershatter, *Dangerous Pleasure: Prostitution and Modernity in 20th Century Shanghai* (Berkeley: University of California Press, 1997, 1998), 3–12; Ruth Rosen, *The Lost Sisterhood: Prostitution in America, 1900–1918* (Baltimore & London: Johns Hopkins, 1982, 1983, 1994), 38–50.

3. "Human rights" as a concept had originally been used by the Nationalist government in Taiwan mainly to highlight the notorious human rights records of its rival, the Communist government of the People's Republic of China. The concept was gradually appropriated by Taiwanese political dissidents during the 1970s and 1980s as they tried to draw attention to Taiwan's own record of political oppression during those years.

4. The Presbyterian Church of Taiwan has been actively and openly promoting the independent nation-state status of Taiwan for the past 40 years and is quite closely linked to the opposition party, the Democratic Progressive Party. Its conception of human rights has

always been framed in a nation-state status claim as the Church urges the government to "face reality and take effective measures to make Taiwan a new and independent nation" (Taiwan Presbyterian Church Declaration on Human Rights, 1977, http://www.pct.org.tw /humanrights30th/, accessed April 30, 2011). Believing that there is no dichotomy between the sacred and the secular, and that the social, economic, and political are all within the field of interest of religion and religious bodies, the Church takes active measures to intervene in social issues, child prostitution being one of them. Admittedly, it was not easy to advocate issues related to sexuality among conservative churchwomen; issues such as AIDS advocacy (which was seen as only teaching foreign laborers how to use condoms in sexual intercourse) and sex education (which was read as encouraging the young to learn about sex) met with great difficulty (http://women.dpp.org.tw/publication/public2–12–17.htm; webpage now removed). The issue of underage prostitution, in contrast, had a much easier time winning support among churchwomen, probably because of its Armageddon rescue/relief posture against demonized lustful/greedy men. Also, during the politically repressive era of the early 1980s, the Church saw firsthand the continued oppression of marginal ethnicities, exemplified in the existence of underage aboriginal prostitutes, and read it as echoing the oppression of the politically marginal, the Church itself included.

5. It was rumored at the time that in any poor aboriginal family, the sons would be shipped off to sea to work as sailors on fishing boats and the daughters would be sold into brothels in the big cities and become prostitutes. Researchers had even estimated that in one aboriginal village, 20 percent of the women were involved in prostitution. See Yi-Yuan Lee, "Teenage Problems among Aborigine Tribes during Social Change," *Journal of Institute of Ethnography*, 48 (1979): 1–29.

6. In response to the setting of the 1979 International Year of the Child, Defense for Children International organized an NGO Ad Hoc Group in mid-1983 to draft the Convention on the Rights of the Child. In 1987, the NGO Ad Hoc Group joined with UNICEF and prepared a Convention which was finally adopted by the General Assembly of the United Nations in 1989. Overall, the 1980s was a decade in which children's rights violations such as torture, prostitution, economic exploitation, arbitrary detention, and trafficking and sale became highly profiled issues (http://www.child-abuse.com/childhouse/childrens_rights/dci_crc.html).

7. Significantly, the aboriginal boys who were shipped off to sea in order to pay back family debts or to improve living conditions for the whole family rarely received much attention, even under the rubric of children's rights. Though involving much exploitation, it was never characterized as a human trafficking or even a labor issue. In contrast, aborigine girls who were sold off for the same purposes became central concerns of Presbyterian ministers and social workers. This urgent concern over the sex of the girls reflected a specific appropriation of the concept of exploitation that would come to dominate later developments in the anti-trafficking cause.

8. The double bind of the highly esteemed Chinese family ideology of filial piety helped make it "natural" for the girls to sacrifice themselves for the family out of love, as well as to return to the trade after they had been rescued by well-wishing NGOs. The church groups, however, put the blame only on the ruthless traffickers and heartless parents.

9. The picture of a poor, powerless girl crying helplessly in the hands of ruthless traffickers captured the imagination of the public and became a powerful symbol for prostitution even when it no longer involved such victimization.

10. One underlying basis of consensus has to do with the fact that many of these groups overlapped one another in membership and in their common commitment to opposition politics (better known as "democratization" in Taiwan). The cause thus carried strong ethnic, age, gender, and (most significantly) religious connotations, mixed in with political concerns. All of these factors would play significant roles in the future transmutation of the anti-trafficking cause.

11. Feminist thought was first introduced into Taiwan with Hsiu-lien Lu's pioneering book, *New Feminism*, in 1973, but it was more of a one-person intellectual crusade than

a social movement. In fact, the book was widely read, not by women, but by dissident intellectuals at the time as a declaration of human rights in general—it is ironic that under martial law, political dissidence could find legitimacy only in discussions of gender inequality. The first overtly feminist journal, *The Awakening,* was not published until 1982; the emergence of the first feminist movement group had to wait until 1987 due to restrictions on the right to associate under martial law, which was finally lifted that year. Significantly, feminism as a concept might have been known to some progressive intellectuals at the time, but "feminists" were stigmatized as ugly, undesirable, angry spinsters, butches, and lesbians. Due to the nature of their own membership—namely, heterosexual, marriage-bound women—most "women's" groups that took part in the anti-trafficking effort chose to describe themselves as "children's welfare groups"; they wouldn't even want to bear the title of "women's groups." Only one group adopted the term "feminist" to describe itself, but whether its individual members did so is another matter.

12. What had begun as a relief effort that depended mostly upon charitable donations would later evolve into a mega-business that receives huge sums in subsidies from a Taiwanese government that, in the name of social welfare, increasingly franchises its functions to various NGOs and thus transforms parts of civil society into power adjuncts of the government.

13. The choice of the wording here certainly did not derive from any pro-sex-work imperative; the latter would emerge much later in 1997 with Taiwan's first prostitutes' rights movement. In reality, the declaration of "universal human rights" for prostitutes at this historical march in 1987, when martial law was still in place, only thinly veiled the demand for "human rights" (understood mostly in political terms) by the highly diversified march participants, who were distinctly opposed to the authoritarian regime as the root of all social evil.

14. The contingent coupling of a feminist group that believed in empowering women through political action and a women's rescue group that aimed to restore peace and security to families was symptomatic of a time when a loosely united opposition front was needed in order to resist a quite authoritarian political regime.

15. Such "effective" means to stop the traffic of aboriginal girls would also prove to be an effective means to greatly enhance the (financial and political) status of those groups working exclusively on the anti-trafficking cause, to the extent that quite a few rescue/relief groups that aimed at rescuing "unfortunate" girls (or women) were established by various religious denominations in the few years just before the 1990s. The Catholic Good Shepherd Sisters (est. 1987) were affiliated with the Catholic Church, while the Garden of Hope (est. 1988), the Rainbow Center (est. 1988), and End Child Prostitution in Asian Tourism (ECPAT) Taiwan (est. 1990) were all closely related to Protestant denominations. As these groups later took up the work of running halfway houses or halfway schools and providing spiritual education/counseling for the rescued girls, their voices and their religious-moral standards also became viable forces in the social framing of the problem of underage prostitution.

16. Garden of Hope (GOH) even hired a new Director for Special Projects, Hui-Jung Chi, to coordinate such efforts. Chi had been a journalist for 7 years and knew how to work the media; she had also been trained in social marketing for nonprofit organizations by international groups and was eager to try out her skills in lobbying and media management. Incidentally, GOH aimed to broaden its influence and power by upgrading the anti-trafficking cause to an anti-child-prostitution "social movement." As Chi recollected recently, "Six months before I came to the Garden of Hope, the Board had passed a resolution [in 1992] to start the Anti-Child-Prostitution Social Movement. In other words, the Garden of Hope was transforming from a charitable organization into a social movement organization. However, due to the sensitivity toward the word 'social movement,' we masked our transformation as 'Anti-Child-Prostitution Special Project'" (Cf. http://www.goh.org.tw/english/english.htm). The reference to "social movement" here had more of a religious connotation—a this-worldly vision of *social reform*—than what is usually considered to be social activism. For over the years

GOH had also done the most actual damage in stigmatizing and shortcircuiting the efforts of sex-rights groups to advocate human rights for marginal sexualities. In fact, in the name of "protection of children," GOH had repeatedly impeached feminist sex radicals for the latter's against-the-grain discourses on teenage sexuality, abortion, occasional sex work, or zoophilia.

17. UNICEF had reported numbers of children involved in sexual tourism in 1993: Thailand had more than 800,000; India had 500,000; Taiwan had 100,000; Philippines had 60,000. Between 1993 and 1994, Taiwanese researchers and officials alike repeatedly disputed the validity of such figures.

18. Their testimonies of having joined the trade "willingly" were consistently read as resulting from financial pressures or from threats against the safety of their families. No room was left for any consideration of the girls' own agency.

19. Garden of Hope itself cited a study of teenage girls in April of 1993 that showed that over 30 percent of junior-high-school girls already had sexual experience, and more than 70 percent of the "rescued" teenage prostitutes "willingly" entered the trade. This new generation of girls, growing up in a social atmosphere quite different from that of the pre-martial-law days were much more daring and assertive when it came to their own sexuality. Consequently, such studies often evoked mass hysteria that resulted in more stringent laws regarding contact with teenagers.

20. The basic spirit here would be carried over to other amendments to the Criminal Code in 2000 that made sexual intercourse with teenagers under the age of 14 (girls) or 16 (boys) a sexual crime no matter what the circumstances are. Many teenage couples have suffered because of this new legislation.

21. This fiercely protective motherly figure would become the key gender position assumed by child-protection groups. The Presbyterian Rainbow Project gradually withdrew from rescue work to turn to more education-oriented work, which was believed to truly enhance the economic status of the aboriginal tribes so that trafficking could be stopped at its origin.

22. GOH's CEO Hui-Jung Chi remembers the event fondly in one interview: "In order for everyone to feel they were a part of the event, I designed it as a massive jogging event. You know, a very healthy activity for everyone. I had thought we could jog around this red-light district seven times, just like what the Israelites did to the city of Jericho, and it would disappear from the face of the earth. It would be a humorous ritual, a pledge of some sort" (http://www.ccea.org.tw/soc/17.htm, accessed April 30, 2011). It was not clear whether all those who joined the event were aware of this Christian underpinning.

23. Feminist sex radicals had long noted the contrast between the two marches and had criticized the assumptions that underlay the erasure of teenage sexual subjectivity by such self-proclaimed children's welfare NGOs. See Xiau-Ling Zhao, "Standing on the Shoulder of Patriarchy: The 'Anti'-Child Prostitute Movement," *The Awakening Monthly* 159 (1995): 12–14.

24. The trend toward the proliferation of sexual ads, commodities, and the liberalization of sexual values and morals was already quite obvious in Taiwan in the early 1990s. As the Feminist Sex Emancipation Movement intervened in 1994 by bringing forth a new liberating discourse for women's and teens' sexualities, the anti-child-prostitution Christian NGOs began lashing out against feminist sex radicals for the alternative stand the latter took on issues ranging from sex work, surrogate mothering, sex education, and cybersex, to teenage sexuality.

25. The annual revenue for Garden of Hope, the largest of the child-protection NGOs, reached US$11,000,000 in 2010, fifty times what it was in 1987, with hundreds of full-time staff members stationed across the island and even overseas in the U.S. The abundance in resources and manpower also greatly increased its power to promote issues and campaigns.

26. I have put "women's" in quotation marks to highlight the fact that in a much earlier historical context, these NGOs actively avoided the label "women's" and its accompanying stigma. But as the gender analytic came to be adopted as a state policy in the late

1990s, these anti-prostitution NGOs have increasingly assumed the position of "women's" groups. And, as dissenting voices rose among sex-positive women in protestation against the retrenchment of sex-related laws, the groups are now resorting to their old titles of child-protection groups to take advantage of the new and seemingly unchallengeable imperative.

27. The struggle of the prostitutes' rights movement in 1997 also marked the formal and summary schism within the Taiwanese feminist movement over the issue of female sexuality, with sex-positive feminist activists being fired from the staff of the once-progressive Awakening Foundation. Feminist discourse was also stymied when faced with female sexual subjects significantly different in age and class, not to mention sexual sentiment and preference, from the underage aboriginal girls trapped in forced prostitution which had come to frame most mainstream women's groups' representation of sex, not to mention sex work.

28. The statement is prominently featured on the back cover of the book that documents the whole legislation process of the Law to Suppress Sexual Transaction Involving Children and Juveniles, signaling the plan of the anti-child-protection NGOs to further utilize this law for future purposes.

29. The law may have been designed to protect teenagers from being tempted into sex work, but "causing people to be involved in sexual transactions" never specified the age of the "people" referred to, nor whether it excluded the person putting up the ad, which effectively makes the law applicable to *anybody* who is sending out sexual invitations, not to mention messages for sexual transaction, on the Internet. As it stands now, Article 29 has proven to be a most potent law against both professional and occasional sex workers.

30. Whether minors were actually involved in the communication is of no consequence, for the mere "possibility" that juveniles might stumble onto such postings on the Internet and become "negatively affected" is enough cause for prosecution.

31. The statistical figure is quoted in Mei-Hua Chen, "Sex Work Rights," *Taiwan Human Rights Report 2002*, Taipei: Avant-Guard Press, 2003, 115–116. For an analysis of *enjo-kosai* as an emerging sociocultural phenomenon in Taiwan, see Josephine Ho, "From Spice Girls to Enjo Kosai: Formations of Teenage Girls' Sexualities in Taiwan," *InterAsia Journal of Cultural Studies* 4.2 (Aug. 2003): 325–336.

32. "*Enjo-kosai*" may have come to stand for any form of casual sex work in Taiwan, but Article 29 addresses not actual sexual transactions, but the *communication* that *may* lead up to such transactions. From 1999 to 2008, more than 20,000 netizens were indicted for their speech and self-expression on the Internet; whether any rendezvous or transaction had taken place was of no consequence to the law. In January 2003, a pregnant wife posted *enjo-kosai* messages in her husband's name to see, as a test of loyalty, if the husband would give in to the many calls of inquiry from women. The husband never made any move, but the wife was prosecuted for posting *enjo-kosai* messages.

33. The Center for the Study of Sexualities at National Central University had a website that collected relevant news, debates, panel discussions, and academic research on the issue of *enjo-kosai*. When it posted satires of police entrapment of Net citizens for possible *enjo-kosai* charges in 2002, the Center received formal warning from the Ministry of Internal Affairs, as well as the Ministry of Education, for possible violations of Article 29: using electronic signals and the Internet to publish or broadcast messages that "cause people to be involved in sexual transactions." The warning had been prompted by none other than the child-protection NGO the Catholic Good Shepherd Sisters.

34. The Internet has also proven vital for marginal sexualities and communities, including gays, lesbians, transgenders, etc. See Chris Berry, Fran Martin, and Audrey Yue (eds.), *Mobile Cultures: New Media and Queer Asia* (Durham, NC: Duke University Press, 2003). Of course, under the auspices of the newly amended law, communications within such sexual communities are also susceptible.

35. http://www.web547.org.tw/nessite/about.htm.

36. In her study of prostitution in Victorian England, Judith R. Walkowitz has already noticed that empirical studies and investigations are often done on the so-called deviant

behavior so as to pave the way for policy suggestions that aim to correct such behavior. See Judith Walkowitz, *Prostitution and Victorian Society: Women, Class and the State* (Cambridge: Cambridge University Press, 1980), 37.

37. ECPAT International's mission statement describes the organization as "a network of organizations and individuals working together for the elimination of *child* prostitution, *child* pornography and trafficking of *children* for sexual purposes." Yet ECPAT Taiwan's monitoring activities often extend beyond the scope of children. Out of the 7 completed monitoring reports posted on their website, only 1 has direct bearing on children. In the end, the reports function only as justification for more obscenity sweeps on the Internet. The Ministry of Education is already citing Web 547's reports to justify new restrictions imposed on postings on the education Internet.

38. For example, Garden of Hope's CEO Hui-Jung Chi has been a member of the Ministry of Education's Gender Education Committee since the latter's founding in 1997. Other such NGOs have also had their delegates on this committee that oversees gender- and sex-education-related matters nationwide.

39. See http://www.ecpat.net/eng/Ecpat_network/index.asp.

40. Following upon the 2nd World Congress Against Commercial Sexual Exploitation of Children held by ECPAT International in Yokohama in December of 2001, the First ECPAT-Taiwan Forum Against Commercial Sexual Exploitation of Children was held on October 14–15, 2002, with three speakers from ECPAT International and SAGE (Stand Against Global Exploitation). Government officials are fully aware of the amazing progress that could be made in such events, considering Taiwan's repeated defeats in other diplomatic channels. In fact, when the Ministry of Foreign Affairs' Research and Design Committee Chairperson tagged along with ECPAT representatives to the World Congress in Yokohama, she was so touched by the opportunity to attend international conventions, as well as so impressed by ECPAT Taiwan's international connections, that she wrote to praise the latter for conducting successful "citizen's diplomacy" (http://www.ecpat.org.tw/html/view01_05.htm; webpage now removed).

41. The Ministry of Interior explains that major revisions of the Children's Welfare Act in 1993 had greatly enhanced relevant laws for the protection of children; the recent fusion of the Children's Welfare Act and the Juveniles' Welfare Act aims exactly to revise both in accordance with UN definitions.

42. Incidentally, the expansion of teenager-related laws often entails establishments and expansions in halfway houses or shelter institutions, many of which are run by the Christian NGOs. In 1988 when the anti-trafficking legislation process began, one halfway institution (Taipei Municipal Kuang-Tze Care Home) built partly to shelter "unfortunate girls" petitioned the government saying that over 700 such girls had been found by the police in the first 6 months of the year, but the institution could keep only seven girls on their roster and was on the verge of being dismantled by the government. They were hoping amendments to the laws would help keep more girls at the institution. Not surprisingly, the Law to Suppress Sexual Transaction Involving Children and Juveniles effectively increased the number of high-risk or already fallen girls to be kept there for rehabilitation. Likewise, when the joint amendments to the Children's Welfare Act and the Juveniles' Welfare Act were being proposed in 2002, the Taiwanese Association of Orphanages admitted that they had the capacity to house 3,500 kids but only 2,300 beds were filled at the time. They thus urged the age of protection be raised to 18 so that more children from "dysfunctional families" would fall under their auspices, not to mention an increase in funding that is required by the law they helped put into place (http://www.ettoday.com/2002/11/19/327–1377473. htm).

43. Scholars have noticed that the new amendments aim to strengthen parental duties, but warn that such amendments depend on a family-centered ideology that aims to consolidate the natural bond between children/juveniles and their parents, which may no longer be viable in the late modern society. See Shuen-Min Wang, "Some Thoughts on

the Combinatory Amendment of Children and Teenagers Welfare Act," *NPF Commentary* 092–046, National Policy Foundation, March 27, 2003.

44. The number of alien workers in Taiwan, totaling 150,000 in 1984, reached almost 400,000 by 2010. Gender distribution used to favor male alien workers but dovetailed toward the end of 2000 due to changes in the industrial structure as well as public fear that male alien workers may sexually assault local women. Last count in May 2010 put male alien workers at 150,000 and female alien workers at more than 240,000.

45. By the end of 2010, the total number of foreign brides in Taiwan totaled 440,000, out of which the brides from Mainland China make up 280,000.

46. After repeated petitions and protests, more than 3,000 Mainland brides took to the streets in Taipei on September 20, 2003, to demand human rights and equal treatment as the independence-minded government moved to change the waiting period of ID cards for Mainland brides from 8 years to 11 years.

47. For historical reasons, Mainland China and Russia (reminiscent of the Soviet Union) have long been considered Communist menaces to the world. Migrant sex workers from these countries who have come to Taiwan seeking better incomes are thus always characterized as, on the one hand, a demonstration of the thoroughly bankrupt rule of these regimes, but on the other hand, embodiments of conspiracies by these regimes to disrupt Taiwan's moral values and economic stability.

48. Since 1999, the Collective of Sex Workers and Supporters (COSWAS), the only prostitutes' rights group in Taiwan which evolved from the 1997 Taipei Alliance of Licensed Prostitutes (TALP), has struggled to keep the right-to-sex-work initiative alive in public debates. COSWAS has organized four International Action Forums on Sex Worker's Rights, three Sex Worker's Cultural Festivals, and numerous dialogs between sex workers and urban residents so as to educate the public about the realities of sex work and to push for decriminalization. Their struggle and efforts have not only effectively challenged the anti-sex-work agenda but also spurred decriminalization initiatives elsewhere in Asia (http://coswas.org/).

References

Barlow, Tani. "Asia, Gender and Scholarship Under Processes of Re-Regionalization." *Journal of Gender Studies*, No. 5 (2002): 1–14.

Berry, Chris, Fran Martin, and Audrey Yue (eds.). *Mobile Cultures: New Media and Queer Asia.* Durham, NC: Duke University Press, 2003.

Bland, Lucy. *Banishing the Beast: Sexuality and the Early Feminists.* New York: The New Press, 1995.

Chen, Mei-Hua. "Sex Work Rights." *Taiwan Human Rights Report 2002.* Taipei: Avant-Guard Press, 2003, pp. 103–124.

Chi, Hui-Jung, and Yi-Shi Zheng. "An Analysis of the Non-Profit Organizations' Strategies at Legislation." *Legislative Action by Taiwanese NGOs.* Taipei: Monitor Alliance over the Law to Suppress Sexual Transaction Involving Children and Juveniles, 2002, pp. 32–62.

Fang, Hsiao-Ding. "The Emergence and Transformation of Relief Rationale: 1987–1996." Paper presented at Revisiting East Asia: Third Convention of Cultural Studies Association, Taiwan, 2003.

Hershatter, Gail. *Dangerous Pleasure: Prostitution and Modernity in 20th-Century Shanghai.* Berkeley: University of California Press, 1997, 1998.

Ho, Josephine. "From Spice Girls to *Enjo-Kosai*: Formations of Teenage Girls' Sexualities in Taiwan." *InterAsia Journal of Cultural Studies* 4.2 (Aug. 2003): 325–336.

Lee, Yi-Yuan. "Teenage Problems among Aborigine Tribes During Social Change." *Journal of Institute of Ethnography*, 48 (1979): 1–29.

Rosen, Ruth. *The Lost Sisterhood: Prostitution in America, 1900–1918*. Baltimore and London: Johns Hopkins, 1982, 1983, 1994.

Shen, Mei-Jen. "Characteristics of the Law to Suppress Sexual Transaction Involving Children and Juveniles: An Introduction." *Legislative Action by Taiwanese NGOs*. Taipei: Monitor Alliance over the Law to Suppress Sexual Transaction Involving Children and Juveniles, 2002, pp. 16–31.

Walkowitz, Judith. *Prostitution and Victorian Society: Women, Class and the State*. Cambridge: Cambridge University Press, 1980.

Wang, Shuen-Min. "Some Thoughts on the Combinatory Amendment of Children and Teenagers Welfare Act." *NPF Commentary* 092–046, National Policy Foundation, March 27, 2003.

Zhao, Xiau-Ling. "Standing on the Shoulder of Patriarchy: The 'Anti'-Child Prostitute Movement." *The Awakening Monthly* 159 (1995): 12–14.

other. These opposing approaches result in a recurring debate whenever trafficking is discussed. The first view sees all sex work as a form of trafficking. The second holds that conditions of labor in all industries, including the sex industry, should be addressed. The debate as to whether prostitution is slavery per se, and therefore equivalent to trafficking in persons, was related most directly and vehemently to the definition of trafficking in persons in this protocol. I describe these debates and the influence exerted by various factions lobbying legislators and presenting at negotiations in order to interpret and criticize the discussion of this new legal document.

I analyze the definition of trafficking in the UN protocol with an eye to the use that is likely to be made of this document. Two Optional Protocols on smuggling and trafficking in persons address mobility, but with different levels of agency. Trafficking in persons defines a victim of crime rather than an agent, while smuggling necessarily implicates the person who has engaged the services of a smuggler. A smuggled person, like a trafficked person, has clandestinely crossed a border or been transported, but unlike trafficking, smuggling is not linked to work. A smuggled person is not a victim but a criminal, an illegal immigrant, an undocumented alien, while a trafficked person is assumed to be an innocent victim. This conception of agency divides in the imagination—if not in reality—along gender lines. This division is reflected in the title of the protocol addressing trafficking, which is the Optional Protocol to Prevent, Suppress and Punish Trafficking in Persons, *Especially Women and Children* (emphasis added). This contorted language was sought by a network of feminist organizations that view all sex work as a violation of women's human rights. They initially advocated for the title "Trafficking in Women and Children," omitting men entirely. The Smuggling Protocol has no such coda and no specific emphasis on gender. Smuggled migrants are assumed to be men seeking work elsewhere without proper documentation, while trafficked persons are assumed to be duped victims, usually women. This gendered distinction follows long-standing stereotypes of women as victims and men as less able to be victimized. As well as presenting a distorted view of women, such an ideology harms men. Trafficked men are invisible and their situations continue to be less recognized and therefore more difficult to address. These distinctions may also significantly affect enforcement, depending on the way that they are interpreted. They are also visible in laypersons' interpretations and in the crafting of this protocol.

The association of trafficking with victimization is commonly reflected in the language used, where the term "victims of trafficking" is frequently encountered. This may in part be encouraged by law enforcement agencies—in dealings with law enforcement, it is always preferable to be perceived as a victim of crime rather than a criminal.

The use of "victims of trafficking" rather than "trafficked persons" may serve as a handy guide that helps to make it clear who is a criminal to arrest and who is a victim to protect.

Another problem with the use of the term "victim" is that it fails to reflect the complexity of this issue or the experiences of all people who have undertaken to leave their homes and families to pursue a better future via economic migration (Finkel 2001; Human Rights Watch 2000; Skrobanek, Boonpakdi, and Janthakeero 1997). Trafficked persons are not simply and solely victims; they are often the go-getters of their home communities. It is ironic that in this framework the ambitious and industrious poor who undertake migration are unrewarded, while "pathetic" victims garner greater sympathy.

This insistence on the title of victim has historic precedent. DuBois and Gordon (1984) wrote that feminists of earlier eras

> consistently exaggerated the coerciveness of prostitution. In their eagerness to identify the social structural forces encouraging prostitution, they denied the prostitute any role other than that of passive victim. They insisted that the women involved were sexual innocents, women who "fell" into illicit sex. They assumed that prostitution was so degraded that no woman could freely choose it, not even with the relative degree of freedom with which she could choose to be a wife or a wage earner. (33)

Definitions of this sort, with their focus on women's role as victims and on the coercive nature of the sex industry, are convenient for those whose definition of traffic in persons views traffic that does not involve the sex industry as being, at best, ancillary to the phenomenon of trafficking. But such a restrictive viewpoint touches on only one aspect of trafficking, and plays down the real pivotal issue; namely the question of migration.

Migration lies at the heart of international traffic in persons. Trafficked persons are for the most part migrants—usually undocumented—seeking work elsewhere, who find themselves in untenable working conditions. A typical recent trafficking case involved some dozens of Asian men and women relocated to the US territory of the Northern Mariana Islands for work in sweatshops and brothels, for which they were either inadequately paid or not paid at all, and were brutalized by their employers if they dared to protest about their conditions. Sex featured in the Marianas case in that some of those trafficked were employed in brothels, but many trafficked persons were not involved in the sex industry at all. Testimony to the US Congress by the Director of the Global Survival Network described thousands of people in debt-bondage and slavery-like conditions in the garment industry.[3] The crucial factors that determine a case of trafficking are the conditions in which trafficked persons find themselves, and the means—deception, coercion, outright enslavement—by which they are brought into those conditions. These are the criteria that are used to distinguish, for example, cases of smuggling from cases of trafficking.

UNITED NATIONS PROCEDURES AND PARTICIPANTS

Lobbying Blocs

Lobbying factions at the deliberative meetings during the drafting of the UN protocol were drawn largely from two main non-governmental organizations working with outside allies. One bloc was led primarily by the International Human Rights Law Group (IHRLG), which worked with the Global Alliance Against Traffick in Women (GAATW), Women in Law and Development in Africa (WILDAF), and the Asian Women's Human Rights Council (AWHRC). These organizations and others distributed documents with recommendations for the protocol under the name of the Human Rights Caucus. The other main bloc, calling itself the Human Rights Network, was chiefly represented by the Coalition Against Trafficking in Women (CATW), working with the European Women's Lobby (EWL), Soroptimist International (SI), the International Human Rights Federation (IHRF), the International Abolitionist Federation (IAF), and Equality Now (EN).

The Human Rights Caucus and the Human Rights Network held diametrically opposed views about whether prostitution is inherently trafficking in persons. CATW and their Network allies proposed an abolitionist approach to sex work to make the sex industry more illegal and to prosecute and punish men involved as clients and otherwise. They sought specifically to include prostitution and other sex work in the definition of trafficking in persons. The International Human Rights Law Group and other members of the Caucus sought to separate sex work and trafficking, and to define trafficking based upon working conditions. In this, they were influenced by the groundbreaking inclusion in their ranks of sex workers and advocates for sex workers' rights. The approach of the Caucus reflected the position of the sex workers' rights advocates, who recognize sex work as a form of work, albeit a difficult one that is not always performed in ideal conditions.[4] While sex workers' rights advocates are the first to recognize that there are abuses within the sex industry, they seek to correct and to address the problems not by abolition, but by improving conditions and affording legal recognition to the sex industry. The Caucus also advocated for the inclusion of other human rights protections such as witness protection and health care.

The issues discussed in this protocol, especially whether to define prostitution as trafficking per se, evoked emotional responses. It is difficult to convey the rancor that existed between feminist factions addressing trafficking in persons. However, malice between feminists on the issue of prostitution is neither new nor unique, and can take extraordinary forms. For example, an earlier Coalition Against Trafficking in Women newsletter (1998–2000) described Jo Doezema, Marjan Wijers, and myself, all members of the Human Rights Caucus, as "pro-prostitution" advocates. This language is akin to the use of the term "pro-abortion" by activists who seek to ban abortion. It is also similar to earlier factional infighting within the feminist movement. Alice Echols, in her article about the sexuality debates in the larger feminist movement, described the use of similar discrediting and silencing tactics when she wrote

> Anti-pornography feminists have tried to silence their intra-movement critics with the same red-baiting tactics of feminist capitalism. Recently, Kathy Barry characterized the feminist opposition to the anti-pornography movement as a cabal of leftist lesbian and heterosexual women who want to destroy the movement so that "male leftists can continue their sexual abuse of women without fear of censure." (Echols 1984, 54)

It is unfortunate to note that such tactics are reproduced twenty years later.

Good-faith efforts to overcome factionalism failed, even on issues that every NGO agreed upon. In one attempt to find common ground for working together, my organization invited the International Abolitionist Federation, a member of the Network, to jointly distribute suggestions for the inclusion of human rights protections for trafficked persons.[5] These suggestions were not a point of dispute between NGO factions because they were not related to the definition of trafficking or similarly loaded issues. But even this olive branch was declined.

I was disappointed that the Network made no efforts to address human rights protections for trafficked persons. In fact, when one Caucus representative asked a Network representative why her group made no efforts to promote human rights protections in the protocol, she was told that the Network chose to focus their limited resources on the definition of trafficking alone.[6] This response suggested that the Human Rights Network prioritized anti-prostitution activism over and above human rights. This order of priorities prevented NGOs from presenting a united front, which in all likelihood prevented the inclusion of mandatory human rights protections in the protocol.[7]

The Human Rights Network and the Human Rights Caucus were both largely composed of self-proclaimed feminist organizations, or organizations with feminist leanings. Their stances on what are often deemed women's issues, particularly those addressing female bodily autonomy, such as reproductive rights, abortion, family planning, and promoting the use of condoms against HIV, were generally similar. Yet despite the potential common ground, the two groups were most often bitterly divided. This division contrasts dramatically with the rapprochement that took place between the Human Rights Network and American right-wing and religious organizations. On the face of it, these two groups should have practically no point of agreement, as the position of the conservative organizations on the issues described in the paragraph above is usually diametrically opposed to that of any feminist organization. Yet the Human Rights Network was able to join with conservative American politicians in promoting a definition of trafficking in persons formulated in such terms as to include prostitution. Apparently, the need for an alliance on this one issue proved stronger than all the other potential sources of disagreement.[8]

This outwardly incongruous alliance was most apparent in media pieces advocating their position. Media pressure as a lobbying tactic usually took the form of op-ed pieces and letters in large newspapers timed to coincide with decisions on particular issues. Both the Caucus and the Network used their media contacts in the United States to promote their views. The US delegation to the UN grew progressively more cautious in their speech during the last few meetings as any comments favorable to the Caucus position were presented as "pro-prostitution" to media and government representatives by Network members and affiliates. William Bennett and Charles Colson, noted American conservative standard-bearers,[9] wrote that "Over the past few months the Clinton administration has lobbied for the United Nations to adopt a protocol that would lend legitimacy to prostitution" and "the White House delegation has worked to narrow the definition of sexual trafficking, in a way that would allow certain prostitution rings to flourish" (Bennett and Colson 2000). This was countered by a letter from Ann Jordan, Director of the Anti-trafficking Initiative of the International Human Rights Law Group and a member of the Human Rights Caucus, in which she highlighted the inaccuracies of these statements, adding that debating about prostitution would bring about the collapse of these negotiations and result in a lost opportunity to combat crime and assist the victims of crime. Echoing the Bennett and Colson view, a *New York Post* article (De Russy 2000) erroneously stated, "Hillary Clinton chairs a presidential task force that is lobbying the United Nations to redefine prostitution in a way that would effectively legalize it—and make it impossible to fight the 'sexual slave trade.'" The *Los Angeles Times* ran an article advocating a definition of trafficking that included workplace abuses, citing a 1995 case in which 75 people were enslaved in a sweatshop (Cho and Salas 2000). Activists on both sides of the debate were aware that media pieces carried considerable weight, with the abolitionist movement being particularly adept at using this tool, albeit at the price of making some strange associations.[10]

The nature of the alliances made and positions taken also became clear in meetings between the US delegation and NGO representatives. In one meeting, James Puglio, a member of the US delegation with a strong law enforcement background in his capacity as Special Assistant to the Assistant Secretary of the International Narcotics and Law Enforcement Department of the US State Department, stated that the inclusion of a definition of sexual exploitation would prevent any accord and so would be scrapped. The Network representative angrily said that she was disappointed, adding that Senator Jesse Helms would also be very disappointed with this.[11] At this time, Jesse Helms—a conservative American politician most famous for the 1973 Helms Amendment prohibiting the use of US funds for abortion services outside the US—wrote to then-US Secretary of State Madeleine Albright:

> I am being deluged with telephone calls, faxes and letters about the incredible US position in the UN negotiations relating to the [Trafficking Protocol]. Those contacting me are shocked, as am I, that your State Department negotiators are on the verge of reversing the official US opposition to prostitution.[12]

These contacts illustrate the "strange bedfellows" phenomenon in which certain feminists work with the radical right (Chancer 1998). The phenomenon continues: More recently, the conservative, anti-choice Representative Chris Smith of New Jersey sponsored new funding restrictions for the US Global HIV/AIDS Fund, apparently motivated by the same conflation of trafficking and sex work. The continued collaboration between opponents of abortion and opponents of sex-work projects reflects the strong focus on sexuality and women's autonomy in policies addressing trafficking.

Definition of Trafficking in Persons for This Document

One of the most hotly disputed elements of the protocol was Article 3, which defines trafficking in persons. Ideologies resembling those of the NGO blocs were visible among the different government delegations, leading to protracted discussion of the definition of trafficking. Consensus was extremely difficult to achieve. Rather than list all the proposed definitions, I will use examples of the more contentious dialogue.

Debates about the definition of trafficking typically centered on whether to include all sex work, an issue on which the different camps were deeply divided. This was demonstrated not only by the expression of opposing views but also by the sacrifices that proponents were willing to make to ideology. The discussion of prostitution eclipsed the plight of trafficked persons—including men—in other industries. Additionally, examples of a willingness to sacrifice women's autonomy were evident during these discussions. For some feminists, sex work and the exchange of sex for goods or money, as in prostitution or possibly even dating, is a re-inforcement of male social elevation over female. While most feminists and certainly most women do not take this much further than acknowledging that an exchange for sex exists and that they may not approve, a minority make this a core issue. This is reflected in some of the recommendations which were offered for the definition of trafficking.

The sacrifices that certain factions were willing to make in the name of ideology were illustrated by some of the emotionally charged pleas made on the floor of the UN in favor of certain proposed definitions. For example, a written suggestion from the Philippine delegation was circulated on June 6, 2000, which suggested a definition of trafficking that included the formula, "with or without consent of the victim by legal or illegal means, for all purposes of sexual exploitation including prostitution, marriage, employment..."[13] If adopted, such a definition would have criminalized as trafficking not merely prostitution, but also marriage and even employ-ment. While this is clearly an extreme, not to say ludicrous example, it is one of the dangers of an obsessive and myopic focus on prostitution that it opens the door to the willing sacrifice of other essential liberties and rights in the name of eradicating prostitution.

In a UN protocol, definitions necessarily afford a certain interpretive leeway for enforcement by signatory nations, in order to allow consensus to be achieved in such a large meeting. The Trafficking Protocol does not prohibit additional measures and/or sterner enforcement, thereby allow-ing signatory nations to enforce additional domestic legislation regarding these crimes and to assess punishment for them as they see fit. Such an allowance for domestic legislation affords great variation in the possible enforcement of this document nation by nation. Thus nations are able to legislate prostitution as they see fit. Australia, Germany, the Netherlands, and New Zealand, among others, were very clear that they would not sign a protocol that would require them to change their national laws to outlaw prostitution. Their sentiments on this matter are in line with the Human Rights Caucus. Similarly, nations such as Iran, Iraq, the US, and the Vatican would not have signed a protocol requiring them to decriminalize prostitution in their jurisdictions.

The definition of trafficking adopted in the protocol specifies that the threat or use of force or deception is a necessary component of traf-ficking persons into any situation. It goes on to make clear that consent is irrelevant when these means have been used. In other words, a person can consent to work but not to slavery or servitude. The definition ad-ditionally specifies that any recruitment, transportation, or harboring of a person under 18 is to be considered trafficking in persons, regardless of the means used. The inclusion of men in this definition constitutes a significant legal breakthrough.

The issue of consent, crucial to the definition, provided fertile ground for the exercise of agendas. Under international law, children—defined as any person "under 18 years of age"—are not able to give consent. During the October 2000 meetings, a member of the Philippine delegation who is also the director of the CATW in the Philippines made an intervention (spoken suggestion), the apparent intent of which was to redefine prostitutes as children. IHRLG representative Melynda Barnhart summarized this statement by saying that the delegate "essentially said that [for] all women making decisions that [this delegate] doesn't agree with, i.e., prostitutes, others should have the legal ability to override their decisions."[14]

Suggestions of this kind echo the way in which some earlier feminists patronized other women during the white-slavery panic of nearly a century ago. In 1913, Jeannette Young Norton, for example, wrote: "The big sisters of the world [want the] chance to protect the little and weaker sisters, by surrounding them with the right laws for them to obey for their own good."[15] The written proposal, distributed October 2, 2000, was significantly refined, but seemed also to include people with disabilities.

> Article 2bis(d) [this article is numbered 3 in the final document] Definition of Child
>
> "Child" shall mean any person under 18 years of age provided that those over 18 years of age but unable to fully protect themselves from abuse, neglect, cruelty, exploitation due to mental or physical incapacity be considered for the purpose of this protocol.

Whatever the intentions behind this proposed definition, it is legally very dangerous. During the 1950s, women in the United States could be institutionalized for being "promiscuous" (Keefe 1994). It would be all too easy, using the definition above, to see a return to that state of affairs with adult women being judged unable to "fully protect themselves" due to "mental or physical incapacity" if they engage in unapproved activities such as promiscuity or prostitution. The definition betrays a readiness to sacrifice many of women's hard-won gains, including independence, legal majority, and the ability to make enforceable contracts, solely in order to render prostitution more criminal.

Definitions of this kind, in which the normal presumption of adult autonomy can be overruled by a subjective, external judgment as to the desirability of an activity, are essentially perilous. They call to mind Rubin's "brainwash theory," which "explains erotic diversity by assuming that some sexual acts are so disgusting that no one would willingly perform them. Therefore, the reasoning goes, anyone who does so must have been forced or fooled" (Rubin 1984, 306).

Abolitionist reasoning proceeds from the same starting point. Prostitution as a condition is assumed to be so inherently intolerable that no rational person could freely choose it for themselves; therefore if anyone appears to have chosen it for themselves, it can only indicate that they are either not rational, or they are victims of coercion or deception; that is to say, victims of trafficking. The perils of such an argument lie precisely in the way that it opens the door to a paternalistic interpretation of "what is best for women." Such interpretations have historically had a very negative impact on women; the gains made by the modern feminist movement have been in large part concerned with escaping from such paternalism and forcing the recognition of women's autonomy and their ability to make their own decisions. To roll back those gains in the interests of pursuing a war on prostitution is perilous indeed.

New USAID Funding Policy

Feminists have shaped not only international law, but also United States foreign policy. Here too, ideological positions have led to some strange alliances and even to efforts directed toward the defunding or discrediting of projects whose effectiveness is undeniable but whose positions are unpalatable. Ironically, even while trafficking is a key concern, it is sometimes precisely those sex-work projects that are recognized for their excellent and effective anti-trafficking projects that may find themselves under attack.

Once again, certain feminists have chosen to work with far-right politicians and other conservative figures to promote an agenda that actually limits women instead of empowering them. Their allies in this case include groups such as the Vatican, the Salvation Army, and other religious groups; their targets include organizations whose efficacy in combating human rights abuses of sex workers and trafficked persons has been confirmed by their selection to receive funding from the United States Agency for International Development (USAID). It is very clear that grassroots efforts have affected policy.

For example, on June 19, 2002, the abolitionist feminist Donna Hughes addressed the US House Committee on International Relations specifically to denounce sex-work projects that she declared "promote prostitution," and to demand efforts to prevent funding of these organizations. The organizations named included the Nobel Prize–winning Doctors Without Borders, as well as the International Human Rights Law Group. Hughes has since followed this up with a number of press pieces and conference talks. Since then, the US administration has been very clear in its determination that projects that "promote prostitution" will not receive further anti-trafficking funds from USAID. Unfortunately, this seems to include projects that work with sex workers in productive ways to promote both their human rights and their health, including working to prevent the spread of HIV.

The shift in focus from trafficking in persons to attacking funding for sex-work projects indicates an interest in promoting anti-prostitution ideology at the expense of health and human rights, particularly the health and human rights of women and others in the sex industry. Whatever the nature of the ongoing debate, ideology should not be permitted to over-ride effective HIV prevention efforts or to interfere with treatment of HIV-positive people. Unfortunately, that is exactly what is occurring with these vindictive efforts to defund sex-work projects. There is as yet no way to quantify the number of infections such policy will promote, yet it is clear that sex workers are put at risk and equally clear that they are not the only people to be adversely affected by such misguided policy. The children and families of sex workers and their clients will all be affected, and there will be a knock-on effect in the broader area of public health. When the alliance between certain feminists and American right-wing politicians affects HIV prevention for the worse, it ceases to be merely incongruous and becomes positively dangerous.

The recent sea change in the administration's attitude was reflected in a cable sent in 2003, signed by Colin Powell and circulated to USAID field officers. The Powell cable stipulated that organizations amend their websites to promote abstinence over condom use in the struggle against HIV and AIDS. This gained widespread notice; a less noted stipulation was that USAID anti-trafficking and other funding should not support sex-work projects, needle exchange, and abortion services.[16] These activities are all legal in the US; it is the Bush administration's position, however, that they must not be supported outside the US, regardless of their proven effectiveness in saving lives or improving public health.

The language of the Powell cable—which stresses the unsuitability of non-abolitionist sex-work projects as recipients of US aid, before going on to stress that taxpayer funds must not be used to support "trafficking of women and girls"—reveals that, once again, the conflation of prostitution with trafficking has resurfaced (so too has the restriction of trafficking to females; the cable does not explicitly forbid using US taxpayer monies to support trafficking of males). If this conflation has proven so durable in the minds of many people, it is in part due to its promotion by certain anti-trafficking activists who have worked very hard to reinforce this association to Congress and the public, through speaking engagements and in print. It is ironic that the activists in question are often strong radical feminists, when the consequence of their efforts is the encouragement of a general protectionist stance toward women, a stance that is more than likely to be highly detrimental to women in general.

This ideological agenda has the potential to affect effective projects whose success has been widely recognized. Projects that involve sex workers are the most successful at combating abuses within the sex industry around the world, but because such projects often advocate legalization of prostitution, they may find themselves cut off from funding. An example of a project that may suffer under this new policy is the Durbar Mahila Samanwaya Committee of Kolkata, more widely known as the Sonagachi Project. This is considered one of the strongest success stories of HIV prevention among vulnerable populations in South Asia, and USAID has supported their presentations at the International Conference on HIV and AIDS in the past. The negative ramifications of excluding exemplary projects such as the Sonagachi Project from USAID contracts would be enormous.

The Sonagachi Project is one of many projects that exemplify pragmatic and effective approaches to reducing not only transmission of HIV, but also abuses such as trafficking within sex work. The prevalence of HIV among sex workers is far lower in Kolkata than elsewhere in India. Their anti-trafficking initiative relies on the participation of red-light-district residents, especially sex workers, to prevent trafficking into the red-light districts. As of June 15, 2001, 43 trafficked persons had been assisted by the Sonagachi Project, 35 of whom were minors (Durbar Mahila Samanwaya Committee 2001).

Another potential victim of current policy is Empower, a Thai project that enables sex workers to get high school equivalency diplomas. Diplomas are important for those who want to leave the sex industry and seek other work. If Empower's attitude to sex work disqualifies it from receiving funding under the terms of the Powell cable, the people who will be hurt are not policy makers, lobbyists, or activists—they are poor women far from the people who make these decisions, women whose voices and needs were not considered when these decisions were made.

The potential ramifications of the policy are far-reaching. Sex workers' groups are at the forefront of proposing specific, practical solutions to the many problems faced by sex workers. A policy that defunds these projects because they fail to measure up to the ideological yardstick used by the current administration will harm the health of sex workers, their human rights, and their ability to organize. It is likely to deny them education and vocational training that would allow them to exit the sex industry.

Sex workers are not the only group likely to be affected by policy that is formulated based on a conflation of prostitution and trafficking. In the first place, whether the administration likes it or not, sex workers are members of a community that includes other people, including the clients or dependents of sex workers. Any decision that impacts their health or economic options also impacts others. Moreover, as the logic of the Powell cable suggests strongly that the administration has "bought in" to a worldview that includes a restrictive focus on sex trafficking as the principal area of concern in trafficking, there is a real danger that other anti-trafficking initiatives dealing with less "sexy" areas, such as trafficking into sweatshops or domestic labor, or trafficking of males, will also find themselves starved of support.

The list of potential losers continues. While specific groups may be directly targeted because their outlook is incompatible with that of the Bush administration, other sex-worker rights organizations around the world are also likely to suffer by association.

The current trend in policy is likely to affect other organizations as well. However distasteful the idea may be to certain groups, sex work is a form of labor. It is also a significant portion of the economy: the ILO estimates that the sex sector accounts for between 2 and 14 percent of GDP of four Asian countries; namely Indonesia, Malaysia, the Philippines, and Thailand (Lim 1998, 7). In common with other economic sectors of marginal legality or low social acceptability it also employs many undocumented workers. A crackdown on sex work may be implemented through a more general attack on sectors employing undocumented workers or, conversely, broad initiatives to crack down on undocumented labor may gain impetus from a policy that favors repression of sex work. In either case, unions and other groups that support undocumented workers will feel the chill of the new policy.

So too will organizations dealing with migrants. Undocumented workers are clustered most heavily in particular industry sectors, such as the sex industry, agriculture, construction, and clothing production. A large proportion of these undocumented workers are migrants, drawn into these specific sectors because they lack the formal qualifications (educational or administrative) necessary for entry to other sectors. If organizations working with migrants are seen (rightly or wrongly) to be facilitating clandestine or illegal employment, they too are likely to be singled out for increased scrutiny, legal harassment, or withdrawal of support.

Feminist groups that address gendered labor issues are a third group that will potentially be affected by present policies. The sex industry employs more women than men, so conditions in the industry are necessarily of interest to feminist groups. But if the formula that they propose for improving conditions of female workers happens to be at odds with the prevailing policy, they are also likely to suffer negative consequences.

The impact of new directions in policy is felt initially by groups that work in specific sectors but ultimately, and far more damagingly, by workers in those sectors. Punishing unions or NGOs for being "out of step" with policy begins by depriving workers of services or support offered by those groups. It also hampers the attempts of those groups to address problems such as the exploitative conditions (including low wages and unsafe working environments) endured by marginalized workers across the sector. Furthermore, because no one sector exists in isolation, trends in one sector affect others. Low wages for undocumented workers in one field will depress wages across all sectors for all workers, documented or undocumented (Kwong 1997). Lastly, the sex industry supports other individuals or sectors. Sex workers have dependents, including children, and sex businesses are supported or serviced by other businesses that are not part of the sex sector but are nonetheless economically dependent on it. For example, a 1997 survey in Thailand suggested that of approximately 100,000 workers in just under 8,000 establishments providing sexual services, more than a third were "support staff" (Lim 1998, 9).

The sex sector does not exist in isolation. Issues surrounding the sex industry are part of a larger complex of issues related to the labor market as a whole, particularly with respect to gender issues and migration. As a consequence, any policy that targets the sex industry will necessarily have a much broader impact, as measures proposed to address one particular sector "spill over" to affect other areas. Trafficking in persons has a long history of conflation with the sex industry. Responses to trafficking that exclusively focus on the sex industry affect a broad range of people and issues, sometimes in unanticipated ways.

Recent years have witnessed significant progress in expanding approaches to trafficking in persons to address working conditions and to include men. In this light, the new US and USAID policy represents a step backward. This return to a restrictive focus on women trafficked into the sex industry is illustrated by a February 2003 conference entitled "Path-breaking Strategies in the Global Fight Against Sex Trafficking," which was sponsored by the US government and attended by international activists. Although mandated "to underscore the commitment of the United States to fighting trafficking in human beings,"[17] this conference exclusively addressed the sex industry, neglecting the larger numbers of people trafficked into domestic work, construction, agriculture, and sweatshops. This backsliding is further illustrated by the fact that USAID anti-trafficking efforts are now managed by the office of Women in Development—trafficking is once again a "women's issue." Male trafficked persons, or those whose experiences do not neatly fall within a narrow focus on sex trafficking, risk being left out in the cold.

The current attitude toward trafficking, promoted in part by specific groups within the women's movement and their *pro tem* right-wing allies and expressed by statements of policy such as the Powell cable, has the potential for doing serious harm. Because of this attitude, organizations with a proven, positive impact at the grassroots level risk losing support because their policies are politically unpalatable to the current US administration and those who have influence over it. Other organizations, while not in direct conflict with Washington's new directions, also risk being starved of support, simply because their primary areas of concern fall outside an increasingly narrow focus on one aspect of the trafficking problem. These ideological policy shifts are not abstract or without consequences—they translate to a very real human impact, and the potential to cause significant suffering to real people.

CONCLUSIONS

Trafficked persons have gained and lost from new attitudes toward trafficking. Progress has been made in the expansion of trafficking to address slavery-like conditions more generally. This has drawn attention to a variety of cases, including ones involving sweatshops, Thai children, and Bangladeshi domestic workers. But trafficked persons and sex workers have also lost ground if prevention efforts by sex-work projects are defunded. All of Asia and beyond will lose out if anti-trafficking efforts are undermined because sex workers are deliberately deprived of access to friendly and supportive services. The most effective sex-work projects are precisely those which address sex work as labor, such as the much heralded Sonagachi Project in India and SHAKTI in Bangladesh, both of which have been noted as "best practices" projects by UNAIDS. Yet these are also the types of projects that the US administration is not currently amenable to funding.

New US policy on funding is part of a continuation of the debate on whether sex work is trafficking in persons per se. This recurrent ideological schism is seen whenever trafficking is discussed,[18] including the recent deliberations of delegates to the UN working to define trafficking for the UN Optional Protocol. The debate hinges on two opposing positions. One position recognizes trafficking of all kinds as a grievous violation of human rights, but holds that sex work is real work and needs to be addressed as such. The other position views sex work itself as a human rights violation and that policy on trafficking is a vehicle to use to address this violation. There is also a third view on the issue, which was neatly summarized by Meillón (2001, 156–157). This view recognizes that forums such as conferences or negotiations of legal protocols are not arenas in which it is possible to conclude one way or another, and that they are therefore not the right places for such discussion. This third view has come to the fore in other discussions of trafficking, including the negotiations of the Trafficking Protocol. This possibly pragmatic realization led to the final definition, which left the legislation of prostitution to the individual nations, rather than capturing it as part of a UN-backed definition of trafficking.

Short-sighted policy in this area risks causing greater damage. Policies that restrict travel, and especially women's travel, actually encourage the practice of trafficking in persons by closing legal avenues of migration. Would-be migrants of both sexes are forced to fall back on the services of traffickers and smugglers, increasing the potential risks that they run (Meillón 2001; Kwong 1997). New restrictions are evident throughout the world, whether they take the form of an increase in scrutiny of young women leaving certain nations, such as Thailand and other Asian nations, or entering them, such as Japan, or simply increased control of borders in general, as in the case of the United States.

Despite a continuing tendency to see trafficking simply in terms of "white slavery," it is a complex issue that involves issues of migration and labor. Faced with this complexity, some advocates see a need to simplify the issue. The temptation of simpler analysis is obvious but it comes at the expense of specificity and accuracy. While simplifying issues may help some people understand them, this is to the detriment of complex problems—an overly simplistic solution is not a solution but a seed for new problems. The anti-prostitution stance is an example of oversimplified and inefficient analysis that claims a moral high ground while obscuring the plight of trafficked men and women in other industries. This is too great a sacrifice. When this attitude manifests itself in policy decisions affecting international aid, it comes at a very real human cost. Cambodian sex workers use the slogan "Don't talk to me about sewing machines, talk to me about workers rights" to emphasize the need to address working conditions within the sex industry. Their voices—incompatible with an abolitionist stance that is unable to accommodate the idea of better conditions within the sex industry as a valid human rights issue—have been ignored by US policy makers.

Despite protracted debate about trafficking and prostitution, there are reasons for cautious optimism. Radhika Coomaraswamy, UN Special Rapporteur on Violence Against Women, has rightly referred to the protocol's definition of trafficking as a "breakthrough"[19] because it established trafficking as a crime that extends beyond the realm of prostitution. This was made possible by a recent shift toward consideration of actual conditions and crimes against persons, rather than focusing narrowly on sexuality and morality. Recent US foreign-policy shifts have taken a dangerous turn, one that has its counterpart in trends directed at reducing women's autonomy in other areas, particularly in the field of reproductive rights, and in the paternalistic approach to new funding to combat HIV and AIDS. But this is in part balanced by the existence of a growing base of supporters working to direct policy in more positive and enlightened directions. These supporters have developed an increased recognition of human rights issues and of trafficking as a multifaceted problem of which sex trafficking is only one aspect, and by no means the defining one.

NOTES

1. United Nations 1949 Convention for the Suppression of the Traffick in Persons and of the Exploitation of the Prostitution of Others, which came into effect in 1950.

2. The Protocol was crafted by the UN Crimes Commission, to supplement the Convention Against Transnational Organized Crime. I attended these meetings in 1999 and 2000 as a lobbyist with the Human Rights Caucus, representing the International Human Rights Law Group and the Asian Women's Human Rights Council.

3. Testimony by Steven R. Galster, Global Survival Network, before the House Committee on Energy and Natural Resources, September 16, 1999, concerning the US Commonwealth of the Northern Mariana Islands, http://www.house.gov/resources/106cong/fullcomm/99sep16/galster.htm.

4. See Sprinkle, and Leigh, both in Nagle (1997). See also "Addressing Sex Work as Labor," presented by the author to the U. N. Working Group on Contemporary Forms of Slavery during the June 1999 NGO Consultation. The text of this talk is available at http://www.swimw.org.

5. This invitation was intended to build bridges after an unpleasant incident. In lobbying, I left a note with suggestions about the definition of trafficking on the desk of the Caucus-friendly delegate from an antipodean nation. A representative of the International Abolitionist Federation, a member of the Network, asked for a copy of the note, and I replied honestly that I had only enough for specific government representatives and not other NGOs. When I returned to the room, the note was gone and the delegates had not yet returned. I confronted the IAF representative and she took the paper I had left from her purse and returned it to me.

6. Private conversations and correspondence with a Human Rights Caucus representative.

7. Human rights protections are included with qualifying language like "in appropriate cases" in articles 6 through 8 of the Protocol. The anticipated consequences of this weak language are described in Jordan (2002).

8. It should be noted that this is not the first time that such an alliance has been observed. Feminists have worked with Christian groups on trafficking in Victorian England and America (Walkowitz 1983).

9. Bennett served in the administrations of Ronald Reagan and George H. W. Bush. Colson served seven months in prison for actions related to the Watergate scandal.

10. For example, Donna Hughes, former webhost of the abolitionist Coalition Against Trafficking in Women, continues to publish regularly in the extreme right-wing *National Review.*

11. Private conversation with a Caucus member from the International Human Rights Law Group.

12. Letter from Senator Jesse Helms to Secretary of State Madeleine Albright, January 2000, on file with author.

13. Text copy of the intervention circulated by the Philippine delegation during the UN Crimes Commission meetings, Vienna, June 2000, on file with author.

14. Discussions with Melynda Barnhart, International Human Rights Law Group representative, October–December 2000.

15. Norton, Jeannette Young. "Women Builders of Civilization." *Women's Political Civilization,* September 1, 1913: p. 5. Quoted in Dubois and Gordon 1984, 38.

16. The text read:

Organizations advocating prostitution as an employment choice or which advocate or support the legalization of prostitution are not appropriate partners for USAID anti-trafficking grants and contracts, or sub-grants and sub-contracts

and continued:

> *Careful review of all programs and publications should ensure that* USAID *is not perceived as using US taxpayer funds to support activities that contradict our laws or policies, including trafficking of women and girls, legalization of drugs, injecting drug use, and abortion.*

The first part of this is repeated on p. 9 of "Trafficking in Persons. The USAID Strategy for Response," February 2003, www.usaid.gov/wid/pubs/pd-abx-358-final.pdf.

 17. http://www.state.gov/g/tip/c8628.htm.

 18. This has been the case at other meetings, such as Beijing + 5 (Mitchell 2000) and the United Nations Working Group on Contemporary Forms of Slavery (Ditmore, forthcoming).

 19. Talk delivered at Columbia University Law School, April 2001.

REFERENCES

Bennett, William J., and Colson, Charles W. "The Clintons Shrug At Sex Trafficking." *Wall Street Journal*, January 10, 2000.

Chancer, Lynn. *Reconcilable Differences*. Berkeley: University of California, 1998.

Cho, Hae Jung, and Salas, Angelica. "Trafficking in Humans Isn't Behind Us Yet: A Proposed Bill Is the First Step in Combating the Modern-day Version of Indentured Servitude." *LA Times*, February 11, 2000. http://www.latimes. com/news/comment/20000211/t000013596.html.

Coalition Against Trafficking in Women. "CATW Debates Pro-Prostitution NGOS." *Coalition Report* v. 5–6 (1998–2000): 8–9.

De Russy, Candace. "Clinton & the Slave Trade." *New York Post*, July 12, 2000. http://www.nypost.com/postopinion/opedcolumnists/7735.htm.

Ditmore, Melissa. "Feminists and Sex Workers: Working Together." In Amy Elaine Wakeland, editor, *Feminist Visions for the Twenty-first Century*. Lanham, MD: Rowman and Littlefield (forthcoming).

———. "Addressing Sex Work as Labor," presented by the author to the UN Working Group on Contemporary Forms of Slavery during the June 1999 NGO Consultation. http://www.swimw.org.

DuBois, Ellen Carol, and Gordon, Linda. "Seeking Ecstasy on the Battlefield: Danger and Pleasure in Nineteenth-century Feminist Sexual Thought." In Carole Vance, editor, *Pleasure and Danger*. Boston: Routledge & Kegan Paul, 1984: 31–49.

Durbar Mahila Samanwaya Committee. Background Report on Trafficking, 2001.

Echols, Alice. "The Taming of the Id." In Carole Vance, editor, *Pleasure and Danger*. Boston: Routledge & Kegan Paul, 1984: 50–72.

Finkel, Michael. "Is Youssef Male a Slave?" *New York Times Magazine*, November 18, 2001: 43–47, 62.

Galster, Steven R. Testimony before the House Committee on Energy and Natural Resources, September 16, 1999. http://www.house.gov/resources/106cong/fullcomm/99sep16/galster.htm.

Human Rights Watch. *Owed Justice: Thai Women Trafficked into Debt Bondage in Japan*. New York: Human Rights Watch, 2000.

Jordan, Ann. *The Annotated Guide to the Complete UN Trafficking Protocol*. Washington, DC: International Human Rights Law Group, 2002. http://www.hrlawgroup.org/initiatives/trafficking_persons/default.asp.

Keefe, Timothy. *Some of My Best Friends Are Naked*. San Francisco: Barbary Coast, 1994.

Kwong, Peter. *Forbidden Workers*. New York: New Press, 1997.

Leigh, Carol, AKA Scarlot Harlot. "Inventing Sex Work." In Jill Nagle, editor, *Whores and Other Feminists*. New York: Routledge, 1997: 223–231.

Lim, Lin Leam, ed. *The Sex Sector*. Geneva: International Labour Organisation, 1998.

Meillón, Cynthia, editor, in collaboration with Bunch, Charlotte. *Holding on to the Promise: Women's Human Rights and the Beijing + 5 Review.* New Brunswick, NJ: Rutgers, 2001.

Mitchell, Grace. "Disputed Subjects in the Global Movement for Sex Workers' Rights." 2000. Unpublished paper.

Nagle, Jill, ed. *Whores and Other Feminists.* New York: Routledge, 1997.

Norton, Jeannette Young. "Women Builders of Civilization." *Women's Political Civilization,* September 1, 1913: 5. Quoted in DuBois, Ellen Carol, and Gordon, Linda. "Seeking Ecstasy on the Battlefield: Danger and Pleasure in Nineteenth-century Feminist Sexual Thought." In Carole Vance, editor, *Pleasure and Danger.* Boston: Routledge & Kegan Paul, 1984: 31–49.

Rubin, Gayle. "Thinking Sex." In Carole Vance, editor, *Pleasure and Danger.* Boston: Routledge & Kegan Paul, 1984: 267–319.

Skrobanek, Siriporn, Boonpakdi, Nattaya, and Janthakeero, Chutima. *The Traffic in Women.* London and New York: Zed Books, 1997.

Sprinkle, Annie. "We've Come A Long Way—And We're Exhausted!" In Jill Nagle, editor, *Whores and Other Feminists.* New York: Routledge, 1997: 66–69.

United Nations Convention for the Suppression of Traffic in Persons and the Exploitation of Others (1949).

United Nations Optional Protocol to Prevent, Suppress and Punish Trafficking in Persons, Especially Women and Children (2000).

US Department of State. "Pathbreaking Strategies in the Global Fight Against Sex Trafficking." 2002. http://www.state.gov/g/tip/c8628.htm.

Walkowitz, Judith. "Male Vice and Female Virtue." In Ann Snitow, Christine Stansell, and Sharon Thompson, editors, *Powers of Desire.* New York: Monthly Review Press, 1983: 419–438.

Pepsi and the next thing she knows she's blearily looking out a dirty bus window at a customs post on the Indian border. Another Pepsi later, she wakes up in a filthy padlocked room in Mumbai.

Despite the rows of beckoning girls she sees on the street below, innocent Gita has no idea what's in store for her. When her snarling madam brings in her first customer (a sickly, festering man who's convinced that sex with a virgin will cure his AIDS) she nobly refuses. Trouble, Gita. In comes the *goonda* for her "training." After being raped fifteen or twenty times a day for a week, Gita gets the picture: she's supposed to be a sex worker.

Finally accepting her fate, Gita starts to work. She has to service thirty customers a night, is not allowed out to see Hindi movies (even though it's Mumbai), and has no idea that she owes the horrible fat madam 25,000 rupees for her purchase at 80 percent interest compounded daily.

Now the saviors appear. An inspired NGO leader, aided by cops with humanitarian consciences, beats down the door of the brothel and finds Gita hidden away in a mattress. After a pleasant holiday in a government remand home, she's repatriated to Kathmandu. But alas, she can't go home any more, as the song says, because she's HIV positive. Luckily for her, there's room in a kind barracks where she learns to embroider placemats and lives her last days in dignity.

The Gita myth is comprised of a sequence of "scenarios," which generally correspond to situations and events in a real trafficking episode. These scenarios also correspond to what are today considered most of the basic areas of direct anti-trafficking intervention.[3] Thus, the scenarios "Gita and Her Socioeconomic Situation Before Trafficking" and "The Trafficking of Gita" correspond to prevention interventions, "The Transportation of Gita" to interception, "The Destination and the Withdrawal" to prevention, "The Rehabilitation of Gita" to rehabilitation, and "Gita Returns to Society" corresponds to integration.

THE RECENT EVOLUTION OF THE TRAFFICKING MYTH

Gita and Her Socioeconomic Situation Before Trafficking

The Gita of the original myth was from the Tamang community, a diverse ethnic group from the hills of central Nepal. The Tamang of the districts north of the Kathmandu Valley were the first ethnic group to be identified with trafficking, in the 1980s by ABC Nepal, the first NGO to raise awareness of trafficking in Nepal (ABC n.d.). ActionAid was the first international NGO to address trafficking in Nepal, also in the 1980s. The Tamang people and the several "danger districts" surrounding the

Kathmandu Valley became established as the cast and setting of the early trafficking myth in film, semifictional "case-studies," newspaper articles, and donor agendas.[4] Historical justification was provided to identify the Tamang as "the first trafficking victims."[5]

In the last several years, Gita has lost her Tamang heritage in the trafficking myth, in part due to objections from the Tamang about being labeled "trafficking-prone," but primarily due to the recognition that many other districts in Nepal have been affected by trafficking. Today, Gita can be Gurung, Magar, or one of the other "Mongolian" hill ethnicities,[6] or she can be from one of the marginalized ethnic groups or castes such as the Mahji. However, Gita is rarely identified as being from the Hindu higher-caste groups such as Brahmin or Chettri, despite the fact that the heavily impacted districts of Western and Far Western Nepal are predominantly Brahmin or Chettri.

In the myth, while Gita's bloodline is "ethnic hill-tribe" rather than Hindu, her gender-disadvantage and socioeconomic status are based on the "disempowered Hindu woman" paradigm that predominates in the gender and development discourses in Nepal. Gita and her sisters are portrayed as second-class citizens, confined to the home, a dowry burden on their parents, and raised to be given over to the husband's family—all strongly Hindu stereotypes, applicable to Southern and Western Nepal and to India, but less applicable to the Mongolian woman of the hills, Gita's mythic bloodline. Nepali hill women have relatively more freedom from the patriarchal constraints of Hindu culture than their lowland sisters. Many women of hill ethnic groups conduct business, they have greater control over household economy than their lowland sisters, dowry is still rare, choice in marriage (by elopement) often prevails over arranged marriage, and, significantly, hill women—like hill men—routinely migrate for employment to supplement their family's income.

Gita and her family are rural and poor, scraping by in a subsistence economy. The economic and social settings of the original myth—the "causes of trafficking"—reflect the simplistic "rural poor" paradigm that has predominated in Nepal development for the last forty years. This paradigm does not recognize a number of socioeconomic factors that exacerbate baseline poverty and make the poor more vulnerable to trafficking.

The Gita myth, as with development in general, denies the caste/ethnicity power imbalance that has long existed in Nepal. While Brahmins and Chettris comprise approximately 30 percent of the national population, they make up more than 95 percent of government employees and, with the exception of the Newars of the Kathmandu Valley, the vast majority of landholders, professionals, media persons, and senior development workers in the country (HMG Nepal 2002). The marginalization of ethnic and lower-caste groups by the dominant Brahmins and Chettris, resulting in unequal distribution of arable land, employment, and opportunity, has not entered the discourse. The prevalence of indebtedness to moneylenders throughout the country has been generally ignored, and has not entered the trafficking myth as a cause of trafficking. As well, the original myth does not recognize the social and economic disruption of families who have migrated from the countryside, and the greatly increased potential for abuse and trafficking of girls and women in highway, small-town, and urban environments.

The Trafficking of Gita

In the abduction scenario of the original myth, usually an outsider kidnapped Gita (often using drugs) or duped her or her family with the promise of employment. In recent years, the myth of Gita's abduction from her village has aligned more with what is known of the abduction or recruitment process. Promise of employment is now the most common ruse of traffickers in the myth, distantly followed by promise of marriage, and the more sensational "drugged and dragged" scenario has receded.

This change has been brought about by NGOs' greater experience with returned trafficked girls, many of whose accounts have been printed in the local media. In a study based on interviews with returned trafficked girls, few claimed to have been drugged, and the majority claimed to have been lured either by promises of marriage or of employment (K.C., B.K. et al. 2001). As well, the recent emphasis on promise of employment is due to increased recognition of girls being trafficked from away-from-home workplaces, and the nascent recognition of Nepali female labor migration. The promise-of-marriage ruse, although common in reality, still does not occupy a major place in the myth. This perhaps reflects a cultural resistance to criticizing the institution of marriage, as well as a denial of marriage by elopement, common to hill ethnic groups, as opposed to arranged marriage, an aspect of the patriarchal construction of the Hindu woman.

In the original Gita myth of a decade ago, NGO, media, and donor scenarios almost unanimously cast the trafficker as a person from "out of town," frequently an Indian or a Nepali from the south or from Kathmandu. For years the myth maintained the innocence of the rural Nepali community, despite the common knowledge of NGO workers and villagers that abduction in an insular village setting would be virtually impossible without inside support. The Nepal government had no wish to accuse their constituents of trafficking their children or to draw attention to the possible collusion of government officials in trafficking. Donors and NGO leaders wished to maintain an easy path of intervention—awareness messages cautioning villagers to avoid the evil trafficker—and were reluctant to confront criminality in the villages they were trying to protect.

From the beginning, the Gita myth has stereotyped the impacted family as uneducated, naïve, and upright. Although it is increasingly recognized that some families are complicit in the sale of their daughters into prostitution (K.C., B.K., et al. 2001; Fichtl 2003), the myth prevails that the parents have been duped. This has caused some inconsistencies in presenting Nepal trafficking in the media. For example, a hillside of houses with new tin roofs purchased with money from the sale of girls has become a common visual symbol of trafficking impact in Nepal, although common sense suggests that a hillside of families cannot all be ignorant of the destination of their daughters.

Although still not held culpable for their daughter's trafficking, in the last few years the probity of Gita's family has been challenged. Since the early 1990s, hundreds of rural women's groups have been started throughout the country to promote income generation, basic literacy, and legal awareness. Many of these groups are now well established and have independently turned to social mobilization, coming out against drinking, gambling, spouse abuse, and most recently trafficking in their villages. These natural grassroots responses have not gone unnoticed. Family dysfunction and indebtedness as a result of male behavior are now beginning to enter the technical discourse on trafficking as one of the "causes," but have not yet been incorporated into the common myth.

In the past several years, however, the myth has accommodated the reality of local citizens and returned sex workers being recruiters for the traffickers. This change is the result of the groundswell of social activism of women's groups and of recent NGO efforts to promote legal awareness and mobilize communities to resist violence against women, including trafficking. These efforts have led to a number of incidents in which community members (usually groups of women) have apprehended a local person attempting to traffic a girl and reported that person (usually a male) to the police.

This change in the Gita myth is significant. As mentioned above, much of the Gita myth has developed in the absence of (and because of the lack of) knowledge about the trafficking episode through direct experience or research. In this case, the positive results of NGO interventions have placed new actors in the Gita myth, resulting in a greater alignment of myth with reality.

The Transportation of Gita

The transportation scenario in the Gita myth has remained firmly unchanged. According to the myth, a trafficker-transporter carries Gita from her village or workplace to a major Nepal-India border point, and with the customs official's eyes averted, takes her across to India. Despite unanimous awareness of the movement of narcotics, weapons, and consumer goods across the open Nepal-India border, and despite years of neighboring Bangladesh addressing the problems of trafficking across its own porous border with India, the Nepal government, NGOs, and donors maintain the myth that traffickers take their victims across official border points.

This is an illustration of how myths are established and maintained by the agendas of mythmakers. India-Nepal government discussions on cross-border trafficking focus on official border crossings, avoiding the uncomfortable subject of the unofficial transportation of goods between countries. Although there is little evidence of success and considerable evidence of human rights violations, "intercepting traffickers" is a widely publicized anti-trafficking activity in local and international media,[7] bringing publicity and funding to the government and to donors, thence to NGOs. Donors now support NGOs to maintain more than ten "transit homes" and interception posts at official crossings, and more are rapidly being established. Mobilizing communities living in border areas to resist trafficking, as has been done in Bangladesh, is far more difficult and less likely to produce numerical results, although at this writing one NGO— Maiti Nepal—is making plans for community sentinel activities along the Nepal-India border.

In part, maintaining this aspect of the myth in order to justify interception is a response to the need of the government, NGOs, and Nepal-based donors to appear proactive in the war against trafficking. There is a frequently expressed feeling of helplessness in the Nepal anti-trafficking community because "their girls" are in India, Nepali NGOs (and most Nepal-based donors) cannot work in India, and India is not helping, having enough problems of its own. Interception allows the Nepal anti-trafficking community to take an aggressive and punitive role, rather than being limited to the more passive roles of prevention and rehabilitation.

The Destination and the Withdrawal

The portrayal of Gita's brothel destination, her clients, and the horrors she undergoes has not changed since the inception of the myth. The brothel is physically modeled on "The Cages" of Mumbai, a small, unrepresentative strip of working-class brothels in Kamathipura where donors and media persons are routinely taken to view the streetside solicitation of sex workers. Gita's resistance to sex work and her subsequent rape and torture are routine in the myth. The personalities of the clients are blank, with the exception of mention of their acts of violence or their HIV-positive status. The madam, or *gharwali*, is abusive, and order in the brothel is maintained by thugs. The other sex workers in the brothel are invisible, or mirror Gita's experiences of torture. The only notable change in portrayal of the destination in recent years is the addition of Delhi as a destination city, primarily due to the publicity given to brothel raids conducted by a Delhi NGO.[8] Kolkata, Pune, other Indian cities, and border towns have not entered the myth.

This part of the myth has clear advantages to mythmakers in being the most evocative and sensational scenario, provoking moral outrage and generating funding. However, the lack of change is also due to continued ignorance of the destination or "demand side" by those in the anti-trafficking field. This lack of knowledge stands in contrast to the considerable knowledge of sex workers and brothel operations in India by those conducting HIV/AIDS interventions, reflecting a lack of information-sharing with the HIV/AIDS community that continues to hamper anti-trafficking interventions. As indicated by bibliographies in NGO and donor publications and situational analyses, the anti-trafficking community in Nepal has utilized few of the available sources of information on the destination. With the exception of one study of the demand side conducted in India (O'Connell-Davidson and Anderson 2002), two narratives by researchers in a book on sex work in South Asia (Frederick 2001), and one well-researched fictional narrative (Friedman 1997), almost all "data" have been taken from newspaper accounts and from case studies of rescued trafficked girls.[9] Unutilized sources of information include studies by HIV/AIDS researchers, studies by Indian anti-trafficking NGOs and research organizations, and a number of pieces by Indian writers.[10]

Despite recent identification of human rights abuses during and after brothel raids, the rescue part of the destination scenario remains firmly in the myth for two primary reasons. As with interception, it casts NGOs and police as dramatic heroes, and provides the illusion, particularly for the public and donors, that something is being done. And it remains because the anti-trafficking community—because of lack of knowledge about, and lack of interaction with, the destination side—has not recognized alternative ways of withdrawing girls who wish to leave the brothels or ways to reduce the demand for trafficked persons.

The Rehabilitation of Gita

This episode of the Gita myth has changed the most in the last few years. In the early 1990s myth, the "Gita returned" scenario was relatively unformed: after her rescue, Gita returns HIV-positive to Nepal, where she is provided with some job skills and lives the remainder of her life in care, or just disappears from the picture. Several reasons account for the anticlimactic ending of the early myth. The Nepal public, government, and media at first resisted the return of trafficked girls, primarily because as many as 50 percent were HIV-positive. An undercurrent of cultural prejudice prevailed during that time, unexpressed except in newspaper editorials, that returnees were perceived to be "ruined," no longer representative of pure Nepali womanhood, and might possibly act as traffickers if they were allowed to return to Nepal. Returnees were accepted only after their highly publicized defense by NGOs.[11] Governments, NGOs, and donors had little experience working with psychosocial cases, and had no ready interventions to assist them, except care homes and job skills. And for many years, the publicity value of rehabilitation was unrecognized; this scenario providing far less response and funding than abduction, rape, and rescue.

The "Gita returned" scenario has developed greatly in the last five years, primarily due to donors and NGOs entering a broad new area of intervention: the rehabilitation of trafficked girls. A precedent for rehabilitating children had been set a few years earlier in South Asia when donors and NGOs began to address the needs of street children and child laborers. Gita's rehabilitation quickly became established as part of the myth because of the obvious need to provide a positive outcome to the trafficking episode, despite the fact that the real outcome—Gita's integration back into society—remained unclear.

For the first time, a small dimension has been added to Gita's personality: traumatized. Because of her experience, Gita is psychologically damaged and needs to be rehabilitated. Damaged Gita has successfully supplanted her previous outcome in the myth—a former prostitute and HIV-positive—which was somewhat uncomfortable, particularly for the government and the public. Now that Gita has been typed as psychologically injured, her HIV-positive status has generally been dropped from the myth. The recent addition of rehabilitation enriches the myth with another actor: the Florence Nightingale figure (or NGO) who helps the helpless, a character with the same theatrical power as the heroic NGO leader of the brothel raids.[12] The repairing of damaged Gita has proven a powerful fundraising tool, and the rehabilitation sector of anti-trafficking programming has now become nearly as large as the prevention sector.

Gita Returns to Society

Both the original and the present Gita myth have inconclusive endings. In the original myth, HIV-positive Gita simply died, usually in care, occasionally back in her village. Most often, her end—or her future—was absent from the myth. The village ending didn't prevail in the original myth because of the harsh reality of returned girls being routinely rejected by their families and communities. Gita's end, or future, is similarly absent in the present myth. When Gita is last noted, she's "recovering." While the "she lived happily ever after" scenario would be an attractive and functional conclusion to the Gita myth, its absence reflects the lack of attention placed on the integration of trafficked girls into Nepali society. To date, there is little conceptual clarity about integration, and interventions are almost entirely absent.

Gita's social integration is not part of the myth because the reality of her return to society is neither simple nor heartening; it is not myth material. At this writing, the subject has been avoided by donors, NGOs, and governments, and only one part of one workshop on trafficking survivors has focused on social integration (ILO-IPEC 2002). The real Gita has few options, none of them positive. Acceptance by her family, and especially her community, is extremely difficult unless she returns with wealth. The stigmatism of sex workers in South Asia is strong, and she faces harassment and possibly rape in any social situation in which she cannot hide her past.

The myth cannot readily accommodate Gita living independently, as such is not part of the South Asian cultural norm. Rather, the culture readily suspects girls who live independently to be sex workers, which is inappropriate for the myth's conclusion. Finding a husband and living happily ever after doesn't fit the myth either, for although the rehabilitation scenario provides Gita penance for being a sex worker by casting her as psychologically damaged, she can never be the model of Nepali womanhood; the highly idealized wife. Consequently, the original and present Gita myths are inconclusive, and in this sense jibe with reality: Gita remains institutionalized.

The Myth and the Interventions

Prevention: Gita and Her Socioeconomic Situation Before Trafficking

Interventions to strengthen the resistance of communities and families to trafficking have taken several approaches: general economic empowerment of the "poor"; preventive support focused on at-risk girls; community mobilization (sentinel activities); awareness raising; and the strengthening of government bodies such as police and local anti-trafficking committees.

Prevention activities, naturally, are based on addressing the "causes of trafficking." The Gita myth was both created upon and has maintained a simplistic definition of causes: poverty, lack of education, and lack of awareness of trafficking dangers. This has been reflected in simplistic criteria for being at risk, criteria that encompass the majority of Nepal's rural population. Many donors have opted for a primary strategy of general economic empowerment of the poor as a means to prevent trafficking.[13] This has been convenient for donors, NGOs, and the government, as criteria for being at risk encompass populations already being served by interventions, and they have been able to "address trafficking" without substantially altering their activities.

Preventive measures targeted at at-risk girls have suffered from the same constraint as those targeted at at-risk communities: lack of criteria for being at risk. These activities have been generally adapted from existing interventions that prevailed throughout the 1990s on behalf of the "girl child": non-formal education and skills training. "Prevention centers" provide day instruction for at-risk girls, varying little in target group or curriculum content from earlier centers for "disadvantaged girls." The establishment of residential "prevention homes," in which girls supposedly at risk are placed for their protection, has caused some concern among members of the NGO and donor community due to reports of girls being institutionalized without adequate evidence that they are in danger of being trafficked.

Over the years, NGO fieldworkers have been able to better identify impacted communities and families. They have unofficially established their own criteria for being at risk, which they are now using in their prevention activities. These include marginalization of ethnic and lower-caste groups, arable land versus size of family, and access to land and alternative sources of income. Recently, NGOs have recognized the possible negative effects on girls within the family from domestic violence, stepparents or second wives, substance abuse, and gambling. Although recognized by NGO fieldworkers, these criteria have not been assimilated by the government or by most NGO leaders or donor partners, nor have they entered the myth. This provides an illustration of the conservative character of the myth, and an example of members of the anti-trafficking community (in this case NGO fieldworkers) "bucking the myth" and conducting interventions based on their own knowledge and experience.

Community-mobilization and awareness activities have generally been conducted in unison, some with positive results. In Nepal, the most successful of these activities have not been those conducted in the name of anti-trafficking. Rather, they have been older, well-designed programs for generating legal awareness for women and for reducing violence against women and girls.[14] Trafficking issues have been highlighted in these programs in recent years. Due to their success, accounts of communities identifying and apprehending traffickers have recently entered the Gita myth.

In the case of awareness raising, however, the myth has supported interventions which have had negative effects on the women and girls it has sought to protect. The denial of Nepali women's migration and the patriarchal "Hindu woman" paradigm inherent in the Gita myth have manifested in migration policies and awareness messages which discourage migration and women's freedom of movement, even that of a girl going alone to a local marketplace. Awareness messages communicate danger and generate fear, using illustrations of a girl abducted by a trafficker at a local festival or disappearing en route to a job "in the city." Utilizing characters such as "loose women" who encourage the freedom and movement of village girls, the messages assert patriarchal Hindu values with the implication that "good women stay home" (The Asia Foundation 2002).

Prevention: The Trafficking of Gita

Although, for all of its generalities and inconsistencies, the Gita myth clearly presents different ruses of the trafficker, no specific method of recruitment or abduction is addressed in the majority of interventions.

In most interventions, the promise-of-employment ruse has not yet been placed in the context of female migration. However, cross-border trafficking by promise of employment from destinations of internal migration is now being addressed. One small NGO of trafficking survivors conducts awareness activities in urban carpet and garment factories, where working girls without family protection are sometimes sexually abused and trafficked by male factory workers.[15] In the last year several donors and Nepali NGOs have been airing issues surrounding "safe migration," and the relationship between trafficking and migration is at this time entering the general discourse. There has been discussion of addressing the trafficking-migration issue by the registration and documentation of women and girls wishing to migrate for employment. Critics of this action state that because the power of registration will be primarily in the hands of male family members and corruption in the registration process is inevitable, this will add to the present restrictions on women's migration.

The promise-of-marriage ruse has received virtually no attention in the strategies and action plans of donors and NGOs. The marriage ruse has been little discussed, and neither researched nor placed in the context of varying marriage patterns in the country. Unlike Bangladesh, in which a study in the Rajshahi District showed promise of marriage to be the primary trafficking ruse in the communities observed, neither the Nepal government nor donors (and consequently NGOs) have developed specific strategies of, for example, encouraging formal marriage registration and background checks on potential husbands.

The Gita myth simplifies the trafficking process, ignoring the critical role of the local recruiter, a person from the community with commercial links to the transporter and the purchaser. This has been reflected in government policy and donor agendas, the strategy being to strengthen communities to resist traffickers, rather than to apprehend traffickers from within. As with general prevention awareness activities, however, NGO fieldworkers and mobilized community members have "bucked the myth." Working on the ground, they have identified and at times apprehended local recruiters. Although some of the recruiters have been identified as family members of the trafficked person, in accordance with the myth families are still not held to be complicit by donors or NGO directors. However, in another example of "bucking the myth," NGO fieldworkers are aware of communities with families who knowingly send their daughters to earn money by sex work, and have directed interventions (primarily economic support) at them.

Interception: The Transportation of Gita

The transportation side of trafficking interventions is probably that most affected by the Gita myth. The strength of the myth, as explained above, continues to maintain a basically ineffective intervention: interception of potentially trafficked girls and women at official border posts on the India-Nepal border. The long-term commitment of considerable funding by donors makes them reluctant to assess the effectiveness of interception (no assessment of interception has yet been conducted), let alone adopt new strategies. Estimates of the number of border interceptions are only a few hundred girls over ten years and most significantly, it is unclear how many of the girls "saved" were actually being trafficked.

Only since late 2002 have doubts been cast on interception, although these doubts refer to human rights abuses rather than the unlikelihood of traffickers crossing at official border posts. This has risen from greater awareness of the prevalence of migration of Nepali women, coupled with reports of intercepted girls and women who claim to have been crossing the border willingly, for economic or for personal reasons. Interception is conducted by NGO "Border Guards," whose assumption of the role of government immigration and police officials has been questioned. Some of the Border Guards are trafficking survivors, others are girls who have been institutionalized at transit homes for being "at risk." There are no established criteria for "being trafficked," and the Border Guards identify traffickers and victims from "their own experience." It has been reported that a female accompanied by a male non-relative is a criterion for "being trafficked." Girls who are intercepted are either returned to their families or placed in transit homes.

At the moment of this writing, one of the major NGOs conducting interceptions is retooling its strategies to address transportation, shifting its emphasis from interception to safe migration.[16] This is a significant example of an NGO "bucking the myth" (as well as bucking donor agendas) and changing interventions due to challenges from human rights, expanded knowledge, and self-evaluation of its activities. Recognizing that trafficking must be placed in the context of women's migration, the NGO is changing its awareness strategy from "trafficking dangers" to supportive safe migration messages. In response to perceived ineffectiveness of interceptions at official border crossings, it will now develop sentinel activities among communities living along the open border, as has been done with some success in Bangladesh and Thailand. It remains to be seen if this development will change the myth.

Withdrawal, Prevention: The Destination and the Withdrawal

As with interception, the Gita myth continues to determine interventions on the destination side. Brothel raids are at present the only form of intervention to withdraw girls from brothel situations. Brothels are identified as places of violence and oppression, and the assumption is made that any person working in a brothel should be "rescued." Although purportedly rescuing trafficked children (notably, non-trafficked children and bonded laborers are not targeted for rescue), adult women are routinely removed from brothels during the raids, often against their will. Media portrayals of brothel raids abuse women's rights to privacy and confidentiality, with the implicit assumption that prostitutes forgo those rights.[17]

Most particularly, brothel raids contravene the law, which in India does not directly prohibit sex work, and by denying the fact that the brothel is a workplace—and often the only available environment for abused and stigmatized women—the raids deny women's rights to choose their employment or place of residence. The publicity of the raids cast all brothels—and by implication, all sex workers—as "evil," legitimating police and community violence against sex workers. And they obfuscate the consequences for women and girls after their rescue: incarceration in remand homes, abuse by police and caregivers, forced repatriation, and detainment for perhaps years during "legal processes."

Notably, the myth supports an intervention which itself discourages more effective alternative interventions. By antagonizing brothel communities, raids restrict the entry of outsiders into those communities—not only HIV/AIDS workers, but also potential researchers on trafficking. Interventions to prevent traffickers' activities at the source, to address debt servitude, and to provide economic alternatives to sex work are all dependent on gaining knowledge of trafficking economics and brothel operations by accessing the voices of sex workers, madams, and clients.

Mobilization of sex-worker communities to resist trafficking, as has been successfully demonstrated in Kolkata,[18] necessitates acceptance of the brothel as a workplace, not a place of criminality as the myth portrays. Working with clients to reduce demand for trafficked persons (as well as for children and indebted laborers) necessitates putting a human face on clients. And the heroic role of the police in the rescue scenario masks routine abuse of sex workers by police—the reason why those in abusive brothel situations do not seek asylum with the police. This discourages the creation of alternative places of asylum for those who are able to escape abusive brothel situations.

There are substantial constraints for the Nepal anti-trafficking community to work on behalf of Nepali women and girls in the brothels of India. Intergovernmental talks on the issue are sensitive, and have resulted in very little to date. Local NGOs are dependent on Indian NGOs to conduct interventions, with consequent problems of funding, administration, and conflicting agendas. For donors, direct interventions are generally conducted from their country offices, and counterpart offices in India may be nonexistent, or may not agree with or be permitted to execute the agendas of Nepal country offices. At this time, alternative means of withdrawal and prevention are not yet on the horizon.

Rehabilitation: The Rehabilitation of Gita

The "Gita returned" scenario of the original myth was unformed, and had only one direct effect on early anti-trafficking interventions: it stimulated the establishment of institutions to place Gita. This has continued to this day, and has resulted in the establishment of dozens of "care homes," "shelters," and "transit homes." Most provide little more than craft activities, residence, and food. Few of those supporting the rapid expansion of facilities have questioned the social and psychological problems resulting from prolonged institutionalization, nor have they yet explored alternatives to residential care, such as foster homes, group homes, or outreach units.

A decade's emphasis on institutionalization has posed some rights concerns. Rescued and intercepted girls are often held in institutions without their or their families' permission. Participation is minimal, the girls' voices concerning their institutionalization are unheard, and the frequency of girls escaping from confinement is not mentioned by NGOs or donors. Systems and practices of confidentiality and privacy are lacking, and institutionalized girls are routinely observed by donors and "experts," and photographed by media persons without their permission.

In the mid- to late 1990s, "psychosocial" interventions drew the attention of the anti-trafficking community. Psychosocial interventions, like child protection activities, became established in development agendas as a part of "children in especially difficult circumstances" (CEDC) activities of the early 1990s, which focused on the needs of street children, disabled children, child prostitutes, and other extremely disadvantaged children. Psychosocial rehabilitation was an entirely new field for the development community, but it answered the question of what to do with returned trafficked children. (Significantly, donor concern for nontrafficked children in prostitution waned.) Gita's "trauma" was identified and incorporated into the myth.

The identification of psychological problems as an area of intervention was a major advance for the development community, and in the last few years has made profound positive changes. It has given a human dimension to development recipients like Gita, added meaning to buzzwords such as "well-being" and "best interests of the child," and expanded awareness of a wider spectrum of human rights. And it has opened up new areas of concern regarding children, such as corporal punishment and domestic sexual abuse. However, in the absence of conceptual clarity and research, the development community has addressed the psychosocial concerns of trafficked girls as it addressed prevention and interception: with dependence on the myth rather than with knowledge or experience. Thus, the constraints inherent in myth—its simplicity, its conservatism, and its ready influence by agendas and cultural prejudices—have made themselves felt on interventions.

The recognition of Gita's trauma supported the welfare paradigm which prevails throughout development: "Gita (or the poor, or the nation) is passive, helpless, and damaged, and needs to be fixed." Although there are very recent challenges to the paradigm (Protacio-De Castro 2002), trafficking returnees are generally treated as victims and beneficiaries, their capabilities and resiliency are not recognized, and they are not given the right to participate in decisions about their lives, including returning to society. Token participation activities, such as selection of menus or daily chores, are provided in some institutions.

The simplification of Gita's brothel experience and her resulting personality as "traumatized" has resulted in a simplification of her needs, and a single-minded focus on a narrow area of psychosocial intervention: counseling. Counseling is seen as the only cure, and to date peer activities, experiential therapies, living skills, and communication skills are scarcely included in the roster of psychosocial interventions. Today, counseling is routine in action plans and proposals; more than twenty counseling courses are offered in South Asia, and numerous NGOs profess to conduct counseling.

In essence, the myth has legitimated the conducting by inexperienced (but well-meaning) NGO workers of what should be professional activities: the operation of caregiving facilities, psychological care, and social work interventions. Counseling is not seen as an activity, like medicine, law, or nursing, to be conducted by professionals. Donors have been eager to build the capacity of NGOs with short orientations called, erroneously, "trainings." Beyond some university courses, professional training in counseling (which by definition includes extensive monitored clinical practice) is provided by only one organization in South Asia.[19]

While the majority of the orientation courses are of relatively good quality, providing an introduction to communications skills and an overview of trauma, depression, and other psychological problems related to abuse, NGO workers are given the impression that they have been trained to be counselors. Numerous cases of "retraumatization" have been reported when NGO workers have attempted to conduct in-depth explorations of survivors' abuse history without adequate skills. To date, none of the facilities in Nepal conduct psychosocial assessment or operate under basic case management principles.

Integration: Gita Returns to Society

Gita's integration back into society is not yet part of the Gita myth, nor at this writing are there substantial interventions to promote her integration. This scenario of the myth is at this time forming, and it appears that interventions will create the myth, rather than vice versa, as in the case of the transportation/interception scenario. Although interventions are as yet unformed, and although many donors, and in particular the government, are maintaining institutionalization as the optimal ending for Gita's trials, a strong demand for effective integration strategies has recently arisen from the NGOs and a few members of the donor community.

Integration is constrained by a major lack of conceptual clarity. The term used by the Nepal anti-trafficking community, "reintegration" (as opposed to integration), is itself problematic, implying that Gita can return to her original state, which she cannot. Integration is generally conceived to be a state of being—that is, Gita back home and normalized. This static view obfuscates the reality of integration as a process: preparation during her residence in a facility; intermediate residential situations, such as group homes; outreach support activities provided after she enters society; and finally, assessment of her self-sufficiency and closure of her case. The "damaged Gita" paradigm, as mentioned above, also denies the resiliency of many Gitas—the fact that many women and girls are not damaged by the brothel environment, and have the ability (and wish) to return to society almost immediately after being rescued. That is, rehabilitation and reintegration interventions are sometimes not necessary.

The history of anti-trafficking interventions in Nepal has shown repeatedly that the hands-on experience of NGO workers has resulted in "bucking the myth" and creating interventions that work. In the case of integration, the decade's experience in rehabilitation has helped

NGOs recognize the downside of institutionalization and identify integration needs of rescued girls. These include market-researched functional job skills, group living situations, community assessment, family interventions, and outreach mechanisms, among others. However, donors have not recognized these needs, or developed the tools or provided support to effect such activities. This is strongly illustrated by the "missing link" in the discourse on rehabilitation and integration: social work. Although the role of social workers is imperative in social assessment of trafficking survivors upon intake and throughout survivors' integration, they are absent in donor considerations. While local Nepali NGOs cannot be expected to identify "social work" as the name for the needed activities they have identified, donors can be expected to do so, but have not.

CONCLUSION: CHALLENGING THE MYTH

In the very short history of anti-trafficking activities in Nepal, the myth still dominates the design and implementation of interventions. The myth has valid and important purposes in being a "consensus description" of a typical trafficking episode upon which to conduct the trafficking discourse, and in encapsulating the issues so that they can be easily communicated. However, the role of the myth in determining anti-trafficking interventions has been shown to be counterproductive.

Over the last ten years, it can be seen that the myth has perpetuated unrealistic stereotypes of the Nepali woman, the Nepali family, sex workers, and the intervention actors themselves. It has maintained incomplete and sometimes false descriptions of the trafficking episode, including the causes of trafficking, the transportation of trafficked persons, and the destination environment. And it has validated activities that have abused the rights of women and girls, including removal of women from their workplace, restricted migration, forced institutionalization, and psychosocial malpractice. The majority of positive changes in anti-trafficking activities have arisen in spite of, not because of, the myth. Local NGOs, with assistance (and sometimes pressure) from human rights activists, have led these changes. From the ground, they have created clearer criteria for being at risk of trafficking, refined prevention activities, responded to the need of women's migration, and encouraged rapid and effective integration of returned trafficked girls.

At this writing, the myth is being challenged from many directions. Knowledge of the trafficking episode is increasing as donors and the general anti-trafficking community absorb the experiences of NGO workers. Research is still lacking, although while donors remain reluctant to support careful research, several small studies of quality have recently been conducted.[20] Increased sensitivity to human rights issues is perhaps having the greatest impact on the myth. The assertion of rights-based perspectives in interventions has stimulated a shift from the discouragement of migration through fear messages and interception toward safe migration strategies. In very recent renditions of the myth, Gita is trafficked during the act of going to a genuine place of employment, due to lack of awareness of how to migrate safely.

A broader understanding of children's rights, along with recognition of poor caregiving practices, has brought about a concern for quality of care in rehabilitation. The government of Nepal is leading an effort to develop national minimum standards for care facilities, donors are developing practices for child protection and participation, and some NGOs are promoting the activism and social involvement of trafficking returnees. Increased recognition of Gita's strength and resiliency is manifest in some of her recent myth portrayals as a returnee-turned-activist who works on behalf of girls at risk.

Certain dramatic aspects of the Gita myth will likely remain. The heart-wrenching, money-earning episode of her trials in the brothel is unlikely to change, much because the basic cruelty of trafficking—if not sex work—needs to be portrayed. Whether the noble brothel-buster will be replaced by the compassionate client or the sex worker with a heart of gold has yet to be seen. The Florence Nightingale NGO character of Gita's rehabilitation scenario will remain. Like the destination hero, she will continue to play a necessary role in the myth, although perhaps she will become a less patronizing figure.

The myth will continue its descriptive and communicative function for the public, media, and participants in the general trafficking discourse. It is hoped, however, that it will lose its role in guiding interventions, to be replaced by a complex picture of reality based on knowledge, experience, and human rights.

NOTES

1. Donor partners include international nongovernmental organizations (INGOs), multilaterals, bilaterals, and foreign governments.

2. Trafficking Thematic Group, *Revisiting the Human Trafficking Paradigm: The Bangladesh Experience* (Dhaka, Bangladesh: Trafficking Thematic Group, April 2003).

3. Areas of anti-trafficking intervention not discussed in this essay include policy development, legal instruments, arrest and prosecution, international repatriation, and training for police and government officials.

4. For example, *The Selling of Innocents,* produced and directed by Ruchira Gupta (1997); *Under the Tin Roof,* produced by the Center for Women and Development Nepal (mid-1990s); and Pradhan, G., *Back Home From Brothels: A Case Study of the Victims of Commercial Sexual Exploitation and Trafficking Across Nepal-India Border* (Kathmandu, Nepal: CWIN, 1996).

5. The Tamang as "the first trafficking victims" have been repeatedly provided with the "historical justification" of their women having been used as consorts by the Rana ruling class of the Kathmandu Valley in the late nineteenth and early twentieth centuries. The historical justification is tenuous, however. The link between the early-twentieth century Kathmandu consort and late-twentieth-century trafficking victim to India has not been established, nor does the history consider trafficking from the eastern Rai and Limbu ethnic groups to Kolkata, which likely preceded trafficking to Mumbai. The trafficking of Nepali girls to Kolkata has not been entertained in the trafficking myth, nor have any interventions of note been focused on the large number of Nepalis in Kolkata. It has been suggested that modern trafficking originated in the 1950s and 1960s as an offshoot of the large recruitment of Nepali men to work in India in road building and urban construction, but this has not entered the myth.

6. "Mongolian" is a term frequently used today, particularly among young people from hill ethnic groups, to distinguish themselves as the original non-Hindu residents of Nepal from the Hindu castes originating from India and southern Nepal.

7. The documentary film *The Day My God Died,* produced and directed by Andrew Levine (2002), contains almost all of the clichés of the early 1990s Gita myth.

8. Stop Trafficking, Oppression and Prostitution of Children and Women (STOP), New Delhi, India.

9. The frequently identical content of published "case studies" of trafficked girls, considering the vast range of potential destination experiences, casts some doubt on the veracity of the accounts. Possible reasons why the accounts may not represent "reality" include NGOs editing, amending, or omitting non-negative accounts; the narrow sample of girls interviewed (only girls who have been rescued); the casual and sometimes abusive manner in which case studies have been collected (usually from girls in rehabilitative confinement); and the probability of some girls' inclination to alter their stories to deny their voluntary entry into sex work or their families' income from their labor.

10. For example, All India Institute of Hygiene and Public Health, *Assessment of Sex Trade in Calcutta and Howrah* (Calcutta: AIIHPH, 1993), and Sinha, I., *A Study of Child Prostitution in West Bengal* (New Delhi: National Commission for Women, 1997).

11. Particularly by Ms. Anuradha Koirala, Director, Maiti Nepal.

12. For illustration of "heroic NGO leader saving trafficked child," refer to documentary *The Day My God Died,* directed by Andrew Levine.

13. ADB and USAID among others.

14. Two legal programs with significant impact have been conducted by Saathi and Lawyers for Human Rights and Legal Aid (LHRLA), both based in Kathmandu, Nepal.

15. Shakti Samuha, Kathmandu, Nepal.

16. Maiti Nepal.

17. It is noteworthy that in the brothel scene of Levine's film *The Day My God Died,* only the white visitor to the brothel had his identity pixilated out.

18. The "Self Regulatory Board" of the Durbar Mahila Samanwaya Committee, Kolkata, West Bengal, India.

19. Centre for Victims of Torture Nepal, Kathmandu, Nepal. Also noteworthy are courses recently being developed at the Department of Clinical Psychology, University of Dhaka, Bangladesh.

20. For example: The Asia Foundation and Population Council/Horizons, *Prevention of Trafficking and the Care and Support of Trafficked Persons* (Kathmandu, Nepal: TAF/ Horizons, 2001); Clawson, V., *Application of the Positive Deviance Approach to Anti-trafficking Programming in Nepal: A Trial in Nuwakot District* (Kathmandu, Nepal: Save the Children US, 2002).

REFERENCES

Agroforestry, Basic Health and Cooperative (ABC) Nepal. *A Situation Analysis Report on Girls Trafficking in Sindhupalchowk: Mahankal and Inchowk Village Development Committee.* Kathmandu, Nepal: ABC Nepal, n.d.

All India Institute of Hygiene and Public Health. *Assessment of Sex Trade in Calcutta and Howrah.* Calcutta: AIIHPH, 1993.

The Asia Foundation. *Our Decision, Our Protection.* Kathmandu, Nepal: The Asia Foundation, 2002.

The Asia Foundation and Population Council/Horizons. *Prevention of Trafficking and the Care and Support of Trafficked Persons.* Kathmandu, Nepal: TAF/Horizons, 2001.

Clawson, V. *Application of the Positive Deviance Approach to Anti-trafficking Programming in Nepal: A Trial in Nuwakot District.* Kathmandu, Nepal: Save the Children US, 2002.

Fichtl, R. *Child Trafficking in Nepal: An Assessment of the Present Situation.* Kathmandu, Nepal: Terres des Hommes, 2003.

Frederick, John. "Deconstructing Gita: The Discourse on Trafficking in South Asia." *Himal Magazine,* 1998.

Frederick, John (ed.). *Fallen Angels: The Sex Workers of South Asia.* New Delhi: Roli Books, 2001.

Friedman, M.S. *Tara: A Fleshtrade Odyssey.* New Delhi: Vikas Publishing House, 1997.

HMG Nepal (His Majesty's Government of Nepal). *Population Census of Nepal 2001.* Kathmandu, Nepal: HMG Nepal, 2002.

ILO-IPEC South Asia Technical Seminar on Psychosocial Rehabilitation and Occupational Integration of Child Survivors of Trafficking, Kathmandu, Nepal, June 2002.

K.C., B.K., et al. *Trafficking in Girls with Special Reference to Prostitution: A Rapid Assessment.* Geneva: ILO-IPEC, 2001.

O'Connell-Davidson, Julia, and Anderson, Bridget. *The Demand Side of Trafficking: A Multi-Country Pilot Study.* 2002. Unpublished.

Pradhan, G. *Back Home From Brothels: A Case Study of the Victims of Commercial Sexual Exploitation and Trafficking Across Nepal-India Border.* Kathmandu, Nepal: CWIN, 1996.

Protacio-De Castro, E. "Integrating Indigenous Knowledge and Practices into Psychosocial Help and Support for Child Survivors of Trafficking and Sexual Abuse." In Frederick, J. (editor). *Creating a Healing Environment: Volume II: Technical Papers.* Kathmandu, Nepal: ILO-IPEC, 2002.

Sinha, I. *A Study of Child Prostitution in West Bengal.* New Delhi: National Commission for Women, 1997.

Trafficking Thematic Group. *Revisiting the Human Trafficking Paradigm: The Bangladesh Experience.* Dhaka, Bangladesh: Trafficking Thematic Group. April 2003.

8

Sex Workers' Rights Organizations and Anti-trafficking Campaigns

Edited by Kamala Kempadoo

Despite the shift in international definitions of trafficking, from prostitution to broader migration processes and situations of forced labor, the global sex trade remains a target for many anti-trafficking policies and agencies. In the following we present excerpts from public statements and appeals by sex worker rights organizations about anti-trafficking interventions and politics. The excerpts reveal dimensions of the violence and terror sex workers are subject to in the name of anti-trafficking, yet also offer alternatives for policy and action to address the multiple dimensions of the problem of trafficking. The organizations represented here—Zi Teng, Durbar Mahila Samanwaya Committee, and Empower—are located in, respectively, Hong Kong, China; Kolkata, India; and Thailand. Their experiences and perspectives are similar to those expressed by sex workers' rights organizations elsewhere in the world.[1]

REDEFINING TRAFFICKING IN NGO PRACTICE

Zi Teng is a non-governmental organization established for the purpose of providing much needed services to Hong Kong and Mainland Chinese sex workers. It was formed in September 1996 by a group of local women activists with diverse backgrounds, yet all sharing the common goal of assisting and empowering Hong Kong sex workers. It aims at raising the public awareness on issues impacting sex workers through legal advocacy work, and targeted programs and services. Sex workers are among the most marginalized groups, facing various forms of political, legal, and social oppression in Hong Kong. Their marginalized legal and social status means they are largely without police or other legal protections and have very limited access to social welfare, health benefits, and legal and health information. They are therefore among the most vulnerable segments of the Chinese society. These problems are particularly urgent in Hong Kong as there are only a few support groups focused on their needs, and no union has ben formed to give voice to their problems and fight for their rights. The executive committee members of Zi Teng believe that every human being should have the same basic human rights regardless of her/his gender, sexual orientation, class, race, age, or occupation, and should have the right to live and work with dignity. This is why we continue to fight against discrimination, marginalization, and criminalization of sex work and sex workers in Hong Kong, and struggle to assist these women in their own empowerment through education, network development, and providing immediately needed services, such as legal advocacy, health assistance, and hotlines.

In addition to its primary concern with sex workers in Hong Kong, Zi Teng also has implemented joint projects with related organizations in different parts of Mainland China since the mid-1990s. Zi Teng has assisted in the development of sex worker–related service centers, and set up a sex worker hotline in collaboration with local organizations in various provinces in China. In addition, migration and cross-border "employment" became a major phenomenon for sex workers in Mainland China over the past decade. There has been a dramatic increase in the number of women crossing borders working as migrant sex workers. Many migrate from the central and southern provinces into Shenzhen, and make their way to Hong Kong and other South East Asia countries. We have many chances to get in touch with those migrant sex workers in Hong Kong through our outreach program and other services.

Through the interaction with migrant sex workers during our outreach program, we realize that many have little knowledge about the industry and related health information. Consolidation of existing experiences and services provided to sex workers tell us that there is a pressing need for more groups and organizations to provide health information and immediate help for those sex workers in need. Our programs are not only aimed at informing the health and livelihood issues to sex workers, but also cover topics on women's sexual autonomy and their rights to self-determination. As China will soon join the World Trade Organization (WTO) and it is foreseeable that there will be an increasing number of under-employed and unemployed women workers due to the restructuring of many enterprises for competitiveness, the number of sex workers will be on the rise. However, as the problem of migrant sex workers is always confused with the trafficking problem, service providers fail to be aware of what information and help the sex workers really need.

In the past decade, the problem of international trafficking in Asia has aroused much attention from international organizations and governments. At the same time, the expansion of the sex industry also worries some of the local and overseas governments. Policies and governments have done a lot to combat some forms of trafficking, such as sex trafficking, while on the other hand, they ignore the existence of other forms of trafficking. From our experience, however, the worst part is that they fail to distinguish between sex trafficking and migrant sex work. This pushes the most deprived and marginalized groups—women sex workers—into an unpleasant and dangerous situation under globalization. Employing a new approach with relevant strategies is the only way to produce more effective and practical programs and practices.

From our local experience, we find no difference between people working as factory workers, domestic workers, sex workers, or people wanting to marry abroad. Sex work is a job or simply a way for women to increase their and their families' living standard. They are women who take initiatives to improve their living conditions. This is quite the opposite of the "passive victim" stereotype that is widely circulated about them.

As an organization that cares about sex workers, we oppose all forms of trafficking—forceful activities against one's will. If women are forced to sell their labour or sex, it is immoral. If women willingly sell their labour or sex, but are grossly exploited in the process of selling, it is also immoral. However, we have to understand that combatting trafficking is different from controlling and suppressing the sex industry through the legal system. Only when we accept sex work as a job, actively engage with the lives of women in the sex industry, we may understand the unfairness of current sex transactions and enable sex workers to gain legal protection. . . . We should not treat sex trafficking and other forms of trafficking differently. If we only consider sex trafficking as evil but overlook the others, sex workers will have to face even greater stigmatization and exploitation. Actions against trafficking within this approach will only put sex workers at risk of punishment. Sex can be sold, but should be sold under fair conditions, in a fair context. "Sex trafficking" applies only when sex is sold under the control of triads or pimps, or when women are sold irrespective of their consent.

Under this approach, governments and NGOs should employ both repressive and supportive strategies to fight trafficking. On one hand, repressive strategies aim at suppressing organized crime, forced migration, and exploitation. On the other hand, there should be also strategies that aim at supporting the women concerned and strengthening their rights. We may employ a labour framework in this issue that would make visible commonalties and shared forms of exploitations between sex workers and other workers. Trafficking in women can be understood as the result of the poor legal and social position of women: as women, as workers, and as migrants. This approach calls for labour opportunities and working rights: protection from unpaid work, pensions, state benefits, etc., to women sex workers. What we need to do now is to make this industry become fairer in its operation.

YimYuet-Lin and Anita Koo, for Zi Teng
December, 2003

DMSC under Attack Once Again

We, the sex workers of Sonagachi and of other red light areas in West Bengal have collectivised ourselves under Durbar Mahila Samanwaya Committee (DMSC)—an organisation of and for sex workers. As DMSC, we run one of the most successful STD/HIV Intervention Programmes in the world—the famed "Sonagachi Project." Besides DMSC, we have our own micro-credit society, Usha, our cultural wing, Komol Gandhar, and our trade union, Binodini Srameek Union. We also run Self-regulatory Boards in red light areas to prevent trafficking and entry of minors into the trade. Every new entrant to the sex trade, adult or minor are [sic] interviewed and counselled by the DMSC Self-regulatory Boards. We actively help all unwilling adults and minor girls option out of sex work.

As a result of DMSC's successful intervention activities among sex workers, Sonagachi had forgotten police raids for a while. However, of late, a group of policemen from the Kolkata Police Headquarters have, in the pretext of searching for and rescuing minor girls trafficked into the trade, been raiding brothels and harassing sex workers who are of age, and also picking up, arresting and harassing, in the name of "rescue," girl children of sex workers. We at DMSC had lodged formal protests about the matter but the government did not take any action to stop this.

[Recently] a posse of police . . . raided a brothel in Sonagachi red light district and forcibly picked up Payel Mazumdar on charges that she is a "minor" and "has been trafficked recently" into Sonagachi. Payel Mazumdar is a sex worker who is "of age," has two children and has been working as a sex worker for the last six years in Sonagachi. When women in the house and neighbourhood protested strongly to this harassment the posse of police resorted to an unprovoked and brutal baton-charge. A large number of our sex worker activists and staff of the intervention project suffered body blows and had to receive medical care. Innocent bystanders, notably children of the neighbourhood too did not escape the brutal police third degree—around fifteen of them received baton injuries and had to be hospitalised.

We immediately protested these acts of barbarism by the police and gave a deputation to lodge a formal complaint with the local police station requesting it to take action, stop their brethren from continuing violence against sex workers, and restoring normalcy within the area.

. . .

We of Durbar strongly condemn this act of terrorism perpetrated on us by Kolkata Police! We at Durbar strongly feel that this kind of violence by the police on us reveal their utter callousness about our human rights, and infringe on our right to livelihood. In addition, such acts of violence by "upholders" of "law and order" on sex workers only manages to marginalise us more, makes us suspicious of "mainstream" interventions and sets back by a quantum leap the gains DMSC had made in STD/HIV prevention efforts among us. In short such police atrocities, take away not only our livelihood, but also our health and our lives!

DMSC, 2003

A Report by Empower Chiang Mai on the Human Rights Violations Women Are Subjected to When "Rescued" by Anti-trafficking Groups

Empower Foundation is a Thai Organization since 1985. Empower promotes opportunities for women workers in the entertainment industry. Empower strives to promote these opportunities and rights to all women workers regardless of their country of origin. Far from being a "bold new method" . . . Empower Chiang Mai has been dealing with the issue of "raids and rescues" of women working in brothels for the past eleven years. Empower abhors the trafficking of any person, forced labor including forced sex work, and the sexual abuse of children, whether for commercial exploitation or not.

Over the past three years there has been an increased international and national focus on the situation of women who have been trafficked. However, the focus on trafficking in persons has meant many groups with little or no experience on the issues of migration, labor, sex work or women's rights have been created to take advantage of the large sums of money available to support anti-trafficking activities. Their inexperience and lack of contact with the sex worker community has meant they are unable or unwilling to differentiate between women who have been trafficked and migrant workers. They also show a great deal of trouble differentiating between women and girls, often applying identical standards and solutions for both. It is obviously inappropriate to treat an adult as a child.

Empower has monitored the methods and results of these group's activities and we are very alarmed at the increasing violations and inhumane treatment women are subjected to by unworkable and unethical methods. . . . [we therefore appeal] to anti-trafficking campaigners, funding bodies and policy makers to urgently and very carefully consider these recommendations and ensure that they protect the rights of the women they propose to assist:[2]

- No person should be trafficked, or forced to work in work they have not chosen to do and that no child under the age of 18 years should be abused sexually either commercially or domestically . . .
- Methods to combat trafficking must be revised and solutions found that do not violate the rights of workers . . .
- The rights of adult trafficked victims as workers must be acknowledged. We should receive recognition of our work and compensation, so we are not financially worse off after our "rescue."
- All women affected by trafficking or anti-trafficking measures must receive adequate compensation . . .
- The primary goal of prosecuting traffickers must be altered to a primary goal of assisting trafficked women and children . . .
- Anti-trafficking groups must work toward improving the human rights situation in Burma, securing the ability for women to travel independently, and fully supporting the recognition of refugee status . . .
- Anti-trafficking dialogue and groups [should] consider us as anti-trafficking workers and human rights defenders. . . .

Empower June 2003
http://www.nwsp.org/mobility/mpower-0306.html

NOTES

1. See, for example, writings by a coalition of sex workers' rights organizations in Australia, "Alleged Trafficking of Asian Sex Workers in Australia" (http://www.bayswan.org/Austraf.html); the "Statement on Trafficking, Stigmatisation and Strategies for Alliances" by Carol Leigh and Marjan Wijers, prepared for The Transnational Trafficking Seminar on Trafficking in Women, June 20–24, Budapest, Hungary, 1998 (http://www.bayswan.org/alliances.html); the electronic article by Anna Louise Crago (2003), writer, activist, artist, and founding member of the sex worker political action group "La Coalition pour les droits des travailleuses et travailleurs du sexe" in Montreal, Canada (http://www.breakthrough.tv/news/news-details.cfm?id_News=117); analyses and commentaries by activists in the Network for Sex Work Projects (NWSP) (http://www.nswp.org/mobility/analysis.html); the journal article by the director of SWEAT (Sex Worker Education and Advocacy Taskforce)

in South Africa: Jayne Arnott, "SWEAT: Engaging with Trafficking in Women in South Africa—an NGO Perspective," *Canadian Woman Studies* 22, no. 3–4 (2003): 188–191; and News Item # 8 with comments by Kara Gilles of the Toronto migrant sex worker advocacy group, on the Canadian police raids on massage parlors in the Greater Toronto Area, December 19, 2003 (http://www.sexprofessionalsofcanada.com).

For more perspectives from sex-workers' rights groups, see *Partners in Change: Stories of Women's Collectives* (Bangkok: GAATW, 2002); the "Legal Agenda for Migrant Prostitutes and Trafficked Women," compiled by a coalition of European organizations, at: http://www.femmigration.net; and the website "Connexiones para Migrantes/Connexions for Migrants," that offers comments, articles, and links, with an emphasis on Latin America: http://www.nodo50.org/migrantes.

2. The recommendations came out of a meeting held by Empower on May 12, 2003, on trafficking and anti-trafficking responses, in which sixty-four entertainment workers from three different centers in Thailand participated. A majority of the participants were from Burma, "some of who had at some time been 'victims of trafficking' and all of who had at one stage or other enlisted help to migrate for work in Thailand."

PART III

REPORTS FROM THE FIELD
Participation, Research, and Action

9

Migration, Trafficking, and Sites of Work

Rights and Vulnerabilities

Jagori

Jagori, a women's center based in New Delhi, India, has worked on issues of trafficking, migration, and rights of sex workers for over six years. In our work so far, we have consistently come across problems in the availability and reliability of data on these issues, which render intervention either impossible or ineffective, and uninformed. In an effort to begin addressing this gap, Jagori conducted a study in 2000 in two states of India, Rajasthan and Gujarat, which led to a larger action-research project.

This paper reports on the study and presents some of the initial findings and Jagori's perspective on the issue of trafficking. During this short study to map trends, we felt that it was critical as a first step to focus on movement per se; that is, migration in itself, and explore its causes and implications for women in particular. Only through such a "lens" would we be able to locate elements of trafficking in the process—such as coercion, deceit, abuse, and slavery-like practices. Using this approach enabled a more acute awareness of the need for women to move in search of work, and the concomitant vulnerabilities inherent in the process of their movement. Second, the context within which trafficking has been conceptualized is across borders, thus it is enmeshed in issues of illegal migration. It is therefore more difficult to apply it in cases of migration within borders, from one state to another, or between districts, and its

159

applicability is immediately reduced. We did find, however, that by breaking the concept into *elements* of trafficking, or understanding it as a continuum of violations, it could be used to analyze internal migration processes. Moreover, while the notion of illegal migration is redundant in internal migration, violations of rights of migrant workers can take place under different circumstances. The concepts of citizens' rights and human rights need to be invoked to address these violations. As the UN Special Rapporteur on Violence Against Women, Radhika Cooma-raswamy, notes in her report of her mission to Bangladesh, Nepal, and India: "Trafficking of girls and women often follows the same route as legitimate migration...'traffickers fish in the stream of migration'...." The focus of inquiry and of the report itself has been on unraveling and understanding these very streams of migration.

METHODOLOGY

The study was conducted over five months in selected districts of Rajast-han and Gujarat. It involved State-level consultations, a series of informal meetings with NGOs and other stakeholders, interviews with women migrant workers, and field visits, in order to understand the dominant trends and key issues and share the concerns of the project with NGOs and other civil-society organizations working in the region. It was critical to identify existing gaps in data, understand the issues of concern, and exchange ideas and strategies that would optimize the scope and utility of the study with the active involvement of groups and experts working in the area. In addition, an extensive survey of literature was undertaken to gauge the gaps and missing links in migration research, particularly with reference to women and migration, in order to contextualize the study within existing debates.

Our initial consultations and forays into the field were conducted within the conceptual framework of trafficking. However, increasingly we found that such a framework was too limiting for us to understand, analyze, and engage fully with all the emerging issues. The NGOs and field sites we visited threw open entirely new areas and ideas to explore, which hinted at possible intersections with discourses of trafficking. Discussions with the NGOs, as well as within our team, helped us reflect on the debates surrounding the trafficking discourse.

THE FOCUS ON MIGRATION

Migration has been a feature of all societies historically. There have been different forms of migration—nomadic migration, migration for labor, migration due to war, displacement, etc. Perhaps today it is the changing context of the world and the extent and scale of migration which makes it a key feature of the times. Globalization has today precipitated the process due to increased opportunities at one level and disruption of livelihoods and food security on the other. The reality is that people today and women in particular are moving in search of survival and fulfillment, in search of ways to create new identities and a better life for themselves and their families (Karlekar 1995; Lingham 1998; Pedraza 1991; Sweetman 1998). Migration indeed has been an extension of women's everyday lives in many regions.

The extremely high level of mobility of capital has led to freedom to choose labor from any part of the world. The devaluation of human labor and the simultaneous increase in the value of capital is the context for the increase in mass-level international migration. These changes in the global economy have brought more women into the realm of paid labor. The transnational character of industrial production has created a market for female labor, especially migrant women.

It has been increasingly documented that women face several kinds of vulnerabilities during the process of movement. In some cases, especially of cross-border movements, studies have shown that there are serious issues of human rights violations that need to be dealt with, the more severe being cases of trafficking (Coomaraswamy 1997, 2000). However, in order to tackle the issue of trafficking we need to make clear conceptual distinctions of the different elements involved. Trafficking has been defined as "all acts involving recruitment and/or transportation, moving, selling and buying of women and children within and/or across borders through coercion and/or deception, for sexual services and/or work, for the purpose of profit" (Coomaraswamy 1997).

It is important to challenge the perception that whenever women move out alone in the world they are forced into the sex industry. While it is true that this is valid in many situations, it is neither correct nor useful to assume this is always the case. The focus on sex work as the ultimate site of work of a trafficked woman leaves aside a large number of other sites into which women migrate and face abuse, coercion, and sexual exploitation. We found that in many of the sites of work which we visited there was abuse and exploitation of different kinds, which might not be labeled as trafficking. It therefore became more relevant to examine the kinds of vulnerabilities that women face during the process of movement, finding work, and at the different sites of work.

Our study therefore focused on a broader canvas, looking at the process of migration and sites of work, point of origin, and the places to which they migrate. It is important to recognize that inequalities, discrimination, and violence within the home, during the journey or movement, and at the sites of work make women vulnerable to being coerced, deceived, and violated. Patterns of violence and exploitation within the family also play a role in women's decisions to migrate in search of work.

Migration Trends in Rajasthan

In parts of Rajasthan, migration has historically been a way of life. People from different castes in Rajasthan move for different reasons with different results. Social structure mediates all access to resources. The caste composition is distinct and has shown great tenacity in surviving the effects of modernization and urbanization. Mechanisms of caste accommodations and networks and local understandings have also been built over generations. As a result migration often occurs in clusters or networks, rather than individually. Structural conditions also may marginalize entire communities, as a result of which they are forced to move.

Pastoral groups also usually migrate in big groups of hundreds or thousands, with cattle and all belongings. The ecosystem in Rajasthan is intricately linked to migration patterns. The pastoral region to the west of the Aravalli Range is a totally separate ecosystem from the rest of Rajasthan; in fact Western Rajasthan is ecologically a part of West Asia. Pastoral migration is an essential part of the ecosystem of Rajasthan (Kavoori 2000).

The role of the State in the context of migration has been ambiguous. While on one hand it plays an enabling role, helping the flow of labor and creating labor markets, at the same time it has also tended to focus on settling people (sedenterization) and on efforts to reinforce ethnicity and "Statehood."

Rajasthan exhibits tremendous regional variation, in terms of ecology, agrarian structure, caste, class, and ethnicity. Southern Rajasthan has a history of bonded labor and exploitation within the tribal institutional framework. In Shekhawati, for instance, the Jajmani system has been very popular, as a result of which people migrated in groups. Thus along with the Marwari patron, the castes which provided services to them would move also—such as the barber, cooks, and so on. Border districts such as Dhaulpur and Sawai Madhopur show a particular type of migration, in which case the construction labor sector becomes important. There is also the phenomenon of migration to Gulf countries in Churu and Jhunjhunu, areas where there is a dominant Bohra Muslim community. The occupational diversity along caste lines is also important to understand. With its rich traditions, Rajasthan has always witnessed migration of one sort or the other; in the case of performing arts groups like the Nat, Mal, and Mirasi, they travel from village to village as entertainers.

The process of industrialization and opening up of markets has had an impact on peoples' livelihood options. For example, in the Alwar area over the past 15 years, a large number of locally run industries have closed down due to their non-viability, which has led to severe unemployment. This has meant loss of livelihoods for families and there has not been a commensurate opening up of other livelihood options for them. This has led to women entering sex work, a phenomenon which we found both in Alwar and in Ahmedabad where textile mills have been closed down in large numbers (Bremen 1996).

In Rajasthan the continuous drought conditions between 1999 and 2002 have been devastating, with over 3 million people having been affected. Livelihoods have vanished, and many villages suffered from acute crises—malnutrition, death of livestock. News came of the Chittor region in January 2000 where 40 villages were so badly affected that as many as 1,400 people were leaving a single village. In some villages only old people had been left behind—men, women, and children had all moved in search of work and survival. In the cities there was increased begging and an increased number of rickshaw pullers, women in prostitution, labor in the *choktis*, and swelling suburbs and slum settlements. "Choktis" is the local name given to the assigned places in the city where laborers, most of whom have migrated from the rural areas, assemble in the early morning to provide their services to contractors who come looking for casual, daily-wage labor. Where there were once 100 people in one place, it has increased to 250 to 300 people in the same place. Often the whole family was there to provide labor. While the number of laborers coming to the *choktis* is on the rise, the work available is falling. Due to inflation the construction industry suffered, so laborers are able to get work for only around ten to fifteen days in a month. There are also different scales of wages among the laborers; the unskilled laborers are paid less and women are usually paid 30–40 percent less than men. Contractors come with work usually for construction, laying of telephone lines and cable lines, and so on. There are thirty-five such *choktis* in Jaipur, of which twenty are very large. The laborers live in slum settlements, where they have to pay rent of about Rs. 200–500 (approximately US$4–10) a month. Some live temporarily in the semi-constructed houses they are being contracted to build. Almost 60 percent of migrants in this kind of situation return to their native place when they are able to. Women are also vulnerable to sexual exploitation; often, delaying payment is the pretext under which women are recalled by the contractors and harassed. Most women and men accept the abuse, as they see no choice. Women workers are usually in the range of fifteen to forty years of age. Ninety-nine percent of the women are accompanied by men. Only some women, like widows, may be on their own.

Many communities have been put out of work by changing economic policies and conditions. The Regar community, for instance, which was a shoemaking community, was affected badly by the entry of Bata, a multinational shoe company, and other large shoe companies; even villagers would no longer come to them for their shoes as options that were cheaper (and sometimes perceived as higher status) were now made available.

Some traditional entertainment tribes such as the Nats, Bedias, and Kanjar have increasingly become impoverished as they can no longer support themselves with their trade. Women who used to work as entertainers are now working as prostitutes to support themselves and their families. They migrate within the State and also to other cities. In recent years a new route has also begun in which women are going, or being taken, to Bombay and then to countries in the Gulf for work, often domestic or sex work.

Family Labor in Brick Kiln Factories

Banwari Lal and Kishandas live in Meda ka Vaas, approximately fifty kilometers from Jaipur, near Choma village, off the Jaipur-Delhi highway. They belong to the Raiger community. Although some members of the community own small pieces of land, the majority are landless. Traditionally they worked on other people's fields as casual seasonal workers when the work was available, but of late it is becoming consistently harder to find regular work in their villages. With the state fighting severe drought for the last three years, work in the fields has become scarce. So to make a living, they migrate to nearby and far-flung cities to work as laborers on brick kilns. The last contract they had was on a kiln near Bijaipur on the Jaipur-Alwar road. They generally travel with their families because the whole family can get work on the site. The women and children all get involved in the work. In the past few years they have traveled to many places in Punjab, e.g., Pathankot, Jammu, Tilwada, Ambala, Chandigarh; many towns in Rajasthan—Jaipur, Alwar, Ajmer; and also Himachal Pradesh.

Nearly 500 people are needed to work on a medium-sized kiln. They come from many states but the majority of them are from Rajasthan and Bihar. An organized network of contractors and brick kiln owners operates in the area, moving from village to village, hiring workers, and then transporting them to the site of work. They contact the workers for contractual labor year after year. The wages are not paid at the end of the day's work, or even at the end of the week. Instead, the contractor gives each family a small sum for daily expenses (Rs.500–600) once in fifteen days. The contractor also arranges for a place for them to stay near the kiln area. These are generally *katchcha* mud huts or tents for which they are not supposed to pay any rent. The settlement is quite large, almost like a small village because many families migrate together, sometimes from the same village also. They generally migrate with eight to ten families in a group. They are usually not allowed to return home in between, or, at the most, for a day or two, but they cannot leave the work in between and take up other work elsewhere. The final payment is done only at the end of the work period when the rainy season starts.

The work is very hard and backbreaking and endless. A typical working day begins early in the morning at 6 a.m. and stretches right through the day till 6 p.m. There are no holidays. All the workers including women and children have to work seven days a week. The wages depend on the number of bricks made by the family. The men prepare the clay, the children transport it to the site, and women fill the mold and prepare the bricks for drying. An average family of four (husband-wife-two children) can prepare up to 4,000 bricks a day. They are paid Rs. 25 for every thousand bricks. This averages to 100 rupees a day (approximately US$2) for the whole family. They do not get paid per person. After meeting their expenses, they can save between 500–700 rupees (US$10–14) in a month. At the end of the contract, which can extend up to a year or more the final payments are made. They return with 5,000–7,000 rupees (US$100–140) after ten months, generally during the rains because there is no activity during this time in the brick kilns.

Besides making the bricks there is other kind of work in the kilns, e.g., loading the firing hearth, firing the bricks, loading and unloading of trucks etc. For this some workers are paid according to the number of bricks, while some are paid daily wages also. But Banwari Lal and Kishandas were not sure of the amount the workers were paid or the terms and conditions in these cases as they had never done other work themselves. However, they were sure that all the workers were paid at the end of the contract and no final payments were made at any other time. They felt that the contractor did this to ensure that they did not leave the job in between.

Women do not migrate alone; they only travel with their families. If there is a single woman (widow) she will also move with relatives. The working conditions are harsh but there is no sexual harassment at the workplace because they migrate in large groups, which is safer for women. The life in the village is much better, but there is no work. The children do not go to school because each year the family moves to another town, another location.

The tribal belt in Southwest Rajasthan exhibits distinct traits from the rest of the State. Badly affected by the depletion of the forests, the tribal blocks are increasingly impoverished and are an ecologically, economically, and socially vulnerable group. The central issues in the area are those of land rights and environmental degradation, and the resultant loss of livelihoods, health, and education. There has been very little investment in the area—for example, literacy rates for women in the last census was 2 percent. Ignorance and lack of facilities, as well as erosion of local healing systems, make health a critically neglected issue.

While seasonal migration of men for wage labor in the cities has been the norm in the last decade, the volume of migrants has increased phenomenally, and now includes women going into the cities to look for wage labor. A unique phenomenon is the seasonal migration of young tribal adolescent girls to work primarily in the cotton-picking fields in Gujarat, and also other sectors such as the tobacco industries and oil pressing mills, and for cleaning machinery. The young girls—from thirteen years of age onward—go in groups, with a contractor from the village or with a group of young boys going to work, and are particularly vulnerable to exploitation by the contractor or the *Seth* for whom they work, or even by some of their village boys. Cases of girls being sexually exploited and "kept" by the *Seth*, and her family's subsequent rejection and violence when she returns are common, but the Panchayat (local governing bodies) are intolerant of engaging with this issue. The silence around the issue and the pressure on the girls to continue this earning, as well as little knowledge of women's bodies and reproductive health issues, make it all the more difficult to address these particular vulnerabilities.

MIGRATION TRENDS IN GUJARAT

In Gujarat, the spectrum of migration stretches from seasonal migration of pastoral communities at one end to large numbers of Gujaratis migrating out of the country at the other. Rajasthan and Gujarat share a common border and common geographical areas and there are many commonalities in trends of migration in the two states. The migration patterns in the state can be broadly divided into four major patterns: pastoral migration, migration from tribal areas, migration to coastal Gujarat, and migration to the industrial belt that includes Ahmedabad, Surat, and Alang.

Pastoral movements in Gujarat, as in Rajasthan, have been the traditional form of migration. Before partition, people moved toward the northwest, to the banks of the Indus River. Now they migrate to the southeast, toward neighboring states. Over the years their access to grazing lands has been restricted due to deforestation and policies which restrict open access. Thus, over the past fifty years the migration patterns have been changing and adapting to availability and access.

Fourteen percent of Gujarat's population is tribal, mainly consisting of the Bhils, Rathwas, and Kolis. The tribals of the Panchmahals migrate as families to other parts of Gujarat—both to nearby cities to engage in work within the informal sector and to agricultural fields nearby. Though many may own small landholdings, they are unable to earn enough to support themselves due to several reasons, including the small size of these landholdings and lack of irrigation. Tribals of the hilly Dang district migrate to the plains of south Gujarat (to the Surat and Valsad areas) in search of employment. Usually they are hired by the sugar factories and are paid according to the piece-rate system (on the basis of the quantity of sugarcane they cut). But this migration is seasonal and lasts for six to eight months. They return to their villages as soon as the monsoon begins in order to carry out the agricultural activities. Migration is undertaken in families or larger units and thus women do not migrate alone.

In the 1980s the export-oriented fish processing zones grew and expanded in Gujarat. According to one local NGO, there are around forty to fifty units along the coastline starting from Veraval up to Dwarka. Gujarat boasts 25 percent of the total continental shelf for fishing and 20 percent of the country's total coastline. This is a major site of work for migrant women. Local women who were previously from fishing communities and other lower castes are employed in these units. They travel up and down the length of the coast each season. They work at the ports where the fish are downloaded from the trawlers and they are involved in storing and transporting. Some women work in the processing plants. Women involved with storing and transporting live near the workplace in temporary makeshift shelters provided by the owners of the units. They have long working hours and can be called at any time of the day and night as required. The majority of workers inside the processing units are women, many of them migrant contract workers hired from the southern state of Kerala who specialize in shelling, peeling, and grading prawns. They handle frozen prawns for hours at a stretch, working in damp and dirty halls. At night, they sleep in dingy hostels located above the units. A large chunk of the wages is deducted as charges for the food provided (Warrier 2001).

The hostels ensure that the factory owner has a captive workforce, which can be put on the job at any time of the night or day, whenever the fish arrive. The units have been given a special exemption from the ban on night work for women. The average worker works for 12 hours at a stretch. The majority of the workers are young girls (preferably unmarried and childless) between sixteen and twenty-five years old. They generally work for eight to ten years in this trade, saving up money for dowry for their marriage or to support impoverished families. Most women are unaware of the method of recruitment, the name of the company for which they work, or the name of the contractor. They only know the sub-agent who recruited them from their villages. Since the units close down during the monsoons, the industry claims that it is seasonal and thus escapes the provisions of the Factories Act, which would include more rights and benefits for the workers. It has also lobbied for relaxation of all labor legislation. Many units are run in mafia style, with security guards who do not permit free entry or exit. The workers are virtually captive.

The saltpan workers migrate in families and sometimes as a group of families from the same village or nearby villages. They travel to the various sites (Jamnagar, Bhavnagar, Kutch, among others) of saltpan plants, where they are employed in couples. The wages are paid to each couple (a man and a woman) and not to individuals. The majority of the workers come from the lower castes. They leave for work at the salt plants after the festival of Diwali (November–December) and return to their villages before the monsoons, when the saltpan work stops. The work is contractual, the Mukadam or contractor comes to the villages and collects them and transports them to the worksite. They live in makeshift shelters near the saltpan fields, made from polythene sheets and bamboo, which are supplied by the owner of the plants. Here they live, braving the vagaries of the harsh weather. While the smaller fields employ twenty to thirty workers, at least 200–300 men and women work the larger fields. Most of the workers were not sure of the amount of wages paid. The wages varied from Rs. 25 to 50 (approx 50 cents—US$1.00) per couple per day. Working in the saltpan exposes them to high levels of concentrated salt as they have to stand in the salt water. They develop sores and many women complained that their hair steadily thins and falls off. Some young girls showed bald patches on their head. The main problem they face is the lack of clean drinking water.

In 1982 there were sixty-five textile mills in Gujarat, which have now dwindled to only ten. Of these most were in Ahmedabad. Nearly 50,000 workers were rendered jobless by the closure of these mills and of these, 36,000 were in Ahmedabad alone. The job of a mill worker was a prestigious job and for those who were thrown out, taking up petty jobs was very problematic and a matter of shame. Some started petty businesses and set up small kiosks, shops, etc. But this was not enough to sustain the family and keep up the middle-class lifestyle. The women in these families were gradually pushed out into the work force, mostly in the unorganized sector. In a situation of scarcity of jobs, women did take up sex work or work related to prostitution, such as renting out rooms. Though there are no red light areas in Ahmedabad, there is a flourishing sex trade, involving housewives, college girls, and others who are brought in from West Bengal, Orissa, and even from Bangladesh. Gujarat, being a relatively wealthy state in India, has always attracted migrant workers from other states. We found organized networks for women coming in from the eastern states of Orissa and West Bengal for different kinds of work, including domestic work and sex work. The conditions under which these women migrate are often very precarious, and facilitated by layers of middlemen. This does sometimes lead to women being deceived or exploited in the process, especially as these are very poor and often uneducated women. The women find work in the cities of Ahmedabad, Surat, and Alang.

Surat has emerged as the city of the migrant with nearly half its population comprised of migrants. Surat attracts workers from all over the state as well as from Bihar, Orissa, and eastern Uttar Pradesh. The city is highly industrialized and known for its power looms, artificial silk factories, diamond cutting, and other industries. Nearly 100,000 migrants work in the power loom factories. There are three kinds of migration to Surat—those who come to set up industry, skilled workers coming to work in the industry, and the unskilled migrant workers.

Finally, Alang, the port near Bhavnagar, is a unique place to study migration of men. The port which is famous for its ship-breaking yards attracts migrant workers from eastern Uttar Pradesh, Bihar, and Orissa. The work is backbreaking and very risky. The workers are exposed to tremendous danger as they are untrained for such a specialized job. They have to use sophisticated machinery for cutting through the hard steel of the ship and in the process become victims of numerous accidents (Abdi 2003). The material taken from these ships and the steel sheets have to be transported to various locations in the country. Because of the heavy traffic, a large sex industry has flourished along the highways to Alang in addition to catering to the men working in Alang.

CONCERNS AND CONCLUSIONS

The study reveals broad trends, yet also provides a glimpse of the various kinds of migration, sites of work, and vulnerabilities that women in India face, both in the process of migration and at sites of work. Globalization and neoliberal economic policies have precipitated migration due to increased opportunities for finding work in certain areas and impoverishment and disruption of livelihoods in others. The growth of export-oriented industries like garments and electronics, and practices such as outsourcing and flexible labor, have created a demand for female labor in certain locations. In addition, migrant women are in demand in jobs of care, specifically domestic work, child and elder care. Another feature of contemporary migration which has contributed to the demand for female labor has been the growing sex, entertainment, and tourism sector.

Our initial study in the two states shows that women's migration is a very complex issue and needs to be analyzed both within a broad

A Saltpan Worker in Gujarat

It is a hot scorching day as we approach the village of Kharchia, near Jhodia in Gujarat. As we bump along the practically non-existent road we can see the white, salt-ridden soil through the fresh green grass. This area has had good rain after three years of drought. Soon one can see the red tiled roofs of the temporary shelters made for the villagers who have lost all their houses and possessions in the earthquake.

Vijayaben Karsan Bai has been working in the saltpans for the past twenty-two years. She is forty-five years old. She goes with her family every year to work on different sites. The *Mukadam,* or contractor (who could sometimes be from the same village), contacts them and offers them work with a certain company. This could change every year. Vijayaben has traveled to Bhuvaniya Taluka in Rajkot, Khejadia, Gagwa, and Sikka in Jamnagar. She has also migrated toward Bhavnagar, Surat, and to Kutch. Her family, consisting of one son, one daughter in law, and three children, moves every year for eight months to work in the saltpans.

The work is hard and painfully slow. Vijayaben says: "First we have to fill the saltpans or fields when the tide is high. Then we make the boundaries to keep the water in. Guarding the boundaries is also a major work. They keep breaking down and a constant vigil has to be kept up. After about a month the salt gets 'cooked.' During this time there is not much work and we have to wait. The Mukadam gives us expenses but these are later deducted from our wages." After the salt starts crystallizing, it has to be taken out and pulled along the sides to be kept in huge mounds. This is then loaded on the trucks to send to the plants where it is cleaned, iodized and packed. Each truck can carry up to 62,400 kilos of salt. The women and men both work on loading.

On the saltpan or field, Vijayaben works as a pair with her husband and, together, they are paid 700 rupees at the end of fifteen days. On probing further about the wages, she seems confused.

"The women do not know what they get as wages," one of the men explains. "As long as there is food to feed the families." The majority are illiterate so they do not know how much their wages come to at the end of the fortnight. Feeding the family is the major concern.

"In the beginning we eat bajra roti (bread) with potatoes and onion sabzi (curry), sometimes daal (lentils), also urad, and chana. But the money is not sufficient to keep this up every day. Then we eat only bajra roti and chillies or onions. We never get milk, not even for the children. Even our tea is black!" Vijayaben grimaces. "When the money is over we just go hungry... What can we do? If we get a little time, we go to catch fish and eat it roasted with salt when we have no more money."

The workers have to stand for long hours in the salt water, which is very harmful for their health. Most develop sores and rashes on their skin. "See?" She shows us the scars on her hands and feet. "We all have them." The scorching heat coupled with salt water burns their skin black. "We are thirsty all the time and our hair starts falling off." She pulls her granddaughter toward us to show the bald patches on her head. Vijayaben herself has lost a lot of hair. "What will we do with long hair if our stomachs are empty? This is a small price to pay," she says philosophically. "Salt gets into every pore of our body—on our skin, in our hair, our mouth, noses and eyes. In our clothes. We feel nauseated at times and sick. Even when we sleep we feel the itching and irritation from the salt. We have to bathe at least twice a day or our bodies will itch terribly and the skin will get rashes." Bathing and washing clothes needs clean water and that is a valuable commodity for the workers. The owner sends one tanker of water every three or four days and this has to be used for everything—bathing, washing, cleaning and cooking. The women have a tough time. They have to bath and defecate in the open. The stark surroundings, sometimes with not even a bush in sight, add to their exposure and shame. They sleep on the hard floor, which becomes like stone in the harsh winters. Sometimes, when the sand gets soaked with dew, sleep can be a punishment.

Life for Vijayaben is not easy when she returns home. Most of her earnings and that of her family have already been spent during the eight months they lived away. When she gets back she has to find work on the fields of the landed people, mostly Patels, in the area. Her two daughters have gone to work in the fields. There is not enough work for all the members of the family. "We have to live somehow," she says. "We have started making coal from the wood we cut from the thorny shrubs around." The wood is burnt in closed furnaces and then water is poured over it to make coal. This is sold to the Patels in the next village who take it in bulk from them. Vijayaben knows that the Patels do not pay them enough for the coal and that they make much more money out of this business, but she and her family have no way of selling it themselves.

macro framework and at the level of the experience of migration and work. It is as important to locate how globalization has led to increasing impoverishment of many people as it is to understand the actual experience of working at a construction site (for example). It is a fact that women are moving today, on their own and with their families, in order to earn a livelihood. There is indeed a feminization of poverty and migration: women's migration has increasingly become a prominent feature of globalization. In our study, we found women in a variety of worksites. The experience of the process of migration, of finding work, and conditions of work all told stories of vulnerability to exploitation, and different forms of abuse.

The debate in the South Asian context over the past decade on women and migration has to a large extent been framed within the discourses of trafficking for sexual exploitation. While completely agreeing that trafficking is an extreme violation of women's human rights, women face different kinds of abuse, exploitation, and violation of rights almost routinely in the process of migration or finding work. Particularly, the state looks at women as victims who must be protected from trafficking, and such protection often becomes a tool for the violation of women's rights by restricting their right to move. Moreover the focus on prostitution as the main site of trafficking has diverted the debate from one of rights and vulnerabilities to issues of morality.

The contexts within which trafficking takes place are similar to those within which migration takes place and include economic compulsions, social and cultural practices, historical and political factors, and the systemic gender discrimination and violence that girls and women face. There are multiple factors that increase women's vulnerabilities which are enhanced because of their structural position within patriarchal society. The conditions which allow for deception, coercion, bondage, violence, and exploitation of labor are the daily realities of the lives of many girls and women. The inherent vulnerability that women face is enhanced when it operates in conjunction with other factors that limit the rights of workers in general—for instance, the nature of work (sex work, domestic work, dangerous work, prohibited work, and so on) and the location of work (own country/foreign country, at home/outside home, and so on).

Our study shows that a focus on migration and informal and non-regulated sites of work allows us to take up such issues as labor rights and sexual harassment at the workplace. It is therefore through a vulnerabilities and rights framework, such as the one employed here, that we can begin to identify issues that frame the lives of migrant women and build strategies for change.

REFERENCES

Abdi, R. "India's ship-scrapping industry: Monument to the abuse of human labor and the environment." *IIAS Newsletter* no. 32, November 2003.

Bremen, Jan. *Footloose Labor: Working in India's Informal Economy.* Cambridge: Cambridge University Press, 1996.

Coomaraswamy, Radhika. *Report of the Special Rapporteur on Violence Against Women, Its Causes and Consequences on Trafficking and Migration.* Submitted in accordance with the Commission on Human Rights. New York: United Nations, 1997.

————. *Report of the Special Rapporteur on Violence Against Women, Its Causes and Consequences. Addendum: Mission to Bangladesh, Nepal and India on the Issue of Trafficking of Women and Girls (October 28–November 15, 2000).* New York: United Nations, Economic and Social Council, 2000.

Karlekar, Malavika. "Gender Dimensions in Labor Migration: An Overview." In Loes Schenk-Sandbergen (ed.), *Women and Seasonal Labor Migration.* New Delhi: Sage, 1995.

Kavoori, P. *Pastoralism in Expansion: The Transhuming Herders of Western Rajasthan.* Oxford University Press, 2000.

Lingham, Lakshmi. "Locating Women in the Migration Studies: An Overview." *Indian Journal of Social Work* 59 (3), 1998: 715–727.

Pedraza, S. "Women and Migration: The Social Consequences of Gender." *Annual Review of Sociology* 17, 1991: 303–325.

Sweetman, C. "Gender and Migration." *Gender and Development*, vol. 1 (6), 1998.

Warrier, Shobana M. V. "Women at Work: Migrant Women in the Fish Processing Industry." *Economic and Political Weekly,* Sept. 15, 2001.

10

Feminist Participatory Action Research in the Mekong Region

Jan Boontinand,
for the Global Alliance Against Traffic in Women

Over the past decade, the issue of trafficking in persons, especially women and children, has gained increasing attention at the national, regional, and international levels. In the Mekong sub-region, the socioeconomic and political changes that have taken place in countries like Cambodia and Vietnam in the past decades have been accompanied by greater mobility of people internally as well as across borders. Experience from a country like Thailand has shown that the movement of people, particularly women, into various types of labor and service sectors, including marriage, has been increasingly accompanied by deception, coercion, and exploitation.

The Research and Action Project on Trafficking in Women in the Mekong Region—in short, the RA Project[1]—was a response to the growing concern over the increasing number of women who had been "trafficked" in Cambodia and Vietnam in the late 1980s and early 1990s. At that time, there was a general lack of reliable data on the trafficking situation as well as a lack of appropriate strategies to provide support to affected women. The main objectives of the RA Project were to document the situation of trafficking in women in Cambodia and Vietnam and to develop appropriate strategies to address the problems and support the women concerned. The methodology employed was one of action research with a feminist and participatory approach. This methodology had been shown to be effective in giving involved women a voice and a chance to improve their conditions through taking actions for themselves. The project was divided into two phases: a research phase and an action phase. It was implemented by four partner organizations: the Cambodian Women's Development Agency (CWDA) in Cambodia, the Youth Research Institute (YRI) based in Hanoi for the work in Northern Vietnam, the Women's Union of Ho Chi Minh City, and Tay Ninh Women's Union in Southern Vietnam. The Global Alliance Against Traffic in Women (GAATW), based in Bangkok, Thailand, acted as a coordinating agency, providing assistance and facilitating the project. When the RA Project was implemented in early 1997, there had been very few projects or studies about trafficking in this region, and in addition the issue was perceived to be very sensitive in certain political environments. These factors impacted on the implementation, as well as the outcome of the project. In this sense, the project as a whole was challenging and a learning process for all involved. Nevertheless, this four-year-long project (1997–2001) brought about a number of tangible positive outcomes.

One special feature of the project was that it was an initiative of local organizations. GAATW recognized that there had been a number of research projects carried out and reports published on the issues related to trafficking in women in the Mekong region. However, many of these research projects were completed by external consultants rather than by local organizations working in the country. Such research reports contained useful information on the situation of trafficking (e.g., experiences of trafficked women, their families and communities, forms and patterns of trafficking, trafficking networks, and working conditions). They also made policy recommendations and suggested programs to address the problem. However, the discussion in the reports did not always reflect the perception of the issue by local groups and the women concerned.

The RA Project was probably the first of its kind in the region. The project set out to achieve many objectives. The process toward achieving these objectives was certainly a challenging one due to the complexity of the issue as well as the particular sociopolitical contexts of Cambodia and Vietnam. The overview of the process and outcome of the project, including an analysis of the research findings, is presented and discussed in the full report (GAATW 2002). This paper describes the complexities that surrounded research on trafficking, discusses the challenges in using the Feminist Participatory Action Research (FPAR) methodology in particular sociopolitical contexts, and reflects upon some of the main research findings.

THE IDEA OF TRAFFICKING: AN EVOLVING DISCUSSION

The conceptual understanding of the issue of trafficking is perhaps one of the most important factors that influenced the RA Project. However, when the project was conceived in 1995–1996, there was no internationally agreed-upon definition of trafficking in persons. For the project partner in Cambodia, the concept of trafficking was understood in the context of a human rights violation, connected to the growth in prostitution. For the project partners in Vietnam, trafficking was perceived as related to women being forced or deceived into prostitution or into becoming wives of foreign men. While the perception of the issue by the project partners may reflect the actual trend of trafficking phenomenon at that time, it must be recognized that the understanding of the trafficking issue by project partners—particularly those in Vietnam—also followed the legal concept of trafficking in each country. This understanding was largely based on the historical understanding of trafficking in international law that focused on the recruitment and movement of women across borders for the purpose of prostitution, as in the 1949 Convention for the Suppression of the Traffic in Persons and of the Exploitation of the Prostitution of Others.[2] Thus, despite the absence of an internationally agreed-upon definition, trafficking was often associated with the crime of harboring or facilitating prostitution. In Vietnam, trafficking was also linked to kidnapping, false adoption, illegal migration, or immigration, as well as illegally staying abroad. All of these acts are considered a crime under the Vietnamese Criminal Code (YRI 2000, 166–167).

To set a common conceptual framework for the research, GAATW as the coordinating agency shared an analysis of the issues of migration, trafficking, and prostitution based on the research experience in Thailand (Foundation For Women 1996). After the initial phase of data collection GAATW organized a meeting to synthesize and share the findings. During the presentation of the findings by each team, it became clear that there was a need to discuss and analyze the terms and concepts that each research team was using. Terms such as trafficker, brothel owner, pimp, matchmaker/recruiter, buyer, and prostitute/sex worker were used to imply a trafficking case although it was not always clear that there were situations of deception, coercion, or exploitation taking place. For example, there was generally no or little distinction made between voluntary migration and trafficking. As there seemed to be a lack of a clear understanding of what constituted trafficking, GAATW provided a two-part definition that was used in the International Report Project on Trafficking in Women in 1997.[3]

The researchers were also cautioned that although the term *trafficking* was often used to describe situations of illegal migration and/or situations of women going into prostitution, they needed to recognize that each of these phenomenon was separate, although they may be interrelated. It was important for clarity, therefore, that the research team be very specific (or give detailed explanations) when describing a situation. To be able to be specific, a number of elements were identified and discussed as follows:

1. Deception (usually about the nature of work), coercion in recruitment;
2. Force, coercion, and/or the threat of violence during transportation process;
3. Force, coercion, and violence or threat of violence at destination, e.g., worksites;
4. Deprivation of freedom (of movement and personal choice);
5. Abuse of authority/dominant position—e.g., a mother may use her position to get her daughter to work in prostitution. She may or may not know what it involves. It may also be government officials, teacher, village head, etc.;
6. Debt bondage—a situation where a woman is told that she is now indebted to the person who facilitated her travel and that she must pay back the debt by working. Equally, a situation where the deduction of the debt was not done in a reasonable manner (possibly in order to ensure that the woman remained in debt for as long as possible).

It was also explained to the researchers that not all of the above elements have to be present in order to talk about trafficking—it was important to consider that there were two key processes in trafficking, i.e., the abusive, coercive recruitment/movement and the exploitative condition at the end point. The research teams were encouraged to identify these elements through their research.

Gaining conceptual depth and clarity on the trafficking issue has been an evolving process, both for GAATW and for the project partners. In the last few years, discussion on the definition of trafficking, and measures to combat it, has been progressing at the international level. The Special Rapporteur on Violence Against Women commented in her report to the UN Commission on Human Rights during its 56th session in April 2000, that the definition of trafficking should focus on forced-labor and slavery-like practices rather than narrowly focusing on prostitution or sexual exploitation. She also noted that "the 1949 Convention for the Suppression of Traffick in Persons and of the Exploitation of the Prostitution of Others . . . [which] seeks to criminalize acts associated with prostitution . . . has proven ineffective in protecting the rights of trafficked women and combatting trafficking" (Coomaraswamy 2000).

COMPLEX REALITIES

Recognizing that the scope of trafficking in women included more than just forced prostitution or sexual exploitation, GAATW encouraged the project partners in Vietnam and Cambodia to look beyond the original research scope. This was done during a monitoring visit in the first phase of the project. In Cambodia, the local partner (the CWDA) already had a good grasp on the elements of trafficking although the actual level of understanding may have varied among the project staff. The director of CWDA was instrumental in giving direction and training to the project staff regarding the broader areas of trafficking. During the first phase, researchers in Cambodia found many cases of trafficking of women for forced labor or for begging in Thailand.[4] In Vietnam, the discussion and understanding of the issue was more complex because the implementing agencies had to operate within the existing legal framework and the official perception of the trafficking issue in the country. In this regard, it was also more difficult to expand the scope of the research here and it was particularly clear in Vietnam during the course of the project that the official perception of the trafficking issue influenced the research process and the nature of the research findings. There were also other challenges related to the project in Vietnam. First, at the start of the research process trafficking was perceived as a sensitive, cross-border issue with China. It took almost one year after the project was actually launched to get official approval for the project from the government. The lack of official status of the project created some negative impact on project activities, particularly those involving the support of GAATW (which implied the presence of foreigners). Second, training for researchers and monitoring of fieldwork during the initial research stage by GAATW, for example, could not take place as planned. Much of the preparation and the actual research process had to be undertaken by the implementing agencies themselves without added support from GAATW.

The conceptual conflation between trafficking in women and prostitution that was employed had some impact on the quality and character of data collected. This was particularly the case with the initial research in Southern Vietnam, in which much of the findings only described the situation of women who had to resort to prostitution because of their difficult circumstances or that of their family. Although the project partners in Southern Vietnam generally agreed on the basic elements of trafficking such as deception, coercion, the use of violence, abuse by authorities, debt bondage, forced labor, and slavery-like practices, these elements were not always highlighted in the project reports. This was perhaps because of the focus on prostitution rather than on elements of trafficking. The Northern Vietnam research team also discussed living and working conditions of prostitutes as those of trafficked women, without making any distinction between the two groups.

The conflation between trafficking and illegal migration, which was consistent with the official line in Vietnam, also had an impact upon the quality of the research findings and analysis presented in the reports. For example, the statistics on "trafficked" women cited in the final report largely referred to the number of women who had migrated clandestinely. The researchers included data on women sent back by the Chinese authorities, those who had gone away and lost contact with their families, and those who did not give official notification to, nor receive permission from, local authorities before migrating. No distinction was made between these different groups. Researchers obtained these figures mostly from local authorities, the border police, or the local Women's Union and cited them in the report without further explanation. Cross-checking with local authorities by GAATW during a monitoring visit clarified the detail of these figures. Moreover, at the beginning of the project, it was difficult for the researchers to gain support for women returnees from the local authority. The women returning from China, especially those in rural Northern Vietnam, were seen as law-breakers by local authorities. This was because local authorities viewed trafficking and illegal migration only as a matter of law-and-order, in line with the country's legal framework. Most of the women and their families did not approach local authorities for help because they were afraid of punishment.

In rural Northern Vietnam, the general community attitude toward migration, especially to China, did not seem to be a positive one. Thus, researchers encountered some resistance from community people when they tried to set up women's groups to support returnees from China. Some people asked the researchers why the project was helping those who had left their homeland to seek a better life in China while many people were trying to make ends meet at home.

In spite of these complications and the fact that trafficking and prostitution were conflated—and that illegal migration was an ongoing issue—some changes in the perception were noted on both individual and organizational levels. In the context of Northern Vietnam, the researchers were instrumental in engaging in discussion with local authorities concerning the latter's view on the status of returnees. Instead of seeing them as criminals, the local authorities gradually developed an understanding about the situation of women who had been cheated and had to leave the country illegally. In the later stage of the project, this shift in perception resulted in the involvement of local authorities in the provision of support to the women returnees and their families, as well as to the women's support groups that had been formed. Similarly, more openness and a change in perception about trafficking were developed during the project in Southern Vietnam. For example, both the researchers and the local authorities initially saw the phenomenon of Vietnamese women in the southern provinces marrying Taiwanese men through arrangement of agents only as a disguise for trafficking. However, through further survey and discussion, the later project report from the Southern Vietnam team remarked that there were also cases of happy marriages. In both Ho Chi Minh City and Tay Ninh province, local authorities and researchers also acknowledged the fact that there were many women who voluntarily worked as prostitutes to earn a living. Nevertheless, the general attitude toward these women remained that they had chosen the wrong path and needed to be reeducated. Developing conceptual clarity of trafficking with the local partners in Vietnam was a challenging and interesting process.

METHODOLOGY: FEMINIST PARTICIPATORY ACTION RESEARCH (FPAR)

The project framework was one of action research with a feminist and participatory approach, which would give women a voice and a chance to improve their living conditions (or to address their situation) through taking actions themselves. The research methodology included both quantitative and qualitative techniques. Questionnaire surveys were carried out during the project extension period on the situation of Vietnamese women marrying foreigners. Secondary information was also collected from published reports and newspapers. However, the project relied mostly on primary data gathered from interviews with women and other informants. The concepts of participation, participatory action research, and feminist research as understood by GAATW for the RA project are summarized below.[5]

Participation

Participation is a powerful but slippery concept. Within the context of development projects it may mean anything from having people contribute to the project with cash or labor, to involving them in planning and decisions, or taking part in research and evaluation of projects. Clearly this last type of involvement means that people are able to share ideas about problems and possible solutions. The participants are seen as "insiders"—they are not simply sources of data or sanctioners of studies and reports, but actively codetermine every phase of the research process. Through this form of research the participants' knowledge and experiences are valued and their confidence in their ability to analyze their situation themselves is enhanced.

Another very important aspect of participatory research is the involvement of participants as a group, not just as individuals. By encouraging participants to share information and analyze problems among themselves, it is possible to develop an even clearer view on the issues being studied. In this way, the research process can function as a conscientization process. The importance of working with groups of participants, rather than with individuals only, is reflected in the methods specifically developed for participatory research. Almost all of these methods, or techniques, have been adopted to be used in group discussions. Such techniques are also useful in social-science research. They can yield very valuable information, not only for the researcher but notably also for the participants themselves. As each of them contributes to the activity, they will share views and discuss and clarify their ideas. At the same time the techniques can assist in clarifying ways of taking action.

Participatory Action Research

The purpose of participatory research is not only to describe and interpret social reality in a more reliable way, but to radically change it as well. Moreover, it aims to transform reality *with* rather than *for* oppressed people. This is the concept of "partnership approaches." Participatory action research combines three activities: investigation, evaluation, and action. The link between research and action is the most important aspect—when people are directly involved in an analysis of their situation, it follows that they want to find solutions to the problems they have identified. In the action process new insights and new solutions may emerge. Not only the participants, but also the researcher can change ideas about social reality. By taking action, the participants and the researcher can work together to change the existing social structures.

An important aspect of action research is its cyclic nature: it starts with studying, learning, and analyzing the situation and problems. From this emerges planning of possible solutions, and then action is taken. The result of the action is then evaluated, a new analysis of the changed situation is made, new planning with new action follows, and so on. These repeated assessments further improve and consolidate the action. By bringing research and action together in this way, it is possible to study the process of change over a long period of time. This type of research is supposed to break down the distinction between the "knowers" (researchers, scholars, experts) and "not-knowers" (peasants, women, poor people; in short, all those who are "subjects" of research). Outcomes and knowledge coming from the research are directly processed and used by the participants, with support and assistance of the researcher.

Participatory action research contrasts sharply with the conventional model of research, in which participants are treated mostly as passive subjects only, and sometimes as receivers of the results. It is not always recognized that this still unconventional type of research can also enhance the validity of the findings. Causal inferences about the behavior of people are likely to be more valid and able to be acted upon when the people themselves take part in developing and testing them. Clearly, participatory action research not only requires considerable skills of the researcher in using participatory techniques as indicated above, but also open-mindedness and a pleasant manner with the participants. Her attitude and her role are different from that of a "traditional" researcher—she not only gathers information, but also clarifies, stimulates, supports, and assists. Her work will always include a transfer of organizational, technical, and analytical skills from the researcher to the participants.

Feminist Research

The most important premises which govern this research can be summarized as follows:

- a focus on the lives, the opinions, and the experiences of women; this includes women's relations with children and men;
- a focus on possibilities for changes in thinking and behavior, in order to fight against oppression and exploitation and to improve living conditions and interpersonal relationships;
- to abandon the conventional idea that knowledge is something that exists by itself and for itself, free of the scientist or researcher and his or her background and environment (sex, culture, language, position, etc.);
- knowledge should be accessible to everyone, not only to the researcher or the scientific community.

Comparing these premises with the principles of participatory research and action research described above, it becomes clear that there is a considerable overlap in basic thinking for all three research modes. Feminist research is mainly different in its main focus on women, and in rejecting any male bias or androcentrism in research. This grew out of the feminist critique of social sciences, when it was found that in many theories and studies women's experiences are omitted or falsely represented. It is believed that looking at the world through the eyes of women and studying women's experiences will adjust the male-biased view on reality which is still not uncommon in the social sciences.

An important aim of feminist research is to understand the extent, the dimensions, the forms, and the causes of exploitation and oppression of women. Then, it is also thought important to study the means through which women may already challenge systems and institutions which limit their choices. Oppression is an extraordinarily complex process in which women (and people in general) are not necessarily totally powerless, in that they may utilize a range of resources—verbal, interactional, and others—as forms of everyday resistance.

Because feminism is committed to changing the conditions of exploitation and oppression, a large section of feminist research focuses on possibilities for such changes. This requires new methodologies and new approaches in doing research, as have been developed in the participatory and action research approaches. Central in these approaches are, firstly, sharing of data and findings with participants, and secondly, using the research as a means toward conscientization, for both the women participants and for the researcher. A heightened awareness, and enhanced skills to analyze their situation, will then encourage and empower the women to take action, to find solutions to their problems, and to change their lives. These concepts are far from those usually accepted in conventional research, where knowledge and theories are supposed to be detached from any practical use. Not only feminists, but also those advocating participatory and action research take the opposite view: research should be executed to serve the interests of the participants in the first place, who will use the knowledge gained for their own empowerment.

Another important requirement in conventional social science is that researchers must be objective—their personal ideas are not supposed to color the research. Feminist scholars point to the impossibility and even the undesirability of this view. Researchers should not only look at their own "hidden" values on moral issues, but take a clear stand in reciprocity and solidarity with the participants in their research. It is also generally agreed that it is preferable that women researchers should be working with women participants. Female researchers usually have an advantage over males in communicating with other women; in addition they may share a set of common experiences with other women and therefore be able to identify with their situations and problems.

The development and application of feminist participatory action research in projects on trafficking and migration is still at a stage of infancy. Prior to the RA Project, it was applied and tested out in the Research and Action Project on Traffick in Women in Thailand that was implemented by the Foundation For Women between 1992–1994. Experience in the earlier project had shown that FPAR was a useful methodology for research on the trafficking issue. Through its "bottom-up" approach, the views of women were heard and their rights promoted. Nevertheless it was thought that application of FPAR in the research in Vietnam and Cambodia could further validate the concept and methodology.

The FPAR Methodology in Action

First and foremost, the understanding of FPAR itself by the implementing agencies was a crucial factor. To really understand the principles and practice of the methodology, extensive training, discussion, and hands-on experience in practical exercises were required, especially for those who were not familiar with such a concept. Given the limitations of the training, it could be expected that the understanding and the use of FPAR by the implementing agencies might not have been optimal.

The application of FPAR was challenging in the particular sociopolitical contexts of Cambodia and Vietnam. Specifically, these contexts determine the structure of the society and the degree of openness and control within that society. Such factors influence the freedom to which a research methodology can be applied in that situation and the success of its outcome. Moreover, the sensitive nature of the issue of trafficking in these countries and confusion over the understanding of what it involved further complicated the application of FPAR (see earlier discussion). The role of researchers, local project coordinators, and implementing agencies was also critical in the application. This included the dynamics and relationships between the researchers and research participants, and between the project coordinators and the researchers. In addition, the mandate and experience of the particular organization as the implementing agency of the project also influenced the way in which the FPAR methodology was applied.

Cambodia

In Cambodia, data collection was done in the first phase of the project in order for researchers to have an understanding of the situation and problems of trafficking. This period was also an important time for the researchers to establish contact with research participants and community people. All of the researchers were either local social or development workers. Some of them were involved in HIV/AIDS education programs at the community level or in brothel areas. With the use of a checklist developed at the start of the project, the researchers were able to make contact with, and interview people in the villages and women in brothels. The researchers reported some difficulties in talking to local people in the villages due to the situation of political unrest during the time of the research (CWDA 1997). The local leaders and the village women perceived them as working for a political group and thus did not trust talking to them. Furthermore, security of the researchers and of the women they talked to was of concern since the trafficking network were connected to some powerful people including some in the armed forces. As for interviews with sex workers, some researchers also found it difficult to talk in detail to the women in brothels because of the close watch kept by the brothel owners. After the process of data collection, the researchers arranged for meetings to share and discuss research findings with the women concerned, i.e., those in the villages and brothels.

In the villages, sharing of research findings, namely the situation of trafficked women from the villages, led to discussion on causes of the problems and actions that needed to be taken to address them. Consequently, information-sharing groups were formed to monitor what was happening to women locally. Subsequent activities that developed in the communities, including literacy classes, a reading room, and income-generating activities, can be seen as responses to some of the problems identified—i.e., low literacy rate and high levels of poverty. Although the focus on and participation of women was central in all activities initiated, the impact of this approach could also be seen at the family and community level in terms of increased gender awareness. In most of the project villages, the number of domestic violence cases has reportedly declined.

Researchers also tried to arrange such sharing sessions with sex workers in the brothel areas. However, this process proved to be more difficult, especially in the area where the majority of the sex workers were under strict supervision of brothel owners. Nevertheless, researchers were able to negotiate with brothel owners to allow some of the sex workers to gather for one or two hours during the days when they were not working. In the red-light district of the Toul Kork area in Phnom Penh, there were more women who operated as "room-rented girls" rather than sex workers in brothels under control of owners, although previously many of them had worked in brothels. These women had more freedom of movement and they were able to meet when researchers invited them to the meeting. Through the facilitation of the researcher, these women shared and discussed their problems and the problems of sex workers in brothels. Such problems included trafficking women from one brothel to another, violence and abuse of women by brothel owners, police harassment and crackdowns. All sex workers also faced problems of discrimination from the community. This sharing and discussion among sex workers in the Toul Kork area led to the formation of the Cambodian Prostitute Union.

In this way, the application of FPAR in the project in Cambodia contributed to the conscientization of women sex workers to demand their rights. In the villages, the use of FPAR also contributed to the empowerment of women to address some common problems. The women felt that they were involved in identifying problems and in the planning and initiating of activities which addressed some of those problems. For both women in the villages and sex workers, impacts and changes could be seen at different levels in different project sites. In general, the use of FPAR in the Cambodian project was seen as a positive experience by the project partners and the women who participated in it.

Vietnam

As in the project in Cambodia, data collection took place during the first phase of the project in Vietnam. Unlike the Cambodian researchers however, in Northern Vietnam the researchers were not locals of the project communities. They were based in Hanoi and they traveled to the research areas in the provinces. Initially, the researchers relied on assistance from local authorities in providing information on the situation in the villages and in identifying research participants. In order to get to know the research participants in the communities, researchers stayed in or near the villages for 10–14 days at a time. They engaged in daily activities with the research participants in order to become familiar with their life situations and to talk to them. The researchers felt that, despite some difficulties, the process was successful in helping them to gain the trust of the women and that the information obtained was accurate and useful in understanding the situation of trafficking and the conditions that the women faced.

For Southern Vietnam, the research team contacted women who had engaged in sex work (those returned from "reeducation" centers), or families with daughters working in prostitution. This identification of research participants was done largely through VWU (Vietnam Women's Union) staff at the district level (in the case of the two research areas in Ho Chi Minh City), and through local VWU offices (in the case of the villages in Tay Ninh province). Because of their background as social workers of the VWU, some of the researchers already had contact with some of the research participants. When making a visit to the women and interviewing them, the researchers offered a small amount of money to the women or their family as a token of appreciation for their time. According to the researchers, this gesture was necessary because most of the women were in difficult economic situations.

In the project in Vietnam, the process after the completion of the research phase was somewhat different than in Cambodia. Sharing of research findings with the research participants did not happen in the first step as in the Cambodian project. In Vietnam, the focus at the beginning of the second phase was on the formation of women's groups. Researchers and project staff invited potential participants (returnees, mothers of trafficked women, high-risk women) to a meeting and to join the group. They informed the women of the objectives of the group including the aim of helping one another both financially and personally. Researchers also told the women that they would be entitled to take a loan from the project. It seemed that formation of women's groups in

Vietnam required active facilitation by the researchers in comparison with the more spontaneous coming together of women in the Cambodian project.

For the project in Northern Vietnam, the observation regarding the formation of women's groups was made based on the fact that many women refused or were hesitant to join the groups at the invitation of the researchers. In the researchers' view, this was because the women were busy making a living and also because they had inferiority complexes and therefore were not open to and avoided the researchers. However, looking at it from the women's perspective, some of them were afraid that the researchers were making investigations in order to arrest them (YRI 2000, 211). There was also a negative perception about the women's groups that would be formed. Some parents remarked that if they let their unmarried daughter join the group of "social evil" women, then the daughter would "lose her honour." Another woman said that "if I need a fund I can borrow anywhere, it is not necessary to join your meetings" (YRI 2000, 237). The researchers, however, were very patient in trying to explain the purpose of the group to the women. It appeared that some women did not see the need to come together with other women and the researchers had to convince them to join the group by offering benefits for the women themselves.

For the project in Southern Vietnam, the process of bringing women together to form groups was similar to that in Northern Vietnam. However, the VWU was already running a number of programs, including some credit schemes, skills training, and HIV/AIDS and health education. The researchers and project staff already had contact with many women, including former prostitutes, those still working in prostitution, and women in difficult circumstances who were identified as high-risk women. Many of those women were invited to come together and form a group of "women in especially difficult circumstances" and told that they would be eligible to take out a loan from the project and participate in other activities. In this regard, the establishment of women's groups was nothing new for the VWU. It was only that in the context of the RA Project, groups of women with different specific needs became the focus. Nevertheless, there was a new element in the work of both research teams, i.e., the use of participatory techniques. Sharing and discussion took place after the group formation. Women who joined in the group were encouraged to share and discuss their situation and problems. Together, they also tried to identify some possible ways to address the problems.

Whilst the major activities of the women's groups that were formed during this RA Project were similar among the groups in Northern and Southern Vietnam, the impact and the outcomes were somewhat different. Most evidently, there seemed to be more cohesion and the sense of bonding among members of the women's groups in Northern Vietnam. This was an interesting outcome considering the difficulties and ambiguity in the initial process of group formation. After the women agreed to join the groups, the process of sharing of experiences among the group members helped create a positive impact on the empowerment of the women. Even now, after the project has officially ended, the group members still meet and support one another. The cohesion that developed within the groups in Northern Vietnam was less apparent in the groups in Southern Vietnam, especially in Tay Ninh province.

A number of factors may have contributed to the different dynamics found between the women's groups in Northern Vietnam and Southern Vietnam. The first is the different geographical context of the project sites and the various basic livelihood strategies of the women in project areas. Most of the women in the project area in rural Northern Vietnam had land for housing and basic cultivation. In comparison, the women in Southern Vietnam lived in the city in squatter areas and were trying to make a living from petty trading. They were more interested in the prospect of having regular employment and income. Moreover, life in the countryside moved at a slower pace while poor women in the city struggled to make a daily living. These situations had some impact on the women's ability to participate in the women's groups.

Second, the backgrounds of the members of the women's groups in Northern Vietnam and Southern Vietnam were different. Among the general public, there appeared to be less stigma attached to women who had been trafficked to China than those who had worked in prostitution. It was also the case that discrimination against trafficked women (for purposes other than prostitution) could be removed more easily than that against former prostitutes. While trafficked women were seen as being cheated or deceived, many people saw those who engaged in prostitution as being "greedy," "lazy," or "wanting easy money." It was generally believed too that former prostitutes needed to be "rehabilitated." In Vietnam, this meant that the women were made to go through a period at a "reeducation" center where, aside from learning some vocational skills, they were taught moral standards and the dignity of being "good" women and citizens. The latter kind of teaching also took place during women's group meetings facilitated by VWU staff in Southern Vietnam, including groups that had been formed during the RA Project. In such groups the women may have felt further stigmatized and perhaps were not comfortable to discuss and share their real problems with the group. This factor, together with the fact that for most women group members joining the group served their economic purpose (i.e., they could borrow some funds from the project), funds may have meant that the women's groups in Southern Vietnam did not develop the same degree of cohesion.

Third, the researchers and project staff in the Northern Vietnam and Southern Vietnam teams had different experiences. Prior to the implementation of the RA Project, project staff and researchers from VWU had their own "top-down" approach to working with the women. The old style of interaction with women was still observed, especially during the initial period of the project. It was not very easy for the VWU staff to understand and practice the bottom-up approach that was introduced in the RA Project. To do this, they had to learn to trust and respect the women and to listen to their views. The women themselves were also perhaps used to interacting with the VWU staff in a more reserved manner—i.e., they were not encouraged to speak out or share their views but only to accept what was told. These factors may have had some impact on initial trust building between project staff and the women and the process of sharing and discussion during group meetings. On the contrary, the researchers from the YRI did not have experience working with a community at the grassroots level. In this respect, it was perhaps easier for them to embrace the participatory and bottom-up approach and apply it in the work with the women's groups once they had been formed. Participation and the open sharing among the women certainly had a positive impact on group dynamics.

REFLECTIONS ON THE FPAR METHODOLOGY

To a large extent, the application of feminist participatory action in the project was influenced by the sociopolitical context of the countries in which it was run, especially in Vietnam. In this regard, preparation for the project that took into account the country's sociopolitical context was essential. Similarly, providing orientation and training for researchers and project staff on FPAR and the conceptual understanding of trafficking was crucial for the effective implementation of the project. However, as mentioned earlier, the use of FPAR in a project on trafficking, especially in countries like Vietnam and Cambodia, was new. It was therefore not easy to anticipate the difficulties that would arise from the sociopolitical context of the countries. From the experience in this RA Project, some observations can be made.

The use of economic incentive to attract women to join the group, as in Vietnam, may be thought to be inappropriate or in conflict with the concepts of real participation and empowerment. However, once the groups formed, women became involved and participated in sharing and discussion as well as in other activities. The changes that were seen among women in the groups, particularly in Northern Vietnam, included an increased confidence to take action to improve their situation and an increased ability to support one another. This can be considered as an empowerment. Even among the women in the groups in Southern Vietnam, one could observe changes during the course of the project. One criticism of the project in Southern Vietnam could be that it focused mostly on providing economic support to the women. However it should be mentioned that for many women, the ability to generate income could be an empowering process. Some women said that they felt more confident and that their families saw them as more capable when they had a loan to start a small business. For other women, more earning capacity meant more decision-making power for them. Nevertheless, the limitation of focusing the project on economic activities alone must be recognized.

The use of feminist participatory action research in a project like this can have different impacts on different people involved in the project. For the women, it allowed their voices to be heard and their needs and problems addressed. For the researchers, FPAR meant learning to listen to and to respect and trust the women as participants of the project. They learned to work *with* rather than working *for* the women and the process became *bottom up* instead of *top down*. These changes were more significant for some researchers and project staff than for others. However, all project teams felt that experience gained from the use of this methodology in this project could be transferred or adapted to apply in other areas of work of the organizations.

For members of GAATW, coordinating this project was a rewarding and challenging experience. We felt that our role in facilitating the learning and understanding of the issue of trafficking and the sharing of ideas and experiences on participatory approach was positive. Nevertheless, we also realized that while the key premises and the methodology of feminist research in combination with participatory action research can offer an excellent base for the research on trafficking in women, the actual implementation of the methodology was not always easy and the results may not be the most desirable. Experience from the project shows that there is a need to be flexible in developing responses to the problems identified, particularly at the policy level. Such flexibility depends greatly on the country's political system and the existence of local non-governmental organization/civil groups that are able to challenge state policies. An important lesson learned from the project is that while policy responses may be more rigid and slow to change (especially in a country like Vietnam), some changes can be seen at the individual and local levels. In such a case, action at the grassroots level can bring about tangible positive outcomes. Finally, the experience in working with FPAR in countries with different sociopolitical contexts like in Vietnam and Cambodia has taught us that we need to be able to use this approach innovatively without compromising its principles and aims.

REFLECTIONS ON THE MAIN RESEARCH FINDINGS

One important issue that a number of research projects on trafficking, including the RA Project, seek to identify is the cause of and contributing factors to trafficking. In the findings and discussion in the project reports from both Northern and Southern Vietnam, poverty and lack of education were identified as important causal factors.[6] For Northern Vietnam it was concluded that "poverty and hunger constitute a socio-economic basis for the formation and development of social evils including trafficking in women" (YRI 2000, 55). Poverty was measured here in terms of rice production capacity and annual income per person per year. A "very poor person" had below 50 kg of rice per year or an equivalent of VND 100,000 (approximately US$10).[7] It should be noted, however, that the perception of poverty in the Vietnamese context was not confined only to "absolute" poverty. The importance of the widening income gap between the rich and the poor as a result of changes in the economic structure was also discussed by both the Northern and Southern teams.

In the research in Northern Vietnam there were some indications of a number or a certain percentage of "trafficked" women who were considered "very poor." For example, the researchers cited statistics provided by Quang Ninh police which indicated that 40 percent of women trafficked during 1991–1997 came from very poor families. It was also stated that thirteen out of fifty-four women trafficked in Kim Xuyen commune were very poor, with an annual income equivalent to VND 100,000 (YRI 2000, 67). A problem with linking poverty and trafficking is that the actual context of trafficking is simplified. In addition, statistics of trafficked women as given by the authorities were questionable. "Trafficked" women were largely identified as those who had left home without official reporting or those who had been "pushed back" from China because of their undocumented status. An important pattern observed in Northern Vietnam, although not always clearly formulated as such in the final research report, was that women were moving in order to look for ways to earn a living. However, because they lacked information about travel and contacts at the proposed destinations, or because of a general lack of experience, many of the women relied on friends or strangers to facilitate their movement and many times they were cheated. In this regard, poverty may well be just one of the causes of female migration while other factors make these women vulnerable to deceit and exploitation during the travel process and at the destination. The situation was similar in the context of Southern Vietnam and Cambodia.

For Southern Vietnam, the research indicated that a percentage of the women interviewed during the first phase of the project entered prostitution due to poverty and indebtedness. In this regard, poverty was one reason for women to resort to prostitution as a means of living, or in order to get out of a difficult economic situation. Nevertheless, it is important to note that poor women are placed in especially difficult circumstances because they have very limited access to assistance from the state. According to the researchers, poor women were unable to obtain a loan from the official sources with low interest rates. This was because they could not guarantee their ability to pay back the money. On the other hand, if they used moneylenders, the interest rate could be as high as 50 percent per month (VWU 1997). In this context, increased access for the women to a suitable credit scheme could help them in such difficult situations and reduce their need to migrate elsewhere.

For Cambodia, poverty was referred to as one of the main factors pushing women and girls into leaving home. The majority of the interviewees stated that they left home because of the promise of a job or because they were looking for work or additional income in order to improve the family's plight or social status. In this regard, there seems to be a clear indication of the desire of women and girls to improve their life and their family's situation through migration.

The research findings from both Vietnam and Cambodia indicated that many women chose migration as a means of escaping domestic violence, boring or abusive marriages, or relationship problems. Women told stories of having had to endure drunken and irresponsible husbands, and they felt compelled to look for what they perceived as a "better" alternative. While these underlying causes need further research and analysis, they have often been explained under headings such as failed love affairs or broken marriages. Such terminology appears again to have negative connotations for women, reflecting the attitude of society at large toward them. There is a social stigma associated with such breakdowns in relationships, especially for women. However, it should be noted that not all women were compelled to migrate by difficult circumstances. Findings by the implementing agencies showed that there were also a number of women coming from well-to-do families who still made the decision to migrate for some adventure.

A low level of education has often been cited as a contributing factor to women being trafficked. For example, the report from Northern Vietnam stated "Our research findings show that women with low educational level are more likely to fall into the trap of traffickers" (YRI 2000, 57). The research in Southern Vietnam also indicated that "girls who fell victims to women-trading rings and who were forced to work as prostitutes were often very poor, with low education level" (VWU 1997, 40). It is important to note here that the low level of education referred to in the Vietnamese context was a primary school level of education. Among the women interviewed, very few were illiterate. However, the majority of them only had a primary school level of education.[8] In contrast, the majority of girls and women interviewed in Cambodia were illiterate, as they had no school education at all.

Lack of or minimal formal education alone may not be the most important factor contributing to the vulnerability of women to deception, or to lack of choices in life. The research in Northern Vietnam indicated that a lack of information and services—for example; TV, radio, and newspaper—in poor rural areas prevented many women from being aware about trafficking; hence they were easily deceived. Indeed, in most of the cases interviewed, the women had never left the village before they were cheated. Lack of experience made them dependent on friends/neighbors who may want to take advantage of them. It should be noted, however, that even when informed about the risk of being trafficked, many women still took the chance, since staying in their villages was not always a good alternative.

Education may provide access to a better opportunity. However, one needs to question the kind of education and skills that really give that option. Having literacy skills is certainly an advantage which helps the women in many situations. For example, a sex worker in Cambodia was under debt bondage because she had signed a false contract with brothel owners without being able to read it. In another case, literacy skills saved a Vietnamese woman who had been forced to marry a man in China, since she was able to write to her friend to ask for help. Nevertheless, simply being able to read and write does not seem to be adequate in giving access to better life conditions, especially in Vietnam where the standard of education is relatively high. However, in a country like Cambodia where the education level is low among the general population, literacy may be a very important factor in assisting women in gaining access to better opportunities. In any case, what is necessary is education to empower women. It is probable that providing access to a combination of formal education and appropriate vocational and life-skills training could assist in reducing the vulnerability of women and girls to being trafficked. The impact of the level of education in preventing trafficking requires further study.

Lessons Learned

The Research and Action Project on Trafficking in Women in the Mekong Region (Cambodia and Vietnam) that was implemented during 1997–2000 was probably the first of its kind. The project set out to achieve many objectives, including the generation of reliable information on the situation of trafficking in women in Cambodia and Vietnam. It aimed as well to develop strategies, both at a local and policy level, to address the problem of trafficking. The process to achieve these aims was certainly a challenging one due to the complexity of the issue as well as the particular sociopolitical contexts of Cambodia and Vietnam. Despite many difficulties and limitations, the RA project generated interesting and useful information that can contribute to further understanding and discussion on the phenomena of trafficking in women, female migration, and prostitution in Cambodia and Vietnam. This contribution is important considering the significance of trafficking at the international and regional levels, and would also have implications on national and local level responses.

An important lesson learned from the project is that while changes at the policy level may be more difficult and slow to take effect, actions can happen more quickly at the individual and local levels. In such cases, initiatives at the grassroots level can bring about tangible, positive outcomes. The RA Project with its specific methodology contributed positively to strengthening individual and community support of women returnees as well as empowering women. This was particularly evident in the project outcomes seen in Northern Vietnam and Cambodia. Furthermore, the formation of the Cambodian Prostitute Union (CPU) can be seen as action by an "affected" grassroots group to challenge policies and practices that violate and discriminate against women in prostitution.

The RA Project provided an important learning ground for the implementing agencies in the understanding and application of feminist research and participatory methodology. While the use of the FPAR concept and methodology in a project like this was considered innovative, particularly in Vietnam, the implementing agencies felt that this new approach brought about many positive results. Nevertheless, experience from the RA Project has also pointed to the need for further validation and consolidation of the use of FPAR in the context of trafficking in women.[9] Finally, the project was essentially about the lives of women in particular contexts and circumstances. These are women who have lived and are still living. Their lives are real and their voices need to be listened to. The Global Alliance Against Traffic in Women concluded that research with and for women must continue in order that the types of violations of women's human rights that were uncovered through this project can be successfully challenged.

Notes

1. The basic framework of the RA Project was based on a project—"The Research and Action Project on Trafficking in Women in Thailand" (RATW)—that was an action-oriented research project carried out by the Foundation For Women (FFW). This project was designed to develop a reliable database about trafficking in women in Thailand and to define workable strategies to fight this problem. When the results of the RATW Project were presented during the International Workshop on Migration and Traffic in Women held in Chiang Mai, Thailand, in October 1994, participants from Vietnam and Cambodia

expressed their concern over the emerging problems of trafficking in their countries. They also expressed a strong interest in, and a need to carry out, a similar project to the RATW in their own countries. This was the inception of the RA Project.

2. The 1949 Convention did not give a definition of trafficking but described punishable acts related to prostitution.

3. This report was coordinated by GAATW and the Foundation Against Trafficking in Women (STV) and created the following definitions:
Trafficking in Women:

> All acts involved in the recruitment and/or transportation of women by means of violence or threat of violence, abuse of authority or dominant position, debt bondage or other forms of coercion.

Forced Labor and Slavery-like Practices:

> The extraction of work or services from any woman or the appropriation of the legal identity and/or physical person of any women by means of violence or threat of violence, abuse of authority or dominant position, debt bondage or other forms of coercion.

See Marjan Wijers and Lin Lap-Chew, *Trafficking in Women, Forced Labor and Slavery-Like Practices in Marriage, Domestic Labor and Prostitution* (Utrecht: STV, 1997).

4. However, information regarding other forms of trafficking was not discussed in detail in the CWDA report.

5. This section relies on a preliminary paper written by Mary Boesveld for an internal GAATW discussion on the research methodology. The paper was revised in collaboration with Jan Boontinand. See Mary Boesveld and Jan Boontinand, "Practicing Feminist Participatory Research Methodologies." *GAATW Newsletter* no. 11 (January 1999):14–17.

6. In Vietnam, Kelly and Le (1999) comment that description of root causes of trafficking becomes rhetoric with the focus on "poverty," "lack of education," and "doi moi." While this may be rhetorical description, the examination and analysis of these factors by implementing agencies contributes to further understanding of the complexity and contextuality of the root causes of trafficking.

7. However, the indicator varies by geographical areas.

8. 50.9 percent in Southern Vietnam and 57 percent (30 of the 57 interviewees) in Northern Vietnam had less than 6 years education.

9. A separate review and evaluation of the project was conducted, and a sharing of this review with external audience was organized in December 2001. During this external sharing, the three implementing agencies also made their presentations on process and outcome of the project as seen in their own context.

REFERENCES

Boesveld, Mary, and Jan Boontinand. "Practicing Feminist Participatory Research Methodologies." *GAATW Newsletter* no. 11 (January 1999):14–17.

Coomaraswamy, Radhika. "Integration of the Human Rights of Women and the Gender Perspective: Report of the Special Rapporteur on Violence Against Women, Its Causes and Consequences." Submitted in accordance with Commission on Human Rights resolution 199/44, E/CN.4/2000/68.

CWDA (Cambodian Women's Development Agency). "Report." 1997.

Foundation For Women. "Final Report of the Research and Action Project on Traffic in Women." Bangkok: Foundation For Women, July 1996.

GAATW (Global Alliance Against Traffic in Women). "The Research and Action (RA) Project on Trafficking in Women in the Mekong Region." Bangkok: Global Alliance Against Traffic in Women, 2002.

Kelly, Paula Frances, and Duong Bach Le. "Trafficking in Humans From and Within Vietnam." 1999.

VWU (Vietnam Women's Union). "The Research and Action Project on Traffic in Women in Ho Chi Minh City and Areas of the South." Ho Chi Minh City: Vietnam Women's Union, 1997.

Wijers, Marjan, and Lin Lap-Chew. *Trafficking in Women, Forced Labor and Slavery-Like Practices in Marriage, Domestic Labor and Prostitution.* Utrecht: STV, 1997.

YRI (Youth Research Institute). *Prevention of Trafficking in Women in Vietnam.* Hanoi: Labour and Social Affairs Publishing House, 2000.

11

Using a Dynamic, Interactive, and Participatory Process to Develop and Redefine the Human Trafficking Paradigm in Bangladesh

Aftab Ahmed

For the past ten years, the phrase "human trafficking" in Bangladesh has been used to address a wide variety of crimes and human rights abuses associated with the recruitment, movement, and sale of people into a range of "exploitative" and/or "slave-like circumstances."[1] A basic problem with the "human trafficking paradigm" in Bangladesh is that many of the elements and definitions for this social phenomenon are often limited in their scope and do not adequately reflect the totality of the problem. Likewise, few attempts have been made to develop usable conceptual frameworks that allow for the many variables to be encompassed under a single umbrella.[2] For example, when several professionals in Bangladesh who were directly associated with addressing the "human trafficking" sector were asked what the phrase really meant to them, a wide variety of different descriptions were given. Depending on the person questioned, trafficking was defined any number of ways—as a legal problem, a human rights problem, a gender problem, a child labor problem, a health problem, a migration problem, or a combination of one or more of these. Those who felt that trafficking was a legal problem indicated that if adequate laws were established and law enforcement agencies and systems were further strengthened, then traffickers could easily be arrested and prosecuted and the problem would go away. Those focusing on trafficking as a migration problem indicated that if appropriate migration policies could be established, implemented, and monitored systematically within Bangladesh, a less irregular, less vulnerable movement of people would occur, thus resulting in a reduction in trafficking. Similar explanations were given for the other problem classifications. Thus, depending on how a given person defined the problem, his/her definitions often dictated what solutions were proposed—legal problems required legal solutions, gender problems required gender solutions, etc. In summary, even after nearly ten years, the sector has continued to lack a standardized and consistent conceptual clarity among those who are working to reduce the problem.

In order for our responses to this sector to grow and expand, the frameworks we use to describe and define it must keep pace with our basic understanding of the problem. For example, over the past twenty years, the HIV/AIDS sector has "reinvented" itself many times to take into consideration new information and insights that continually arise. In Bangladesh, it was felt that a similar process was needed in the "human trafficking" sector—for us to move from "first generation" thinking on trafficking to a new, refined, and expanded "second generation."[3] The purpose of this chapter is to describe a process that was carried out in Bangladesh that has allowed those working in the anti-trafficking sector to develop a comprehensive "human trafficking" paradigm for adults and a clearer sense of conceptual clarity; and to provide an expanded framework for better articulating a concept of "second generation" thinking for the trafficking sector within Bangladesh.[4]

Addressing the Need for Conceptual Clarity

Over the years, as many issues and inconsistencies in the trafficking sector in Bangladesh came to light, a regular pattern emerged at anti-trafficking meetings and workshops. As part of routine discussions, various ideological problems regularly came up that would often result in long, drawn-out debates. These arguments focused on the definitional problems, the issue of migration and trafficking, the question of trafficking and the sex industry, etc. In other words, they focused on inconsistencies that were brought about because there appeared to be a lack of consistent conceptual clarity within the trafficking sector. As it became clearer to many of the regular attendees that this was becoming a dysfunctional situation, it was decided that some kind of a process in Bangladesh was needed to tackle this recurrent impasse.

To help address some of these issues, on September 26, 2001, the International Organization for Migration (IOM) organized a roundtable discussion, entitled "Anti-Trafficking Initiatives: Bangladesh and Regional Perspectives." The meeting included representatives from various Government of Bangladesh ministries, donors, nongovernmental organizations (NGOs), and community-based organizations, as well as private institutions and universities. The main objective of this event was "to review various conceptual and definitional aspects of the human trafficking sector in Bangladesh and South Asia." The initial suggestion for this specific event came up during an informal discussion at IOM during which several donor and NGO representatives expressed a strong desire for more conceptual clarity in the trafficking sector.[5]

Following a series of presentations that were made during this roundtable, the assembled group discussed and debated long-standing problems that they felt presently existed in the trafficking sector. As one person stated, "I sometimes feel like we have the same meeting over and over again when we talk about trafficking. Within the first fifteen minutes, we end up arguing about the same things that have come up in past meetings. This is why I think we need to really sit down and sort what we mean by trafficking once and for all." Another person indicated, "It is time that we re-look at what trafficking is after ten years. We need to be thinking about a 'second generation' understanding of the trafficking problem."

During the discussions, a number of relevant "inconsistencies" that often arise in the human trafficking sector in Bangladesh were discussed in detail. For example, several participants noted that many definitions used in Bangladesh to articulate the human trafficking problem include statements that focus almost exclusively on what "occurs" as part of this process of moving and placing a person into a particular "slave-like condition." The UN Protocol to Prevent, Suppress and Punish Trafficking in Persons, which is used by most of the multilateral donors in Bangladesh, was cited as an example. Several participants pointed out that this definition, along with others, tended to focus on three basic elements: the movement and trade/sale of a person; the techniques used to bring about a condition for this movement (e.g., deception, fraud, violence, etc.); and a listing that relates to the "purpose" for the above-mentioned actions (e.g., forced labor, slave-like practices, etc.). By stating it this way, however, they felt that the definitions did not directly "include" or focus on the outcome of this placement—the "slave-like condition" itself. Thus, although the "outcome" is often implied within "trafficking paradigms," technically, for many, it is not explicitly present within the definitions.

Second, another basic inconsistency that was discussed focused on the fact that while most definitions implied that the process is open to a

range of different exploitative outcomes, there seemed to be a dispropor-
tionate emphasis on "human trafficking" into the sex trade.[6] In the absence
of more research and programming in Bangladesh regarding most of the
other "slave-like" conditions, the emphasis on "sex work/prostitution"
continues to grow at the expense of addressing the full range of exploitative
outcomes. The participants felt that in the years to come, it is imperative
that the "human trafficking" framework place an emphasis on addressing
all of the abuses inherent, not just the trafficking of women and girls into
the sex industry—which represents a subset within the overall human
trafficking sector.

Third, the group felt that in Bangladesh and throughout South
Asia, illegal or irregular migration is often confused with trafficking.
In some ways, many trafficking events are defined by the endpoint of a
migratory process—if the process goes well, it is migration; if the process does not, it is trafficking. While most trafficking has an element of
migration involved (at least for adults), there are many migration stories
that have happy endings—e.g., the person is content with the outcome.
To better understand the violation of human rights, prevention, rescue,
rehabilitation, and integration interventions for trafficked survivors, the
participants felt that the sector must be explored in the context of migration, migratory trends, patterns, and outcomes. To achieve this goal, they
felt that policy guidelines to address trafficking for adults must have
provisions for subverting trafficking by enabling access to affordable
and safe migration.[7]

Fourth, another problem in the "human trafficking" sector that was
discussed was the regular association of women and children in the same
category as if they shared the same level of dependency and inability
to exert their own "will" or "agency." The group felt that when women
and children are combined together under the same heading like this, it
implies that women are unable to make any choices for themselves and
that they are totally dependent on others for their life decisions. This
does a disservice to women and tends to underestimate their ability to
make major life choices. Likewise, the interventions that are required to
address the needs of women versus children in the trafficking sector are
often very different.

Finally, several participants mentioned that there was a tendency in
the trafficking sector to look at a trafficking episode as an "event." A person
is trafficked—an event has occurred. In reality, the trafficking experience is
seldom a single event. Instead, they felt that it was a series of interrelated
steps along an extended continuum that spans from when a person is recruited, the movement of that person to the "trafficking harm/outcome,"
and through the recovery and integration process. The participants felt that
the trafficking sector needs to recognize the importance of understanding
this extended continuum.

At the end of a two-hour, in-depth discussion, the representatives concluded that many trafficking definitions being used in Bangladesh tended to be limited in their scope and did not reflect the totality of the problem; that there were many inconsistencies in the existing human trafficking paradigm that had yet to be resolved in Bangladesh; that the sector lacked conceptual clarity among even those who were working to reduce the problem; and that there was a need to "rethink" some of our previous assumptions to restructure and revise/expand our understanding of the problem.[8]

To begin addressing these conclusions, the participants attending the roundtable recommended that a systematic process be adopted to formally "come to terms" with the trafficking paradigm in Bangladesh. As an outcome of this suggestion, a series of thematic subgroups were formed, which would meet monthly to review various elements of the trafficking paradigm. The themes of the subgroups included: definition and conceptualization; prevention; rehabilitation, recovery, and reintegration; and prosecution.[9] IOM was selected to coordinate the initiative. To help manage the process, the Canadian International Development Agency (CIDA) provided a small grant to IOM to hire a project coordinator to help with the day-to-day coordination of a thematic group secretariat. It was decided that the program would last between fourteen and sixteen months.

The first set of meetings for each of the four subgroups occurred in October 2001. Each subsequent meeting took place every three or four weeks. To begin the first session, a conceptual diagram with boxes and arrows was created for the specific subgroups to initiate the discussion. From the first set of meetings, it was decided that these "visual representations" (diagrams) would be emphasized. The participants reviewed the diagrams and made suggestions that often resulted in complete revisions. Each subsequent meeting further refined these materials. After four meetings of each of the subgroups, the "definition," "prevention," and "rehabilitation" representatives decided that these three groups should be combined together. It was felt that there were too many overlapping issues that needed to be addressed together and not in separate meetings. Thus, from this point onward, the subgroups were merged and a combined thematic group was formed (entitled the Bangladesh Thematic Group).[10] The "prosecution" subgroup, however, remained separate since this subject was considered more technical and required more detailed discussions to better understand the dynamics of the legal system.

From the beginning, the new "combined" Bangladesh Thematic Group set the following guiding principles for each session: a) the "process" itself was as important as the outcome; b) the outcome of the process had "no ownership" (e.g., diagrams, text, flowcharts, etc.)—anyone could use the materials for whatever purpose they wanted; c) anyone was welcome to attend the meetings; d) the conceptualization process should be based on what the group felt was important and relevant, not necessarily what existed within the literature; e) anything and everything should be questioned and debated until a consensus was reached;[11] f) there was no limit to what element of the problem could be introduced; g) all views were welcomed and would be given due consideration; and h) there would be three different paradigms produced over time: one for adults (18 years and older), one for adolescents (13–18), and one for young children (1–12).[12]

The participants attending these meetings included representatives from the Government of Bangladesh, donors, INGOs (international non-governmental organizations), NGOs, universities, and law enforcement agencies. The numbers ranged from twenty to fifty, with each meeting lasting approximately two hours. On occasion, guest speakers were asked to make short presentations related to a specific trafficking subject. This added new insights to the discussions. Between October 2001 and June 2003, a total of forty-one meetings were held.

The persons regularly attending these meetings offered a wide range of different experience and expertise, and included donor fund managers, NGO program officers, counselors, lawyers, teachers, researchers, law enforcement officials, medical doctors, health professionals, sociologists, migration experts, and generalists. While it was clear from the beginning that many of the participants were not like-minded, over time most issues discussed were agreed upon by consensus—thus, the process itself helped to standardize the thinking of the overall group.

To manage major ideological differences, the group offered sufficient time for discussions to take place, often breaking down concepts into their component parts. For example, when addressing the issue of trafficking versus prostitution, the members of the group repeatedly returned to the "trafficking harm/exploitation" definition derived by the Thematic Group in the early sessions. This helped the participants to see that trafficking issues must focus on generalized "exploitation" in a generic sense. This also helped to ensure that everyone clearly understood what was being argued from the differing perspectives. In many cases, when this process was followed, a breakthrough, of sorts, occurred when it became clear that the differences between the participants were merely a matter of perception, not substance.

By the fourth set of meetings, what started off as a series of single-sheet conceptual diagrams began to change into a large flowchart made up of ten pages that were taped together. Each page contained boxes and circles, which had text inside that was linked with arrows and lines. The advantage of this consolidation was that it allowed for all of the conceptual elements to be brought together in one place. This change helped the representatives to better understand the linkages that existed throughout the entire trafficking process. As one person stated: "I can now see the relationships between prevention and rehabilitation when I look at the flowchart. I am also better able to understand the elements that make up the problem." Another person made the statement, "after seeing the various elements that motivate a person to migrate, I can now see that poverty is just one contributing factor—this will help us to come up with information campaigns that allow us to really tailor our messages." During each meeting, the Thematic Group revisited the flowchart. If there were elements that were unclear, which required changes, the participants made suggestions. This helped to ensure that the flowchart truly reflected Bangladesh and South Asia's trafficking realities.

Outcomes of the Thematic Group Process

There were two basic outcomes of this project—the "process" itself and the "flowchart." For many, the discussions that took place during these meetings were found to be invaluable. As one participant stated, "I really enjoy attending these meetings. They help me to understand things that I was confused about." Another person stated, "This is the first forum I've sat in that has people who used to argue all the time, agreeing with each other. Since the elements of the problem are discussed from a logical and rational perspective, it is easier to get a consensus." Thus, the flowchart development process itself had considerable value in enabling people to better understand and visualize the complexities of the trafficking phenomena.

From the beginning, the group immediately recognized the usefulness of a flowchart as a conceptual tool. Unlike detailed reports that describe a problem using text (often in an abstract way), a flowchart can help a person to instantly visualize the interrelated elements of a problem. Like a road map, 100 percent of the information a person needs is available right in front of them. This allows for a group of people to be brought "up to speed" very quickly.

Another important difference between the Thematic Group's flowchart and most others is that it is "person-centered." In other words, the various boxes and arrows are used to depict that a person goes through a particular process from the point at which they are recruited to the point at which they are integrated back into society. This makes it easier for people to understand the overall trafficking experience, with its multitude of steps. To test the validity of the flowchart, real-life case examples were regularly identified and then tracked on the flowchart. If the case didn't seem to fit, there were two explanations for this: 1) it was not a trafficking case; or 2) the chart was wrong. This process allowed the group to revise and improve the flowchart to ensure that it was consistent with reality.

Since most trafficking frameworks try to take a macro-level perspective, they tend to overgeneralize the problem—thus creating confusion.

Such approaches make it more difficult to clearly define the many factors that make up a trafficking experience and also make it difficult to integrate "human rights" principles (many of which are person-centered) into the conceptualization. An attempt was made to avoid this problem during the flowchart development process by making the chart "trafficked-person-centered."

From the first meeting, the Thematic Group members felt that their findings should be shared with others. To date, the adult version of the flowchart has been developed into an "interim flowchart" (poster size), which is being circulated within Bangladesh and throughout South Asia. This flowchart is in both English and Bengali. The purpose of this step was to collect feedback to further refine and improve the overall product and to offer others a tool that would help them to better understand the problem.

In November 2002, a two-day "Expert Meeting" took place to bring together nine professionals from within the South and Southeast Asia to further refine and conceptualize the elements presented in the flowchart. Following this event, the adult paradigm went through another round of revisions. To help explain the rationale and justification for the various boxes/arrows that make up the flowchart, a detailed, comprehensive report was written. In addition, a PowerPoint version is also being developed that can be used as a tool to educate managers who are working in the trafficking sector. Since this first flowchart focused on the trafficking paradigm for adults, beginning in June 2002, a second "child trafficking paradigm" was initiated.

The flowchart itself has become a useful tool. For example, a woman in Canada who works with exploited persons has taught them to use the flowchart to teach others about exploitation. She stated in an email, "The chart (flowchart) helps these women to organize their thoughts and also provides them with some credibility—to show that they have a brain and know how to use it." Several women from this group traveled to a UN-sponsored youth conference in The Hague (January 2002). There, they presented the flowchart to 500 high school students from around the world who spent several hours discussing and debating its elements to help them to better understand the trafficking problem. The program was considered a great success. The High Commissioner for Human Rights also used the flowchart as a reference while developing the United Nations Principles on Human Rights and Human Trafficking.[13] In addition, researchers working for the Asian Development Bank have used the material in formulating an overview conceptual approach for Bangladesh and South Asia. Some of the participating organizations regularly use the flowchart in preparing documents and papers relating to trafficking for national and international forums. Thus, as a reconstruction of the trafficking paradigm, the flowchart offers a comprehensive set of reference points that help guide agencies seeking to better understand the concept of trafficking.

In addition to the work being done to develop the trafficking paradigm, the Thematic Group also came together on several occasions to prepare an Action Plan for the South Asian Association for Regional Cooperation (SAARC) Secretariat that would address its recently signed Convention on Trafficking.[14] During this process, the need for a set of policy guidelines for the trafficking sector in Bangladesh came up and a decision was made that the Thematic Group would work closely with the government to help formulate them. Since the group had developed a good working relationship in coming up with conceptual clarity, this was able to be transferred to the program realm.

SECOND GENERATION THINKING

From the first day the Bangladesh Thematic Group was formed, the concept of addressing "second generation thinking" for the trafficking sector within Bangladesh was introduced.[15] For the Thematic Group, first generation thinking in Bangladesh included ideas such as: trafficking and migration are unrelated; women and children should be treated the same when addressing trafficking outcomes; trafficking should be treated separate from other developmental issues; trafficking is predominately related to prostitution; the "movement" of people within a trafficking event is the major issue; trafficking is a specific event; etc. As the Thematic Group progressed, this concept began to take on a life of its own, as the various conceptual elements were refined and expanded. During a major anti-trafficking conference held in Hawaii (November 2002), Bangladesh's second generation concept was introduced to others working in the anti-trafficking movement as part of several Bangladesh presentations.[16] Based on these presentations, a number of other presenters repeatedly made calls for having other countries move from their own "first" to "second generation thinking" within the trafficking sector.

During a South Asia regional conference entitled "Workshop to Explore a New Paradigm for Addressing Trafficking in Persons" (March 2003),[17] thirty-five participants from throughout South Asia came to Dhaka to debate and contribute to the development of a second generation conceptualization of trafficking for Bangladesh. Some of the key outcomes of the workshop were 1) a consensus on the parameters/guidelines on Bangladesh's second generation thinking; 2) an agreement that the Bangladesh Thematic Group would now be expanded into a South Asian Thematic Group; and 3) an agreement that other countries in the region would initiate a similar country-specific process.

To better articulate the basic components of Bangladesh's "second generation thinking" as expressed in the expanded thematic group, a number of specific suggestions emerged. First, the Thematic Group felt that "second generation thinking" needed to begin by focusing on all of the various steps involved in the trafficking process—from when a person is recruited, to the movement of that person to the "trafficking harm/outcome," and through the recovery and integration process. The idea is to avoid presenting "trafficking" as a single event—but to present it instead as a series of interrelated events along an extended continuum that spans a given period of time.

Second, the group felt that more approaches were needed to visually present the process (e.g., through mapping, flowchart development, etc.) so that those addressing the problem can better see and understand the complexity of the various elements that make up a trafficking episode. For example, the flowchart format can be used to: link appropriate "interventions" with the various stages of a trafficking episode; link research needs/gaps to the various stages of the trafficking episode; and introduce indicators and methods of measuring impact as a part of everything the sector does to address the trafficking problem. This approach allows for more "science" (supporting research, focus group testing to create targeted messages, etc.) to be introduced into the sector in terms of what interventions should be used to reduce the problem in an environment of limited funding. Since trafficking scenarios differ from country to country, however, each flowchart should be adapted to accommodate the specific needs of a given setting.

Third, the group felt that all trafficking outcomes (e.g., domestic servitude, camel jockeys, beggars, factory workers, and prostitution) should be given equal attention when addressing the trafficking problem. In the past, there has been more emphasis on trafficking into the sex trade, at the expense of other exploitative outcomes. For this change to happen, more research is required to further explore other trafficking outcomes, especially in the destination countries.

Fourth, the group felt that there was a need for a clear distinction between the approaches and interventions used to address the different needs of women who have been trafficked versus children who have been trafficked, as separate target groups. When addressing trafficked persons, women and children are often combined together in the same category as if they share the same level of dependency and inability to exert their own will. When women and children are put into the same category like this, it implies that women are unable to make any choices for themselves and that they are totally dependent on others for their life decisions. This does a disservice to women and tends to underestimate their abilities to make major life choices.

Fifth, the Thematic Group felt that more time and effort is needed to show how the migratory process coincides with many trafficking events for adults (this does not always hold true for children). This is not to legitimize the problem, but instead to help provide a better understanding of how traffickers "deceive" victims through a promise of migratory benefits or outcomes (e.g., a marriage, a good job, etc.). As noted above, our present traditional, theoretical understanding can no longer resolve the ambiguities and uncertainties concerning migration and trafficking. It warrants a new theoretical framework for providing a clear picture and analytical understanding of the issue.

Sixth, the Thematic Group felt the need to further emphasize the importance of "demand" factors in understanding the trafficking phenomenon. Human trafficking is driven by two basic factors: a) the available supply of people who can be tricked, manipulated, and/or forced into slave-like situations; and b) the demand created by those who use these people to fill a need for cheap, vulnerable, and highly exploitative commercial sexual services and/or exploitative labor. Up until recently, most reports related to the human trafficking sector have focused only on the supply side—the trafficked persons, their experiences, what happens to them, etc. In contrast to this, only a handful of studies have tried to address the question of "demand dynamics." In this case, demand refers to those people/organizations/syndicates that create or influence an environment that allows for exploitative commercial sexual services or exploitative labor to exist.

Other elements discussed included that the health of trafficked persons should get special attention; the recovery process in trafficking can have both progressive and regressive elements; the integration process can be facilitated or self-initiated; that participation of trafficked persons is necessary at all stages of counter-trafficking interventions; power relations and a person's own level of "agency" need to be understood in the context of trafficking events; and that trafficking is a development concern and should not be treated as a "political" one.

CONCLUDING REMARKS

As a conclusion to this chapter, there are three overarching observations that the Thematic Group has repeatedly emphasized. First, the Thematic Group has shown that an effective, positive process can be established to reconceptualize and outline a new way of looking at the human trafficking sector in Bangladesh. Second, this participatory and interactive process can help to educate and bring about increased conceptual clarity for those who participate in the process and move people forward in their thinking about human trafficking. And finally, a Thematic Working Group–format can be used to reduce "political/ideological" tensions that often plague the trafficking sector. The overall experience has demonstrated that by structuring group dynamics, a process can be productive, educational, transferable, and conducive to building strong alliances and coalitions in anti-trafficking work. While significant advances have been made in creating a new paradigm, it is important to note that over time this outcome must continue to be developed, refined, and redefined—in other words, this is an open-ended process.

NOTES

1. Other related phrases that are often used include "girl trafficking," "child trafficking," "women and child trafficking," or simply "trafficking."

2. Informal survey carried out among managers overseeing trafficking programs in Dhaka, Bangladesh, May 2001 (unpublished).

3. The "Second Generation" concept was first formally introduced at a conference entitled "Anti-Trafficking Initiatives: Bangladesh and Regional Perspectives." The event was sponsored by the International Organization for Migration (IOM) on September 26, 2001.

4. The concept of "Second Generation" thinking was further refined during the conference entitled "The Human Rights Challenge of Globalization in Asia-Pacific-US: The Trafficking in Persons, especially Women and Children," in Honolulu, Hawaii, USA, November 13–15, 2002.

5. Those present at this meeting included IOM.

6. Jyoti Sanghera, "Towards the Construction of an Empowered Subject: A Human Rights Analysis of Anti-trafficking Legal Interventions and Trends in South Asia." Technical Consultative Meeting on Anti-Trafficking Programs in South Asia, Kathmandu, and Nepal, September 11–13, 2001: 2.

7. "Revisiting the Human Trafficking Paradigm: The Bangladesh Experience," Bangladesh Thematic Group, Dhaka, Bangladesh, IOM, unpublished work.

8. Proceedings of the "Anti-Trafficking Initiatives: Bangladesh and Regional Perspectives," IOM, September 26, 2001.

9. Each subgroup had its own chairperson. All were invited to attend these meetings.

10. The "Bangladesh Thematic Group" name was discussed and decided by the group after several individual meetings had taken place.

11. In some cases a vote was taken to break a deadlock. But this was the exception, not the rule.

12. From the beginning, these guiding principles served to ensure that the process was all-inclusive and open to anyone. This offered all the participants a safe environment in which to express their views and opinions. This was one of the most important outcomes of the overall process.

13. Experts Group Meeting, March 24–25 2002, HCHR, Geneva.

14. The Bangladesh Thematic Group met four times to develop a paper to provide recommendations for how SAARC should begin addressing the trafficking problem in the region, (July 2002).

15. "Revisiting the Human Trafficking Paradigm: The Bangladesh Experience," Bangladesh Thematic Group, Dhaka, Bangladesh, IOM, unpublished work.

16. "The Human Rights Challenge of Globalization in Asia-Pacific-US: The Trafficking in Persons, especially Women and Children," Honolulu, Hawaii, USA, November 13–15, 2002.

17. IOM-sponsored event in Dhaka from March 4–6, 2003. A total of fifty-six participants representing forty-two organizations, including the Ministries of Bangladesh Government, UN agencies, donor agencies, INGOs, intergovernmental agencies, and NGOs participated in the workshop. Apart from the participants from Bangladesh, thirteen participants from other South Asian countries also joined in the workshop: two from India, four from Pakistan, and seven from Nepal.

12

Trafficked Persons or Economic Migrants?

Bangladeshis in India

Natasha Ahmad

A study of the situation of trafficked Bangladeshi women and children in India was carried out during 2000 and 2001, sponsored by IOM (International Organization for Migration)–Bangladesh chapter.[1] Through the research we found that for every "trafficked" person from Bangladesh, there are hundreds who migrate "illegally" to the same destination, and who often face similar conditions. Whether considered trafficked or not, all arrive in India because of a dream: a dream to feed themselves, and a dream to have more options in life. Through the study we interviewed sixty-five migrants, mostly women. The main objective of the original study was to research trafficking in women and children with a view to examining how people from Bangladesh move to India, what they do after their arrival, what their work and living situations are like, and what their future plans are. We also wanted to investigate their socioeconomic background and reasons for leaving home—the circumstances under which people decide to leave their country of birth and move to an unknown place. The main idea was to understand the pull and push factors and also the reasons a person stays in India. Most importantly the study was to be focused on the views, needs, and wishes of the persons concerned.

To track down and identify the trafficked women to India, investigations were carried out in brothels, rehabilitation centers, and slums. It was in the slums in the big cities that we came across a large number of migrants who did not have legal status and who often faced harsh treatment from the authorities. However, due to the initial focus of the study, and the original idea that trafficking was attached exclusively to the sex trade, there was an overrepresentation of women from the brothels in the research population. Further research on migrants, within and outside the sex trade, would help to further our understandings of the differences and similarities we found in this study, and about where, or whether, a clear distinction can be made between trafficking and illegal/undocumented economic migration.

REASONS FOR LEAVING

In our study most movements, involving men and women, appeared to be voluntary. But behind each voluntary movement there were reasons that ranged from sheer poverty, to deception by known persons, to legal complications. Individual reasons for leaving the home country were also influenced by persons who were involved with the respondent's movement. These were people who, for various reasons of their own, held information (sometimes incorrect) regarding the options and opportunities across the border, and who helped others to be smuggled out of the country. Specific reasons might have been different for women and men, but economic compulsions remained a major factor that triggered the undocumented, but voluntary, movement across the border. In our sample of sixty-five, as much as 61 percent (thirty-nine persons) claimed to have migrated for direct economic reasons.

While poverty and therefore economic factors were important in motivating people to migrate or in making them easy targets of "trafficking," the economic factor may be compounded by other social factors or special circumstances. In real-life situations, it was not always possible to identify the relative importance of the various factors. Keeping this in mind, the term "economic factors" is used here in a very broad sense.

An important factor was that for a large segment of our research population (44/65), the rural family did not have any agricultural land. For those who had agricultural land, the amount possessed was very small. Some respondents reported loss of land to meet such basic expenses as medical treatment and social compulsions of dowry. There were also a few families who had lost their land due to river erosion. Although these were not unique cases, as the national picture (in Bangladesh) regarding landlessness is more or less similar, in a country where the vast majority of the people are directly dependent on agriculture, loss of land for any reason can be devastating. A major section of the sample came from a background of poverty, landlessness, and unemployment. For such people, the economic factor took various forms.

It was also found that a vast majority of the women were poorly educated. For men also, the basic level of education was low. One important issue is that the specific factors of illiteracy, landlessness, and poverty are not unique to those who migrate to India. For every such migrant person, there are many more who stay in Bangladesh. There may be, then, some critical factors that influence the process in an environment of general poverty. Following is an attempt to discern a pattern from our research findings. The case studies illustrating the various reasons and factors behind leaving home have been drawn from the three cities of Kolkata, Mumbai, and New Delhi.

Marital Status of Women

For many women, against the general background of poverty, certain social factors compounded their vulnerability. Marriage is universal, especially in Bangladesh, and the marital status of a woman is a very important determinant of her standing in the family and in the society. For some, divorce, desertion, or remarriage by the husband, or even the death of the husband, leaves them with a status that is mostly to their disadvantage. The changed status leaves them with few options and they are forced to return, mostly with the children, to their parental homes for support. However, parents or brothers are often reluctant to take care of the woman. The situation is further exacerbated by the presence of step-parents/-mothers at home. Even in some families where the woman owns land, she has little effective right over it. Soon the women discover that they have to leave home and support themselves and the children alone. Migration to India seems to be an easy option for such women.

However, poverty and a lack of education make the women easy targets for traffickers. Moreover, the pressure of getting married on one hand and the prevailing dowry system on the other makes it easier for the traffickers to attract unmarried young women out of their homes. Taking advantage of their situation, some men pretend to become lovers, promise marriage, or even go through the process of marriage. Later the women are persuaded or deceived into going to India with the promise of a better life. Often the parents aid in their decision to cross borders. In our study we came across two women who were forced into marriage and sold as brides.

Among the sixty-five respondents we identified three cases of kidnapping/abduction. With the abducted and then trafficked cases into India it was apparent that women and/or girls were taken away with the help of people who they knew—as a sequence to enmity, or with the explicit motive of selling them. Not every kidnapped girl or woman ended up in the brothels. While visiting a NGO-run Rehabilitation/Short Stay Home where trafficked persons, especially women and young girls, stay after their rescue, we came across a Bangladeshi woman who was kidnapped from her home in Bangladesh, smuggled to India, rescued by the Indian police, and sent back to her country of origin.

Loss of Land

In a country like Bangladesh, where land as a resource is of prime importance, landlessness is a major problem. Despite people trying to "hold on" to whatever amount of land they have, many are compelled to dispossess it for various reasons. Along with meeting medical treatment expenses or paying dowry for marriages, land loss to river erosion leaves hundreds of households in utter destitution. Homeless and landless—these are desperate people. A workplace with a semblance of shelter is all that they look for. Thousands throng the big cities within the country while tales of prospects on the other side of the border lure many to cross over to India.

Supporting the Family

Gone are the days when a man's world comprised a few adjoining villages along with his own, while a woman's activity was restricted within the four walls of her *bari*/homestead. Today women, along with other family members, have been observed to migrate to India and elsewhere, for work and income, and remit as much as they can to the remaining family members at home in their country of origin. Take Sohana, for example. She belonged to a poor peasant family. Because of their poverty, the mother had migrated to India (New Delhi) in the early 1980s and sent money home from time to time. Sohana married, but after the birth of her first child, her husband deserted her. With her child of one year, Sohana returned to her father's house. Seeing the poverty of her family, Sohana decided that she too would go to New Delhi, join her mother, and help her father's family in Bangladesh. At the time of the interview, both Sohana and her mother worked as domestic help with relatively low-income families, who themselves worked as darwans (doormen), ayahs (childcare domestic workers), cooks, or domestic help, and both sent money to Sohana's father through the *dalals* who frequented India.

THE MICROCREDIT TRAP

There is yet another category, which should be a matter of concern for those who advocate microcredit programs for women. In our sample, there was at least one case where the woman had borrowed money from three well-known microcredit schemes and had to run away from her debtors. Kohinoor, over forty years old, used to live in Jessore. She was married when young but was ill-treated by her husband, who had already been married and divorced. Kohinoor went back to her parent's family with one child. Desperate to earn some money, Kohinoor became a member of a microcredit program offered by BRAC—the largest development NGO in the world—for buying cattle. After some time, she joined two other microcredit programs under local NGOs. She took loans for poultry and for leasing land. She was doing well and was also able to buy some land. Her credit worthiness was rated high. That Kohinoor could take a loan of 10,000 Bangladesh Taka (US$1 = 63 BdT) at a time from BRAC is an indication that she was prompt in her repayment. During this time, she entered into a business deal with a person who was married to a girl from her village. The man persuaded her to take a loan of 10,000 BdT from BRAC and another NGO (RRC Samity/Islamic Samity). The money was handed over to the man in good faith. But soon the man fled with the money. For a loan of 10,000 BdT, Kohinoor had to pay 800 BdT per month as repayment. She could pay for only two months, which she did by selling off her land and cattle. Unable to repay the rest of the loan and meet her debt obligations any further, and afraid of the probable consequences, she decided to enter India with her son, leaving her country behind. She virtually fled from Bangladesh. When we interviewed her, Kohinoor worked in Mumbai as a domestic helper. She regularly sent money to Bangladesh from her earnings in India in order to clear her debts (loans and interest) incurred with BRAC and other local NGOs.

INDIA AS A GATEWAY TO GREENER PASTURES

According to some respondents, India was a stepping stone to realizing all their future dreams. They treated India as the first lap of their aspirations for going further. It was also revealed that some aspiring to go to Pakistan and the Gulf countries felt it was easier and less expensive for them to try from places like New Delhi or Mumbai than from Bangladesh itself. In our sample, there were two men in Mumbai whose wives were able to get five-year contracts as domestic workers in Saudi Arabia through agents and organizations in New Delhi and Mumbai specializing in this business. According to Noorjahan of New Delhi, agents approached them with job offers and the rate for going to Pakistan was as low as Rs.600 (approximately US$12). For Gulf countries and Malaysia, the rates were Rs.10,000 for women and Rs.30,000 for men. There were thus some people who went to India to earn and save enough money so that one day they could go further. The countries/cities where most respondents aspired to go were Saudi Arabia, Dubai, Riyad, Italy, and Malaysia. Greece is a new addition to the list of countries, and the rates for Greece vary from Rs.80,000–100,000. Going to Pakistan was not a problem. One only needed a passport and a visa, which were available in New Delhi for only Rs.600.

In Search of Dreams

For many, the dream of making it good in India does not die easily. Take the case of Khadija. She and her husband had reached Mumbai just the day before the interview for this study. This was their second visit to Mumbai in eight years. Eight years earlier, when they had arrived for the first time, they were able to stay for seven to eight months before they were arrested and "pushed back" to Bangladesh. Back in Bangladesh, they tried to make a new life by starting a shrimp farm, but due to local rivalry the farm was poisoned and the shrimp perished. The couple took another loan to start afresh. This time, the entire crop was washed away by floods. After the second disaster they found it impossible to continue with their investments at home any further and decided to go to India. Khadija had already started working as a daily laborer at the fish market (peeling shrimp). Her husband was still looking for a job. They did not have any shelter yet. They had spent the first night on the pavement on newspapers. But she was optimistic. With the first day's earnings (Rs.40) in hand, she was planning to buy a stove and cooking pan. She had already started looking for a job as domestic help. She had heard from a "reliable" source that a room in another slum would be vacant and that they could possibly rent it.

Occupations Pursued

Case studies gave an insight into the conditions of the respondents in terms of the occupations that they pursued. For the women, a fairly large segment were associated with the sex trade (45 percent, or twenty-three women). Of these, two had "risen" to the position of brothel owner and another two had jobs as peer educators for HIV/AIDS projects. Most of the sex workers interviewed were based in Kolkata. After sex workers, the next most common category was domestic workers. In this group, five were based in Mumbai and seven in New Delhi. Three women did not get anything better and became ragpickers, two begged on the streets, while three others managed their own households. One became a drug peddler and another a wholesaler of scrap metals and waste paper.

Of the fourteen men in our sample, around a third had started their own business, however small. Three had joined the workforce as wage laborers, either skilled or unskilled. Two boys were students, and others became self-employed as doctor, taxi-owner/driver, or tailor. One became a ragpicker.

Starting Life Anew

Other than the three women who had been physically kidnapped and taken to India, all others had gone "voluntarily" to start a new life. It is another matter that many women were victims of deception and were taken to India for a life that was not of their own choice. Still others had gone with expectations that turned out to be different from the reality they now faced. However, leaving behind one's own country and roots—all familiar faces and places—and making a new life in an unfamiliar environment in another country was not an easy task.

For the respondents, apart from becoming engaged in remunerative activities, there had to be a search for accommodation, and struggles to overcome problems of language, to get to know the surroundings, and to enroll children in school—activities all aimed at (gradual) assimilation into the mainstream. The process of assimilation was difficult and drawn out. Time was an important factor in terms of adaptation and blending. When asked how long the respondents had been living in India, most, presumably to assert their rights for residents' status, stated a time span of ten to fifteen years.

As soon as the migrants reached their destination the priority was a place to stay. Most often the persons who accompanied them allowed them to stay under their care at least for a few days. Respondents also stayed with people known to them from before, including people from the same village and relatives (if any), until such time as they could find independent accommodation. Staying on footpaths by spreading out newspapers was also observed. Almost simultaneously, the search for a job began. For those who were brought with the explicit intention of the sex trade, there was no search for accommodation or occupation—they were almost immediately handed over to the brothel owners.

To get a job and to communicate with the locals, on the job or elsewhere, respondents were required to learn the language (Hindi), especially in Mumbai and New Delhi. In Kolkata the problem of language was not so great, as the language spoken in Kolkata is Bengali. There, however, for those involved in the sex trade, a conscious effort was needed in the use of certain words (*jal* instead of *pani*, for water; *Bhogoban* and not *Allah*, for God; etc.) in their daily parlance. Muslim names were also changed, in order to attract less attention and more easily integrate into the new society. For women, a name change could help them to get jobs as domestic help in Hindu families. In Mumbai and New Delhi, language proved to be the greatest barrier for all in merging with the locals. Apart from learning the language, all women in New Delhi were found to have discarded their *saris* and changed over to *shalwar kameez*—this too was an attempt to fit in, observed also in Mumbai but not to the same scale. Such a scheme was not necessary in Kolkata.

Evidently most of the children (girls and boys of migrants) had been enrolled in *Madrasahs* (Islamic schools) functioning within the slums. Some NGO-run schools in New Delhi and Mumbai were frequented, mostly by the boys. The main reason for this discrimination was the Hindi medium of instructions in these schools. The parents aspired to have the girls married in Bangladesh and wanted them to be fluent in Bengali by staying home. Moreover, the girls helped with the household chores.

In the Indian context, the ration card is a document used for buying certain food grains and other commodities from the (subsidized) public distribution system. It is widely accepted as an identification document (ID). For many undocumented migrants, getting a ration card through the help of corrupt politicians and officials is thus a high priority. In our study, seven of the thirty-four respondents in Kolkata, ten out of the fifteen in New Delhi, and two of the sixteen in Mumbai had been able to procure ration cards.

Another important ID that legitimizes one's stay in India is getting one's name on the voters list. Like ration cards, those who want to stay in India also try for this. In our sample, two persons in Kolkata, nine in New Delhi, and none in Mumbai had his or her name on the voters list. The information unfortunately could be collected from only twenty-eight respondents. The others were either not asked the question or did not give any clear answer as it was apparent that they were not in favor of giving out such information.

In Kolkata, of the thirty-four people interviewed, five had bank accounts. In New Delhi the number was two, and in Mumbai, one. Of these eight who had bank accounts, five also had ration cards or a voter ID. Five were women. Of the sixty-five respondents, only three had been able to procure the final document legitimizing their stay—an Indian passport. Of them, two were women in New Delhi and one was a man in Mumbai.

FREEDOM OF MOVEMENT

It was expected that undocumented migrant women would have restricted movement, even when they had the advantage of not being easily identified, due to similarity of looks and, to an extent, a common language (in Kolkata). In New Delhi and Mumbai, as stated earlier, language restricted free movement, as did the insecurity of living without immigration documents in a foreign land, harassment of the law enforcing agencies, and the threat of being caught and "pushed back." The respondents, when asked about problems they faced in moving about from one place to another, gave mixed answers. About 77 percent of the women and 64 percent of the men felt they could move about freely. For those who felt otherwise, four men in New Delhi reported restricted movement as two of them lived in a rehabilitation home, and the other two men were worried about police raids. In Kolkata, eight women mentioned experiencing problems. Of them, two young girls were inmates of a rescue home and obviously had restricted movement. The other six were young sex workers who worked under brothel owners, where half of their income was taken by the brothel owner or madam. They felt restricted in their movements due to the control of the brothel owners.

In Mumbai and New Delhi, three women were not comfortable in moving from one place to another. Of them, one was a newcomer. Two others (in New Delhi) were nervous because of increased raids by the police. By and large, there was no problem in movement in Kolkata except for the special circumstances of some sex workers or young girls in rescue homes. New Delhi is the only city where at least a few felt uncomfortable because of the fear of authorities.

STRIKING ROOTS

Of the women and men interviewed for the study, a difference in needs, attitudes, and planning for the future was apparent. There were three distinct groups among the respondents. In the first group were people who had settled themselves comfortably and wanted to stay in the country of destination (India). These were the people who wanted to make India their permanent residence and not go back to their country of origin. The second group, of almost equal size to the first, wanted to return some day. According to them, they could return only if they could get a secure job or better earning opportunities in Bangladesh. The third group was relatively small—eleven persons. They were the ones who had not been able to make up their minds.

Apparently a large segment of the population was in a dilemma. Among them were people who had gone to India destitute, due to dire economic conditions. They had no land or had lost whatever land they had to river erosion and were thus without a place to live or a job that gave a decent income. The women among this group had been deserted or divorced by their husbands and had to make an independent living. Some among them had been deceived and forced into a profession (the sex trade) that was not to their liking then, but they were willing to continue with it. Of all the people interviewed, some were doing well in the place of destination, while others had not fared that well, and between these two groups of people a difference in attitude appeared. The persons who were destitute in the place of origin, but fared well after migration, stated they wanted to stay on at the present place of residence at least while their age permitted them to work and earn. They were the ones who bought land or married their daughters in Bangladesh, trying to maintain a relationship with the home country, and thought of going back someday. On the other hand, the people who were not doing so well, but had also been destitute before migration, were the ones who had not decided about, or did not have any specific plans for, the future. It may also be mentioned that people who worked in Mumbai and New Delhi for several years and had invested in land or business felt that they had a "right" to stay on in their present residence.

All the cases suggest that, at least economically speaking, the respondents were better off than they had been in Bangladesh. Many had settled down, and some were quite satisfied with their work. Thirteen women and two men sent money home. Some had not been able to make it that well, but thought they were still economically better off than they were, or would have been, if they had stayed at home. Twenty of the fifty-one women did not want to change their occupation, ten of whom were sex workers. Among men, this was different. Only four did not want to change their occupation. It is important to note that although nearly half of the women who expressed a desire to change their jobs were sex workers, some women in the sex trade stated they would like to settle down in India with their *babus,* or steady clients with whom they had a special relationship.

ACCEPTANCE IN INDIA

For a migrant, particularly for an undocumented migrant, it may be possible to eke out a living and even to do better economically than at home. But that does not necessarily mean that they feel comfortable in their daily life. The respondents were asked if they felt any problem in mixing with the locals or in sending their children to school. Of the fifty-one women and fourteen men interviewed, twenty-seven and ten, respectively, answered that they had free social access, although about half of the women and a third of the men felt they were not acceptable to the locals. A substantial proportion of the respondents thus felt that they had social acceptance. However, many of those who had problems had them for occupational reasons. For example, in Kolkata, among the fourteen women who stated they encountered problems, ten were sex workers and the inmates of the NGO rehabilitation home. Two others lived in a particular area where people pointed them out as Bangladeshis. The remaining two, who lived on the footpaths of Kolkata as ragpickers, were derided by locals as "Beggar Bangladeshis." As Bangladeshis in Kolkata, some were also not permitted to rent houses, even in slums. In Mumbai, the migrants had no such problem. In New Delhi, however, around a quarter of the women and half the men mentioned that they faced problems. They felt that they were pointed out as "illegal immigrants" from Bangladesh. Because of frequent police raids, this identity enhanced a feeling of insecurity among them. However, in general, with an increasing number of migrants, the attitude of the locals toward those from Bangladesh has undergone a distinct change. In Mumbai in the past, migrants who stayed on the footpaths were fed by the wealthy locals. In 2003 this was rare. Instead, young children, especially boys, were branded as thieves. There were still others, in all cities, who felt that there was pressure on local resources and an increase in the rate of crimes due to the migrants.

POLITICAL SITUATION AND LAW ENFORCING AUTHORITIES

The women and men who lived and worked in New Delhi were very uncertain about their lives and livelihood as the political party in power was against undocumented migrants, especially those from Bangladesh. There were frequent police raids taking place in the areas, mostly in slums, where the Bangladeshis normally resided. According to the respondents, unlike the previous government, the government in power at the time of the study was against them. They however felt that the situation would get better just before the election time. All the people interviewed in New Delhi had some affiliation with political parties. In the past, when there were regular fires in the slums,[2] important political leaders, such as Indira Gandhi and V.P. Singh, would visit the slums and distribute ration cards and money to rebuild their houses. The politicians would go with food, and medical teams would provide health support. In 2002 there was no such thing. The migrants in the slums were identified as "illegal foreign nationals" and instead of receiving government assistance, migrants were subjected to raids and arrests.

Respondents informed us that the police who patrolled the (slum) area harassed and threatened both men and women by saying that they would be picked up during the next raid and that they should leave the country immediately. Once picked up they would be placed in lock-ups for an uncertain period of time, to be shipped to the bordering districts in order to be pushed back to their country of origin. The women alleged that there were cases of police taking the young girls and sexually harassing and abusing them. However they did not wish to talk about it, as the life of the young girl would be stigmatized.

Respondents in New Delhi reported that previously the police would pick up slumdwellers and keep them in the local station lock-ups, releasing them after several days. At the time of the study, the time in lock-ups was more than three weeks and those held were beaten brutally. During the period in which the study took place, there was a raid in the slums of Jamuna Pusta in New Delhi at around 3 a.m. The police picked up the outspoken, prominent leaders of this community, and the residents became scared, fearing that the next time the authorities would be more strict and would drive all Bangladeshis out of the country. The respondents further informed us that the men (ages seventeen and older) did not sleep in the huts; right after dark they would leave their homes and stay on the footpaths away from the locality. They returned around noon and left again in the evenings. The police also verbally abused and harassed the women.

In New Delhi we also visited other slum areas, such as Jahangirpura, and became aware that some slums housing people from West Bengal had been demolished. The homeless people reported that because they were Muslims and spoke Bengali their huts had been demolished—"even the dogs are better treated in this country," they remarked.

The respondents in Mumbai also reported increased police raids and the demolition of many of the slums. There was a constant patrolling of police in all the slums. Some of our respondents and/or their family members had been taken to the police lock-ups. They had been released after their family paid a handsome amount of money (i.e., Rs. 2,500–3,500, approximately US$50–70) to the local police station.

ROOTS OF INSECURITY

The people we spoke to had left behind their countries of origin. Most had gone in search of a new life. Many were successful in striking roots in India. Some were still striving to do so, and very few wanted to return to Bangladesh in the near future.

The process of striking roots was not an easy one. Apart from material problems, there were problems, as stated above, of social acceptance and legality. But apart from this, disaster struck in other forms. For some it was communal riots. The major factor in generating insecurity, however, was the nagging fear that they would be marked as an "illegal foreign national" and pushed back to their own country. From time to time this feeling of insecurity was accentuated because of harassment and raids by the authorities for hounding out people from Bangladesh. This insecurity was very strong among the people we spoke to in New Delhi. In Mumbai also, this fear prevailed, but to a lesser extent. Kolkata is the only place where the people we interviewed did not seem to be under any such threat—there they appeared to have no fear of raids, detentions, or deportations. When asked about why they did not move from New Delhi and Mumbai to Kolkata, where they could feel more secure, our respondents replied that Kolkata was a relatively poor place and had little to offer in terms of jobs or better earnings. To us, this was an indication of the fact that despite all odds, earning a decent living, albeit in a foreign country, was the prime objective of all the respondents interviewed for this study.

FUTURE PLANS AND EXPECTATIONS

Interestingly, people with children articulated their plans and expectations for the future, while those without any children were fatalistic, and left all future actions to "fate." This was emphasized among the sex workers. Those with children expressed their desire to leave the brothels and start anew elsewhere in India or go back home someday—but to what, they had no idea. The others wanted to stay in India in their present trade but wanted to be able periodically to visit parents or relations in Bangladesh, although they were concerned and wary about their present status vis-à-vis their acceptance in the community. Those in rehabilitation centers expressed a desire to go back, but they too were unsure about how they would be received at home due to the stigmatization of sex work and the criminalization and victimization of women within the sex trade. The boys, on the other hand, were studying and receiving skills training. All dreamt of going back home and using their skills for work/trade.

Some migrants had more concrete plans for the future. Those who wanted to stay on in India had bought landed property in order to establish their right to stay. Those who had married Indian men or women planned on leaving their present residence in the city and setting up home in their in-laws' villages. This group of migrants stated they would like their sons and daughters to get married in Bangladesh—that daughters would go back to Bangladesh with their husbands and that sons would take brides from Bangladesh but stay and work in India. There were also those who planned to return to Bangladesh someday because "there is no peace of mind in a foreign country." These people were working toward saving enough, acquiring landed property, and then returning home. However, the migrants who had not fared well, and had not been able to acquire any property, stated they would like to stay on in India and not return.

All the migrants felt that the Indian government could not stop people like them from coming to India. According to them, "at home there is no work, we have no food...people like us...we will come." They had pinned their hopes on the government of Bangladesh to take responsibility and make their life comfortable while in India—"if Hasina [the Prime Minister of Bangladesh from 1996–2000, who Bangladeshis widely believe had a good relationship with the Indian government] had accepted our presence, things would have been better...we would have been spared of our constant harassment."

Economic Migrants

We found that most people had migrated voluntarily to India and were not deceived or coerced into crossing the border. All had undergone a similar process—destitution at home, underground transportation across the border, and work or a new life fraught with bribes, exploitation, harassment, and abuse. Most lived as undocumented immigrants in India. There was a clear distinction within the total population, however, between those who had moved independently and those who came otherwise. The first group went willingly, and with an explicit intention and expectation to make a living, even if it was as a sex worker. They had made the decision to cross the border alone or with consultation with a near relative/friend, after some circumstance (economic/social) at home triggered their decision to move. The other group was forced, deceived, or lured into migrating for various reasons. The decisions about migrating, the destination, and the type of work once there, were often somebody else's. For the first group, the expectation of making a living was more or less fulfilled. Some felt cheated as they had expected more—a result of a lack of proper prior information—but once in India most had a place to live, their jobs/trade gave them a substantial income, some opened bank accounts, saved, and also invested in India and in Bangladesh. Among them many had married in India (mostly men), and were raising a family with their children going to school. Still others had acquired ration cards, enrolled themselves as voters, and had passports. Maintaining ties with their original homes, through investments and the marriages of their sons and daughters, some—after acquiring property and with money in hand—hoped to return one day. The majority, despite an environment of harassment and insecurity including, often, restricted movements and barriers of language, aspired to stay on. They had also invested in India. Evidently, the majority were, in general, better off than they were in Bangladesh.

The second group, who were initially tricked or deceived into leaving home, were mostly women, many of whom were later forced into prostitution—a situation from which one usually "cannot completely come out," due to the stigma attached to it. They had left home with people they knew and trusted, to better their position economically and/or socially, but were turned over to brothel owners instead. Among the sex workers, only those with children looked forward to getting out of the brothels and to starting life anew elsewhere in India and/or to returning home to Bangladesh someday. Those with no such ties had no intention of going back and seemed more or less resigned to fate/*bhaggo*.

A commonality between the two groups of people was that in their movement across the border, the persons who facilitated their movement were the same. Both groups resorted to fraudulent means aided by professional *dalals* and went through the same process in order to be smuggled across the border. The difference that existed was in terms of money spent and sexual harassment. People who had migrated independently had to bear all expenses themselves, while those who were deceived and/or forced did not have to spend any. However, even those who willingly moved to join the sex trade had to pay a price of a different kind—they were often sexually abused by *dalals* and law enforcement agents positioned on both sides of the border, before being passed on to the brothel owners. We were unable to establish whether migrants who worked in India as domestic help, in factories, etc., were subjected to such harassment or abuse.

It became apparent through the study that an organized network was actively engaged on both sides of the border. From the way money changed hands—often openly, from respondent to *dalals* to law enforcement personnel to another third party—transporting or smuggling people across borders appeared to be a lucrative business. People who wanted to better their economic position took advantage of this organized group who helped in their clandestine movement. On the other hand, with a demand for girls/women in the brothels of especially Kolkata and Mumbai, the members of the organized networks on both sides of the border took advantage of the border situation and actively sought out gullible, often unmarried or deserted girls and women from poor households. The primary reason for the majority of the respondents to leave the country of origin was to have a better life socially or economically, in a country that had apparently more to offer. The majority who left were those who did not have food security or a secure livelihood in their country of origin.

India is a vast country and also has many (im)migrants from different neighboring countries, such as Afghanistan, Myanmar, and Tibet, who
have been given refugee status. Having legal status as refugees, they are
not harassed by the law enforcement agencies, nor threatened with deportation, whereas the economically disadvantaged people of Bangladesh
who are working in India, doing various odd jobs, and thereby fulfilling
the demand for certain services for which there is a dearth of local labor,
are harassed and abused at every step. Moreover, while conducting this
study we found hundreds of Bangladeshis living in constant fear. As "illegal foreign nationals" some had experienced brutal behavior from the
law enforcing agencies, some had been arrested and were in the lock-ups
and no one was allowed to visit them. There were still others who were
being threatened with eviction.

The (im)migrants from Bangladesh engage in a variety of activities
and play a major role in managing waste in the big cities of India. It is
often said that had it not been for the migrants, Mumbai would have had
a "smoky mountain" like Manila. India, the receiving country, benefits
from these undocumented migrants who do a great many odd jobs and
form the bulk of cheap labor. In turn, the migrants from Bangladesh are
benefited as they have a secure livelihood that was not available at home.
Migration is acknowledged as a fundamental human right, but there is
no policy or mechanism to recognize the rights to life and security of
livelihood for the "illegal foreign nationals" who have been living in
India for years, and who we would rather term as *economic refugees* or
economic migrants.

Toward a Future

The geographical location of India and Bangladesh is such that despite
wire fences and tight controls, people wanting to cross the border are able
to do so. But had the authorities or law enforcement agencies on both
sides of the border been less corrupt and more honest in carrying out
their duties, the wave of clandestine migrants could have been reduced
from a stream to a trickle. Moreover, inside the countries there is a need
to build up awareness through proper information about the networks
that take advantage of migrants and also about the harsh treatment that
one can confront in the place of destination. Women's freedom of movement should be ensured so that they are not made to be accompanied in
their travel by a male guardian, which could result in further deception
and exploitation. Most importantly, food and livelihood security within
the country has to be ensured for all, irrespective of gender, class, and
religion, through proper development policies and projects, if clandestine
movement is to be combated.

Economic migrants such as the people in our study technically have no legal rights in the receiving country, but viewed from a humanitarian angle they deserve better treatment than what is meted out to them, and it falls on the State to shoulder responsibility so that the migrant's right to life is not at stake. The respondents in the study apparently had easy access to health and legal services, but few had legal status. They were tracked by the police in (periodic) raids, and sometimes detained or arrested. In the courts, cases drag on for years as the countries concerned take their time to determine the nationality of the "rescued victim." Meanwhile trafficking serves as a front for undocumented economic migrants to be hounded and rounded up, followed by forced eviction or deportation by the authorities. Moreover, in the name of rooting out migrants from Bangladesh, Bangla-speaking persons, including Indians, have often become victims of anti-Muslim sentiments from certain political parties and law enforcing agencies. It is important for the countries concerned to create conditions through cooperation and a spirit of accommodation to enable the people—trafficked and/or economic migrants—to live in India and/ or return to the country of origin voluntarily, and with dignity. With a proper policy that recognizes the reality, migrants need not be victims of any communal cleansing, pushed in and/or pushed back, in either India or Bangladesh.

Notes

1. The original report of the study was entitled "In Search of Dreams."

2. A regular event—often an accident but sometimes caused intentionally; during such incidents the firefighters cannot enter the area through very narrow roads and all cardboard and plastic huts are burnt along with the important papers/documents collected with such great difficulty.

PART IV

LOOKING BACK, LOOKING FORWARD

13

Revisiting Feminist Participatory Action Research

Because "A Woman's Life Is Richer Than Her Trafficking Experience"

Rebecca Napier-Moore, for the Global Alliance Against Traffic in Women

In the 1990s the Global Alliance Against Traffic in Women (GAATW—the Alliance) looked at what constituted the term "trafficking." The Alliance and researchers globally at that time were seeking to ascertain what set of experiences made up this particular phenomenon. In 2000, with the establishment of an internationally recognized definition in the UN Trafficking Protocol, trafficking became a rights violation defined and set apart from other violations. Many police officers, immigration officials, NGOs, employers, trade unions, and the public generally have gained awareness of this as a problem for which to be on the lookout and to provide a set of social and legal services. With an eye for this human rights violation, the anti-trafficking field emerged. Ten years on, many have begun to see that things have become too narrow and fairly disconnected from the broader issues that affect trafficking and trafficked persons, that is, women's rights, migration controls, livelihoods, and globalization. GAATW's 2009–2010 Feminist Participatory Action Research (FPAR) was a reaction to anti-trafficking's current over-specialization.

This chapter gives a short history of GAATW's engagement with the FPAR methodology, problematizes anti-trafficking's current segregation from other rights movements, details the methodology GAATW used in 2009–2010, and explores actions as well as findings concerning the complexity of women's identities. An important starting point for the research project was that women's experiences were taken to be far richer and broader than the mono-identity ascribed to them under the label "trafficked person."[1]

CHANGES IN GAATW FOCUS

Before GAATW formed as an alliance in 1994, the Foundation for Women, a Thai nongovernmental organization (NGO), conducted a project in north and northeast Thailand, aiming to understand women's migration and with a view that certain experiences could be identified as "trafficking." "The Research and Action Project on Trafficking in Women in Thailand" was a classic FPAR project in methodological terms, with a researcher living in a community for nearly a year conducting rigorous participatory observation. The aim was to look at migration experiences within the sex work sector, and examine the meaning of *return* for women who had returned home. This research produced initial understandings of trafficking for the organization and others. The research had been quite localized, focusing on a specific region of Thailand, yet Foundation for Women and GAATW took these findings to an international level, hoping to "ground" UN discussions.

The second Action Research project that Jan Boontinand details here in Chapter 10 began with a few organizations from Cambodia and Vietnam showing interest in the findings and methodology of the first project during a 1994 workshop. Understandings of trafficking were more stabilized but certainly not yet set by the time the research took place from 1997–2001. Alongside this, in 1999 and 2000, GAATW conducted two trainings on FPAR methodology for other interested NGOs. The trainings had a heavy emphasis on distinguishing trafficking from other social phenomena and human rights categories, for example, smuggling, labor migration, sex work, forced labor, debt bondage, and so on. This was a time in anti-trafficking's history when definitional politics were at their height. The researchers' main tasks were to collect firsthand information about trafficking, documenting the experiences of trafficked women in Vietnam and Cambodia. The FPAR tried to identify causes of trafficking with an aim to developing appropriate support strategies for trafficked women. GAATW did a lot of work, as Jan points out in her chapter, to clear up conflations between trafficking and prostitution, and trafficking and undocumented migration, conflations that existed among the NGO research partners and in Cambodian and Vietnamese legislation.

In the current era of anti-trafficking, however, the need is not so much to distinguish trafficking as a unique rights violation nor to work on better defining it. Rather, it is to understand overlapping identities of women's lives. As advocates and service providers, we frequently ask whether a woman is a sex worker, a trafficked person, or undocumented, but we must also ask how much these labels matter, if they are not the ones a woman uses herself or identifies with. The labels may help in some cases to allow certain categories of people to access services or help. However too much complexity in women's lives is lost or dismissed when identities are essentialized or distilled to one facet. Critiques of identity politics have taught us this, as has intersectionality theory, but it seems anti-trafficking, as a field generally, has yet to learn these lessons, or yet to figure out how to apply them. Anti-trafficking still depends on the idea of an essentialized trafficked person to justify funding, jobs, special police forces, prosecutions, research, new legislation, workshops, trainings, coordination meetings, and so on.

At a practical level we have observed that the segregation of expertise is impairing our ability to assist people or effect change when rights violations are happening. As earlier research has pointed out, anti-trafficking initiatives have in some instances harmed the very people whose rights they have claimed to protect.[2] Exclusive focus on trafficking without a social analysis also contributes to sensationalism. It creates the false impression that trafficking is a problem that can be solved by merely taking a few legal measures and providing assistance to those identified as trafficked. Thus, as Kamala Kempadoo notes in the Introduction to this book, a group of advocates increasingly feel that the long-term goal of lobbying for systemic and structural changes in society gets overlooked.

Regrettably, while many of us in civil society find ourselves in specialized niche areas, sometimes our advocacy efforts in one area may run counter to the advocacy efforts made by other social movements. For example, our loud condemnation of exploitation of women migrant workers may encourage states to stop women from migrating altogether. Indeed, strict border controls have been touted as anti-trafficking measures (see box entitled "Restricting Migrants to Counter Trafficking?" later in this chapter). How do we then condemn rights violations, but also expose the agenda of states as anti-migrant or as protectionist toward women? How do we uphold rights of migrating people, but not let the state abdicate its responsibilities toward its citizens and their right to livelihood in their own countries? How do we expose workplace exploitation and advocate for standard wages for all, but not let our advocacy result in a large number of people losing their jobs and being replaced by another set of workers in some other place? This complexity goes far beyond the typical anti-trafficking measures of awareness campaigns, brothel raids, prosecutions, and shelter, health, or psychological assistance.

Many migrants and migrants' rights advocates have trouble understanding why trafficking categories are so black and white, defining migrants as solidly trafficked or not, when people not labelled as trafficked are also in forced labor situations or have been deceived by migration brokers. Other migrants receive far less positive attention from legislation or government assistance, and some are sought out for deportations, detentions, and so on. There are people who are "deemed sufficiently exploited in order to get help, versus others who are merely 'an underpaid worker.' If we go to a village, and talk to a 'victim' about the terrible things that have happened to her, others in her village wonder what she has done to receive so much attention. Looking around, it is clear that everyone in the village needs better health care, education, and other state support, yet few qualify under anti-trafficking measures."[3] The tendency to give a lot of attention and support to a trafficked person and much less attention (or negative attention, such as detention and forced repatriation) to others seems arbitrary to many migrants and their families.

Part of the reason this complexity is not often explored lies in the *silo effect,* where different civil society groups operate in different spheres and do not talk to each other. Don Flynn, from the Platform for International Cooperation on Undocumented Migrants, notes that as with any other specialist rights organization, anti-trafficking groups "have claims as to why the people, who are the focus of their concerns, are not to be regarded as 'ordinary' migrants" but as deserving of special attention and exemptions.[4] Flynn bases this statement in the way human rights practically operate by rights advocates having to lobby for a particular group of people's rights:

> The highly conditional way in which human rights law operates means that access to a particular human right has to be negotiated around the public interest reservations which allow national authorities to limit the application of the right. If state objections can be surmounted, it is because arguments are assembled which make the case that for *this* group of people in these circumstances, the right to (say) privacy and respect for family life should override an imputed public interest favouring restrictions on privacy and the respect for family life.[5]

It seems, therefore, that working with rights may inherently involve creating special categories of exemption, and with them specialists and their *silos.* Organizations working against trafficking develop relations with specific government agencies and mechanisms.

The logic behind work rooted in silos arose from the conviction that this segmentation represented something objectively real about migration. The world of the refugee really was different from that of the migrant worker, and the legal migrant from the undocumented, and all these from the trafficked person. In truth this sense of distinctiveness had much to do with international conventions and state administrative practices rather than absolute difference.[6]

While we are seeing this separateness as problematic, we should not, however, throw the baby out with the bath water, remembering that anti-trafficking frameworks do remain useful for some trafficked persons because they flip the migrant from being a law violator to a victim deserving justice and compensation. Anti-trafficking frameworks can exempt migrants from automatic deportations, providing instead some room to seek redress for abuses.

Today, GAATW is *both* working within the anti-trafficking framework to critique bad practice, as well as trying to think outside of it, looking for alternative approaches and alternative ways of arguing for rights that might benefit migrant women. We see that it is now necessary to reconnect trafficking with the very social phenomena we worked so hard to distinguish it from ten and fifteen years ago—migration, work, gendered experiences and identities—and to utilize both Violence Against Women (VAW) and labor rights structures in order to better help a trafficked person. We see that there is a danger in trying to address the problem of human trafficking without understanding the changing context of labor and migration in a rapidly globalizing world. By doing so, trafficking is taken exclusively as a crime and not as the end result of a number of interconnected social factors. And without analyzing social reality from a gender and human rights perspective, we realize that we lack the ability to create progressive political change.

What we ask for is that organizations, states, and service providers work toward a greater *understanding* of a person's wider identities, as a worker, a sister, a Hindu, an indigenous person, as well as an *understanding* of how other fields impact on trafficking, and vice versa. To some, this may sound as if GAATW is losing its focus. However, we are convinced that it is precisely a narrow focus on trafficking that risks promoting policies that harm women in practice. With a narrow focus, we might be unwittingly closing our eyes to the exploitation that does not qualify as trafficking, or to legislation that is restrictive of women's movement in the name of trafficking, and not see the negative effects it is having on other migrant women. This broader perspective, of looking beyond one category, may not be sexy or quite as *sellable* as the neat trafficking category, but it is closer to reality.

Restricting Migrants to Counter Trafficking?[7]

By saying that migration restrictions should be put in place to combat trafficking, NGOs and governments are using the "humanitarian" sentiment behind anti-trafficking to justify deportation or destruction of homes. Governments are claiming that they are helping migrants by restricting them.

Case 1: Senegalese are increasingly migrating to Latin America as European migration becomes increasingly difficult. As seen recently, an Argentinean NGO, the Catholic Committee for Immigration, "is *demanding stricter controls* for new arrivals." They allege that the authorities reject applications for residence permits but do not deport [the Senegalese], who stay in the country "*without proper status, an easy prey for people-trafficking networks.*"[8] The NGO is saying people without papers should be deported, otherwise they might be trafficked.

Case 2: In September 2009 French authorities destroyed the "jungle," a migrant camp in France near the English Channel which was home to hundreds of migrants hoping to reach the UK. The British Home Secretary Alan Johnson said the *camp's destruction* would not only serve to "*prevent illegal immigration, but also to stop people trafficking.*"[9] In all, 287 people were detained, almost half of them minors.[10] An estimated 2,000 migrants spread to other sites on the French coast, and the price of smuggling doubled to 1,500 Euros.[11]

In the two cases above, the NGO and the UK Home Secretary mixed undocumented migration with trafficking, claiming one can *solve* both by making it harder for all migrants to gain entry or stay in destination countries. We advocate strongly that anti-trafficking discourses not be used in this way to negatively affect migrants.

LINKING TRAFFICKING TO MIGRATION, LABOR, AND WOMEN'S RIGHTS: THE 2009–2010 FPAR

With the change in context has come a change in the aim of GAATW's projects. FPAR, however, remains the best way we know to gain an accurate ethnographic picture without being extractive or usurious methodologically. What remains constant between the past and the current projects is an aim that the research be a tool for women's voices to be heard, as well as a platform from which they can take actions themselves to improve their situation. Also constant is the aim of collecting firsthand information about women's migration and trafficking experiences.

Just as the anti-trafficking context changed the aims of our projects over the years, the changing shape of our global network also changed the nature of the projects. The Alliance is quite different from a decade ago. It has a greater international scope with over one hundred member organizations in forty-two countries, and has worked over the last five to eight years on building members' participation and feelings of belonging in the Alliance. Through the process of strengthening the network, some members questioned why some research had taken place *without* them. They demanded greater participation. Further, since the network is stronger on a global level, new research is needed to include more groups and have more than a regional, southeast Asian purview. Although the Alliance realized such a wide geographical remit would be a methodological challenge, it also recognized that such a scope was needed.

Getting Started

The NGOs participating in GAATW's 2009–2010 FPAR were from varying sectors (legal aid, sex workers' assistance, diaspora migrant assistance, migrant rights, women's rights, and anti-trafficking). The projects involved Middle Eastern immigrant women in Canada; migrant women in the informal sector in Kenya (FIDA Kenya); rural returnee migrant women workers in Moldova (La Strada Moldova); Filipino migrant worker activists in Europe (RESPECT); African asylum-seekers in Ireland (AkiDwA); rural returnee migrant women in Indonesia (ATKI and LRC-KJHAM); returnee trafficked women in Thailand (SEPOM); sex workers and migrants in the Dominican Republic (MODEMU and CEAPA); and migrant women in Brazil (Sodireitos and CLD).

The process, much like the one described in Chapter 10, was rich as well as complicated. We faced challenges in terms of ethics, participation, and turning research into action. The GAATW International Secretariat (IS) sent out a call for participation in early 2009 and selected groups based on a number of criteria: geographical representation, understanding of the link between trafficking and other fields, GAATW membership, the grassroots nature of groups, connection to communities the group intended to work with, and capacity to take on a time-intensive research project. We knew that many groups had not used participatory methods, and prioritized involvement of those few that had.

In May 2009 GAATW-IS held a Learning Workshop on methodology and concepts relevant to the project: power, feminism, intersections in identities. The workshop was successful in modeling participation throughout, holding reflection sessions with anyone who wanted to join at the end of each day, and nearly every session included all participants' involvement. The entire GAATW-IS team was present and learning (not just *teaching*).

Both IS and NGO researchers led sessions. Everyone appeared to leave happy and excited about the project.

After the workshop we discovered that our training methods had been more tailored to established and professional NGOs than smaller grassroots groups, impeding the ability of these smaller groups to participate and engage in the workshop. While some of the groups were well versed in research, others were not. We also learned that our five-day workshop was inadequate to meet the needs of all groups. Two less formal groups pulled out of the project upon returning home because members felt unsure about how to facilitate or replicate the positive experience of inclusion and participation they had experienced during the workshop.[12]

When representatives from each group returned home, they needed to consult with their colleagues and the communities with whom they intended to work. Within a few months of the Learning Workshop some groups had significant staff changes, meaning the person who came to the workshop was no longer the main person working on the FPAR. Some groups returned back to other projects that needed to take priority, some simply because they were better funded. And some groups realized they did not really have as good a relationship with the community as they had thought and found it hard to form trusting bonds. GAATW-IS staff also realized that it would need to allocate more time to working with the groups, through visits as well as through email and phone communication. This is where the projects' wide geographical cover became problematic, as it was costly to travel long distances for lengthy periods of time. IS staff stayed with five groups each for longer than one month, and we made shorter visits to six other groups.

Finally, we had assumed that groups would be able to continue their normal work and incorporate the project into it. However, this assumption did not hold for most groups, who turned out to need to spend more time, money, and staff resources than they anticipated. For the most part the FPAR took away from work on other projects, rather than working to enhance them. While the FPAR did not necessarily fit neatly with the NGOs' existing work, the project did open up new doors for knowledge and action, and importantly, though unfortunately retrospectively, GAATW keenly learned that future FPAR work needs to be able to provide much more in terms of resources for dedicated NGO staff time.

Participation[13]

Community participation is central to FPAR in that participants are the primary actors shaping the research; they are *participant researchers*. One of the key principles of FPAR methodology is that it values the knowledge that the community has, prioritizes the experiences of the community (in our case migrating women), and believes in people's ability to steer change they want. FPAR also does not assume that the researcher is disengaged and objective and yet somehow has superior knowledge. Rather it demands that the researcher is an empathetic listener who knows when to act as a catalyst, when to be a fellow traveler in solidarity and when to encourage the women to analyze the patriarchal basis of some of their assumptions.[14] The NGO staff and GAATW-IS were a type of *ally researcher*, not part of the community group, but allies in helping the process along. In a few grassroots groups, the ally and participant researchers were the same people—as the grassroots staff were part of the community as well.

Participation varied. Some participant researchers conducted interviews themselves, while others were interviewed; some hosted focus groups at their houses and some shaped focus group discussions to ensure their concerns and views were addressed; some participated in group analysis or lobbying, while others were unable to do so because of safety issues, limited time or interest, and lack of childcare. Similarly report writing was mostly left to the NGOs and in some cases to GAATW-IS. In most instances, ally researchers and research participants discussed the FPAR process before beginning any problem analysis, interviews, community mapping, or other methods.

Each group selected techniques for participation that complemented the project, as well as organizational capacity and community interest. Some chose in-depth interviews only, while others drew on story writing and focus groups. In some instances ally NGO researchers lived for a time in the community. Safety concerns and confidentiality were pivotal, such as when collective methods like focus group discussions would expose participants to unnecessary risk.

Social and cultural dynamics were a challenge for researchers, especially in communities where social control was strong. This was evident in the FPAR with migrant women in Moldova, where women reported mostly positive experiences in group discussions, though less triumphant and more realistic versions of their stories arose in one-on-one interviews. Similarly in the Canadian case:

> Not group dynamics; but socio-cultural dynamics within the larger Middle Eastern community impacted the research (i.e. the taboo nature of sex work, the sense of communal shame) and could impact honesty. However, I feel like the research process enabled each woman to really tell their stories without holding back—which is quite refreshing for a community that focuses a lot on keeping up appearances.[15]

Just as each NGO undertook research with specific objectives that shaped the nature of participation, GAATW-IS also had a specific objective, namely in terms of being able to do advocacy at the end of the process. Previous FPAR projects by GAATW resulted in findings so disparate that they could

not be collated for advocacy. While allowing space for research participants to adapt FPARs as necessary, GAATW staff had to gather all groups
under a similar rubric for analysis and problem-setting in order to obtain
outcomes that could be used in regional and/or global advocacy. Because
FPAR is a political tool, we also wanted to do some consciousness-raising
around feminism and migrants' rights. Both our agenda-setting and our
consciousness-raising aims left us with questions about whether our own
involvement/participation was too much, and whether we were overly
influencing the nature of others' participation.

Participation in FPAR is more complex than simply "bringing people
together" and expecting that change will "naturally" follow. When the
GAATW-IS planned the FPAR project, we did not expect participation to
be particularly problematic, but we soon learned just how inextricably
linked women's participation was to the complex realities of their lives.
While participation was shaped by women's positions in their communities, intersections with migratory and labor status and family life also
contributed significantly.

Ethics, Representation, and Safety[16]

Among the ethical issues that arose during the projects, the issue of ensuring
participants' and researchers' social, physical, and emotional safety came up
repeatedly. Some groups were socially isolated because of stigmatization or
criminalization. Similarly, women in rural villages who participated were
typically geographically isolated, small communities where women were
concerned about the social consequences of disclosing certain experiences.
Participating in research posed risks for some women who nevertheless
wanted to share their stories and experiences with other women.

For the research projects with immigrant and migrant women in destination, criminalization was seen as a risk of the research process. In these
projects, the migrant categories imposed on women by the government
(e.g., trafficked person, undocumented migrant, asylum-seeker, refugee)
often meant severe restrictions on women's agency. Women's livelihood
options were extremely limited by their migrant status. In Vancouver,
Canada, two local advocates talked to Middle Eastern women who had
at some point engaged in sex work:

> This sample of informants is unique and, to our knowledge, includes the
> only known examination of the struggles of Iranian women in Canada
> who have engaged in sex work at some point post-migration due to
> severe financial constraints. The taboo nature of sex work in general
> coupled with the severe communal repercussions of engaging in sex
> work[17] pose significant challenges to accessing such a hidden, invisible
> community.[18]

Participants had intense fears about being criminalized in Canada—as women in sex work, as migrants, as persons of Middle Eastern origin. Although they wanted to help others by sharing their experiences, talking to anyone about their experiences still posed a tremendous risk to their personal safety, social reputation, and families (risk of child apprehension).

Moving Beyond the Trafficking Category[19]

Can state and non-state actors move beyond singular, fixed categories and do full justice to women's experiences? Taking up this task is quite hard. In discussions with our members and allied groups, we found that some anti-trafficking organizations were reticent. Some found it difficult to conceive of how their organization could operate if they were taking care of trafficked people, plus migrants, plus other exploited people, and so on. They thought they would need to expand their scope, provide more people with more services and thereby "spread themselves too thin."

Moreover, labels for different categories of migrants have different tangible impacts because the labels (e.g., refugee, trafficked person, undocumented, forced laborer, sex worker) often determine what services a person is entitled to, what work a person is allowed to do, how a person is allowed to move, and what rights they can access.[20] This of course was the crux of our FPAR theme—wanting to link trafficking to other fields and identities so that the trafficking label does not end up restricting people's options. It was not surprising, then, that the women participating in the research were adamant about determining how they would be represented throughout the research process. For instance, while GAATW was interested in the Canadian group participating in the project because they were a community of "sex workers," the community did not want to define themselves that way. They referred to sex work obliquely as something they did "to make ends meet." Our problem, they said, is not with sex work (that's how we live and survive), but with lack of childcare, with domestic violence, and with deskilling.[21] In one low-income or "slum" community in Nairobi (Kenya), participants initially emphasized that they were Kenyan citizens and claimed to have Kenyan national identity cards. However, after some time, they disclosed that they were Somali or Ethiopian migrants and had not been born in Kenya: "It is clear that they were originally not comfortable disclosing the fact that they are migrants, perhaps because the law forbids refugees to live in urban areas, and also because of fear of harassment."[22] Participants were emphatic that they were not participating in this project as *migrant* women. In one focus group discussion, one of the community facilitators emphasized that they had been included in the research project because they *were* migrant women. The women were furious, saying that this would only stir up trouble for them. The other research facilitators promptly responded and worked out other ways of engagement.

The small size of villages, the relationships between residents, and changing social norms around migration also meant that many women felt they had to take great care in how they described and shared their labor migration experiences. Disclosing negative migration experiences within a small community could result in negative social and economic consequences. In La Strada Moldova's research with returnee migrant women in rural Moldova, women described residents in one Moldovan village as being "cruel" to those who had negative labor migration experiences:

> Upon return I told about our [husband and wife's] negative migration experience to my old parents ... they were of course unhappy but asked me not to tell anyone in the village about our experience. They were afraid that villagers would laugh at our family ... like we spent so much time working abroad, and did not even earn enough to mend our roof.... [23]

In these projects, women often shared very different information in individual interviews than they did in focus group discussions. Women felt much safer disclosing negative labor migration experiences in individual interviews and felt more comfortable only sharing positive experiences within focus group discussions. Individual interviews provided a safer space to share negative, complicated, or ambivalent feelings and experiences. This was particularly salient for women who felt shame or embarrassment about negative or unsuccessful labor migration experiences or returning home without any savings.

> Women had to frame their labour migration experiences very carefully once they returned to the village. Women described the village community as being "cruel" to those who had experienced exploitation or negative migration experiences. As such, women only dared to share their negative experiences in individual interviews (women mostly shared positive experiences in focus groups). For most participants, exploitation largely meant not being paid for one's labour, although sexual exploitation was also acknowledged as a risk for women (e.g. feeling pressured to endure sexual harassment to keep one's job). [24]

Even though focus groups could not capture the depth and complexities of women's experiences, in Ursoaia village (Moldova) and Limbangan village (Indonesia) they still provided a valuable space for women to share positive migration experiences, strengthen common values, share lessons learned from migration, and promote general discussions about migration as a broader social issue. Focus group facilitators took care not to publicly expose anyone's stories of pain, exploitation, or other negative experiences: "During the focus groups, the researcher's unspoken tasks were to build a sense of togetherness among the women, to encourage them to see migration-related problems from another angle, to accent the positive things in their lives and to help them feel powerful enough to act."[25]

Women of SEPOM (Self-Empowerment Program for Migrant Women in Thailand) used the project to take control of how they were labeled and perceived in their community. The women strongly challenged current assistance paradigms that only supported women who would accept being publicly labeled (and stigmatized) as a "trafficked person," stating: "If we get help, we just want help without using the word 'trafficking' because it makes us feel like we have a defect and, in our hearts, we will never heal...."[26] The women of SEPOM were struggling to rebuild their lives and all that this entailed—building houses, finding work, and gaining recognition and respect in their communities. Their FPAR project found that identification as a "trafficked person" increased obstacles to reintegration. In the research and action phases of the project they worked to redefine social ideas of trafficked persons, including what trafficked persons need and what trafficked persons are capable of. Women from the program, including returnee migrant women and women who had been trafficked, conducted interviews themselves, collected stories for analysis and worked with a photographer, Yoonki Kim, to create a photo essay and exhibit in which empowering images of the women were placed next to their stories and where women of SEPOM determined how they wanted to be represented. The SEPOM photo exhibit was presented and discussed at GAATW's 2010 International Members Conference and Congress, the 14th UN Human Rights Council session, and the 2010 UNTOC Conference of Parties.[27] SEPOM researchers planned to expand the FPAR locally and continue collecting stories as part of their outreach activities to "highlight women's strengths in overcoming social stigma and gender inequity and their efforts to gain recognition from society."[28]

Group formation can also be significant in terms of people taking power and using it to self-define. It often results from the action phase of an FPAR project. In the 1997–2001 GAATW FPAR in Cambodia, for instance, the Cambodian Prostitute's Union (CPU) was formed, a group which we still work with as an active ally in the fight against trafficking and the promotion of the rights of women in prostitution. The FPAR and the continued work of CPU to some extent brought about a change in perception of local authorities in Cambodia and North Vietnam who no longer saw trafficked women as criminals, but as women who needed support.[29] Similarly, several groups were formed out of the recent 2009–2010 FPAR in Indonesia (two groups), Kenya (three groups), and Moldova (one group), while existing grassroots groups were strengthened through the process in the Netherlands, Dominican Republic, and Thailand, or women involved in the projects talked about forming groups to continue some of the FPAR work in the future:

> I think it's good if we continue our rendezvous in the future to collect our problems that are usually faced during migration and try to solve them together. (Participant researcher in Indonesia)[30]
>
> Yes the group is working and it gives me a platform to raise my concerns and those of other members openly. All we need is support and we can reach great heights. (Participant researcher in Kenya)[31]
>
> Who better knows women's problems? And who knows the best solutions? ... Yes ... women ... we should support each other. (Participant researcher in Moldova)[32]

In Indonesia after initial research in 2009, researcher participants and NGO LRC-KJHAM developed an action plan and transformed their project focus group into the Rowoberanten Women Migrant Workers Group. At the time of writing, the group is planning to participate in the local Development Plan Meeting (Musyawarah Rencana Pembangunan/Musrenbang), and lobby village, sub-district, and district officials based on research findings and recommendations. There are plans to create a credit union as well as another FPAR phase focusing on migrant worker health, which emerged as an issue of concern. A second participating NGO in Indonesia, ATKI, also saw group formation in Limbangan Village, Indonesia. The FPAR acted as a catalyst in the formation of ATKI Limbangan, which continues the collective organizing that started through the project. They organize monthly meetings to discuss issues, are developing a migration information center for prospective migrants, and want to expand FPAR to other migrant worker communities.

FIDA Kenya's FPAR with women migrant workers resulted in the formation of three groups in Nairobi slums—Kawangware, Kangemi, and Kiamaiko—to address social and economic challenges the women face. The groups created a space for women to share their experiences and provide support for each other. The Kawangware and Kangemi groups both have rotating kitties, in which each member contributes the same amount of money at each meeting and one member takes the whole sum at once. This access to larger sums of money than the women would otherwise have increases their opportunities for business expansion. The Kiamaiko group has focused its activities on a partnership with Bunge la Wananchi (People's Parliament), an NGO that helps grassroots communities raise their voices in advocacy. Kiamaiko women have held a series of activities, mobilizing women to participate in forums and meetings to lobby for their rights. The Kangemi Group has also reached out to HIV-positive women, providing support to the heavily stigmatized community. There are concerns about sustainability, with time spent at the collectives equating to time away from work and loss of potential earnings. However FIDA Kenya is in discussions with several development organizations in the hope of creating partnerships that will strengthen the collectives.

In the FPAR, women's strength has come from self-definition, storytelling, and group formation, as well as advocacy for oneself and one's community to local or national government. As in the cases above, women chose what labels they wanted to use, choosing ones with less stigma, ones with more political advantage. Sometimes the trafficking label does provide little stigma and a lot of benefits, but this is not always the case. In the FPAR women voiced strong opinions about how they wanted to represent themselves, and they told quite complicated stories of their journeys, work, families, hardships, and strengths.

CONCLUSION

From the standpoint of the migrating or trafficked woman, the specialization of NGOs or the compartmentalization of assistance has little relevance. The migrant woman stands as one unified subject whose concerns as a worker are not separate from her concerns as a woman, or a mother, migrant, and so on. The complexities of women's lives cannot be adequately captured by one approach or framework alone, whether that be anti-trafficking, women's rights, migrant rights, or labor rights.[33]

Some migrant women have told GAATW that they do not understand the divisions that categorize them. They often are unjust. Why should one woman get to stay in a country because she testified against a trafficker, while another did not want to testify or did not meet the trafficking definition? Why should women be identified at borders as potential victims of trafficking and sent back home, while men are not? Why are brothels raided and sex workers detained, while flagrant abuses at factories employing "cheap labor" go unmentioned? Why are wealthy people allowed to migrate with visas, while working classes are more often restricted? Why are men allowed to improve the lives of their family members through migration, while women's "place" is said to be in the home?

In the 1990s our Feminist Participatory Action Research work intended to figure out what the trafficking experience looked like, wanting to know what migration and exploitation experiences constituted this new emerging category. This was useful at that time, as people were asking for service provision and compensation based on having had their rights violated during trafficking. Since then, the process of categorization, not to mention the specific category of trafficking, has proven problematic. The trafficking category is filled with assumptions about gender in migration and work, about women belonging at home, about class. And women, we have seen, are resisting the trafficking category, as well as others such as "migrant," "sex worker," and so on. Acceptance or resistance depends on each context and the specific socio-political discursive arena.

In the 2009–2010 FPAR we saw women defining themselves. In Kenya, outsiders wanted to call women in certain slum areas "migrants"; the women want *any other* label. In Canada, we chose a group because they were "sex workers"; they defined themselves as migrants, as women, as mothers. In Thailand, many have called the women in the grassroots group SEPOM "trafficked women"; the women, however, are creating complex pictures of their identities beyond that. With a photo exhibit, they showed their work life in fishing and at their market stalls. They showed their ordinary home life in pictures and talked about their children, not wanting them to have the stigma that comes with the trafficking label. They wanted to show that they were ordinary—not extraordinary, apart, or trafficked. Service providers and states need to be aware of discursive and political nuances in these contexts, rather than adopting the anti-trafficking framework wholesale and uncritically.

We chose Feminist Participatory Action Research because we needed a methodology that could counter the tendencies in anti-trafficking discourses to assume what women's vulnerabilities, experiences, and limitations are. We needed a framework that could better capture women's holistic experiences and the meaning women made of their own and their community's experiences. This methodology would also allow us to take stock of changes in gendered trafficking, migration, and labor patterns in the context of global economic developments and a strengthened anti-trafficking movement. As a feminist Alliance, FPAR methodologies reflect the principles that guide our everyday work, such as the importance of carrying forward research into concrete action; research processes that are guided by and respectful of women's priorities, aspirations, and concerns; processes that allow sharing of power among all involved in the research; centering the voices of trafficked and migrant women in any activities involving them; and knowledge production that is guided by the research participants rather than the researcher.[34]

NOTES

1. Thanks and acknowledgments are due to all the FPAR participants and IS staff who were involved in the 2009–2010 GAATW project. Before writing this chapter, many of us had done a lot of reflection on the FPAR process, especially for the December 2010 edition of the GAATW *Alliance News*, as well as for a handful of journal articles. This chapter draws on that rich reflection and the work of others is cited accordingly. It also draws from GAATW (2010), "Introduction," in *Beyond Borders: Exploring Trafficking's Links to Gender, Migration, Labour, Globalisation and Security*, Working Paper Series, Bangkok: GAATW; GAATW (2010), *Beyond Borders: Exploring Linkages Between Trafficking and Migration*, Beyond Borders Working Paper Series, Bangkok: GAATW; and GAATW (2008), *Gender-Migration-Labour-Trafficking: Exploring Conceptual Linkages & Moving Forward*, Roundtable Report, Bangkok: GAATW, pp. 17–19. Many thanks are also due to Kamala Kempadoo's fine editorial hand.

2. GAATW (2007), *Collateral Damage*, Bangkok: GAATW.

3. Bandana Pattanaik, "Anti-trafficking and a Rights-based Approach: Are They Compatible?" GAATW Roundtable, *Gender-Migration-Labour-Trafficking: Exploring Conceptual Linkages & Moving Forward,* 6 August 2008.

4. Don Flynn, "Managing (Ir)regularity: Trafficked Persons and Undocumented Migrants on the Spectrum of Global Migration." Roundtable discussion paper, August 2008, p. 4.

5. Don Flynn, "Managing (Ir)regularity," p. 5.

6. Don Flynn, "Managing (Ir)regularity," p. 8.

7. Textbox from GAATW (2010), *Beyond Borders: Exploring Linkages Between Trafficking and Migration* in Beyond Borders Working Paper Series, Bangkok: GAATW.

8. "Africans Test Argentinean Hospitality." Oct 30 2009. *Guardian Weekly.* Emphasis and brackets added by author.

9. "UK 'Won't Take Calais Migrants.'" Sept 22 2009. *BBC News.* Retrieved from *http://news.bbc.co.uk/2/hi/uk_news/8268113.stm.* Emphasis added by author.

10. "French Police Clear the 'Jungle' Migrant Camp in Calais." Sept 22 2009. *Guardian online.* Retrieved from http://www.guardian.co.uk/world/2009/sep/22/french-police-jungle-calais.

11. "Calais Jungle Raids Escalated to Unprecedented Levels." Dec 8 2009. *Migrant 2 Migrant Radio.* Retrieved from http://m2m.streamtime.org/index.php/2009/calais-jungle-raids-escalated-to-unprecedented-levels/.

12. N. Bilbatua and R. Napier-Moore (2011), "Participatory Enough? The 'P' in FPAR," submitted for publication, pending review.

13. This subsection draws from N. Bilbatua and R. Napier-Moore (2011), "Participatory Enough? The 'P' in FPAR," submitted for publication, pending review.

14. GAATW (2009), *FPAR Learning Workshop Report.* Bangkok: GAATW.

15. K. Noushin in personal communication with the author (August 2010).

16. This section is adapted from J. Ham and R. Napier-Moore (2010), "Ethical Concerns in Feminist Participatory Action Research With Geographically and Socially Isolated Groups," presented at Forcing Issues: Re-thinking and Re-scaling Human Trafficking in the Asia-Pacific Region, October 4–5 2010, National University of Singapore, p. 3.

17. The type of sex work described here refers specifically to indoor-based sex work with a few select and regular clients.

18. K. Noushin and Fereshteh (2010), "Understanding Needs, Recognising Rights: The Stories, Perspectives, and Priorities of Immigrant Iranian Women in Vancouver, Canada." In *A Woman's Life is Richer Than Her Trafficking Experience: Feminist Participatory Action Research (FPAR) Series.* Bangkok, Thailand: GAATW, p. 9.

19. This section draws on J. Ham and R. Napier-Moore (2010), "Ethical Concerns in Feminist Participatory Action Research," pp. 4, 6, 8; N. Bilbatua and R. Napier-Moore (2011), "Participatory Enough? The 'P' in FPAR," submitted for publication, pending review; R. Napier-Moore (2010), "Research Into Action." *Alliance News,* December 2010. Bangkok: GAATW.

20. J. Pollock, "The Migrant Worker, the Refugee, and the Trafficked Person: What's in a Label?" *Alliance News* 33 (July 2010), pp. 19–22. Available online at http://www.gaatw.org/publications/Alliance%20News/Alliance_News_July_2010.pdf. S. Kneebone, "The Trafficking-Refugee Nexus: When Return and Reintegration Becomes *Refoulement." Alliance News* 33 (July 2010), pp. 19–22. Available online at http://www.gaatw.org/publications/Alliance%20News/Alliance_News_July_2010.pdf.

21. K. Noushin and Fereshteh (2010), "Understanding Needs, Recognising Rights," p. 9.

22. A. Maranga and N. Laiboni (2010), "The Realities and Agency of Informal Sector Workers: The Account of Migrant Women Workers in Nairobi." In *A Woman's Life is Richer Than Her Trafficking Experience,* p. 23.

23. V. Rusu for La Strada Moldova (2010), "A Look at the Linkages: How Does Gen-

der, Migration, Labour and Trafficking Intersect in Women's Lives? A Qualitative Research Based on Migration and Labour Experiences of Women from Ursoaia, Republic of Moldova." In *A Woman's Life is Richer Than Her Trafficking Experience*, p. 19.

24. V. Rusu for La Strada Moldova (2010), "A Look at the Linkages," p. 4.

25. V. Rusu for La Strada Moldova (2010), "A Look at the Linkages," p. 11.

26. Self-Empowerment Program for Migrant Women (SEPOM) (2010), "'Trafficked' Identities as a Barrier to Community Reintegration: Five Stories of Women Re-building Lives and Resisting Categorisation." In *A Woman's Life is Richer Than Her Trafficking Experience*, p. 8.

27. See coverage, for instance "Permanent Mission of Thailand in Vienna Sponsored the Launching of a Photo Exhibition," *Siam Daily News*. Available at: http://www.siamdailynews.com/2010/11/15/permanent-mission-of-thailand-in-vienna-sponsored-the-launching-of-a-photo-exhibition/.

28. Self-Empowerment Program for Migrant Women (SEPOM) (2010), "'Trafficked' Identities as a Barrier to Community Reintegration: Five Stories of Women Re-building Lives and Resisting Categorisation," p. 6.

29. M. Taguinod and B. Pattanaik (2009), "GAATW's Work in Asia." *Alliance News* 32, p. 9.

30. ATKI (2010), "The Impact of Excessive Placement Fees on Indonesian Migrant Workers (IWMs) and Their Families." In *A Woman's Life is Richer Than Her Trafficking Experience*, p. 26.

31. A. Maranga and N. Laiboni (2010), "The Realities and Agency of Informal Sector Workers," p. 35.

32. V. Rusu for La Strada Moldova (2010), "A Look at the Linkages," p. 34.

33. Adapted from J. Ham and R. Napier-Moore (2010), "Ethical Concerns in Feminist Participatory Action Research," p. 1.

34. Adapted from J. Ham and R. Napier-Moore (2010), "Ethical Concerns in Feminist Participatory Action Research," p. 2.

14

The Anti-trafficking Juggernaut Rolls On

Kamala Kempadoo

It is difficult to close a book such as this, for new events are reported daily in the media, new analyses of trafficking published, new migrant women's and sex workers' experiences heard, and new anti-trafficking organizations created. So to produce a collective reflection on the current state of affairs and new directions I asked the original contributors what concerned and excited them around the issue of trafficking in the specific country in which they work, and what they would like to see happen in the future. Many of the authors have continued to participate in anti-trafficking struggles and interventions, and six—Josephine Ho, Phil Marshall, Natasha Ahmad, John Frederick, Melissa Ditmore, and Matt Friedman (aka Aftab Ahmed)—sent their reflections and updates. Others said they were no longer in the field of anti-trafficking and/or had nothing to add at the time. What follows is a compilation of the responses, as well as some of my own thoughts and some additional ideas from others in the field. Concerns about the ineffectiveness of the main trafficking paradigms remained paramount but some positive developments were noted, and several authors identified areas that they saw as needing (greater) attention.

MAIN CONCERNS

"In South Asia, sad to say," John Frederick starts off, "the anti-trafficking discourse in both the media and the general anti-trafficking community has not substantially changed since the book came out, or since the 90s."

And while this appears to be an unstated assumption in many of the responses, with, as Josephine Ho puts it, anti-trafficking discourses occupying the moral high ground, there is also recognition that there remains little clarity or consensus about what constitutes or is understood under the rubric "trafficking." Matt Friedman, for example, observes, "There needs to be much more conceptual clarity among those addressing the problem. I recently attended an event where half the people didn't have the same understanding of the problem." Phil Marshall adds to this: "A small but telling study by Simon Baker in my view, pretty much obliterated any contention that there is consensus on how to apply the TIP [Trafficking In Persons] definition in real life and therefore on the definition of trafficking itself. Baker gave ten case studies to nineteen practitioners independently and asked whether the case was trafficking. In not one case, did all nineteen people agree. A corollary to that is if we cannot agree on how to apply the definition, it is most unlikely we can get numbers, even setting aside methodological difficulties."

Nevertheless, despite a lack of clarity or consensus, many organizations "continue to flog the trafficking horse," as Marshall puts it. Jyoti Sanghera notes, "I was helping a team from the Women's Ministry with a policy on trafficking ... and saw that they were really floundering with wanting to do the right thing but without a clue on what that 'ephemeral' right thing is."[1] Or, as Friedman observes, "so many projects 'do things' that don't translate into a person being protected, a criminal being prosecuted or a victim being helped." Marshall writes, "I work in one country where a myriad of organisations, including several different US government agencies, continue to provide specialised anti-TIP training to a police force that lacks such basic foundations as recruitment policies, rotation policies, promotion policies, use of force guidelines, handcuffs, etc.—building on sand in other words."

Moving away from a focus on how to understand or conceptualize the problem of trafficking, yet continuing to believe that trafficking must be combated, has given rise to attention to two areas in the debate in Asia: child protection and migration. Marshall sees this move as gradual where, in regards to children, "organisations are starting to place less emphasis on whether or not they can be defined as trafficked and more on the 'best interests of the child.'" In relation to adults, he sees IOM (International Organisation for Migration) and other such organizations "working to broaden the parameters of their assistance to migrants in distress." These moves produce "a focus on child protection in the context of migration," led by organizations such as UNICEF, Terre des Hommes, ILO, and Save the Children through the Children on the Move Initiative, which, in his view, appear to be taking organizations back to their original mandates.

John Frederick sees a similar refocusing. Trafficking, he writes, "is increasingly placed within migration conceptual models," with the most significant change being "the increased attention to trafficked persons, including adult males, in forms of labour other than prostitution/sex work ... with increased attention to the abuse and exploitation of boys." Such shifts in focus, in his view, however, also mean that "a lot of localized 'micro-trafficking' for example within districts, is now being ignored."

In the case of Taiwan, Josephine Ho observes that "anti-trafficking policies are being used as an occasion to expel migrants from economically disadvantaged areas" while at the same time working as a "gesture" to the rest of the world that something is being done. Moreover, "anti-trafficking Christian groups have expanded to cover legislations that deal with issues such as sexual harassment, sexual assaults, and child protection," pushing for new legislation in which "all social space may be patrolled and purified for the sake of 'giving children the best environment possible to develop themselves.'" "It is quite conceivable," she adds, "that child-protection protocols will become universal imperatives, and spread down to the developing countries to evolve into anti-sex-work legislation."

In the US, the country that monitors the rest of the world on issues of trafficking, a shift to a focus on children is signalled as a part of the "domestic turn," as mentioned in the introductory chapter of this book, which also turns the attention to local sex markets and domestic prostitution. Elizabeth Bernstein writes further,

> The issue, at least in the U.S., is that the definition of domestic trafficking that has been incorporated into recent revisions of the TVPA [Trafficking Victims Protection Act] explicitly states that domestic prostitution is to be treated on a legal par with previous cross-border understandings of the crime, and also that *any instance of underage prostitution qualifies automatically*, since force, fraud, and coercion do not need to be proven when the 'victim' is under 18. This can be a useful means of keeping the panic circulating in the face of the embarrassing discrepancy between 14,500–50,000 estimated victims annually, and the reality of < 2,000 T-visas granted in ten years. In fact, it also serves to crank up the estimated numbers of victims. If *any* underage person in the sex industry constitutes a victim of trafficking, then the numbers can easily explode to > 300,000 a year.[2]

She goes on to note that federal laws are now used "straightforwardly and unabashedly" to police local sex work markets, sometimes severing the trafficking issue from migration completely.

Melissa Ditmore's primary concern about the US is that the new efforts are focused on ending the demand for sex work clients, which appear to confirm the trend of an increased attention to the domestic sex market. However, in a recent project, she found that people trafficked into sex work were likely to be helped by clients, leading her to surmise that the new focus of the law would prevent such assistance from occurring and create even greater obstacles for sex workers.[3] Ditmore also sees that such a focus ignores the demand for cheap labor in other sectors in the US, pointing especially to the Signal case in the rebuilding of New Orleans, where Brazilians and Bangladeshis are reported to work in slavery-like conditions and debt bondage.

The "domestic turn" in the US, however, can also be read as a focus on domestic work itself, which returns the gaze to migration issues. Due to inclusion of the US in the State Department's TIP review, forced labor practices within the country and involving its overseas diplomatic personnel have become increasingly visible. Migrant domestic work thus is foregrounded in recent US anti-trafficking interventions, with the 2011 US State Department directive to protect domestic workers taking on greater importance in the fight against trafficking.[4] Migration and migrant labor remain, then, at the heart of US state anti-trafficking interventions, albeit disconnected from the domestic sex industry.

Alongside these shifts that are highlighted in the anti-trafficking industry, the conflation of trafficking and prostitution remains an area of ongoing critique and concern in different parts of the world. According to Melissa Ditmore, "The white slavery/trafficking panic continues to adversely affect sex workers and ignore people in horrible conditions in other industries (and there are so many more of them in fishing, weaving, agriculture, brick making, construction, sweatshops ...)." Phil Marshall explains it somewhat differently: "The confusion between TIP and prostitution continues to create nothing but problems. In Cambodia, the totally predictable impact of the inclusion of solicitation as an offence in the anti-TIP law created carte blanche for police abuse and also messed up HIV programmes. Also, while there are 50-plus organisations working on TIP in Cambodia, it seems only a handful will assist sex workers with other forms of violence such as gang rape, unless what they want is sewing lessons." And on this subject, Josephine Ho notes:

In the years since the 1997 prostitutes' uprising in Taipei, the anti-prostitution (anti-sex) religious groups' power of influence with the government as well as public opinion in Taiwan has been growing exponentially. Globalization has brought a culture of competition in images of respectability and civility among nations that are striving for international recognition, Taiwan especially, which often turns into increasingly stringent laws and delicate emotions. The traditional cultural scripts for trafficking, with pitiful innocent victims and demonized traffickers, lends itself easily to strong moral condemnations by economically comfortable countries that often displace underlying anxieties toward migration and mobility.... The conflation of children exploited in economically backward countries and adults migrating to seek better economic opportunities make it more difficult to battle the underlying realities of anti-sex, anti-sex-work manoeuvres.

With the move away from debates about what constitutes trafficking alongside the shifts and the continuities mentioned above, the rescue and rehabilitation aspects of anti-trafficking interventions are gaining greater significance. John Frederick notes, "Of the different areas of intervention, recovery (aka rehabilitation) has seen the most strengthening. In India, Bangladesh and Nepal, we've done a lot of work establishing case management, service-referral and protection systems in recovery facilities, de-institutionalizing long-term care facilities, and establishing community-based alternatives. 'Shelters' are out of fashion, 'counsellors' are less seen as deities, and much emphasis is being placed on integration." Nevertheless, Phil Marshall writes: "Victim services in the GMS [Greater Mekong Sub-region] countries remain by and large incredibly paternalistic, with victims having little say in the services they receive, forced stays in shelters, lack of consultation on reintegration goals, etc."

The rescue and recovery industry is also not only a preoccupation of various agencies and NGOs, but also increasingly of Hollywood celebrities. Movie stars such as Mira Sorvino, Demi Moore, Ashton Kutcher, Susan Sarandon, Emma Thompson, Ashley Judd, and Sarah Jessica Parker have adopted the cause of trafficking as a way to "save" poor people, especially women and girls.[5] UN Goodwill Ambassador Sorvino is reported to have said at the launch event for a UN grants fund for trafficking victims: "[They] can't speak for themselves—yet. But that's what we're trying to do.... The trust fund will hopefully help emancipate them and give them a voice."[6] This new expression of Western imperialism, or as the report labels it, "The White Hollywood Star's Burden," not only commands a lot of public attention but continues to reproduce the "helpless victim" image. As Jyoti Sanghera writes: "Demi Moore is here now for five days on an anti-trafficking mission to launch a joint campaign with Maiti Nepal, called 'Real men don't buy girls'. It's really quite horrific. The entire Hollywood team with the anti-trafficking sleuths went off to the Nepal–India border and rescued five young girls. The TV cameras rolled and CNN was making a film." She comments, with some indignation, "It just does not stop, does it?"[7]

Aside from the rescue and recovery aspects, concerns are raised about the overall effectiveness of anti-trafficking interventions and policies. Marshall writes, "There remains a major lack of evaluation of the impact of TIP interventions, with the notable exception of the negative impact of programmes on the people they are ostensibly supposed to protect (Collateral Damage, etc.). Almost all evaluations seem to focus on process rather than impact, not least because by the time the evaluations take place, there is nothing the evaluators can actually use to assess the impact—lack of baselines, clear objectives, etc." Matt Friedman appears to concur, noting, "The sector has to accept impact assessments to see what is working. There has been a real resistance to this over the years, as if we don't have to be accountable.... Understanding what works and doesn't work must be explored."

Funding is also of concern. Phil Marshall observes, "On a recent trip to the Cambodian border all government and NGO people told me we need awareness raising." However, he continues, "All the people we met not only knew about the realities of migrating to Thailand but didn't get this knowledge from the thousands of awareness raising activities that have taken place to date, but from word of mouth. With no side benefits ... it [awareness raising] is a real black hole for resources." Moreover, he observes, "Donor support for anti-TIP initiatives is waning, not helped by lack of demonstrable results." Recognizing this tendency, Matt Friedman writes with some urgency, "With the limited funding available, we can't waste a single dollar."

On the ground, Friedman thinks there is also not enough collaboration. "In our day-to-day interactions with partners, we have all seen how collaboration can be paralyzed or hindered by simple misunderstandings, polarized political views, and/or a lack of faith in the process. In the absence of collaboration, people often waste time obsessing over our differences and our perceived failures, instead of on the problem at hand. This wasted energy takes away from our mandate to help and support those we serve. We don't have the time or the luxury to divert any of our attention to anything other than the problem itself."

The lack of attention by the state to the issue of trafficking is also flagged as a recurring problem. Natasha Ahmad, for example, writes, "The issue of 'legal trafficking' is a concern for me! There are many people who are going as migrant workers and most of the time these migrant workers do not get what they were promised. This is becoming a big issue for Bangladesh. The laws to protect the 'migrant workers' are in place but they are not at all effective as there is no mechanism to implement them ... the migrant workers live in a sort of 'no man's land' as the country of origin does not have any effective role to play in the country of destination, and destination countries have their own laws and do not have any respect for the international laws which protect the rights of 'migrant workers'. This is a serious issue."[8]

Bandana Pattanaik explains further that it is not possible to ascribe the concept of "legal trafficking" to any one group or person, and that it is not an official term in anti-trafficking work, yet still, "I have heard migrant rights groups saying that the states that push their citizens to travel abroad for work are the big traffickers.... " She notes that while it is technically impossible to identify states that do this, "regimes such as in Burma make it impossible for people to stay in that country and other states, such as the Philippines and Indonesia, have proactively adopted out-migration policies, with Bangladesh and Nepal following suit." The issue of having proactive out-migration policies but no adequate protection, which potentially fuels trafficking, could be, according to Pattanaik, put on the table for discussion.

Marshall remarks on the state's complicity, "As we start to point more at exploitative aspects of trafficking, the unwillingness of governments to handle destination issues is finally coming out more into the open. Thailand, for example, has traditionally been seen as quite responsive on trafficking, but now people are starting to notice that the government has consistently stopped short of actually apprehending and punishing the exploiters."

The state, then, appears as a very unreliable partner in the war on trafficking, particularly in Asia, or as John Frederick writes about what governments have been doing: "In Nepal, I can say: nothing. The news last week reported that the Nepal Constituent Assembly met for a total of 95 minutes since its formation 365 days ago. But people still go to work and buy their rice.... "

POSITIVE SIGNS

Despite the grave concerns about current anti-trafficking work and state interventions—many of which echo what was said several years ago and are commented on at length in other chapters in this book—some authors have been in the field consistently enough to notice positive developments, as well as the limitations of such developments. Natasha Ahmad, for example, writes:

> BOMSA/IMA/RUMMRU/WARBI—all these organizations in Bangladesh are working to prepare the workers, giving them skill training, talking about hygiene, how to use a toilet etc. Such service was not there earlier and I am sure that this is helping the migrant workers. But is it enough? How do we ensure the migrants' rights? How do we ensure that these migrant workers will not be deceived? Where do they go for help? Most of these people need legal support, but who will provide it? How do we build up links with groups in the destination countries? I know the Middle Eastern countries are going through a huge political change. Many migrant workers have returned home and many new migrants are going there to this new situation. Are there groups interested to work on this issue and do some policy advocacy to ensure rights of migrant workers? In the country of origin there are now some organizations working to help migrant workers to set up small businesses, or to see that the money they remit is used properly. But honestly, these are not enough.

John Frederick also sees some positive developments, noting that "some good research has been conducted in the last few years, particularly in Bangladesh and Pakistan. [However] there are still large gaps in our knowledge base, particularly in Nepal and India. A notable exception is Pakistan, which has conducted significant solid research about trafficking and exploitation in non-sex work labour sectors and in the sexual exploitation of boys." On the subject of research, Matt Friedman adds some cautionary notes, "We need better data to understand the problem—not just qualitative studies, but quantitative ones." Moreover, "It is not just enough to have the research—it has to be reviewed, analyzed and applied. There is often a major disconnect between data collectors and field officials. The two groups need to come together."

In terms of trafficking prevention and response, John Frederick sees that "donors such as UNICEF are placing increased emphasis on the establishment of 'systems'—basically meaning social service systems. Accompanying this is (finally!) a recognition of the role of the 'social worker' in both prevention and response. In some countries, like Bangladesh, government social workers are being developed. However, social work training services remain limited, and will take some time." And Josephine Ho writes,

> More than a dozen years of persistent activism and social education by Taiwan's prostitutes' rights group COSWAS is finally paying off—to a certain extent. With the help of a trial-run process of deliberative democracy that surprisingly revealed a unanimous decriminalization position among participating citizens in 2009, as well as the work of a couple of sympathetic judges who in the same year filed for constitutional interpretation on articles that criminalize only the prostitutes but not the johns caught in conducting sexual transactions, the Constitutional Court has ruled that, on the ground of gender discrimination, those criminalizing articles are to be annulled toward the end of 2011.... However, two years of back and forth contestations are now ending, with anti-prostitution religious groups successfully persuading the cowardly politicians into moving toward alternative laws that would severely punish all parties involved in any sexual transaction that takes place outside designated red-light districts (which, incidentally, are yet to be established, and where sexual and social stigma may hinder local residents' desire to host those districts). This seemingly liberal policy remains blind to existing sex work and their historical habitat yet creates the facade that the government has respected the human rights of sex workers.

Phil Marshall states, "There are some encouraging signs finally with regard to prevention of labour trafficking in the form of increased focus on actual exploitation, including the role of recruitment companies. Also, work is starting to be done on supply chains, tracing the products produced by badly exploited labour. This has already shown success with carpets, chocolates, etc. The beauty of this is that once consumers decide not to buy a product there is nothing that corrupt officials can do about it. Governments and companies can force people to work for them but they can't force people in the door to buy their products." In addition, he says "I am excited about UNIAP's recent study of deported migrants which is a move towards distilling what actually makes people vulnerable to TIP." He also sees the ongoing challenges to existing 'data' about the proportion of trafficking that is for sexual exploitation as encouraging. Finally, he adds, "notwithstanding issues in other aspects of his presidency, the election of Obama seems to have lessened the voice of those who appear to have no interest in either evidence or the views of those they claim to be helping. My discussions with US government officials have been limited, but there has certainly seemed a lot more space."

Melissa Ditmore also critically notes a positive shift in the President's Emergency Plan for AIDS Relief (PEPFAR) under the Obama administration: "The pledge [PEPFAR's Anti-prostitution Pledge for Organizations Working With Sex Workers] is no longer a separate document, and contracts now include that the recipient is 'opposed to prostitution and sex trafficking because of the psychological and physical risks they pose for women, men and children.'"[9] However, guidance remains unclear about what activities are forbidden and what activities are allowed in HIV prevention with sex workers. Enforcement has been unpredictable; when the pledge was first implemented, some representatives of US government funding agencies advised stopping all work with sex workers rather than losing US government money. Other US government representatives cautioned that stopping work with sex workers would mean that sex workers would be discriminated against and denied critical HIV prevention and health services.[10] The Obama administration has stressed that it does not condone discrimination: during the 2010 AIDS Conference in Vienna, Eric Goosby, the US Global AIDS Coordinator (OGAC), said, "If there are examples of anybody being turned away [for being a sex worker], if someone feels that they were excluded from or dropped out of care for those reasons, we would get on that like a laser" and that sex workers would be "embraced" at all locations.[11] Still, Ditmore goes on to caution that "to change implementation but not to change the actual policy ... leaves the rights of sex workers dependent upon political winds; not to do so is dangerous to the health and human rights of sex workers."[12]

These authors thus see some positive developments around the amount of research being undertaken on the issue, support for (would-be) migrants in their countries of origin, and investigation into highly exploitative and discriminatory working conditions and laws in and outside sex industries, as well as an indication of slightly less conservative US foreign policies concerning trafficking and prostitution under the Obama administration. All, however, also indicate that these steps are small and there is a whole lot more to do to stop the abuse, coercion, and hyperexploitation in migration and labor situations.

So, What Needs to Be Done?

According to Natasha Ahmad, "We have to look at this whole issue in a more holistic way. That is what is missing.... I have seen sex workers who have gone to the Middle East who come back more traumatised. What do we have to say about it? We often see that our migrant workers are receiving capital punishment ... and suddenly a dead body comes from the country of destination. Such things are very common and we have not been able to do much. It is high time we stop looking at trafficking in the narrow way but broaden our view point and expand our work area."

Matt Friedman writes, "It is imperative that the private sector be engaged—not just as funders, but as full partners.[13] Kicking in doors and helping a few hundred victims a year isn't going to address the big numbers. Supply chains need to be regularly reviewed and consumers need to get into the game—making choices on products that come to their stores through responsible means." Just as importantly, he notes, "Development efforts need to evolve. So many of our processes are old and tired.... There has to be innovation in the way we address our work." As well, "We need more trained professionals to address the problem—preferably from the local communities." And again he stresses, "We must be held accountable for our work. We must be able to demonstrate tangible, measurable results.... We have to instil a sense of urgency in everything we do." But perhaps, most of all, "What we do, MUST address the needs of real people."

Josephine Ho weighs in on the question: "Work is desperately needed to trace the historical development of anti-trafficking movements and the discourses they used as well as their appropriations or transfigurations in evolving social contexts. Recent backlashes in the Netherlands and elsewhere are also often cited by local officials as the world trend to eliminate sex work. So, more information and possible strategies to fight back are also needed."

In brief, Melissa Ditmore says: "I would like to see the use of evidence-based proven effective strategies to address trafficking in all fields, rather than celebrity hype!" And Phil Marshall writes:

> Most of all, I would like to see sex workers treated as people and given the same opportunities to participate in decisions that affect their lives as everyone else. This is the most basic principle in international development, and is almost completely ignored. In practice in the GMS, I believe this could include working with HIV organisations to include

programmes which deal with legal rights, access to legal services, long-term sustainable exit strategies rather than an obsession with rescue, and with the ability to make complaints on their own terms, as appropriate.... In labour trafficking, while we should continue work to strengthen protection of migrants, I would go after the profit—by supply chains, public pressure, peer pressure, use of justice system, etc. I would also like to see more attention to the factors that create an enabling environment for trafficking. In many countries, there is limited social outrage in relation to violent treatment of migrants. Education systems often nurture, or at least do not address, attitudes that breed dislike/contempt for people from other countries. While anti-migration rhetoric is popular everywhere, there is surely more we can do with regard to the importance of migrants to the host country. And [we could] start focusing anti-TIP education in schools on not exploiting others as well as not becoming a victim.

Alternatively, he suggests, "we could throw out the whole paradigm!"

In short, there is still much, or nothing, to do, depending upon where we stand in relation to the trafficking debate. The discrimination, abuse, and hyperexploitation of migrant workers, the criminalization of sex work and stigmatization and discrimination of those who sell sexual labor, and the use and abuse of children in a range of industries, remain central to the current global economy, with the state proving to be more frequently a partner in the crimes rather than in effecting any real change. Perhaps another round of reflections and evaluations in a few years will tell us something more or reveal something new. For now, after a decade of worldwide attention to human trafficking, it seems business continues much as usual.

NOTES

1. Email correspondence, February 24, 2011, on file with author.

2. Email correspondence, January 20, 2011, on file with author. Bernstein has written more fully about this trend in her earlier work.

3. Melissa Ditmore (2009), *The Use of Raids to Fight Trafficking in Persons.* New York, NY: Urban Justice Center Sex Workers Project. http://sexworkersproject.org/publications/reports/raids-and-trafficking/

4. This emphasis on migrant domestic work within US anti-trafficking policies was made abundantly clear by Amy O'Neill Richard of the US Office to Monitor and Combat Trafficking in Persons, during her talk on the panel "Shifting Populations." *Driving Change, Shaping Lives: Gender in the Developing World,* Radcliffe Institute for Advanced Study and Harvard Kennedy School, March 3–4, 2011. See http://www.youtube.com/watch?v=-j5vWx4tHHs&feature=youtube_gdata_player. See also: http://www.state.gov/g/tip/rls/fs/2011/167235.htm for details about the US Government Action to Address Involuntary Servitude.

5. See for example http://news.change.org/stories/top-ten-human-trafficking-celebrity-activists.

6. See http://www.anorak.co.uk/275916/keyposts/human-trafficking-the-white-hollywood-stars-burden.html/.

7. Email correspondence, April 8, 2011, on file with author.

8. For further comment on this need for protections for Bangladeshi migrant workers in the Middle East, see http://www.thedailystar.net/newDesign/news-details.php?nid=192245.

9. US Department of Health and Human Services (DHHS). 45 CFR Part 89. FR Doc 2010-8378. The Federal Register, April 13, 2010, v. 75 n. 70. http://www.thefederalregister.com/d.p/2010-04-13-2010-8378.

10. Melissa Ditmore and Dan Allman (2011), "Sacrificing Harm Reduction Practice to Moral Ideology: The Example of the USAID Anti-prostitution Pledge." Presentation to the International Harm Reduction Association, April 2011, Beirut, Lebanon.

11. "Straight Talk with Eric Goosby, Head of PEPFAR." *IRIN/PLUS News.* July 26, 2010. http://www.plusnews.org/Report.aspx?ReportID=89965.

12. For a fuller analysis, see Melissa Ditmore and Dan Allman (2010), "Implications of PEPFAR's Anti-prostitution Pledge for Organizations Working with Sex Workers." *HIV/AIDS Policy and Law Review* 15(1):64–65. http://www.aidslaw.ca/publications/publicationsdocEN.php?ref=1138.

13. See as an example "HK Bosses Arm iPods to Fight People Smugglers." *South China Morning Post.* May 8, 2011. www.scmp.com.

Index

ABC Nepal, 129
Abolitionism, xiii–xvi, 73, 111, 117
Aboriginal girls and women: as
    prostitutes, 99*n*5; rescue efforts,
    99*n*8; Taiwan's anti-prostitution
    initiative, 84–88; trafficking of, 100*n*15
Abortion services, 114, 118, 124–125*n*16
Abuses: abuse versus human rights
    violations, 11; addressing of, 202
Accommodations, 217
ActionAid, 129
Adolescent girls: trafficking of,
    in relation to immigration and
    prostitution, 12
Advertising, for sex transactions, 93–
    95, 102*n*29, 102*n*30, 102*n*33, 102*n*34
Advocacy campaigns, 69–70
Age factors, 59; and children's
    welfare in Taiwan, 96–97; consent
    and coercion issues, 17–21, 116;
    underage prostitutes, 89, 89–91,
    99*n*4. *See also* Children
Agency, xxviii–xxx, 21, 209;
    addressing female migration in
    international law, 36–37; exercise
    of, 6, 13–14, 20, 202; levels of,
    109; of migrating sex workers,
    97–98; sexual, 10, 19, 80*n*2; Taiwan's
    prostitutes, 101*n*18; of trafficked
    persons, 59
Ahmad, Natasha, 211–227, 249, 254,
    255–256, 258
Ahmed, Aftab, 199–210
Albright, Madeleine, 114

Aliens Laws, Netherlands, 68–69
Ally researchers, 239
Alternative livelihood options, 48
Anti–child-prostitution efforts, 90–91, 94
Anti-pornography campaigns, 94–95,
    103*n*37
Anti-terrorism laws, 34
Anti-trafficking initiatives, 45,
    129, 134*n*3; and cross-border
    movements, 18–31; and Empower
    report, 152–153, 155*n*2; Europe,
    67–69; and human rights issues,
    xix, 78–80, 86, 100*n*13; intercepting
    traffickers, 133; and international
    government discourse, xii;
    legislation equating children with
    women, 13–14; Nepal, 143; new
    developments and concerns about
    effectiveness of, 249–250; political,
    religious, ethnic and gender issues,
    99*n*10; reflections on, 3–4; restricting
    migrants to counter trafficking,
    236(box); Taiwan, 84, 86–87, 99*n*11;
    Thailand, 69–70; transcending the
    trafficking framework, 241–245;
    USAID funding policy, 117–122,
    124–125*n*16; workshop in the
    Netherlands, 66, 80*n*2. *See also*
    Rescue efforts
Asia, international trafficking in, 151
Asian Ministerial Regional
    Conferences on People Smuggling,
    Trafficking and Related
    Transnational Crime, 50

261

About the Editors and Contributors

Natasha Ahmad is an independent consultant and researcher, presently living in India. She has worked for a number of development organizations, including the International Organization for Migration, and the Centre for Feminist Legal Research, and is a member of the Global Alliance Against Traffic in Women. She is presently working on issues of displacement of migrant workers who are trafficked under a "legal" banner.

Vachararutai (Jan) Boontinand worked with the Global Alliance Against Traffic in Women (GAATW) from 1996 to early 2002, when she also coordinated the Research and Action Project on Trafficking in Women in the Mekong Region. Jan works with civil-society groups on gender and other development issues and is currently a PhD Candidate in Human Rights and Peace Studies at Mahidol University, Thailand.

Lin Chew is a feminist and human rights activist, focusing principally on issues around migration and women migrant workers. She was one of the founders of the Dutch Foundation Against ·Trafficking in Women (STV) and the Global Alliance Against Traffic in Women (GAATW), whose international secretariat is based in Bangkok. She is a program coordinator of GAATW and Executive Committee member of Action for REACH OUT (Hong Kong), an NGO advocating the rights of sex workers.

Melissa Ditmore is a consultant on research and rights-based programming who has worked on gender, mobility, HIV, and sex work. She is the author of *Prostitution and Sex Work* (ABC-Clio 2010), editor of *Encyclopedia of Prostitution and Sex Work* (Greenwood 2006), and co-editor of *Sex Work Matters* (Zed 2010). Her recent research, with Dan Allman of the University of Toronto, addresses ethics and participatory research methods in biomedical HIV-prevention clinical trials with marginalized populations including sex workers and drug users.

John Frederick is the director of Ray of Hope, a consultancy organization that designs research and programming on sex work, trafficking, gender,

279

violence, and sexual abuse in South Asia. He is the author of *A Study of Trafficked Nepalese Girls and Women in Mumbai and Kolkata* (2005) and *Trafficking and Exploitation in the Entertainment and Sex Industries in Nepal* (2010). He is presently employed by Terre des Hommes (Lausanne) to develop service delivery systems for NGOs working with entertainment workers in Nepal.

Matthew Friedman (aka Aftab Ahmed) is a regional project manager for the United Nations Inter-Agency Project on Human Trafficking. He has worked for over a decade in Asia.

Josephine (Chuen-Juei) Ho is Chair Professor in the Department of English and Head of the Center for the Study of Sexualities, National Central University, Taiwan. She has been writing both extensively and provocatively to open up new discursive space for gender/sexuality issues and is known for her research in female sexuality, sex work, transgenderism, and teenage sexuality, as well as for her involvement in social movements. The Center for the Study of Sexualities is internationally recognized for both its activism and its intellectual stamina. http://sex.ncu.edu.tw.

Jagori (meaning "awaken woman") is a training, documentation, and research organization working on women's issues for the past twenty years. Jagori has been involved in issues of violence against women, women's health, sexuality, migration, and rights of women workers. Kalpana Viswanath, a sociologist and feminist activist, revised the paper published here from research conducted by Jagori in 2000. She has been the coordinator of Jagori, based in New Delhi, India since 2000. This research was conducted by Manjima Bhattacharjya, Abha Dayal, and Seema Singh, in addition to Kalpana.

Ratna Kapur is director of the Centre for Feminist Legal Research, New Delhi, Professor at the Geneva School of Diplomacy & International Relations and Visiting Professor, Jindal Global Law School, India. She has also taught at various law schools in the United States and Canada, and written extensively on women's human rights issues and postcolonial and feminist legal theory. Her publications include: *Makeshift Migrants and Law: Gender, Belonging and Postcolonial Anxieties* (2010); *Erotic Justice* (2004); *Secularism's Last Sigh? Hindutva and the (Mis)Rule of Law* (co-authored, 2001), and *Subversive Sites: Feminist Engagements with Law in India* (co-authored, 1996).

Kamala Kempadoo is professor in the Department of Social Science at York University, Toronto, Canada. Her research since the early 1990s has centered on the global sex trade. Her publications include *Sexing the*

Caribbean: Gender, Race and Sexual Labor (2004); *Sun, Sex and Gold: Tourism and Sex Work in the Caribbean* (ed., 1999); and *Global Sex Workers: Rights, Resistance and Redefinition* (co-editor, 1998). In developing this work she has been closely associated with black, migrant, and Third World women's organizations in different parts of the world.

Phil Marshall commenced his career working for New Zealand's Ministry of Foreign Affairs on international development issues. He became involved in anti-trafficking work as the first manager of the UN Inter-Agency Project on Human Trafficking in the Greater Mekong Sub-region (UNIAP), 2000–2003, and subsequently worked as an anti-trafficking consultant. He is currently Director of the Research Communications Group, a small not-for-profit international consultancy firm that focuses on social protection, health communications, and responsible infrastructure.

Rebecca Napier-Moore is Research Programme Officer with the Global Alliance Against Traffic in Women. She is working on a program to enhance smuggled persons' rights, particularly with respect to anti-trafficking measures, and previously worked with others to develop GAATW's Feminist Participatory Action Research project, as well as a series of working papers entitled *Beyond Borders: Exploring Trafficking's Links to Gender, Migration, Labour, Globalisation and Security.*

Bandana Pattanaik is an International Coordinator of the Global Alliance Against Traffic in Women. She is also co-editor, with Susanne Thorbek, of *Transnational Prostitution: Changing Global Patterns* (2002).

Jyoti Sanghera is the Representative of the United Nations Office of the High Commissioner for Human Rights (OHCHR) in Nepal. She has been with OHCHR for close to a decade serving as the Adviser on trafficking in Geneva for several years and subsequently as the Senior Human Rights Adviser in Sri Lanka. Jyoti has worked on human rights issues concerning women, migrants, sex workers, and other discriminated groups in conflict and post–conflict situations for the past three decades in various capacities, including with key UN agencies and NGOs in North America and Asia. She has taught for several years in the Department of Women's Studies at the University of Victoria in Canada.

Susu Thatun is Deputy Regional Programme Manager to the UN Inter-Agency Project on Human Trafficking (UNIAP), based in Bangkok. She has worked on the issue of human trafficking for the past five years; for over three years in Myanmar as the National Project Coordinator. She has been involved in the initiation and facilitation of the Mekong Sub-regional

Ministerial Consultation, better known as the Coordinated Mekong Ministerial Initiative against Trafficking, or the COMMIT Process, an initiative by the six governments in the Sub-region. She is regularly invited to speak on the issue of trafficking at international forums and has been called upon to train NGOs and government officials on the issue.